Chesapeake Gardening & Landscaping

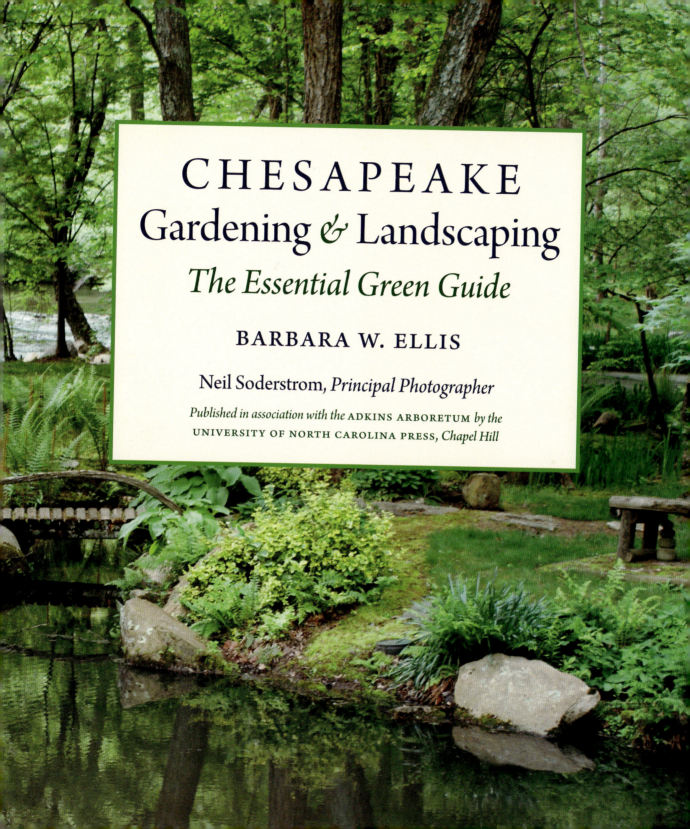

CHESAPEAKE
Gardening & Landscaping
The Essential Green Guide

BARBARA W. ELLIS

Neil Soderstrom, *Principal Photographer*

Published in association with the ADKINS ARBORETUM by the
UNIVERSITY OF NORTH CAROLINA PRESS, *Chapel Hill*

Designed and set in Arno and The Sans by Rebecca Evans
Manufactured in China.

The paper in this book meets the guidelines for permanence
and durability of the Committee on Production Guidelines
for Book Longevity of the Council on Library Resources.

The University of North Carolina Press has been a member
of the Green Press Initiative since 2003.

Photo credits: Front cover: Top: Barbara Ellis; Hardy garden.
Bottom, far left: Barbara Ellis. Center left, center right, right:
Neil Soderstrom. Back cover: All photos by Neil Soderstrom
except bottom center by Barbara Ellis. Title page: Barbara
Ellis; Liesfeld garden. Copyright page: Neil Soderstrom;
Environmental Concern, Inc. Contents page: Barbara Ellis.
Foreword page: Neil Soderstrom; New York Botanical
Garden. Acknowledgments page: Nancy Ondra.

Library of Congress Cataloging-in-Publication Data
Ellis, Barbara W.
Chesapeake gardening and landscaping : the essential
green guide / Barbara W. Ellis ; Neil Soderstrom, principal
photographer.—First edition.
pages cm
Includes bibliographical references and index.
ISBN 978-1-4696-2097-8 (cloth : alk. paper)
ISBN 978-1-4696-2098-5 (ebook)
1. Ecological landscape design—Chesapeake Bay Watershed.
2. Gardens—Chesapeake Bay Watershed—Design. I. Title.
SB472.45.E45 2015
712.09755′18—dc23
2014027846

CONTENTS

FOREWORD

In wildness is the preservation of the world.
—HENRY DAVID THOREAU

In civilization is the hope of preservation of wildness.
—WENDELL BERRY

In gardens is the preservation of the world.
—JOHN HANSON MITCHELL

I settle in comfortably beside nature writer John Hanson Mitchell in a belief in gardening as our salvation. We are what we garden. To garden is to nurture, and what we choose to nurture is where we will live and find support for our lives. Will we choose to live under the shade of mature trees, surrounded by diverse plantings of ground covers and shrubs, native meadows, and woodlands where we can observe and enjoy abundant wildlife? Will we choose to grow greens and berries to harvest in the morning for supper in the evening? Will we have a prospect to view, a spot of refuge to retreat to, and a clean stream where we fish and swim?

In *Chesapeake Gardening and Landscaping: The Essential Green Guide*, Adkins Arboretum on Maryland's Eastern Shore partners with the venerable University of North Carolina Press and seasoned gardener and garden book author Barbara Ellis. The result is an indispensable resource for all gardeners—whether novice or experienced—who wish to hone their craft and take part in making our world a healthier and more beautiful habitat for all creatures.

Not all gardening is green. Enough ill-gotten gardening advice is promulgated through garden centers and all forms of media to confuse even the most sophisticated gardener. Often what falls under the guise of good gardening practices is merely a marketing ploy to sell chemicals and petroleum-fueled equipment. Despite conveying a sense of well-being by lessening your physical effort, riding mowers, backpack leaf blowers, and motorized pesticide sprayers cause environmental harm. This comprehensive guide will build your confidence so that you can make good decisions about how you garden to truly make the world greener.

Gardeners come to gardening with many motivations—to solve a drainage problem, to attract birds to their yard, to decorate their patio, for curb appeal, and for physical exercise and solace for the soul. Whether your priority is improving environmental health, pursuing healthy activities, or beautifying your yard, *Chesapeake Gardening and Landscaping: The Essential Green Guide* offers first steps and next steps that are successful and ecologically beneficial to help you achieve your dreams for your property.

This is not a guide for gardening with native plants, and yet it is a guide for gardening with native plants. Do not let this confuse you. Throughout the book, you will be introduced to native plants not only for their aesthetic characteristics but for their ecological function, such as providing food and shelter for wildlife and nectar for pollinators. You will also learn about non-native plants that are neither invasive nor detrimental to the environment, and that prove beneficial as ground covers to prevent erosion on steep, dry, or shady slopes. You will find that *Chesapeake Gardening and Landscaping: The Essential Green Guide* recommends planting predominantly native plants, but not to the degree that non-invasive non-natives are ignored when they can solve a homeowner's challenge—the need for an evergreen screen, midsummer color, or to tolerate a range of soil conditions.

Chesapeake Gardening and Landscaping: The Essential Green Guide is a clarion call that urges all landowners to become green gardeners. Our ability to survive on this planet depends upon it. Sustainable gardening practices can minimize the use of resources, water, pesticides, and fuels, thus increasing our ability to harness resources, store carbon, minimize soil erosion and pollution, and provide habitat for pollinators and other wildlife. By implementing these practices, we will ultimately create, one yard at a time, a green world that is critical to supporting our health and the health of our children.

Eleanor Altman
Executive Director
Adkins Arboretum
Maryland's Eastern Shore

ACKNOWLEDGMENTS

A great many people have helped me complete this book, which has been a labor of love from the start. Making a list of all the individuals I need to thank caused me to wonder when, exactly, this process began. It seems to have consumed me for years. I did not have to look beyond my computer to figure out when the project started. In November 2009, I received an e-mail from Adkins Arboretum volunteer Carol Jelich writing on behalf of Executive Director Ellie Altman and Adkins Arboretum to ask if I would be interested in writing a book about "conservation landscaping—all the good things that people can do to make their landscapes not only beautiful, but healthy for people and other living things." As a writer, gardener, conservationist, and resident in the Chesapeake Bay region, how could I say no?

From the first meeting, we were all on the same page in our vision for this book. Carol, Ellie, and I met and discussed ideas, and we traded outlines for the book, budgets, and proposals in countless e-mails. We all owe thanks to David Perry, then editor in chief of the University of North Carolina Press, who responded with enthusiasm almost immediately when he received our proposal. I began researching and writing shortly thereafter.

Photographs and illustrations figured prominently from the outset. Principal photographer Neil Soderstrom researched gardens he could visit, and his photographs are a testament to his skills and to the great gardens he found. I would also like to thank Roger Foley for the use of his wonderful photographs, including several of designer Tom Mannion's landscapes. Finally, my friend and fellow gardener and writer Nancy Ondra also contributed photographs to the effort that helped with illustrating several essential plants and points. Thanks also to Kimberly Day Proctor for her illustrations and for being so fun to work with.

A number of people read and reviewed my manuscript, and all deserve heaping thanks for all their constructive comments. Thanks to reviewers Sylvan Kaufman, Mollie Ridout, Ann English, and Nancy Carter. Also, I would like to thank Jodie Littleton for editing the manuscript before the final draft was sent to UNC Press.

Thanks also to Bhaskar Subramanian of the Maryland Department of Natural Resources for his help with the living shorelines section and to Karen

Duhring of Center for Coastal Resources Management for help and advice on wetlands issues.

Senior Executive Editor Elaine Maisner and her assistant, Alison Shay, have been invaluable for helping us prepare the manuscript and, together with Project Editor Stephanie Wenzel, for guiding it through the UNC Press editorial process.

Finally, thanks to my husband, Peter Evans, my sister Janet, and my good friends Sarah Ruckelshaus, Gayle Folger, and Nancy Ondra, who have patiently listened to my updates, ideas, frustrations, and accomplishments throughout the process of developing, writing, and producing this book. I also do not want to overlook the undying support of my Papillion, Bing, who has been curled up under my desk every minute I have spent writing this book, or to parrots Harley and Milo, who have provided essential office comic relief.

My last nod of appreciation is to you, the reader. I hope that everyone who picks up this book will find a wealth of ideas that make sense for you and your garden and inspire you to begin taking steps toward a more Bay-friendly landscape.

Barbara W. Ellis

Chesapeake Gardening & Landscaping

Bay-Friendly Gardens and Landscapes

Where Do We Go from Here?

Open a newspaper, turn on the television, or browse the Internet, and you will discover a host of reasons to live a greener life and create sustainable gardens and landscapes. The news is rife with stories about pollution, invasive plants, overdevelopment, runoff, global climate change, loss of wildlife habitat, missed opportunities, and directions not taken. The stories are especially overwhelming because these are problems that none of us can fix working alone.

What if, one step at a time, we could make our gardens and landscapes greener—or more earth-friendly? What if, one garden at a time, we could create a significant change that improves the overall health of our environment, the quality of our waterways and air, and the diversity of our native flora and fauna? *Chesapeake Gardening and Landscaping* shows gardeners how to do just that. This book contains a wealth of information, projects, and plant lists that help gardeners at all levels, from beginner to advanced, take steps to make their yards and gardens part of the solution.

Designers and landscape architects who practice sustainable or conservation landscaping are a big part of the solution as well. The book includes photographs of their attractive, sustainable designs as well as photographs of equally appealing designs created by backyard gardeners that convey how sustainable or Bay-friendly landscapes are much more than serious attempts to right environmental wrongs. They are stunning, appealing, and wonderful gardens and landscapes in their own right.

This is not just a newfangled gardening fad: Sustainable or eco-friendly landscapes are based on good gardening principles, pure and simple. That means good soil care, good plant choices, planning for wildlife, and more.

The steps toward a greener yard and garden do not have to be daunting or life-altering. Enthusiastic gardeners may elect to plant wildflower meadows or create a native woodland garden, but even simple actions can make a positive difference. For example, removing vines from a volunteer oak or cherry tree gives it room to grow. If enough of us take steps—whether large or small—in the same direction, the results will be positive and significant. Once each of us understands what steps are possible and make a difference, we can influence friends and neighbors to join us on this path, this garden path to a greener, healthier, and more beautiful world. Encouraging local governments to create and protect green space, reduce runoff, and save wildlife habitat are other improvements that have significant impact.

Every situation is unique, so each of us will choose our own steps toward a more sustainable landscape. Properties range from urban to rural, and landscaping budgets run from modest to extravagant. Motivation and physical ability vary as well. Some people like nothing better than puttering in their gardens, while others simply want a care-free landscape that looks tidy with minimal effort. This book is designed to help everyone identify actions that interest them and then map out an approach to the challenge that suits their finances, property, abilities, interest, and time. For enthusiastic gardeners, creating a greener landscape may mean adding as many native plants as possible to their garden and designing and installing flower beds that welcome butterflies and birds. Homeowners who prefer boating or golf to yard work might opt to replace a patch of lawn with low-maintenance ground covers. While it takes work to plan and care for ground covers as they become established, this book contains suggestions for managing that work. In the long run, established ground covers will not require the weekly maintenance, much less the carbon footprint, needed by lawn. Still others may focus on creating plantings that absorb rainfall and help reduce runoff, a major source of Chesapeake Bay pollution.

To avoid leading readers down an unrealistic garden path with a false promise, I must relay an important caveat. Any garden, yard, or landscape takes maintenance. Yet with careful planning, you can reduce the level of maintenance required, sustain the time and energy needed to care for plants and gardens, and have the satisfaction of knowing you are contributing to a healthier environment.

Whether you call this type of gardening green, eco-friendly, earth-friendly, Bay-friendly, or sustainable, some of the book's recommendations are simply to do nothing. Letting the lawn go dormant in summer conserves water, reduces emissions, and saves time by lessening the need to mow. Allowing a dead tree to remain standing (as long as it does not present a hazard) creates habitat for native woodpeckers and a perch for owls and ospreys. Leaving hedgerows or other wild areas untouched when clearing property for new construction means even more space for wildlife.

Bay-Friendly Basics

Deciding where to start practicing a more environmentally friendly style of gardening can be a challenge, whether you want to make a simple change or redesign your entire landscape. Several excellent lists of principles or guidelines exist (see Suggested Resources for links to two different ones). Simply stated, the options are our selection of plants, where we plant them, and how we care for them. In *Chesapeake Gardening and Landscaping*, these are summarized in six basic principles. For more information on each principle, see Chapter 1.

 Reduce lawn. While useful and certainly durable, a well-maintained lawn requires regular mowing, watering, fertilizing, raking, and trimming, as well as pest and weed control. When compared with deep-rooted plants, lawn is not effective at absorbing runoff. Nor does it offer food or shelter for birds or other beneficial wildlife. An excellent first step toward a greener landscape is to start replacing sections of lawn with other plants—ideally a mix of native ground covers, perennials, grasses, shrubs, and trees. Replacing even a small patch of lawn each year helps reduce runoff, hydrocarbon use, and chemicals released into the environment. Ultimately, use lawn only where it is needed most, such as for a play area.

 Build plant diversity. Including a wide variety of plants in yards and gardens helps prevent pest and disease problems that can affect an entire region. Dutch elm disease, which decimated the American elm (*Ulmus americana*) population in the United States, is the best-known example of what can result with monocultures or by over-planting a single species. More diverse home landscapes help to replace wildlife habitat lost due to development. Wild creatures need more than the conventional landscape of a huge expanse of lawn, a tree or two, and a few foundation shrubs. For birds to feed their young and for butterflies to find host plants, a rich, diverse landscape featuring a variety of native trees, shrubs, vines, and perennials is essential. (See "Grow native plants," below, for more on why these are vital to the health of our yards and gardens.) One easy way to diversify your yard or garden is to begin planting three or four different plant species where you would normally plant only a single species. For example, replace sections of lawn with a planting that features sweeps of different native ground covers, or plant a shrub border with various native shrubs and small trees instead of a single-species hedge. Throughout this book, you'll find lots of suggestions for plant combinations. Build-ing diversity also involves removing and/or managing invasive, non-native plants that out-compete other plants. Turn your back on a small planting of English ivy for too long, and it will climb trees and eventually cause their demise.

 Grow native plants. Planting plants that are native (indigenous, not introduced) is important for a variety of reasons. Native plants are naturally adapted to the region's soils, climate, and growing conditions. For this reason, they are generally much less dependent on watering, spraying, and other maintenance than are non-natives. Native trees, shrubs, vines, and perennials support the native insects that form the basis of the food chain. When you attract these insects, you feed birds and support pollinators that are essential to growing plants.

 Manage water runoff. Until recently, directing water away from homes and landscapes as quickly as possible after a rainstorm was standard landscaping practice. Depending on where you live, water runoff travels either via gutters and storm sewers or via ditches and streams. Either way, it ultimately flows into rivers and the Chesapeake Bay. Whatever path it travels, the faster water moves, the more erosion it causes and the more silt and pollutants it gathers and carries. Allowing water to run off the land quickly does not give it a chance to soak into the soil and recharge local aquifers. For these and other reasons, managing runoff means reversing the way water has been handled on sites ranging from yards and gardens to municipal landscapes. Instead of speeding water on its way, the new goal is to retain it on the property where it falls. This prevents erosion, allows water to soak into the soil to recharge aquifers, and reduces or eliminates the flow of silt and pollutants into nearby waterways. There are many ways to accomplish this, but for homeowners installing a rain barrel is an easy first step. Rain gardens are another excellent way to manage runoff.

 Welcome wildlife. Providing wild creatures with the resources they need to thrive can replace habitat that has been lost to development and add immeasurable appeal to your property. While not all wildlife are desirable, the key is to plan for desirable and threatened wild creatures by providing essential food, water, cover, and nesting sites, so they can raise families. While installing bird houses and feeders is a simple first step, the real secret to enticing birds, small mammals, butterflies, and pollinators to your yard requires replacing conventional lawns with a rich array of native plants. Arranging plants in a naturalistic way—in colonies, thickets, and shrub borders—is also important. A wildlife-friendly landscape can begin with planting a single plant or implementing an elaborate plan. Food plants, such as shrubs that produce berries, and trees, such as oaks, that bear nuts, play a significant role. Water is essential, too. Birdbaths are one option, but butterflies and other insects appreciate shallow saucers, pools that are filled with rocks so they can drink safely, or a water garden.

 Garden wisely. This principle encompasses a wide variety of effective, earth-friendly gardening techniques. Replacing high-maintenance plants, making compost, and caring for soil by adding organic matter and mulching are all gardening practices that benefit the environment. Switching to organic sprays and embracing a sensible approach to pest control is important, since the vast majority of insects in a garden are either benign or beneficial. (All are fair game for hungry parents looking to feed baby birds!) Using fewer resources such as water and energy also are ways to garden wisely.

Dividends, Large and Small

The ideas presented in this book pay dividends beyond the environmental benefits. Many reduce landscape maintenance, including mowing, weeding, spreading, and spraying. Attractive landscapes, including those that are well designed and Bay friendly, will increase property values. According to the U.S. Forest Service, trees can increase property values as much as 10 percent, and their value increases every year they are in the ground. (This applies to sturdy, pest-resistant species like native oaks and maples but isn't necessarily true of less-desirable, weak-wooded trees like non-native, invasive Bradford pears.)

All of these ideas pay dividends in terms of the enjoyment a yard and garden can offer, whether a huge suburban landscape or a postage-stamp-size city plot. Bay-friendly plantings are not just environmentally correct: They can be beautiful, soothing outdoor spaces worth enjoying every day. Moving toward a more sustainable yard and garden is something every gardener can be proud of.

Many of the options presented are quite economical. Reducing the amount of herbicides, pesticides, and fertilizers spread on your lawn saves money. There are ideas for using recycled or low-cost materials to make a landscape both greener and more attractive. Finally, while it is harder to quantify, learning how to analyze sites and select plants eliminates much of the guesswork at the garden center. A yard filled with native plants that thrive naturally in the Chesapeake region increases the likelihood of your gardening success.

Since determining what to plant can be an insurmountable hurdle, the book features lists that identify what plants will grow best in particular sites. These lists make it easy to plant shady or sunny areas with ornamental native plants and are helpful for planting challenging spots like wet woods or dry slopes.

How to Use This Book

Whether you are a brand-new homeowner, a beginning gardener, an advanced gardener, or an individual who simply wants a more environmentally friendly landscape, this book is designed to help you find ideas and plants to achieve your goals. Reading it cover to cover is one option, but paging through and finding ideas, either by reading sections or by gleaning inspiration from the photographs of beautiful landscapes and plants, is another.

Part 1, "Creating Your Chesapeake Bay Landscape," begins with a chapter that explains in greater detail the six principles of sustainable yards and gardens. Each principle is accompanied by a list of ten simple steps that help achieve it. Chapter 2, "Creating an Ecological Landscape Design," presents the basics of sustainable garden design, from site analysis and creating outdoor living spaces to measuring the yard and drawing a plan. Chapter 3, "Building Your Chesapeake Landscape," includes information on learning more about garden sites, soil care, proper planting technique, and managing invasive plants.

Part 2, "Recommended Plants and Gardens," contains information on native plants suitable for landscapes in the Chesapeake region. The plants are presented in chapters by plant type or use: "Shrubs, Trees, and Vines for Landscaping," "Ground Covers for Chesapeake Landscapes," "Flowers for Chesa-

peake Gardens," "Plants and Gardens for Shade," "Water, Rain Gardens, and Wet Soil," and "Gardens for Wildlife."

Progress, Not Perfection

Whatever your starting point, think about sustainable gardening as a process, not a destination. While there certainly are individuals with the resources or enthusiasm to redesign their entire landscape to make it Bay friendly, simply taking steps in the right direction will work best for most of us. Thinking progress, not perfection, makes it easier to set goals and keep moving forward without the stress of overwhelming projects that remain undone. Focus on manageable steps to take today, tomorrow, this season, or next season. Many options are suggested throughout this book. Read about the possibilities and then bite off a small, manageable chunk to get started. Follow up, when possible, with a second step, a third, and then a fourth. One option for determining where to start is to pick an area of interest—minimize lawn mowing by replacing patches of lawn with ground covers, or plant a berry-bearing native shrub and discover what birds visit it during the seasons.

A fundamental shift in the perception of what makes an attractive landscape is critical for adopting the practices described in this guide. As the gardens pictured in this book testify, Bay-friendly landscapes are both beautiful and earth-friendly. The shift we need to make is similar to the way hairstyles have evolved, from the beehives and buzz cuts of the 1950s to today's less-formal fashions and acceptance of diversity. Planting more native plants is one part of the formula, but it is crucial to recognize that landscapes that are less sheared, cropped, and manicured are beautiful, too. That means clumps of plants that grow together, leaf litter covering the soil, some damage from insects (because insects are a food source for birds and other wildlife), ground covers that replace closely cropped lawn grass, and patches of wildflowers planted along hedges. A landscape composed of non-native evergreen shrubs and trees—one that looks the same all year round—is no longer an attractive solution. Native landscapes change with the seasons and provide us with a sense of place.

Obviously, every gardener can and will decide what steps he or she can take toward an earth-friendly landscape. Taking the first step will bring rewards that encourage you to take steps two and three. The impact of your efforts will grow exponentially when you share your progress with friends and neighbors and encourage them to do the same. One step at a time, we can create greener, more sustainable, and more diversely beautiful landscapes that improve the quality of our environment.

PART ONE *Creating Your Chesapeake Bay Landscape*

Chesapeake Gardening and Landscaping is a guide to help homeowners create beautiful yards and gardens that contribute to a healthy environment. Whether you live in the country, in the suburbs, along the water, or in the city, landscapes are more than pretty pictures to look at. The plantings around a home can provide food and ornamental flowers, but they also can offer an ever-changing canvas of colors to enjoy throughout the seasons. Shrubs that afford privacy to a patio or hide an unsightly view of the neighbor's backyard can also feed birds and other wildlife. Trees that create shady sitting areas outdoors also cool the air around them, sequester atmospheric carbon, increase property value, and enrich the soil, all while reducing both indoor cooling bills and your carbon footprint. Trees also play a vital role in preventing erosion, as do rain gardens. A commitment to managing the flow of water on your property can yield a hardworking garden and a fascinating and beautiful landscape.

Part 1 describes the tools for creating a beautiful and functional landscape, whether replacing a patch of lawn with shrubs or wildflowers or redesigning an entire property. A well-designed green landscape is not something accomplished in a weekend or even in a season. It requires a series of steps and is achieved by identifying and tackling one project at a time at your own pace.

(overleaf) Native wildflowers, including black-eyed Susans (*Rudbeckia* spp.); water for birds and other wild creatures; and tree and shrub plantings that reduce the size of the lawn are some of the Bay-friendly elements of this simple landscape. Photo by Neil Soderstrom; design by Mary Jo Messenger.

ONE ❧ Gardens and Landscapes That Benefit the Environment

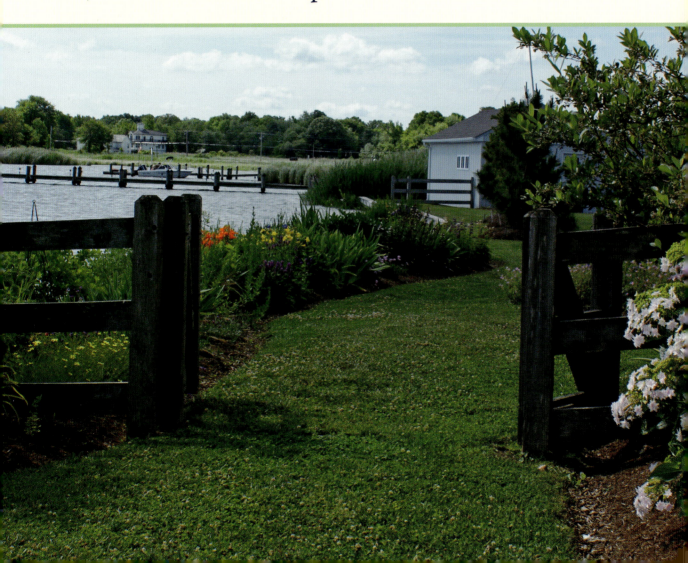

Sustainable landscaping is a way to design and care for yards, gardens, and the larger landscape by creating attractive outdoor spaces that are healthy for humans, wildlife, pets, and the environment as a whole. These landscapes include places to picnic, play games, and enjoy respite in a shady spot. They provide food and shelter for wildlife in addition to outdoor living and enjoyment for people. An added benefit is that sustainable or green landscapes can require less maintenance than conventional ones. This is not a promise for a landscape requiring *no* maintenance, just less. Maintenance tends to decrease over the years in a sustainable landscape, while maintenance for conventional landscapes stays the same.

Think about this style of gardening in terms of landscaping practices and design principles to work toward. Every site is different, and each gardener has different desires and interests; thus every landscape that adheres to basic green principles looks different. Green landscapes come in all styles as well, from wild and natural to snug and orderly. They are fun to design, fascinating to maintain, and wonderful to enjoy. Their variety, however, makes it hard to decide where to begin.

The best place to start is by looking at the techniques and principles used to design, construct, and manage the landscapes themselves. It is important to remember, whether you call it Bay-friendly, environmentally sensitive, or simply green, gardening in a sustainable manner is a process, not a destination. As you explore this book, you will learn about a variety of changes—some simple and others complex—to make in your own landscape. Start a list, and identify short-term changes as well as long-term goals. In the

Planting even a single native tree or shrub is beneficial. The flowers of this species, red buckeye (*Aesculus pavia*), attract ruby-throated hummingbirds to the garden in spring. Photo by Neil Soderstrom; design by George Fenn.

short run, for example, you may plant a native tree or shrub, reduce the use of fertilizers or pesticides, or install a rain barrel to collect and recycle water in your garden. Long-term goals could include creating a rain garden or replacing a portion of your lawn with ground covers or other plants.

The familiar phrase "reduce, reuse, recycle" summarizes what it means to create a sustainable landscape. Reducing runoff, lessening the use of chemicals and fertilizers, decreasing the amount of water used to irrigate, and reducing carbon dioxide emissions by curtailing the use of gas-powered equipment

(overleaf) The path toward a more sustainable landscape can start with steps as simple as adding a few clumps of native perennials to the garden or replacing a patch of lawn with ground covers. Photo by Barbara Ellis; Hardy garden.

are all beneficial objectives. The "reuse" part of the equation comes into play when fallen leaves are used as mulch, wooden pallets become compost piles, and cut branches serve as pea stakes in the vegetable garden. It is appropriate that compost fits into both the "reuse" and "recycle" portions of the phrase, since the compost pile is where kitchen and yard waste becomes gardener's gold. Other examples of recycling in the garden include using newspapers under mulch to squelch weeds and building decks or other garden structures with materials manufactured from recycled products.

Creating habitat for wildlife, encouraging widespread planting of more native plants (for the purposes of this book, this means plants that grow naturally in Maryland, Virginia, Delaware, and the District of Columbia), and curtailing the use of nonrenewable resources are a few more of the essential goals of a sustainable landscape. Every landscape and situation is a little bit different—as are the desires of every gardener or homeowner—thus it is no surprise that deciding where to start is a challenge.

The six general principles presented in the introduction—reduce lawn, build plant diversity, grow native plants, manage water runoff, welcome wildlife, and garden wisely—simplify the decision-making process and help organize the different steps of transforming a landscape. This chapter examines each principle in depth and provides tips and suggestions for implementing each principle.

One way to rethink the lawn is to simply leave sections unmown. When compared to mown lawn, long grass reduces runoff, and less mowing also reduces your carbon footprint. Here, sweeping paths still allow access to sections of the yard where the grass is long. Grass seeds also provide food for birds. Photo by Barbara Ellis; Nobel garden.

Reduce Lawn

Typically, lawn functions as monotonous green wall-to-wall carpeting in the average American landscape. From both design and environmental standpoints, there are better ways to incorporate lawn into the average landscape. Reducing irrigation and carefully managing pesticide and fertilizer applications are options, but there are better choices for landscaping than lawn—choices that require less maintenance; reduce runoff more effectively; do not need weekly mowing; require less water, pesticide, and fertilizer; and are friendlier for wildlife.

Start the process of transitioning from lawn to more sustainable options by considering where you need and use lawn. For example, lawn is desirable for play areas or open space where you can throw a Frisbee. Yet if you want a smooth, green-carpeted area next to a deck or patio, ground covers may be the best option. See "Ten Tips for Reducing Lawn" for ideas on portions of the lawn to target.

With a goal in hand, keep your plan for achieving it manageable. Otherwise, it is too easy to become frustrated and overwhelmed. Replacing just a square yard of turf each year with more environmentally friendly, lower-maintenance options is a change in the right direction. Every square yard of lawn you replace will no longer require weekly mowing. If you replace lawn with ground covers, you will have to weed weekly for a few months, but weeding chores lessen as ground covers become established. Eventually, attention once or twice a year may be all the new area requires.

Keep in mind that you may need to educate neighbors when replacing closely cropped lawn with flower beds or wildflower meadows. If you have neatnik neighbors or prefer a more closely tended landscape yourself, consider beds of lower-growing ground covers. Or install mixed flower beds but balance them with beds of low shrubs or herbaceous ground covers. Even meadow plantings are more acceptable to the uninitiated if they have a clearly defined shape you can maintain by mowing. Cutting meadow plants back by half early in the season helps limit their height and makes the planting look more tended, keeping neighbors happy. You also can cut back plants around the edges of a meadow, leaving plants toward the center untrimmed. Plants in the center will bloom first and be taller, while plants on the edges will bloom later and be shorter.

Healthy Is Bay Friendly

Maintaining a healthy, vigorous lawn helps reduce runoff and the flow of pollutants into the waterways—a dense stand of grass absorbs more runoff than a sparse, struggling one. If you do not mow or care for your own grass, ask your lawn service about environmentally responsible options, such as those below. Consult your local Cooperative Extension Service for suggestions on grass species recommended for your area and soils, as well as for soil testing and organic fertilizer recommendations. Use the following tips to keep your lawn growing vigorously.

Plant the right type of grass. Turf-type tall fescue and zoysia both resist pests and diseases more effectively than other types. They generally require less fertilizer as well. Fine fescues are good choices for shady sites and low-maintenance applications.

Test your soil. A soil test will reveal whether your grass needs feeding or if the pH is optimal for grass plants to absorb existing nutrients. The recommended fertilizer schedule will minimize waste and runoff. Compacted soil can also cause unhealthy lawn. See "Avoid Soil Compaction" on p. 82 for more information.

Cut long. Set your mower to keep lawn grasses at about 3 inches (1 inch for Bermuda and zoysia). Cutting high and frequently, never removing more than one-third of the grass blades, keeps grass healthy. It also helps eliminate weed problems by 50 to 80 percent.

Recycle the clippings. Using a mulching mower and leaving cut grass on the lawn saves time, keeps the grass healthy, and returns nitrogen to the soil.

Minimize fertilizer runoff. Use slow-release fertilizer—organic products are ideal—and fertilize at the proper time for the type of grass and the area where you live. Keep fertilizer off paved surfaces and natural drainage areas to prevent it from washing away. Compost is especially valuable because it both feeds the lawn and improves soil.

Water only as needed. Sprinklers turned on by timers regardless of the weather are not the best

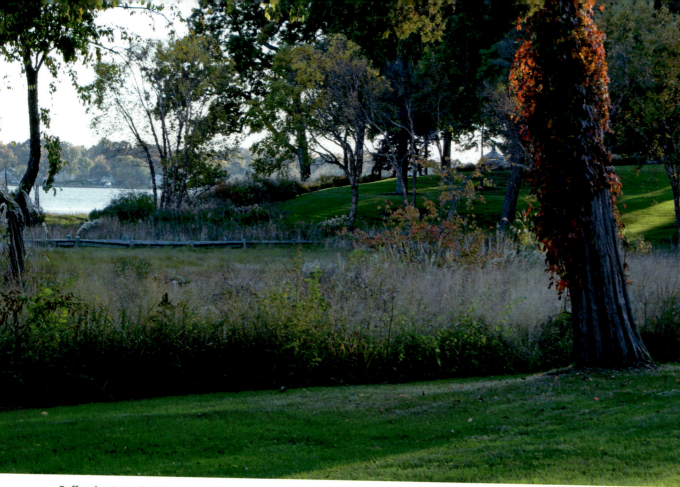

Buffer plantings of native grasses, wildflowers, and other plants along waterways reduce runoff, eliminate the need to mow in soggy soil, shrink the size of the lawn, and provide valuable habitat for birds as well as insects that are eaten by birds and other creatures. Photo by Barbara Ellis; J. Kent McNew garden.

watering option because they will come on even during a rainstorm. Frequent, shallow watering is not ideal, as it results in shallow-rooted grass plants with little drought tolerance. To determine if the lawn needs water, walk on it. If you leave footprints, it is time to water. Water slowly for a long period of time. The goal is to wet the top 4 to 6 inches of soil to encourage deeply rooted, drought-resistant plants.

Plant a buffer. Avoid mowing grass right up to the edge of any body of water—a creek, river, lake, or

the Bay. This helps prevent storm runoff and grass clippings from reaching the water.

Another Bay-friendly lawn option is to stop watering, feeding, and using herbicides altogether. Keep the lawn mown, but at the highest level your mower will allow. This will introduce some diversity into your lawn—clover and a few wildflowers. This practice is cheaper (no chemicals), better for the environment (fewer hydrocarbons from the mower and no chemical runoff), and less work (the grass will grow more slowly without regular watering). It will still look like a lawn to satisfy most homeowners, and it will still be a smooth, unifying element in the landscape—albeit not one resembling a golf course. The Bay will thank you. Another option is to contract with an organic lawn care company or switch to using organic products yourself.

Ten Tips for Reducing Lawn

Use these tips to help determine your overall approach to reducing the amount of lawn currently on your property. Plan on replacing lawn in manageable patches. One easy way to eliminate a patch of grass is to cut it as short as possible, cover the area with 8 to 10 sheets of newspaper (overlap the edges), and top it with 2 to 3 inches of mulch. Do this in spring for fall planting or in fall for planting the following spring. See "Deep Mulching" on p. 92 for more information on this technique.

1. Mulch around shade trees. Smother lawn around shade trees and maintain a mulched area instead. A 2-inch-deep layer is fine. Beginning a foot or more from the trunk, reduce the depth of the mulch gradually toward the tree trunk and keep mulch from touching the trunk. In addition to the benefits listed above, this prevents mowers from damaging tree trunks and helps maintain moisture in the soil near the tree's roots. Mulching all of the area under a tree's canopy helps reduce competition for moisture between the tree and lawn grass.

2. Give your lawn a shape. To create attractive lawn areas with a unifying design function, reduce the overall size and establish a clearly designed shape. Think of lawn as an area rug instead of wall-to-wall carpeting. Edge it with planting beds, ground covers, and walkways. A nicely shaped lawn, instead of one simply covering the entire yard and joining with neighboring yards, becomes a powerful unifying element in a design.

3. Smooth the edges. For fast, efficient mowing, aim for a lawn with gentle curves. Simple shapes are easiest to mow, since you can cut grass without needing to back up and reposition the mower. To accomplish this goal in small steps, start by replacing lawn grass in awkward, hard-to-mow spots.

4. Add edging strips. Edging eliminates the need to come back and trim, since you can mow and trim at the same time, with one wheel on the edging strip and one on the lawn.

5. Create or enlarge buffer zones. If lawn areas extend to the edge of a waterway, reduce runoff and protect the shoreline by replacing the lawn along the water with beds of native grasses and wildflowers. Where the waterway is tidal, consider a Living Shoreline. See "Living Shorelines" on p. 40 for more information. Either way, in addition to reducing the size of the lawn, this eliminates trimming and risking a mower that is bogged down in wet soil.

6. Widen foundation plantings. Eliminate a strip of grass beside foundation plantings by replacing it with low-growing shrubs or perennial ground covers. A necklace of flowers along a foundation adds interest during the growing season.

7. Manage steep slopes. Slopes are among the most difficult sites to mow. One option is to cover them with shrubs or tough, shrubby ground covers. Terracing slopes with landscape timbers, blocks, plantable wall systems, brick, or stone is another alternative that yields flat planting areas. To establish shrubs or ground covers on an unterraced site, create temporary terraces with scrap lumber (2 by 8 inches is fine; hold in place with wooden stakes) to create level planting areas where water can collect and seep down. Once plants have become established, the scrap lumber can be removed or allowed to rot.

Replacing lawn around trees is another way to reduce mowing chores and reap the benefits of a smaller lawn. This simple planting features rounded edges that are easy to mow around and a small garden pool that provides water for wildlife. Photo by Neil Soderstrom; design by Andie Phillips.

8. Make a plan for walkways, work areas, and temporary parking spots. Lawn grass does not grow well on high-traffic sites because of soil compaction and other factors. Consider replacing grass on such sites with permeable pavers, a deep layer of gravel, or bark mulch. This eliminates lawn areas that tend to be unattractive anyway.

9. Create beds of trees and shrubs. Instead of mowing and trimming around individual trees and shrubs, replace the lawn between them with ground covers, additional shrubs and smaller trees, and/or plantings of tough perennials. This creates island beds you can easily mow and trim around. Create one or several beds. If you cannot plant right away, eliminate the grass and simply mulch the area to control weeds and plant at a later date.

10. Plant a meadow. Replacing lawn areas with a planting of meadow grasses and wildflowers cuts mowing from weekly to once a year. A wildflower meadow becomes a wonderful habitat for birds, butterflies, and wildlife. For more information on meadows, see Chapter 6.

Lawn has been eliminated entirely from this front yard, and the plantings feature a diversity of native trees and a variety of native and non-native plants, including drought-tolerant sedums and thymes. While plantings such as this require regular weeding, the amount of maintenance decreases as the planting matures. Photo by Neil Soderstrom; design by Mary Streb.

Build Plant Diversity

Gardeners will be happy to know that planting more and different kinds of plants is a simple way to make a landscape more sustainable. Look closely at any natural area, and it is clear that Mother Nature is a cottage gardener. A natural woodland features trees such as oaks, maples, and beeches in the top layer, or canopy, and beneath them are shade-loving understory trees, along with shrubs, perennials, vines, ground covers, ferns, and mosses filling all the available space. In a sunny meadow, low, ground-covering creepers grow with taller, herbaceous plants above.

Layers of plants work for a variety of reasons. They protect the soil by shading it and keeping it cool, which is important for the health of soil organisms. (Plants, especially trees, are important for storing carbon dioxide, but healthy soil is also an important reservoir of stored carbon. See "Start with the Soil" on p. 74 for more information.) Layers of plants break the force of raindrops. Rain falls on leaves and trickles down stems, and leaf litter below the trees acts like a sponge to absorb water. As a result, there is virtually no runoff from a woodland or meadow during most rainstorms. Layers also form dense cover that benefits wildlife.

Building plant diversity means working toward adding more plants, and a greater variety of plants, to your yard and garden. Ideally, add plants that grow naturally in the region. See "Grow Native Plants" on p. 19 for more on why natives are so important. Plant diversity means avoiding monocultures, plantings that feature a single plant species. Lawn is a monoculture, but so is a street lined with Bradford pears or a hedge of Leyland cypress. Instead of planting hedges or foundation plantings consisting of one or two species, plant a shrub border with eight or more different plants. Consider species that flower at different times of year, produce showy berries, or feature different foliage textures and colors in autumn.

Creating layers of plants to cover the soil helps build plant diversity. Add ground covers under shrubs and plant clumps of different perennials so they can grow together and cover the soil completely. For a more traditional look, plant drifts of five or more of each ground cover or perennial. This will create sweeps of solid color and texture, rather than a free-form cottage garden.

Building plant diversity also means managing invasive plants on your property, since these thugs crowd out native species. See "Managing Invasive Plants" on p. 102 for more information.

Ten Tips for Building Plant Diversity

Whether you inherited an existing garden or a standard-issue developer landscape with fewer than a dozen different plants, the tips below should provide ideas for identifying plants to add to your yard and garden.

1. Fill in under shrubs. On mulched sites along hedges, shrub borders, or foundation plantings, plant ground covers or low-growing perennials. Avoid adding invasive plants that are not native, such as English ivy (*Hedera helix*) or vinca (*Vinca* spp.), also called common periwinkle. See Chapter 5 for more on both invasive and native ground covers.

2. Stop mowing weedy areas. If you routinely mow or trim under trees or along drainage ditches to give

Shade-tolerant ground covers and other plants add diversity to the landscape. Here, northern sea oats (*Chasmanthium latifolium*), a self-sowing native ornamental grass, fills space under a river birch (*Betula nigra*). Photo by Neil Soderstrom; design by Ann Wing.

the area a neater look, consider letting the plants grow instead. You will find that native plants attract desirable butterflies and other insects. Identify the plants when they flower, or ask an experienced gardening friend or neighbor for help if you do not recognize them. You can add native plants that suit the site to give the area a more planted, colorful look. If neatness is a concern, mow around the edges to give the area a defined shape.

3. Start a collection. For a ready-made list of plants, consider collecting plants from lists in this book— berry-bearing shrubs or perennials to attract butterflies, for example.

4. Grow up. Add a second tier of plants by allowing

🍂 Plant a Tree—or Trees

Planting a native tree is a simple way to make a significant step toward sustainability. Trees play a vital role in cooling the air around them, and especially underneath the shade of their branches. They capture carbon dioxide and other pollutants. Carefully locating trees in relationship to the sun can reduce heating and cooling bills. When planted on the south or west side of the house, a deciduous tree creates shade and reduces air-conditioning bills in summer without blocking much-needed sun in winter. Planted on the north side of the house, trees and shrubs, especially evergreens, insulate and offer wind protection. Trees shade and protect the soil, intercept water and reduce runoff, and increase property values. On average-size properties, a mature shade tree comprises a significant percentage of the total plant community biomass, meaning the mass of all species in the plant community. A single tree can have a dramatic effect on the overall percentage of native vegetation when you're calculating total biomass rather than counting individual plants.

If you take only one step toward a more sustainable landscape, plant a native tree. See Chapter 4 for information on native trees.

Working toward a landscape that features a diversity of trees, shrubs, and other plants is a valuable goal. Not only are such landscapes healthier and better able to adapt to factors such as changing weather patterns, but they support more wildlife. Oaks, including scarlet oak (*Quercus coccinea*), are especially valuable for building diversity. Photo by Neil Soderstrom; U.S. Botanic Garden.

vines to climb a fence or trellis or ramble over existing shrubs. Scarlet honeysuckle (*Lonicera sempervirens*), Carolina jessamine (*Gelsemium sempervirens*), and American wisteria (*Wisteria frutescens*) are all good choices.

5. Plant the spaces. If there are expanses of mulch between plants in your flower beds, plant annuals, add smaller perennials, or sow flower seeds. Plants touch each other in nature, and they can do so in a garden, too!

6. Add a water garden. Whether you add a tiny puddle or a large water garden, you will find that water brings life to the garden in the form of dragonflies, frogs, birds, and more. You can add bog plants in the shallow space around the edges. See Chapter 9 for information on water gardens.

7. Build a rain garden. In addition to creating an attractive new site with different growing conditions, a rain garden helps reduce runoff. See Chapter 8 for information on rain gardens.

8. Tolerate lawn weeds. Stop using herbicides and allow clover, violets, and other "weeds" in the lawn. Cutting the lawn with the mower set on high discourages many weeds, and spot-treating can address any problematic ones that appear.

9. Design a mixed border. Instead of planting a garden with annuals or perennials, consider including ornamental grasses, flowering and fruiting shrubs, and small trees.

10. Look for local ideas. Visit local botanical gardens and natural areas to look for demonstration gardens and appealing plant combinations. Many offer suggested plant lists as well as periodic plant sales where you can purchase all manner of natives to suit your site. Many local garden centers also have demonstration plantings. You also will find lots of ideas on local garden tours.

Grow Native Plants

If reducing lawn and adding diversity are good, growing more native plants is even better. Native plants make sense because they are adapted to the soils and climate of the region. They also withstand the extremes of summer heat and humidity and wet winters. They require less maintenance once established, since they can survive with existing conditions, such as rainfall and pests. Do not, however, be misled to believe that native plants thrive with *no* maintenance. Like all plants, native plants require good care at planting time, enough water over the first few weeks or months to become established, and attention through the year to keep them looking their best. For the purposes of this book, a plant identified as native is one found growing naturally within the Chesapeake Bay region, primarily in Maryland, Virginia, Delaware, and the District of Columbia. The plant lists in Part 2 include some "nearly native" plants—excellent landscape choices in our region, but native to other nearby states.

Native plants form the basis of the food chain, which is essential for birds, insects such as butterflies and bees, and other creatures that pollinate crops. (Native plants, which have been growing in the region for thousands of years, have evolved relationships with native pollinators, seed dispersers,

Although they are not maintenance free, native species generally require less maintenance than non-native species. This pairing features New England asters (*Symphyotrichum novae-angliae*) with panic grass or switchgrass (*Panicum virgatum* 'Heavy Metal'). Photo by Neil Soderstrom; design by Mary Streb.

Non-native plants figure prominently in most landscapes today. Because trees add so much biomass, planting them is an excellent way to start the transition to a higher percentage of native plants. This landscape features lawn replaced with non-native ground covers along with large native river birch trees (*Betula nigra*). Photo by Neil Soderstrom; design by Leigh Sands.

and even animals and insects that eat them. Many native animals do not recognize introduced plants as a food source.) The more natives in the landscape, the richer the food chain to sustain wildlife.

Few of us start out with properties primed for growing an all-native landscape. In typical suburban developments, the land is bulldozed before construction starts, often removing fertile topsoil. Invasive plants that are not native, like English ivy (*Hedera helix*), common periwinkle (*Vinca minor*), and tree of heaven (*Ailanthus altissima*), fill many city lots where land disturbance has occurred. A reasonable

goal for these situations should be progress, not perfection. If you are starting with a wooded site where native plants predominate, consider yourself lucky. If you are not so lucky, a realistic short-term goal is to grow more natives than you have at present. Managing non-native invasives is an excellent way to eliminate undesirable plants and create more room for natives. See "Managing Invasive Plants" on p. 102 for more on dealing with non-native invasive plants. The percentage of natives versus non-natives you grow is up to you. Make no mistake—creating a sustainable garden does not mean that non-native peonies,

Designers specializing in native plants can help homeowners select plants that will thrive on a particular site, such as the rudbeckias (*Rudbeckia* spp.), Joe-Pye weeds (*Eutrochium* and *Eupatoriadelphus* spp.), and ornamental grasses spilling down this hillside. Photo © Roger Foley; design by Tom Mannion Landscape Design.

petunias, marigolds, and lavender have to go. Many enthusiastic sustainable gardeners continue to grow a percentage of plants that are not native. The choice is yours. Whatever you create will be a vast improvement over what you started with.

Ten Tips for Growing More Native Plants

Use these tips to add more native plants to your yard and garden and maximize the benefit from every native you grow. You will find information about selecting appropriate sites and plants in Part 2 to maximize success and ensure your new plantings thrive.

1. Look for lists. Plant lists are a good place to start, since sorting through arrays of flowering plants at a nursery or in a catalog is a difficult task. This book contains plant lists for many different types of sites, but asking at local botanical gardens and at your Cooperative Extension office is also helpful. Take your lists, along with a description of your site, to a reputable nursery specializing in native plants, or use it to shop online.

2. Think right plant, right place. Instead of buying native plants for your whole yard in general, study your yard and the particular site you want to plant. Then buy plants for the different sun, soil, and expo-

🌿 Celebrate Your Site

Including native plants in your landscape is an opportunity to celebrate what is special about the area where you garden. Designers call this gardening with a sense of place. Instead of struggling against the site conditions and natural history to create a garden, gardening with a sense of place means using plants that grow naturally on your site. Planting natives helps attract and support the needs of the wildlife that shares our world.

Instead of seeking inspiration in pictures of gardens in faraway places, garden with a sense of place by studying the characteristics of your property, whether it features salt marsh, shady woodlands, rock outcrops, or urban oasis. Those assets become the inspiration for your design.

Native plants support more native insects than non-native plants, which means they supply food for more birds and other wildlife. In addition to providing a food source for larvae of several native butterflies, hackberry (*Celtis occidentalis*) fruit remains on trees and is eaten by birds from winter into spring. Yellow crownbeard (*Verbesina occidentalis*) provides seeds in winter. Photo by Neil Soderstrom; J. Kent McNew garden.

sure conditions characterizing each site. For example, look for meadow flowers able to thrive in dry soil and full sun to create a low-maintenance planting around a mailbox. Or select native woodland wildflowers for a shady spot with rich, well-drained soil.

3. Demand added benefits. Look for natives offering pretty flowers and long bloom time or trees and shrubs, such as viburnums (*Viburnum* spp.), that provide spring flowers, attractive foliage, fall color, and berries for birds and other wildlife.

4. Consult a specialist. Local native plant sales held by plant societies and botanical gardens are good sources for natives. Also look on the Internet for native plant specialists. Specify your state or region when searching to ensure you find natives from your area.

5. Grow from seed. For a garden on a budget, nothing beats starting from seeds. Luckily, many natives are easily grown from seeds. You will find germination instructions on seed packets. Or see the online link in Suggested Resources for more information.

6. Look for replacements. If your landscape features non-native plants you would like to replace, ask your local Cooperative Extension office or area botanical gardens for natives to plant in their place. *Native Alternatives to Invasive Plants* (Brooklyn Botanic Garden All-Region Guide), by Cole Burrell, and *Plant Invaders of Mid-Atlantic Natural Areas* (National Park Service, U.S. Fish and Wildlife Service) are two good sources. For complete information on these titles and more books on native plants, see Suggested Resources.

7. Plant popular perennials. Many popular perennials are native plants. You will find a wide variety of popular ornamental natives in Part 2 of this book. For starters, wild columbine (*Aquilegia canadensis*), New England and New York asters (*Symphyotrichum novae-angliae* and *S. novi-belgii*), blue wild

Many popular perennials found in garden centers are native wildflowers or cultivated forms of natives, including this dwarf purple coneflower (*Echinacea purpurea* 'Kim's Knee High'). Photo by Neil Soderstrom; New York Botanical Garden.

indigo (*Baptisia australis*), thread-leaved coreopsis (*Coreopsis verticillata*), bleeding heart (*Dicentra eximia*), purple coneflower (*Echinacea purpurea*), oxeye (*Heliopsis helianthoides*), rose mallow (*Hibiscus moscheutos*), beebalm (*Monarda didyma*), garden phlox (*Phlox paniculata*), orange coneflower (*Rudbeckia fulgida*), and dense blazing star (*Liatris spicata*) are just some of the popular native plants available at nearly every garden center.

8. Attend a lecture. Learn more about growing and designing with native plants at a lecture or symposium in your area. Many native plant lectures are organized with plant sales. At these events you will have a chance to ask for advice from experts in your area. If they are held at a botanical garden, be sure to tour native plant gardens for more gardening ideas.

9. Coddle babies. When starting with small plants

or preparing to move seedlings out into the garden, consider creating a nursery bed as an interim step. The ideal nursery bed is a growing area located where it can be monitored daily and where there is access to a hose for easy watering. Raised beds and soil amended with organic matter create ideal growing conditions for a variety of plants. A site with some protection from full sun, such as shade during the afternoon, is generally best. Build a nursery bed in shade for growing woodland plants. Also look for a site protected from wind, which can dry out small plants quickly. With a nursery bed, you can grow plants for a season or two so they attain size and maturity and will not be out-competed in the garden.

10. Plant well. To give plants a chance to thrive, select a site with the specific sun and soil conditions the plant needs to grow. Ideally, control weeds with mulch and loosen the soil at planting time. See "Keeping Soil Healthy" on p. 79 for details on soil preparation at planting time. Water regularly until the plants are well established.

Cardinal flower (*Lobelia cardinalis*) is one of many native plants that thrives in average to wet soil. Consider it for rain gardens and other plantings designed to reduce runoff and allow water to soak into the soil. Photo by Barbara Ellis.

Manage Water Runoff

Water that flows off rooftops, over compacted lawns, and down driveways carries with it everything from oil and pesticides to grass clippings and eroded soil, all of which is eventually deposited in streams, rivers, and the Chesapeake Bay. The farther it travels, the faster it moves and the more power it has to pick up soil and pollutants. Water that runs off the land does not have a chance to soak into the soil and recharge water tables. For a gardener, runoff water is wasted water. When it flows away too quickly to be absorbed into the soil, water cannot support growing plants. Taking steps to reduce runoff and clean up water

that reaches rivers and the Bay has both economic and recreational benefits. Studies link healthy plant communities along streams to healthier fish habitat, which means more fish and more wildlife that feeds on fish. Less runoff translates into cleaner water, better boating, better fishing, and better crabbing for individuals and the seafood industry.

One significant step you can take to help reduce the runoff polluting the Chesapeake Bay and its tributaries, or any body of water, is to build a rain garden. A rain garden is a planting in a slight depression that captures rainfall and holds it while it is absorbed into the soil. In addition to being useful for reducing runoff, rain gardens can reduce the size of the lawn and increase plant diversity, and they are especially beneficial when planted with native plants. For more information on rain gardens, see Chapter 8.

Water collected in rain barrels can be transported by watering can to where it is needed or by a hose to nearby garden beds. A base for the rain barrel makes the water more easily accessible. Photo by Neil Soderstrom; American Horticultural Society's River Farm.

Trees catch and hold raindrops on leaves and branches during storms and store water they take up through roots. Tree leaves—and plantings under trees—also slow the speed of raindrops, increasing the amount of water that soaks into the soil. Photo by Neil Soderstrom; design by Oehme, van Sweden Landscape Architecture at Brillembourg estate.

Ten Tips for Reducing Runoff

In addition to creating a rain garden, consider some of these other options for slowing down and retaining water on your property.

1. Redirect downspouts. Instead of directing water from the roof onto the driveway or other avenues to carry it quickly to the street, point downspouts and gutters so they drain into flower beds, onto the lawn or vegetated swales, or into a rain garden. Always direct the flow away from the house to avoid foundation problems or a wet basement.

2. Loosen and amend soil. Well-prepared soil acts like a sponge during rainstorms. Dig soil to at least a shovel's depth and amend it with compost or coarsely chopped leaves. Top prepared soil with 2 to 3 inches of mulch (add a layer of newspaper under the mulch to discourage weeds).

3. Cultivate thick, healthy vegetation. Layers of plants catch more water and prevent it from running off. In areas where plant cover is thin, have the soil tested to determine if pH or fertility is a problem, and then add additional ground covers, perennials, shrubs, or other plants. (Amend soil with compost at planting time, and mulch to protect soil so plants get off to a good start.)

4. Plant a tree. Incredibly important additions to sustainable landscapes, trees act as mini–water reservoirs, and they control runoff at the source by catching and holding rain on leaves, branches, and bark. Tree roots also store water and help rainwater percolate into the soil—especially if they are underplanted with ground covers, shrubs, and other plants. While slowing down the flow of water, trees play a critical role in preventing soil erosion.

5. Mulch. Covering the soil with 2 to 3 inches of mulch—bark mulch or chopped leaves are good choices—protects the soil and slows down rainwater, giving it a chance to sink into the soil. Avoid using artificially dyed mulches, as they may actually be pressure-treated or other undesirable wood.

6. Install rain barrels. Rain barrels collect water from the roof and store it for later use in the garden. Rain barrels can be linked together to provide additional storage.

7. Create buffer plantings. A bed or border planted with flowers, grasses, shrubs, or a mix of all three can reduce runoff when located at the edge of your property. Ground cover or shrub plantings on slopes also help to control runoff if you avoid significant disturbance at planting time by loosening soil at each planting site and cutting small terraces to slow down the water. See "Planting Slopes" on p. 95 for more information.

8. Rethink hardscape. Instead of poured concrete, brick, or mortared stone walkways and patios, consider permeable materials. Bricks or pavers set in sand or gravel are more porous than mortared surfaces. Permeable materials suitable for surfacing a driveway also are available.

9. Consider green roofs, ponds, planted swales, and more. Runoff can be directed into rain gardens, but it is also possible to build a pond that doubles as a huge rain barrel. For more options, see Chapter 8.

10. Plan a water cycle. Instead of thinking about each individual element in your landscape that catches water, consider how water flows through the landscape as a whole. The water cycle can become the theme for a garden's design. Downspouts can flow into channels leading to rain gardens, and drainage ditches can become planted swales able to slow runoff, support ornamental plantings, and give water time to sink into the soil. Cutting-edge designers are creating stunning designs based on how water flows through the landscape.

Welcome Wildlife

While few gardeners yearn for more deer, groundhogs, moles, starlings, Japanese beetles, and brown stink bugs, there are many advantages to creating a landscape that encourages desirable wildlife. Discovering visitors like wrens, toads, monarch butterflies, and box turtles makes a garden special—a direct connection to Mother Nature. Conventional home landscapes with their large lawns, lack of trees, and minimal foundation plantings provide very little that is attractive to wildlife. By considering the needs of wildlife as part of the design, you can help alleviate habitat loss. Having a landscape that supports desirable wildlife honors our site and sense of place.

To create a wildlife-friendly landscape, think about your yard and garden in terms of what it offers wild creatures. The essential elements they need are food, cover, nesting sites, and water. Plant selection is a big part of the picture, both to provide food and to offer cover vital for nesting and roosting sites. Trees and shrubs are especially important in both respects.

Landscapes that welcome wildlife feature a variety of native trees, shrubs, flowers, and other plants that provide food and cover. This landscape includes shingle or laurel oak (*Quercus imbricaria*) and Virginia pine (*Pinus virginiana*). Photo by Neil Soderstrom; J. Kent McNew garden.

Shrubs produce berries attractive to a wide variety of birds and other wildlife, but trees are even more effective. According to Douglas Tallamy's *Bringing Nature Home*, oak trees support 534 species of butterflies and moths. More than 100 species of birds and mammals also feast on the acorns. According to the Georgia Wildlife Federation, eastern red cedars (*Juniperus virginiana*), a common evergreen throughout the Chesapeake region, feed "40 wild species, including cedar waxwings, bluebirds, purple finches, gray squirrels, and opossums." Eastern red cedar also has shredding bark that is an important nest-building material for many birds, and its dense evergreen foliage creates a favorite roosting site for juncos, myrtle warblers, and native sparrows. Unlike native trees, popular non-native trees such as ornamental cher-

Oaks, such as swamp white oak (*Quercus bicolor*), are especially important trees because they support many insects that in turn provide food for birds and other wildlife. Photo by Neil Soderstrom; Green Spring Gardens.

Cardinals and other native birds enjoy highbush blueberries (*Vaccinium corymbosum*) nearly as much as people do, so plant enough for both. Photo by Neil Soderstrom.

Welcome wildlife by providing at least one source of safe, clean water for drinking and bathing. Photo by Neil Soderstrom.

ries, crepe myrtles, and Japanese maples do not support insects that are critical pollinators as well as food for other creatures.

How plants are arranged in the landscape matters. When scattered in a sea of lawn, a few trees and shrubs are not as effective at attracting wildlife as the same plants would be when grouped together. Grouping plants creates safe cover and nesting sites that creatures need to thrive. Layers of plants are ideal: See "Build Plant Diversity" earlier in this chapter for more information on creating layers in plantings.

Food, another wildlife essential, comes in many forms. One of those is bird feeders, but berry-bearing shrubs are important for birds and wildlife. Migrating birds depend on berries to fatten up for their annual flight south to warmer climates. Gray dogwood (*Cornus racemosa*), pagoda dogwood (*C. alternifolia*), nannyberry (*Viburnum lentago*), and chokecherry (*Prunus virginiana*) are a few choices. Birds that overwinter in the Chesapeake Bay region eat seeds and fruits of plants like coneflowers (*Echinacea* and *Rudbeckia* spp.), hollies (*Ilex* spp.), red cedar (*Juni-*

perus virginiana), and bayberries (*Morella* spp.). Butterflies, of course, depend primarily on flowers for their sustenance. See "Butterfly Gardens" on p. 280 for more on creating gardens to attract them.

Ten Tips for Welcoming Wildlife

In addition to grouping shrubs and other plants to create areas for wildlife, use the tips below to transform your yard into a haven for desirable wildlife. For more information on creating wildlife-friendly landscapes, see Chapter 9.

1. Reduce pesticide use. This benefits all wildlife, but especially insects, which form the base of the food chain. The vast majority of insects are either benign or beneficial, and all are an important part of the food supply for birds and other wildlife.

2. Provide water. Install a birdbath. Change water every other day to ensure it is safe to drink. (This also eliminates mosquito larvae.) For insects and butterflies, a shallow dish or water garden containing rounded rocks creates a safe place to drink. A water garden with a shallow end that incorporates a gradual slope allows a variety of insects and other tiny creatures to access water easily and safely.

3. Plant landing sites. Flat-topped flowers become landing sites for butterflies, pollinators, and other beneficial insects so they can easily feed in the garden. One simple way to identify suitable flowers is to look for members of the daisy family, Asteraceae, such as sunflowers (*Helianthus* spp.), zinnias (*Zinnia* spp.), coneflowers (*Echinacea* spp. and *Rudbeckia* spp.), and blazing stars or gayfeathers (*Liatris* spp.). See Chapter 9 for more on butterfly plants and gardens.

🍃 Recruit the Neighbors

One gardener working alone can only accomplish so much, but it is possible to extend your influence beyond your property borders. Your yard and garden fit into your neighborhood and the larger region in which you live. The butterflies that hatch on your property will visit flowers in neighbors' gardens, and birds feeding on berries and insects in your garden will raise the next generation there as well. Talk to neighbors about your interest to help convince them to expand a wild area on the edge of your property onto their property. For an entire neighborhood, the vision of creating corridors for wildlife from yard to yard or to a local park or natural area may inspire residents to do their part. Convincing neighbors to reduce the size of their lawn or pesticide use will support the declining population of bees and other pollinators. Pollinators are responsible for the production of seeds and ornamental berries that benefit wildlife, and they are also essential for the production of a wide range of food crops, from apples to zucchini.

4. Embrace wild areas. Doing nothing can be beneficial. Whether you have a patch of old field, woods, or other wild area, resist the temptation to cut back undergrowth or mow the space to make it neater unless you are managing non-native invasive plants.

5. Erect feeders. Birds visit seed and suet feeders, but if you watch feeders at night, you may also see flying squirrels on suet feeders. To attract the greatest variety of wildlife, hang and install several different types of feeders. To protect birds from flying into windows, either keep feeders 25 to 30 feet away from the house or place them close to windows—2 to 3 feet.

6. Keep cats indoors. Cats that stake out bird feeders or hunt anywhere outdoors kill a great many songbirds every year, along with other wildlife. They are not natural predators, and it is best to keep them indoors to protect both local wildlife and the health and safety of the cats themselves.

7. Create a windbreak or shelterbelt. Planting a hedge or shelterbelt creates an area that provides birds and other wildlife protection from prevailing winds and shelter from the elements. Butterflies also appreciate a protected spot. For winter cover, evergreens such as American holly (*Ilex opaca*), southern magnolia (*Magnolia grandiflora*), eastern red cedar (*Juniperus virginiana*), southern wax myrtle (*Morella cerifera*), and eastern white pine (*Pinus strobus*) are effective. A windbreak also will reduce wintertime home-heating costs.

8. Leave snags, brush, and woodpiles. Snags, or dead trees, are useful to a variety of wildlife. Woodpeckers use them for finding food and nesting sites, but chickadees and other birds visit them as well, hunting under bark and in crevices for insects. Birds of prey such as eagles, osprey, and owls use snags as observation points. Brush and woodpiles also are excellent habitat for insects and larger creatures.

9. Learn to love—or tolerate. Although songbirds and butterflies are universally beloved, some wildlife needs to look farther for friends. Snakes top that list for many. If snakes scare you, locate brush piles and wildlife areas away from your home. Keep in mind that snakes help keep rodent and insect populations in check and that they (snakes, mice, and other wildlife) are far more afraid of people than people are of them. Learning to identify poisonous snakes can lessen your fear of harmless snakes.

10. Look for year-round appeal. To encourage wildlife to visit your landscape, analyze the availability of food during each month of the year. Whether you use a simple paper chart or a computer spreadsheet program, record which plants bear berries or seeds and when they are available. Based on this analysis, you can plant additional fruit-, nut-, and seed-bearing plants to provide food in the months you have identified as not having much available. Consider an inexpensive birdbath heater/deicer to ensure a steady supply of water for wildlife during winter months.

Take time to identify insects that are eating precious plants before spraying to eliminate them. Most are beneficial or benign. In a rich, diverse landscape, pests and predators generally balance each other out, so there is no need to spray. This tiger swallow caterpillar is desirable for the beautiful butterfly it will become. Photo by Barbara Ellis.

Garden Wisely

This catchall category covers all principles of sustainability. Gardening wisely means thinking about what you are doing in the garden today while setting longer-term goals. You will find plenty of short-term activities—all of them green or sustainable gardening practices—under "Ten Tips for Gardening Wisely." When it comes to longer-term objectives, reducing garden maintenance should be on everyone's list. Yards and gardens can—and should—require less maintenance over time. Reducing the size of the lawn and increasing plant diversity by planting more native plants help because these changes mean less

trimming, mowing, watering, and spraying. Planting more densely and in layers reduces maintenance, creates better growing conditions, and reduces the need to weed. Covering soil with mulch, especially with leaves that fall naturally from overhead trees, recycles and feeds the soil and the millions of organisms that live within it. (If the quantity of leaves that fall threatens to smother plants in the garden, use some of them in the compost pile. Shredding also reduces the volume of leaves so they are less likely to smother plants.) Feeding soils with compost has the same benefit. Both of these practices reduce the need to haul materials off site to a dump and diminish the need to water and weed.

A garden's style also affects the amount of maintenance required. Beautiful natural areas do not need pruned shrubs or closely mown grass to appear attractive to the passing public. Accepting a looser, wilder landscape as beautiful not only benefits wildlife but also reduces maintenance. It brings nature into our own yards and gardens where we can enjoy it up close. In some cases, the first step toward wilder, more natural landscapes means changing local regulations, such as "weed" ordinances. In other cases, it means changing a homeowners' association regulations. If a contractor mows your lawn and trims your property, reducing maintenance means reducing *their* maintenance. Talk to your contractor about allowing some areas to grow, or contract for less frequent mowing during summer droughts, when grass is not growing anyway.

Ten Tips for Gardening Wisely

A garden is always a work in progress. By focusing on projects and approaches, you will achieve your vision of a greener landscape without becoming overwhelmed or frustrated.

1. Go organic. Switching to natural, slow-release fertilizer and fewer and less toxic pesticides reduces chemicals in runoff, making your yard friendlier for beneficial insects.

2. Identify before you spray. A bug sitting on a damaged leaf is most likely either benign or beneficial and merely in the wrong place at the wrong time. Determine if insects are actually doing damage before attempting to eliminate them. If you identify a pest, it is best to watch populations for a day or so to see if they are growing. If the population increases, take time to check whether beneficial insects are starting to control the problem. When you do spray, use organic controls, and start with the least-toxic alternative first.

3. Care for the soil. Mulched soil amended with organic matter reduces runoff, and organic matter in the soil helps feed the microherd of organisms busy breaking down organic matter into a form plants can take up through their roots. Larger soil organ-

Protect and care for soil by keeping it covered with plants and/or a layer of mulch. Natural leaf litter is especially beneficial. Photo by Barbara Ellis.

isms such as earthworms, voles, and moles help move organic matter around and dig tunnels through the soil, allowing air and water to infiltrate. Keep well-prepared soil covered with chopped leaves or other organic mulch. Since the organic matter in soil is used up and broken down by the microherd, add more organic matter, especially compost, every time you dig a hole in the garden. Also replenish mulch regularly. If enough compost is available, consider spreading it over the soil, underneath the mulch.

4. Plant along ponds and waterways. Grow native grasses, perennials, shrubs, and trees along streams, ponds, storm drains, rivers, and the Bay. Buffer plantings slow runoff (see "Plans for Waterfront" on p. 37 for information on planting along waterways), absorb nutrients, create wildlife habitat, and reduce the need to mow grass in the soggy soil along waterways. Rich, diverse plantings along streams and other bodies of water have been shown to benefit fish populations, as they support a larger, more diverse insect population.

5. Theme weed. While weeding a bed from one end to the other is the conventional approach, some

The six principles in this chapter will help anyone create a more sustainable garden or landscape. Use them to help guide planting choices, design decisions, and more as you carve a path toward an appealing, exciting, and Bay-friendly design. Photo by Neil Soderstrom; Adkins Arboretum.

days the soil moisture level is perfect for eliminating dandelions, root and all, or pulling up garlic mustard. "Theme weeding"—attacking only one species of weed for whatever reason—can give a great sense of accomplishment. Another reason to theme weed is to eliminate a particular weed before the seeds mature. By pulling as the flowers fade, you can prevent it from going to seed and spreading. Pulling weeds by hand is the most environmentally sound approach, but non-native invasives often require chemical control. See Chapter 3 for more information on eliminating invasive plants.

6. Dispose of weeds properly. If you are removing English ivy, vinca, or other vigorous weeds, do not dispose of them on the edge of a wild area, where they can take root and spread. Instead, pack them into plastic bags (recycled mulch bags work well for this) and take them to the dump. Another option is to spread them out on the driveway until they are dried and completely dead, and then take them to the dump or add them to your compost pile.

7. Replace high-maintenance plants or plantings. This could mean shrubs or perennials that require constant spraying or fertilizing to stay alive or those that need regular pruning to keep their size in check. Remove them and substitute less-demanding native species. Allow a formal hedge that requires shearing several times a year to take on a more natural shape that requires less pruning, or replace it with a more natural, unsheared shrub border.

8. *Test the soil.* Every 3 to 5 years, test your soil to determine fertility levels. Request organic, slow-release fertilizers in the test result recommendations.

9. *Compost.* Recycle kitchen and yard waste in a freestanding compost pile or in a bin or other composting structure. See Suggested Resources for more on composting.

10. *Create your own path.* Ask for help and advice from experts and knowledgeable gardeners, to be sure, but it is important to have your own vision of what your landscape should look like.

TWO 🍃 Creating an Ecological Landscape Design

Adding planted areas under trees is one effective option for starting a landscape design. The beds in this backyard leave a nicely shaped lawn that is easy to mow. The beds include a mix of native and non-native plants, and the design features excellent shade trees, including northern red oak (*Quercus rubra*), redbud (*Cercis canadensis*), and white pine (*Pinus strobus*). Photo by Neil Soderstrom; design by Andie Phillips.

There is more than one way to begin transforming a conventional landscape into a sustainable one. One option is to undertake a series of projects such as those described in Chapter 1: Mulch a square yard of lawn to create a bed of ground covers, install a rain garden, plant a tree, or add native trees or perennials to the garden. While individual projects are a good place to start, some overall planning is valuable and yields a more polished design. Developing a design before planting commences will yield many rewards.

The information in this chapter will help you plan, a little or a lot, depending on your taste. The resources that each of us can dedicate to gardening and landscaping vary according to demands on our time, financial resources, interests, and even physical

(overleaf) Landscape features such as areas of shade or steep slopes play major roles in determining garden design. Existing trees determined the location of this gazebo, and drifts of wildflowers, including mayapples (*Podophyllum peltatum*), edge a moss lawn. Photo by Barbara Ellis; Burnet moss garden.

strength and ability. Even if you prefer minimal planning, there are reasons a simple plan makes sense. At the very least, a basic plan helps to identify the best sites for new trees, shrub borders, and other features. Planning helps to eliminate future problems such as trees that might become entangled in overhead wires or drop debris on the patio or in the pool, as well as shrubs that will quickly overgrow a location or shade a flower bed. In addition, a plan will help you prioritize projects and break them down into manageable tasks.

Strategies that will help you draw your plan include writing down design ideas; listing garden features that appeal to you; collecting thoughts from other family members, magazine articles, and photographs; and then organizing the information. Visiting gardens, especially Bay-friendly ones, can also inspire your design. This process helps if talking to a professional designer is your ultimate goal.

As you gather notes and make sketches, be aware that making lists and drawing on paper can become an obstacle. This is supposed to be about doing something *outside*. If you find yourself endlessly shuffling through files of various versions of property plot plans, plant lists, and notes about potential projects, pick something—anything—from your notes and go outside. Use one of the techniques described under "Planning on the Ground" on p. 63 to plan a project and then start digging and planting. Getting your hands dirty is satisfying, and you will find more inspiration working in the garden than you will moving paper around on the dining room table or making plans on a computer. Accomplishing a project on your list may help you move ahead with your overall plan.

Plans for Waterfront

Whether you live on the shores of the Chesapeake Bay, along one of the rivers or creeks that feed it, or overlooking a wetland or tidal pond, water plays a special role in your design plans. Maintaining a water view is important to every waterfront owner, but without the clean water that sustainable landscaping helps create, a view loses some of its appeal. A closely cropped lawn may seem like an effective way to achieve a water view, but a diverse planting along a waterway both enhances the view and helps keep the water clean. Native plants framing a water view introduce the changing colors of the season, entice wildlife to visit, and add the movement of swaying grasses or other plants and contrasting textures to the landscape.

Anyone who lives within the Chesapeake Bay region can make landscaping choices that improve water quality, but individuals who own waterfront property have a unique responsibility. Legislation is in place to protect water quality and the health of

 Understanding Our Watershed

Gardeners throughout the Chesapeake Bay region can have a positive effect on water quality and the environment, because we all live and garden in the same watershed. A watershed is a land area where all the water flows to the same place, whether it runs off the surface into a stream or infiltrates into the soil as groundwater. The Chesapeake Bay watershed is enormous. The Bay itself is about 200 miles long, but the watershed covers 64,000 square miles, stretching from the headwaters of the Susquehanna River in New York and flowing south through Pennsylvania. The Chesapeake Bay watershed encompasses all or portions of six states—Maryland, Virginia, Delaware, West Virginia, New York, and Pennsylvania—plus the District of Columbia. According to the Chesapeake Bay Program, the shorelines of the Bay and its tidal tributaries total 11,684 miles—longer than the West Coast of the United States—while the surface area of the Bay and its tidal tributaries covers approximately 4,480 square miles. The watershed encompasses 48 major rivers, 100 smaller rivers, and thousands of creeks and streams. Water quality in the Bay and its tributaries affects humans who live in the region, all of our activities, and the health of fish, crabs, insects, and all forms of wildlife. Just as human activity impacts water quality, water quality impacts humans' quality of life.

the watershed. Visit your local planning or conservation office and become familiar with the regulations. Once you are familiar with the requirements in your area, use the design process that follows to develop a plan for your property.

A lawn path edged with evergreens, including eastern red cedars (*Juniperus virginiana*), along with beds of flowers leads to the waterfront. Grading the soil underneath the lawn helps direct runoff so it flows into beds along the path. Photo © Roger Foley; design by Scott Brinitzer Design Associates.

This pool deck overlooks a broad native buffer area where wildflowers have been interplanted with native grasses for added color. On the deck, a sweetbay magnolia (*Magnolia virginiana*) grows in a planting area. Photo by Neil Soderstrom; design by Oehme, van Sweden Landscape Architecture.

Buffer plantings that feature grasses, wild-flowers, and other native vegetation protect the Bay by cleaning water runoff. Grasses along this shoreline are interplanted with spiderworts (*Trade-scantia virginiana*) and great coneflowers (*Rud-beckia maxima*), a native of the Southwest. Photo by Neil Soderstrom; design by Oehme, van Sweden Landscape Architecture.

Critical Area Legislation

Critical Area and Buffer ordinances throughout Maryland, Resource Protection Areas in Virginia, and equivalent laws in adjacent states regulate development activities along the waterfront. This includes restricting the removal of trees and other vegetation in the Critical Area and especially in the Buffer. In Maryland, land within 1,000 feet of the mean high water line around the Chesapeake Bay and the Atlantic Coastal Bays, including tidal wetlands and tributaries in both regions, is designated as the Chesapeake Bay Critical Area and given special protection. In addition, the Critical Area legislation designates a 100-foot-wide buffer (the Buffer) along wetlands and bodies of water. (The Buffer is expanded beyond 100 feet in areas where there are adjacent sensitive resources such as steep slopes or soils with development constraints.) One goal within the Buffer is to protect, restore, and establish diverse plant commu-nities along the Bay, the Atlantic Coastal Bays, and tributaries and wetlands.

If you plan to build a new home or an expansion, add a deck or terrace, construct stairs or a path to the shoreline, implement shoreline erosion control measures, remove trees or other vegetation, or conduct any other development activities, contact your local town or county planning department to learn what local regulations you need to follow. To control stormwater runoff and increase the amount of water that soaks into the soil, municipalities have laws regarding the percentage of a property that can be covered with impermeable surface. Impermeable surfaces, which prevent water from infiltrating the ground, include roofs (except for vegetated or green roofs), gravel, flagstone, pavers, brick, asphalt, concrete, and impervious parking materials. Impervious surfaces decrease aeration for roots, cause water to run off a site rather than percolate into the soil, and absorb heat, which leads to urban heat islands. Water is able to percolate through pervious surfaces such as permeable paving, wood chips, lawns, and garden beds. Pervious surfaces reduce runoff.

Critical Area and Buffer regulations ensure that construction and landscaping in these areas are handled in a way that reduces sediment and erosion, safeguards water quality, and protects the overall health of the Chesapeake Bay, the Atlantic Coastal Bays, or their tributaries and wetlands. Although the purpose of regulating disturbance on the land along waterways is to protect water quality—not to protect your water view—these regulations do not preclude a landowner from maintaining a water view. Implementing the sustainable practices described in this book respects these regulations and helps to ensure clean rivers and streams, the health of the wild creatures that thrive in these habitats, and a healthy habitat for humans. Consider Critical Area and Buffer regulations not as restrictions but as opportunities to add diversity and more interesting plants to your landscape. They do not preclude having a beautiful water view, and a view that overlooks sparkling clean water cannot be bad for property values!

Visiting the local planning department, learning about requirements and regulations, and obtaining necessary permits are essential first steps for any construction activity. Depending on where you live and where your property is located, you will need a permit to remove trees or other plants because of development activity or storm damage. Mitigation is required, which generally means you will need to replant more individual plants than were removed. (Leaving dead trees standing, where possible, benefits wildlife such as woodpeckers, nuthatches, and owls.) Under Maryland law, planting gardens is allowed without a permit in the 1,000-foot Critical Area, provided you do not remove any trees. There are specific requirements for gardens planted in the Buffer, since the goal for this area is a natural plant community, ideally forested with shade trees, understory trees, shrubs, and a variety of herbaceous plants. Traditional flower or vegetable gardens are generally not recommended in this area. Local planning offices have helpful books and pamphlets outlining the options, including lists of recommended plants and garden designs to create handsome plantings in the Buffer—or anywhere else. See Suggested Resources for more on these titles and links for further information.

Living Shorelines

Erosion can be a serious problem for anyone living along the water. Not only do receding shorelines endanger buildings, but erosion also reduces property size. Historically, bulkheads made of wood or concrete and stone revetment (often called rip-rap) have been the primary solutions. These structures often have unintended consequences and can create more problems than they solve, as they do not prevent waves and tide from battering the shoreline. Since wave and tide energy has to go somewhere, erosion commonly continues behind bulkheads and revetment. Solid structures also affect movement of silt and other material along the entire shoreline, and they can increase erosion on either end of the installation. Furthermore, bulkheads eliminate the crucial zone where water and shore meet that provides essential habitat and breeding grounds for wildlife.

A Living Shoreline is an environmentally friendly treatment that reduces erosion and protects land areas while enhancing areas near the shore. Instead of using bulkheads or other hard barriers, this technique uses planted areas to move wave energy and tides away from the land, essentially cushioning the shoreline. (Similar environmentally friendly tech-

niques can be used along rivers or streams with eroding banks. See "Planting along Waterways" on p. 258 for other effective techniques.) The plantings consist of native species, primarily wetland grasses that exist naturally in that area. Plantings are established in areas created by sand fill that is held in place by either temporary or permanent sills or other structures. In low-energy environments, coir logs are a commonly used option. Made of rolled-up coconut fiber, or coir, these last for several years—long enough for grasses and other plants to root deeply and become well established. On sites where the shoreline requires permanent protection, stone sills, jetties, or groins are used to protect planting areas and hold sand fill in place.

Living Shorelines are most effective on sites with low to moderate wave action, although they have been used successfully on high-energy sites in Maryland. Plant selection varies according to the site, but saltwater-tolerant smooth cord grass (*Spartina alterniflora*) is commonly used to restore plantings from the mid-tide to high tide mark. Salt meadow hay (*S. patens*) is commonly used for high marsh areas, which are inundated occasionally but are located above the high tide mark. (Where these two species occur, the line between them marks the high tide line, since smooth cord grass grows on sites that are inundated daily by tides and salt meadow hay only tolerates occasional inundation.) In addition to cushioning the land from waves and tide, plants also filter silt and bind soil and sand in place.

A vital characteristic of Living Shorelines is that

they provide land and water connectivity. Unlike bulkheads and revetment, they allow essential access for turtles and other creatures that nest on land and beaches and in wetlands. Living Shorelines also create vital shallow-water habitat and spawning areas for fish, crabs, and other aquatic organisms. Wetlands are rich ecosystems where decaying organic matter feeds microorganisms that in turn feed shellfish, fish, birds, amphibians, reptiles, and small mammals. A high percentage of endangered and threatened species in the Chesapeake Bay region, as well as two-thirds of commercially important fish and shellfish, depends on wetlands for spawning.

In addition to being a practical way to protect against erosion, a Living Shoreline becomes an attractive, natural-looking extension of a waterfront property that protects and enhances property value.

Living Shorelines do not have to be complex to be effective. Design and planting is not beyond the ability of a dedicated gardener. However, most individuals choose to hire a contractor to help them through design, permitting, and planting. In Maryland, property owners can start by contacting the Department of Natural Resources (DNR). (In Maryland the state owns the land below the *high tide mark*, so it has a vested interest in how the land is developed or modified. Homeowners have the right and responsibility to protect and maintain their shoreline, however.) In Virginia, start with your local permitting authority. (In Virginia the state owns the land below the *low tide mark*, so most wetlands are on private property.) Maryland DNR has resources available to help with planning as well as lists of approved contractors who can design and install. Virginia Institute of Marine Science's Center for Coastal Resources Management also has excellent resources.

For all Living Shorelines, a permit is required from local, state, and/or federal authorities, depending on the site. The design takes into account tidal activity, wave action, fetch (the distance from the site to nearby shores), slope, and grading, as well as factors that affect what plants will thrive on the site, including exposure, water salinity, and soil type. With the exception of sites where a few coir logs will hold necessary planting areas in place, most installations require heavy equipment to move sand or other materials for sills or other protection.

To find someone to install a Living Shoreline in Maryland, start with DNR's list of recommended contractors. Virginia does not have a similar list; see the online resources link in Suggested Resources to find recommendations on where to look.

Interview potential contractors as you would someone who is going to do work in your home. Find out if they have installed Living Shorelines. Ask for references—and check them—and ask to visit at least one installation. Ask references if they were pleased with the quality of the work accomplished and whether the contractor completed the project on time and on budget. Ideally, visit a Living Shoreline installed for another homeowner. Be aware that while these contractors will help you regain property lost to erosion, they are also in business for the money. Contractors buy plants and materials such as fill at wholesale and sell to you at retail. Research wholesale pricing to make sure you are being charged fairly. Stay away from contractors who try to circumvent the permit process.

Keep in mind a Living Shoreline is low maintenance, not *no* maintenance. Think of yours as an extension of your landscape and care for it accordingly. Weed periodically while plantings become established (inform local authorities beforehand to obtain any necessary permits) and pick up debris that washes into planting areas. Observe the site over time—photographs provide a good record of health and status of plants and structures—and consult with your contractor or other experts if problems arise.

Evaluating Your Site

The best way to start a site evaluation is by looking out the windows of your home. Make notes about the views from major windows and doors concerning what is attractive and what is not. Take pictures, too. Try to envision where it would be nice to have a flower garden, a shade tree or patio, or a shrub border to screen the neighbor's backyard. Note what views are worth highlighting—or hiding. Starting to plan indoors is important because it helps you develop a vision for enjoying the landscape both indoors and out. Next, go outdoors and walk around, again with a notebook and a camera. Reducing runoff is a crucial element of any sustainable landscape, so take time to study how water runs off your property. See Chapter 8 for more information on making a plan for handling runoff.

Conventional landscapes feature large expanses of lawn, a few trees, and all-too-common foundation plantings of non-native evergreen shrubs that require annual pruning to keep them in check. The goal of a conventional landscape is to look the same all year round. This arrangement impacts wildlife, but a year-round static green landscape has consequences for humans, too. If everything in the back or front yard is visible at a glance from indoors, there is little reason to walk out into the garden, and still less to enjoy once you are there. Part of site evaluation involves envisioning features that would make a landscape more enjoyable to view and to experience.

Think in terms of quick fixes as well as long-term goals. For example, planting a small grove of trees could make a shady spot for a sitting area or a ham-

This grass-and-brick path leading to a garage reduces paving and runoff, when compared with conventional driveways. The brick strips allow for traffic while preventing vehicles from causing worn stretches of lawn due to compacted soil. Photo by Neil Soderstrom; American Horticultural Society's River Farm.

mock. Perhaps a few carefully positioned shrubs would screen the spot to create a secluded outdoor living space, and berry-bearing shrubs could attract wildlife to enjoy. A shady terrace or deck might provide a space for enjoying coffee or family meals—and reduce the size of the lawn at the same time. Planting shrubs to hide a storage area might be another option. Or perhaps there is space for a rustic, meandering path around the perimeter that one day could wind around a rain garden and into a shady corner.

Whether evaluating sun and shade patterns or visualizing design ideas, a second-story bird's-eye view can be helpful. This stunning garden features lawn surrounded by a water garden, pathways, and beds that gradually blend into the larger landscape. Photo © Roger Foley; design by Oehme, van Sweden Landscape Architecture.

 Tools for Design

Landscape design tools have changed dramatically in the last 20 years. Use whatever makes you most comfortable, whether that means design software on a computer or tablet or graph paper, tissue overlays, and pencils. A digital camera or smartphone is useful for recording "before" views as well as projects in process. Print the pictures to use for sketching options and design ideas. See what your house would look like with an island of trees and shrubs in the front yard, for example, or how a deck might fit onto the back of the house. Choose the recordkeeping tools that work best for you.

For more information on organizing landscape ideas, see "Planning Outdoor Living Spaces," on p. 47.

Keep in mind that none of these plans needs to be accomplished this week, much less this year, or even next year. Your vision may be many years and decades in the making. Looking closely at your property, considering the possibilities, and making a plan will start you moving in the right direction.

Since some digging is inevitable, identify existing easements and utility lines on your property so they can be incorporated into a plan.

Sun and Shade Patterns

Watching the sun travel over your yard is an important part of site evaluation. Understanding areas that

Sun and Shade Terms

Nearly all plants will survive in a range of exposures, but knowing how much sun or shade a plant can tolerate allows you to plant it where it will actually thrive and honors the adage "right plant, right place." Below are the basic terms used in this book to describe sun and shade preferences.

Full sun. This means 10 hours of direct, uninterrupted sunlight per day during the summer months. Most plants recommended for full sun are happy receiving 8 hours of direct sun daily.

Part sun. Also called partial sun, this term is used to describe sites that receive fewer than 8 hours of direct sun daily. Plants recommended for part sun generally need 4 to 6 hours of direct sun for best growth, and the closer to 6 hours the better. In most cases, hot afternoon sun is best. "Full sun to part sun" indicates a plant that prefers full sun but can tolerate less. In addition to sites with afternoon sun, look for spots that are sunny in the morning, shaded at midday, and sunny again in the afternoon.

Part shade. This term refers to sites that receive shade for a portion of the day and direct sun the rest of the day. Sites in part shade differ greatly, depending on the duration and timing of the shade. In general, plants that need part shade should receive no more than 6 hours of direct sun daily. Most will do better with less. Plants recommended for part shade or "part shade to shade" are best in a spot that receives afternoon shade. Most can tolerate direct sun in the morning, but they need shade once the sun is hot.

Dappled shade. This term refers to high, bright shade under a tree, with changing patches of sun and shade throughout the day. Plants that grow naturally on the edges of woodlands and in clearings in the woods are typically plants that thrive in dappled shade.

Shade. Also called full shade, this term refers to sites that do not receive any direct sun throughout the day. Spring bulbs and woodland wildflowers are able to thrive in full shade because they generally sprout, flower, and die back before deciduous trees above them block out all the sun. Few plants survive in the full shade under evergreen trees.

are sunny or shady at different times of day is valuable for locating flower beds, shade trees, and features like sitting areas. In addition, identifying sun and shade patterns is essential for selecting plants that will thrive in different sites.

Observe the sun for a few days to determine where planting beds for sun-loving or shade-loving plants could be located. For an accurate picture of sun and shade patterns, make observations throughout the year, as the sun changes position in the sky seasonally. For example, deciduous trees on the south or west side of a house are useful for casting shade in summer, but since they lose their leaves in fall, they do not block winter sun that helps warm the house during the colder months. Make notes about these preferred locations, so that you can add them to a master landscape plan.

The time of day a particular area is sunny or shady is important, since this affects the temperature of the site. A spot that is sunny in the morning but shady in the afternoon will be cooler than one that receives shade in the morning and sun in the afternoon. Use

This front yard features a small area of lawn on level, easy-to-mow ground. Mixed plantings cover the slopes that run from yard to sidewalk, and flowering dogwoods (*Cornus florida*) provide spring color, summer shade, and fall berries for birds. Photo © Roger Foley; design by Florence Everts & Associates.

this information to site plants that prefer shade but need some sun to bloom well by locating them in morning sun and afternoon shade. Or, on a shady lot, look for spots that are sunny in the afternoon to accommodate plants that thrive in heat and sun but tolerate part shade.

Slope and Other Conditions

In addition to sun and shade patterns, a proper site evaluation takes into account such things as existing slopes, sites that are frequently wet or flooded, and wind exposure. Look for the following as you evaluate your site.

Prevailing wind. Wind direction may affect where shrub borders should be located to mitigate winds and may also determine where plants are planted, since prevailing winds can dry out foliage quickly and break off brittle stems. Wind exposure also plays a role in determining what plants will thrive on a given site. For example, wind can damage the foliage of broad-leaved evergreens during the winter months when the ground is frozen, as the leaves cannot take up water fast enough to protect themselves against this damage.

Topography and soil. Identify slopes where water rushes off and depressions where it settles, since understanding both factors is necessary to locate beds and site plants. For example, replacing lawn on a steep slope with ground covers or shrubs will reduce runoff, and a persistently wet spot may be perfect for moisture-loving perennials or shrubs. Sites where soil is excessively compacted or where gravel has been piled and then covered are also worth noting, so you can accommodate them in your plans.

Tough sites. Record spots where every plant you have tried to grow seems to die and areas where lawn grass does not grow well. These areas will require closer examination of soil and other growing conditions. (See Chapter 3 for suggestions and more information.) They may be good candidates for replanting with ground covers or other plants or perhaps for covering with a thick layer of bark mulch. Also note areas where grass is excessively lush or where other plants grow tall and lanky. These, too, are candidates for replanting, since finding shrubs or perennials more suited to the site will make it more attractive and easier to maintain.

Buried obstacles. Live wires are at the top of this list. Always call Miss Utility (811) or your state's "call before you dig" hotline before starting any project that involves digging. Be on the lookout for buried concrete or asphalt, such as abandoned walkways, parking areas, or driveways. Some yards have dump areas where pieces of concrete or gravel were disposed of and forgotten. Obviously, these are equally challenging sites. Options for handling all three obstacles include uncovering them and removing them or burying them under raised beds.

Invasive plants. Whether you do it as part of an overall landscape plan or because a particular plant is an aggressive grower, be aware of non-native invasive plants on your property. Non-native invasive plants are fast-spreading species that have been introduced from another country or region. They spread rapidly by seed or by vegetative means (ag-

gressive rhizomes, for example) and out-compete native plants. See "Managing Invasive Plants" on p. 102 for more information and a list of some of the worst offenders in the Chesapeake region. Many invasives are still available for sale in garden centers. Identify populations of invasive species on your property that could be eliminated.

Creating Useable Landscapes

Outdoor spaces that are a pleasure to spend time in and explore are rare. The average home landscape contains surprisingly little space that is pretty and appealing, especially since most homeowners maintain far more lawn than they need and use. In the suburbs, large yards make it possible to place houses well away from one another, but often these landscapes offer little else. City lots are often equally unappealing, usually because they are tiny and because it is difficult to decide how to use the space effectively.

Moving toward a more sustainable design means rethinking the way you use your yard. In addition to reducing runoff and adding plants for wildlife, this means thinking about people and how they enjoy being outdoors. Good landscape design means making compelling spaces people want to use, from comfortable sitting areas to areas for play or exploration.

Planning Outdoor Living Spaces

To plan outdoor spaces that appeal to you and your family, make a list of favorite outdoor activities you could enjoy in your yard. Also list features that appeal to you, such as spring-blooming trees or flowers that attract butterflies. While collecting ideas, walk around your property and look for spaces that might suit them. A very simple drawing of your property or

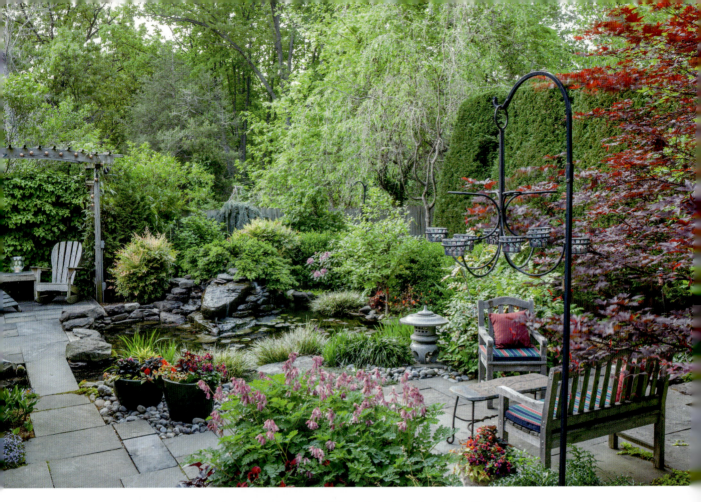

(top) Effective planning is important for any design, but it is perhaps most valuable on small lots where space is at a premium. This well-designed suburban lot is both useful and inviting. It incorporates two sitting areas, a water garden, and clipped hedges for privacy. Photo © Roger Foley; design by Joan McCarthy and GreenSmiths, Inc.

(bottom) A sitting area does not need to be fancy or expensive to be comfortable and useful. Pavers eliminate the need to mow grass under this simple sitting area, and trees surrounding it provide privacy. Photo by Barbara Ellis; Beth Burrell, Giving Tree Garden.

a copy of the property plat may be helpful for note-taking. To use space efficiently, plan spaces that can be used for multiple activities. If badminton, croquet, and Frisbee with dogs are on your list, a fairly large lawn area is in order to accommodate them. On the other hand, a list that includes reading, bird watching, outdoor dining, and coffee with friends may best be accommodated with a landscape that does not include any lawn.

Writing ideas on index cards, in a word-processing program, or with a note-taking program on a tablet makes it possible to sort ideas easily. For example, if a secluded sitting area, more shade trees, and shrubs that produce berries for birds are all on your list, consider combining them into a single area. Make duplicates of ideas you want in more than one place—shade trees or shrubs that attract birds, for example. Note which activities or landscape features can be adjacent to one another, such as a sitting area situated next to bird feeders, or a spectator area next to a lawn area used for volleyball or badminton. To involve the family, post ideas on a bulletin board or share them on a family website.

While collecting ideas, also consider space for utility areas, such as for composting. If vegetables or herbs are in your plan, reserve a sunny area for a food garden.

Creating a private, shady retreat can be a design goal that enhances the overall appeal of a garden. Take note of shady spots that might be perfect for a table and chairs or just a seat. In addition to spaces that are already fully shaded, look for spots where adding another tree or even an arbor would create a shady area. Plans for a sitting area might also include shrubs for screening and privacy. Mulch and pavers, useful for creating a level surface for chairs and tables, also are a great alternative to lawn and eliminate the need to mow under and around outdoor furniture.

Look for spots that are shaded, or could be shaded, in the afternoon and early evening if creating space for family picnics or evening dinner parties is a priority. Consider adding trees on the west side or an arbor overhead to create or augment shade for such spaces. Is your deck or terrace shaded? If not, plant trees or an arbor to make it more comfortable to use. If an existing deck or terrace only provides room for a chair or two, consider ways to enlarge it. For outdoor dining areas, plan for a level path for access from the kitchen to carry food and supplies.

The list of outdoor activities you have developed will determine the framework of an overall garden design. See "Developing a Plan" on p. 59 for information on drawing a design. Making decisions about your landscape is easier once you have a plan, whether general or detailed. It will identify areas where you need lawn for activities. Siting new trees and shrubs becomes easier once you identify spots where more shade or additional privacy is desired. In addition, if expanding the house or building a deck are long-term objectives, you can plan access routes for equipment and materials storage and plant new trees well away from potential construction zones.

Beds, Borders, and Planting Islands

Lawn is the common denominator in most landscapes, and properties dotted with trees and/or shrubs surrounded by a carpet of lawn pose a special design challenge. Incorporating isolated trees or shrubs into larger beds, borders, or planting islands is an effective means to a more lush and unified landscape. Incorporating existing trees into islands of shrubs, perennials, and other plants creates areas appealing enough to visit regularly to view changes or see what has come into bloom. In addition, trees surrounded by mixed plantings are more attractive

(top) Beds planted with a mix of trees, shrubs, perennials, ferns, and bulbs help anchor this house to the landscape. The plantings also decorate the walkway to the front door. Photo by Barbara Ellis; Clarke garden.

(bottom) Perennial borders typically run along a fence, driveway, lot line, or building. This border features a variety of native wildflowers, including purple coneflowers (*Echinacea purpurea*), thread-leaved coreopsis (*Coreopsis verticillata*), liatris (*Liatris* spp.), beebalm (*Monarda didyma*), and non-native small globe thistle (*Echinops ritro*). All are excellent at attracting butterflies and pollinators. Photo by Barbara Ellis; Grotsky garden.

than lawn to birds and other wildlife. This approach also reduces the size of the lawn and eliminates the need to trim around every tree or shrub, thus speeding maintenance and protecting trees from damage by string trimmers.

If you are starting with an empty lot—with lawn and few, if any, trees, shrubs, or flowers—plan to create beds and/or borders from the outset, for mowing efficiency as well as to gain the other benefits that beds and mixed plantings bring to a landscape. Create plantings that do double duty. In addition to creating an attractive framework for your home, beds, borders, and islands can add privacy or shade, attract wildlife, block the wind, and define a path's edge. Mixed beds also sequester much more carbon than a few trees interspersed in an expanse of lawn.

To visualize the shape of a planting island that incorporates two or more existing trees or shrubs, snake a hose on the ground to design the edge of the bed. Or use stakes and string, a sprinkling of lime,

or landscape paint to experiment with shapes. To connect a tree just off the corner of the house with a strip of grass between the house and the tree, plant a bed that extends from the foundation or the foundation plantings. Whatever method you use, look at the shape from several different angles.

Beds can be any size and shape. Square or rectangular beds reflect a formal design, while free-form beds create an informal or natural look. Beds should be anchored to other landscape elements so their function in the landscape is clear. Plan beds that serve as the edge of a pathway, that define a garden room, or that function as an extension of a foundation planting. One effective landscape planning approach is to first determine the location of all the paths and walkways on your property and then design beds that are anchored to them. When determining the shape of a bed, keep in mind that simple, gentle curves are best. Island beds should be about three times as long as they are wide. In general, large

🍃 Bed Types and Terms

There are three main types of garden beds, each incorporated into the landscape in a slightly different way.

Island bed. These plantings are surrounded by lawn and can be viewed from all sides. An island bed can connect trees and shrubs that are already planted in a lawn.

Beds, mixed beds, and flower beds. These terms generally describe gardens located along the edge of a lawn or against a house, sitting area, or structure. These types of plantings are generally viewed from two or three sides.

Perennial borders or mixed borders. As the name suggests, perennial borders primarily are planted with herbaceous (soft-stemmed) plants. Mixed borders, on the other hand, contain perennials, grasses, shrubs, and small trees. Both types of borders generally run along the edge of the yard, in front of a fence or building, or along a walkway or driveway. They are meant to be seen primarily from a distance and from only one direction. For a lower-maintenance alternative to a traditional perennial border, consider a meadow garden that runs along the back lot line adjacent to a natural area.

(top) To visualize what shrubs and trees will look like once lawn is eliminated and the plants have been underplanted with ground covers or other plants, lay a hose on the ground in the approximate shape of the bed. Use newspaper and mulch to smother the grass.

(bottom) This large island bed incorporates trees, shrubs, and ground covers to create a large planting area surrounded by lawn. Photo by Barbara Ellis; Clarke garden.

Stepping-stones set in grass make an attractive path that is also simple to maintain. Since the stepping-stones are flush with the soil surface, a mower can pass right over them, making the area easy to mow and eliminating the need to trim. Photo © Roger Foley; design by DCA Landscape Architects.

yards call for large islands, since a small planting will look puny and insubstantial. Conversely, a large island can make a small yard look too small and the remaining lawn appear too fragmented. In this case, either create a smaller island or plan beds on either side of a central patch of lawn. Or dispense with lawn altogether and fill the yard with plants and paths from which to admire them.

Beds that connect trees to other plants or features can be phased in over time. One option is to first mulch the area that will eventually be planted to eliminate grass and weeds (spread 8 to 10 sheets of newspaper under the mulch to help smother existing vegetation), then wait a season or even a few years to plant. Indicate the locations of existing trees and shrubs on your plan so you can create beds that will connect them sometime in the future. On sites under trees, root competition can make it difficult for plants to thrive. A suitable solution is to maintain an unplanted but mulched area around the tree where leaf litter is allowed to fall and accumulate. (Set large

containers under trees if you want to add color or interest.) Outside the mulched zone, plant compatible ground covers, perennials, shrubs, grasses, and other plants that grow at the same rate and that thrive in similar conditions. With time, they will multiply and grow into areas closer to the tree. When spreading mulch around trees or other existing plants, always feather out the depth of the mulch so that it does not touch trunks or stems. Mulching too closely and deeply around a plant's base or trunk can lead to rot and insect damage.

Plan for Paths

Every landscape has a variety of pathways. There are formal ones, like the walkway from driveway to front door, and utilitarian ones, such as the single track to the compost pile or vegetable garden or the cut-through used to visit neighbors. Paths that wind through the landscape, either around beds or to a hidden sitting area, are valuable and enjoyable.

(top) This informal path winds through a tiny shade garden that features moss, ferns, and other plants. The bends in the path, along with the roots that cross it, cause visitors to walk slowly and pause to enjoy the plantings. Photo © Roger Foley; design by Joseph Krakora and Sheela Lampietti.

(bottom) To accommodate visitors but save plants from being damaged by foot traffic, lay paving stones or spread mulch to create an obvious path through flower gardens or mixed beds.

A well-designed landscape plan takes both kinds of paths into account.

As you design, think about paths that will take you to new gardens and spaces. Incorporate existing pathways into your overall design. When planning utilitarian paths, remember that a direct route is nearly always best. Family and friends inevitably cut across paths that wiggle and wander in a meandering fashion, trampling beds and other plantings in the process. The best course of action is to plan beds and other features around existing informal paths, or lay pavers or maintain a mulched section through a bed to accommodate an existing traffic pattern.

Although a direct route is best for utilitarian paths, not all routes through the landscape need to be straight. Consider a route with gentle curves or a walkway that dips out of sight behind a shrub or other feature when designing a path for touring the property or a particular garden. This creates intrigue and beckons visitors farther into the yard. For walkways that lead to outdoor dining or picnic areas, plan a smooth, safe surface that is as level as possible, so people carrying trays of food can walk without incident.

Garden Mapmaking 101

A fully developed landscape plan starts with a base map drawn to scale. The base map should show property boundaries, the location of the house, the driveway, and outbuildings such as sheds or garages. It should also identify the location of major trees or other plantings, as well as any easements that exist.

An existing survey of the property is a perfect place to start. If you do not have one, check with your municipality's planning office, local property tax office, or county courthouse to see if one is available. Internet map sites such as Google Earth offer another option for obtaining a base map. To create a base map from a survey, take measurements from the survey and redraw it on a sheet of paper, make a large photocopy, or trace the boundaries and features of the existing survey onto a new sheet of paper. To avoid drawing or writing on the original base map, use tracing paper overlays, as described below, to do the actual design work.

If an existing survey does not exist, you will need to draw a map to scale. Use the directions in "Geometry in the Garden," below, to draw an entire map, locate trees accurately on an existing survey, or create a plan for just one section of the yard. Large sheets of graph paper are another mapping option, but using some simple geometry skills is easier.

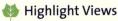

Highlight Views

Every property has something that makes it unique, whether a nice mature tree, a woods edge, or a view of the water, mountains, or even a nearby building or landscape. As you consider your property, look for views to highlight. Trees and other plantings can frame and accent views. A meadow may be a great option for ensuring a water view is visible from multiple directions. Be sure to consider the topography of a site, however. Trees and/or lower shrubs can add interest and frame a view and are invaluable for blocking or screening views. One way to experiment with positioning trees is to drive stakes or fence posts into the ground and then observe them from several angles to determine if plants in these positions will achieve the intended purpose.

Balance Maintenance

Enthusiastic gardeners may want to garden on every square inch of their yard. To tend gardens everywhere and manage this ambitious workload, think in terms of maintenance zones. Balance high-maintenance areas such as conventional flower or herb gardens with areas that require less attention to look their best, such as a naturalistic garden of native meadow plants. It is possible to create a gardenlike feel in a low-maintenance ground cover bed by underplanting it with spring bulbs and adding drifts or groupings of different ground covers to create a patchwork quilt of texture and color.

A base map helps ensure an effective design because it records views to highlight, existing trees, and other important features. This informal garden features a small, beautifully shaped lawn for playing with resident dogs and a meadow overlooking the Chesapeake Bay. Photo by Barbara Ellis; Lang garden.

Geometry in the Garden

Mapmaking Supplies

To draw a base map from scratch, or to mark the location of trees on an existing survey, gather the following supplies:

Clipboard

Rough sketch of your property (not necessarily to scale)

Pens in two different colors

100-foot measuring tape

Scratch paper

Map Drawing Supplies

To draw the map, you will need the following:

Several large sheets of paper (an 18- by 24-inch sketchbook, for example)

Large drafting compass (the type with a pencil on one side and a point on the other that is used to draw circles) that reaches at least 10 inches

Ruler

Pencil

Masking tape

Triangulation is an invaluable tool for drawing a base map from scratch or for accurately locating boundaries, trees, or other features in the yard on an existing map. To triangulate, you will need a rough sketch of the property that indicates the various features to be included in the final design. Also make a list of these same features—trees, property corners, sheds, etc.—on a piece of scratch paper. Scale is not important at this point.

Next, pick two points that will be consistent reference points. For example, the two back corners of the house will serve this purpose well if you are mapping the backyard. Measure the distance between these two points and write this measurement on the rough sketch. Select points that allow you to see and measure to all the features in one area of the yard from both reference points. (Eventually you will need a

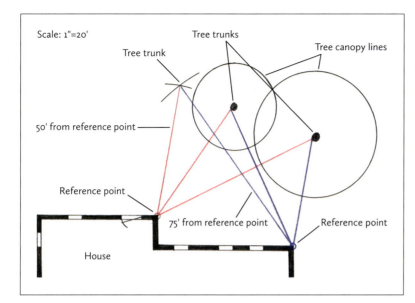

Scale: 1"=20'

Tree trunk

Tree trunks

Tree canopy lines

50' from reference point

Reference point

75' from reference point

Reference point

House

Locate features, such as the trees shown here, on a base map using triangulation from two reference points to each feature (trees). Select a scale for the map. Then, using a drafting compass set at the proper distance according to the scale, draw arcs on the map from each reference point. The arcs meet at the correct location of the feature.

pair of reference points for each section of the yard that is mapped. For large yards and for ambitious designs, measure and draw the house first, so all of its corners can serve as reference points.)

Starting with the first pair of reference points, use the following steps to triangulate:

1. Circle each reference point with a different color ink. Measurements from each point will be listed in the same ink color.
2. From one of the reference points, measure to the first feature being mapped. Record the distance from the point to the feature on the rough sketch, using the ink color used to circle that reference point. (You may also note measurements on scratch paper or a hand-held tablet.)
3. Measure from the other reference point to the same feature. Record the distance in the color ink used to circle the second point. When measuring to trees or other features that are hard to pinpoint (unlike the corner of a garage, for example), measure to the same spot from each

reference point. For example, measure to the same point on the front of a tree trunk. Also note the diameter of the trunk or the overall size of a clump of shrubs.

4. Continue measuring to other features that will be included on the base map. List distances from both reference points, each in the correct color.

If you prefer, you can make all the measurements from one reference point to the various features, then make measurements from the second point. Either way, the end result is a list of features with pairs of measurements in two colors.

Making a Map to Scale
Bring your sketch map and other supplies indoors and spread them out on a table to draw the base map. Protect the table with a sheet of cardboard to avoid poking holes in the table surface with the compass point.

Next, decide what scale to use. To determine what will fit on a sheet of paper, divide the longest bound-

🍃 Using a Grid for Design

Landscape professionals often use a grid as the basis for a design. In its simplest form, the grid is two sets of parallel lines—arranged perpendicular to each other like the grid formed by streets in a city—used to establish the framework of the design. Designers use "lines of force" to establish the grid. Primary lines of force run along the sides of the house and extend into the yard. Lines of force can also be drawn out along garage walls or other structures. Lesser lines of force extend from either side of doors and windows. Perpendicular lines that extend across the grid radiate from other landscape features—a garage, for example—or their location can be determined by a logical measurement, such as the width of a porch or picture window. The grid lines are then used to establish the location of walkways, beds, focal points, and other landscape elements. Because they are drawn in relation to existing buildings, they help link the garden to the house in a logical and pleasing manner.

To create a grid for your property, draw lines of force on an overlay of your base map, using a single color for all primary lines and a second color for lesser lines of force. Pay attention to lines that extend from windows and doors, since they are useful for locating landscape features such as focal points.

Next, select a prominent dimension, such as the length of an addition on the house or the width of a picture window. Draw lines out from the house that mark this dimension, then establish an imaginary square using the same dimension. Extend lines of force into the landscape from the corners of this central square. To determine the location of paths, beds, or other features, divide the central square into equal spaces. For example, a 12-foot-long addition would establish a 12-foot-square central square that could be used as is or divided into four 3-foot by 3-foot smaller squares. Use these lines to determine the location and size of other landscape elements.

For more information on using a grid for landscape design, see the design books in Suggested Resources. Or search "grid landscape design" on the Internet. For a more informal style that uses curved lines to create a design, search "arc and tangent landscape design."

ary of the yard (or the space being mapped) by the scale. For example, if you have a 250-foot lot line and are using a scale where 1 inch equals 20 feet, divide 250 feet by 20. That equals 12.5 inches, so a 250-foot lot line would easily fit on a page from an 18- by 24-inch sketchbook.

Once you have settled on a scale, use the following directions:

1. Draw the reference points first, locating them on the paper so there is plenty of room to fill in the rest of the area being mapped. Draw the reference points to scale and the proper distance apart. For example, for reference points at either corner of a 150-foot-long house and a 1-inch-equals-20-feet (1″=20′) scale, the points should be 7.5 inches apart (150÷20=7.5).

2. Note the proper ink color next to each reference point.

3. Next, set the drafting compass to the correct distance from the first reference point to the first feature. Place the point of the compass on the

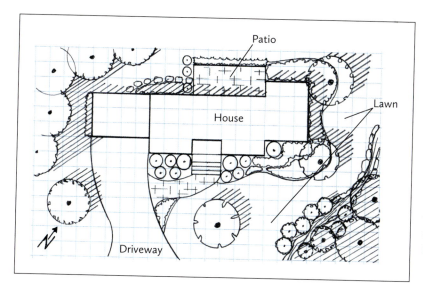

Patio

Lawn

House

Driveway

Landscape designs can be simple sketches or finished drawings. Overlay sheets of tracing paper on your scaled base map so you can experiment with ideas without drawing on the original map. This drawing indicates where afternoon shade will fall and planting beds that will be easy to mow around. Longer-term goals may be to plan plantings that will create more afternoon shade for the back terrace and less lawn overall.

reference point and draw an arc with the other end. For example, to locate a tree that is 50 feet from the first reference point on a map drawn with a 1"=20' scale, set the compass at 2.5 inches (50÷20=2.5). Put the point on the first reference point and draw an arc on the base map with the pencil end.

4. Reset the drafting compass to correspond to the correct distance from the second point, place the point of the compass on the second reference point, and draw a second arc. To continue the example above, if the tree is 75 feet from the second reference point, set the compass at 3.75 inches (75÷20=3.75), place the point of the compass on the second point, and draw a second arc.

5. The point where the two arcs meet indicates the location of the feature being mapped, in this case, a tree. To finish adding the tree to the map, draw in the diameter of the trunk, to scale, using the measurements you gathered. It is also a good idea to indicate the spread of the branches, or canopy, on your map.

Continue adding features. Be sure to mark "North" on the map and note the scale you are using. If you need to add a feature that is farther away or difficult to reach from your initial reference points, triangulate from the existing points to establish new reference points and then measure from those points. Any of the points you have previously identified can be used as new reference points.

Developing a Plan

Organizing a collection of ideas and dreams into a plan for a garden is a creative and inspirational activity that each gardener approaches differently. Depending on your style, you may decide to base your plan on a list of ideas and a rough sketch of your property. See "Planning on the Ground" on p. 63 for methods that do not depend on paper and pencils. To develop a design from a finished base map, first buy a supply of tracing paper. Place a sheet of tracing paper over your design so you can experiment with

Garden style is more than just formal or informal. This modern-looking landscape features a round swimming pool, a shape characteristic of formal gardens, paired with informal, naturalistic-style plantings. Photo by Neil Soderstrom; design by Oehme, van Sweden Landscape Architecture.

The rectangular central lawn and clipped hedges that surround this garden are formal elements, but exuberant plantings in the beds surrounding it create a lush, informal feel. Photo © Roger Foley; design by Arentz Landscape Architects.

ideas without drawing directly on the original map. Trace a line or two from the base map onto the tracing paper overlay to make it easy to line up sheets accurately. When one sheet of tracing paper becomes too messy, add another and trace elements onto the new sheet that are worth keeping. Then discard the sheet underneath.

An overlay identifying general sun and shade patterns and the location of major shade trees is useful, although noting this information on the base map as a permanent record is also helpful. Also record wet or low-lying areas, slopes, and other troublesome sites that need special design attention. Mark the location of views worth highlighting or hiding as well. Even if all this information is on a separate overlay(s), you can add it to the stack and then add a third piece of tracing paper on top to experiment with designs. You might also set it aside and use it as a reference or return it to the stack later for considering plants or determining exact locations for particular features.

Selecting a Style

Think about the style of garden that appeals to you. While every gardener's preferences are unique, there are two general styles of gardens, and both can be sustainable. Understanding both styles makes drawing a plan easier. Remember, there are no strict rules you must follow—many gardeners mix elements of both styles. Formal designs generally require more maintenance than informal ones because of the need for regular pruning, edging, and other tasks.

Formal gardens. These feature a balanced, symmetrical design, with pairs of matching plants marking pathways and, for example, mirror-image shrub borders on either side of the front entrance. Planting beds are geometric, square, round, oval, or rectangular, and if a path bisects two beds, the beds on either side generally look identical or at least include the same edging plant around the outside edge. Formal designs tend to use fewer, but carefully selected, species of plants. These plants are repeated throughout the design to create a sense of unity and a balanced harmony. Formal gardens highlight stone, gravel, and brick, along with classic details such as metal gates and urns or stone statuary. Clipped hedges are another common characteristic of formal gardens.

Informal gardens. Gardens with an informal style feature beds with a natural, free-form shape. They tend to be unstructured and are more dynamic than formal gardens. Informal gardens lack the predictable repetition of plants, shapes, and materials. Plantings are balanced asymmetrically, meaning that two or three smaller plants may balance one large one, for example. But that is not to say that informal gardens look messy or disorganized. Despite the variety and free-form shapes, plants can be arranged in bold drifts or groupings of color that give the design a handsome, tended, and intentional look. On the other end of the spectrum, informal gardens can feature a jumbled, one-of-everything style, as in a cottage garden.

To create a sense of unity, an informal design uses repeated plant colors, forms, and textures throughout a bed or across the entire landscape. Informal designs can feature walls made of rough stone or landscape ties, paths covered with mulch or flagstones, and board fences or shrub borders as boundaries. Statuary is selected and arranged in a free-form fashion, with a classic or whimsical style, or however the garden's creator prefers.

Mixing it up. Sometimes using both formal and informal elements makes the most sense. In a small front yard, beds of ground covers in a formal arrangement may be easier to care for and give the

(top) The exuberant flower beds surrounding this rustic shed have an informal, cottage-style flair. Photo by Barbara Ellis; Clarke garden.

(bottom) Grasses, spiderworts (*Tradescantia virginiana*), and great coneflowers (*Rudbeckia maxima*) planted in a naturalistic style echo wild areas beyond the bounds of this ground-level deck. Photo by Neil Soderstrom; design by Oehme, van Sweden Landscape Architecture.

entrance a handsome, orderly appearance. Formal elements are useful for lending order to an otherwise informal design. Matching beds of ground covers on either side of a path could define the entrance to a wilder, informal garden, for example.

Drawing a Plan

To start experimenting with your garden plan, lay another sheet of tracing paper on top of the base map and begin sketching in ideas—beds, sitting areas, rain gardens, shade trees, and other features—on your list. Draw the area in plan view—looking down on the property from above. Drawing in ovals or rectangles is fine to determine locations, sizes, and approximate shapes of different areas. When one overlay gets too messy, add another on top of it and trace the reference lines to make sure everything lines up. Trace any parts of the previous drawing that you would like to continue working on and discard the rest. By using tracing paper overlays, you can experiment with ideas as much as you like, discarding what does not work and building on what does.

Keep scale in mind during this process to allow sufficient room for features and plants. A table and chairs or an old-fashioned picnic table requires more space than one might imagine. A rectangular table that seats eight needs at least an 8- by 12-foot space. Paths should be at least 4½ feet wide to accommodate a garden cart or two people walking side by side. Check the mature dimensions—width as well as height—of trees and other favorite plants to make sure the areas designated for them are large enough.

Once you are satisfied with your design, make a clean copy of the drawing. If you plan to do all the work yourself, identify projects to undertake in the short term as well as those planned for the future. Use the plant lists in Part 2 to develop individual garden plans, and read the information in Chapter 3 on developing sites and caring for soil. If you will use contractors or other professionals for some or all of your garden's installation, use the plan to review design options with these professionals. Experienced contractors are undoubtedly familiar with similar projects and sites and will have valuable suggestions.

Planning on the Ground

If paper planning is not your style or if visualizing your plan is difficult, try the techniques below to experiment with designs in the yard.

Stakes or hoses. Experiment with bed shapes, path locations, and even the size and shape of patios or decks by marking them out with stakes and string or "drawing" them on the ground with hoses. Revise until the design suits you. Then, to eliminate tripping hazards, mark the design with lime or landscape paint and coil up hoses and remove the stakes and string.

Enlist stand-ins. To determine the best location for a particular tree or to decide where to site a shrub border, enlist family and friends to act as stand-ins. Ask participants to stand where you think specific plants need to be located and evaluate each from all sides. Fine-tune the placement of each plant by having stand-ins adjust their positions, then mark the final locations with stakes. Leave stakes in place for at least several days to evaluate the location from all angles. Transfer this information onto your plan, if you have one. Inanimate stand-ins are also effective: Set out lawn chairs or garbage cans to determine shrub positions or use fence posts for trees.

Space out plants. If you already have plants, space them on your site and then stand back and visualize them at their mature sizes. You can find this information on plant labels when plants are purchased.

A large feature, such as this water garden, requires planning as well as construction expertise, unless you are an experienced do-it-yourselfer. Plan a large feature like this one first, then develop plantings around it and add other details as time and budget allow. Photo © Roger Foley; design by Joan McCarthy and GreenSmiths, Inc.

Plant descriptions in this book include mature height and width as well. Rearrange until you have a design that suits. Mark final locations with stakes or landscape paint. This method also is useful for locating shrubs and perennials in a bed.

Plan on Pictures. Photographs printed from the computer offer another way to experiment with design. Select shots of a particular area, print out a few copies, and use pens or pencils to sketch in trees, shrubs, or other features to evaluate. Be aware of scale, and draw plants at mature or nearly mature sizes to anticipate their impact as they grow.

Growing with Your Design

Do not allow the process of designing your garden to become overwhelming and prevent you from planting and enjoying your landscape. If necessary, go back to Chapter 1 and pick a simple project. Select-

ing and planting a native shrub or replacing a patch of grass with flowers for butterflies will give you experience and confidence to tackle another task. Many projects can be completed in a weekend. Digging and planting in your own yard helps develop a better understanding of conditions that exist there and plants that will thrive.

Ideas and inspiration are everywhere: Find photographs in magazines and on the Internet and garden designs in books like those listed in Suggested Resources. Local botanical gardens are another valuable resource. Participating in garden tours offered by garden clubs or horticultural or environmental organizations can be especially helpful, since you will be able to see the mature size and shape of many natives that can look puny when they are growing in containers in a nursery. Tours also offer an opportunity to talk to fellow gardeners and gain from their experience.

To create plantings that are diverse and natural looking, consider planting in layers. This illustration shows trees forming a canopy layer and large shrubs forming a lower, understory layer in the shade of the trees. A variety of perennials and other low-growing plants covers the ground. Soil and roots are a vital fourth layer.

Above all, remember that garden design is a creative process. It takes time and experimentation. Gardens are always changing, and there are no correct answers. All that matters is that you are pleased with your landscape.

Layered and Matrix Plantings

There are several ways to achieve layered plantings characteristic of natural areas. Planning and planting garden beds is one option. Another is to look for remnants of natural areas on a property and then build plantings by adding suitable native species, controlling invasive plants, and expanding the boundaries of the planting by gradually replacing lawn. See the general principles "Build Plant Diversity" and "Grow Native Plants," which are covered in Chapter 1, for ideas to help create natural areas in your design. Tips for adding diversity to shady areas are found in Chapter 7.

Matrix plantings offer yet another option for developing gardens that thrive with minimal interven-

tion from their creators. Like other successful planting strategies, they are based on matching plants to the site where they are to grow, although in the case of a matrix planting the emphasis is on developing a community of plants that is matched to the conditions on a site.

The first step in creating a matrix planting is to carefully observe the site and learn about the growing conditions that exist naturally. The next step is to select plants that will grow in those conditions. Many matrix gardeners combine non-native and native species to create suitable plant communities, although using all native plants is an excellent option as well. For example, in addition to native woodland wildflowers like Canadian columbine (*Aquilegia canadensis*), wild blue phlox (*Phlox divaricata*), and wild ginger (*Asarum canadense*), matrix gardeners may add non-native, non-invasive species that thrive in similar conditions, such as epimediums (*Epimedium* spp.) and European wild ginger (*Asarum europaeum*) to create a community of plants.

The goal is to select plants and to build a community that will look attractive and gardenlike yet sustain itself as much as possible. In a successful matrix community, the selected plants will all thrive, and they will out-compete most or all weeds. Plants selected for a matrix community need to have similar growing conditions, grow at similar rates, or fill different niches in the community—ground covers or shrubs, for example—so they coexist without the need for excessive intervention (weeding) from the gardener. This mirrors plant communities in nature, since wild plants grow and reproduce without intervention from humans. Unlike conventional gardeners, who plant with a preconceived design in mind, matrix gardeners strive to develop communities of plants that self-sow and spread on their own to create thick, natural-looking areas.

To create plantings that function as much as possible like natural areas, matrix plantings echo both the vertical and the horizontal aspects of natural landscapes. In a typical Chesapeake Bay woodland community, large trees form the canopy or topmost vertical layer, including American beech (*Fagus grandifolia*), oaks (*Quercus* spp.), and tulip poplars (*Liriodendron tulipifera*). Understory trees fill in just beneath the canopy, including flowering dogwood (*Cornus florida*), redbud (*Cercis canadensis*), and American hornbeam (*Carpinus caroliniana*). Shrubs form the second layer under the canopy and include viburnums (*Viburnum* spp.), dogwoods such as gray dogwood (*Cornus racemosa*), and deerberry (*Vaccinium stamineum*). The third layer consists of perennials, ferns, bulbs, grasses, sedges, and ground covers. These plants cover the ground and form the planting's horizontal dimension. Matrix gardeners recognize a fourth layer: the soil and roots beneath the ground. The use of deep mulching to avoid disturbing the soil layer is one reason matrix gardening is a low-maintenance approach. Dense planting is another.

To create a matrix garden, start by studying conditions on the site you are going to plant to identify the natural communities that might grow there. Another option is to identify the habitat (or habitats) that most closely fits your own landscape and learn about characteristic conditions and plants that exist there naturally. Remnants of habitat may still exist on your property, and these can provide inspiration as well. Make notes about plants that could form the vertical and horizontal dimensions. Trees for a canopy layer may already exist. Plan on adding understory trees, along with shrubs and a variety of plants to comprise the third or ground cover layer. On a sunny site, shrubs and tall perennials may form the canopy layer.

Use mulch to prepare the site for planting (see "Deep Mulching" on p. 92 for details) and wait until the following season to plant. For planting that mimics a wild area, visit local botanical gardens or natural areas, or look at photographs of your chosen habitat, then use the ideas you gather when arranging the perennials, grasses, and other plants that form the horizontal layer. Arrange plants in similar, natural-looking drifts. Spacing plants densely and planting in large drifts, along with combining plants that grow at similar rates, is important to success. Paying attention to traditional garden design principles like repeating colors and forms, mixing textures, and planting species with a variety of forms helps ensure an attractive garden.

Time is the last dimension that is important to matrix gardeners. Once plants are in the ground and are well established, watch how they grow and interact. Some will thrive and others will die out. Eliminate any that are aggressive, especially if they are not native. With time and good plant choices, the planting should reach a balancing point and form a stable community that requires minimal maintenance.

THREE ❦ Building Your Chesapeake Landscape

Nearly every yard has a variety of sites that will accommodate different plants and activities. Terraces in this backyard create level planting beds, sitting areas, and a small lawn, plus plenty of space for shrubs, trees, and wildflowers. Photo © Roger Foley; design by Tom Mannion Landscape Design.

It is easy to overlook the fundamentals that underlie a successful garden. Beautiful flowers, lush color combinations, interesting textures, and handsome foliage all catch the eye and start us dreaming. But filling a wagon with the prettiest plants at the local garden center or picking selections from a magazine photo does not necessarily lead to success. Both approaches overlook the fact that selecting plants on looks alone is not the best way to find the plants that will thrive in your garden and make it beautiful.

To create plantings that benefit from good gardening fundamentals, learn about the conditions a particular site offers the plants that grow there. Consider the amount of sun or shade a spot receives, along with soil type, average moisture level, exposure, and any other aspects that make that site unique. Use these characteristics to help determine what you plant there. Using site characteristics as a primary factor in plant selection makes it easier to have lush plantings filled with striking perennials and handsome shrubs, because the plants you select will naturally be adapted to conditions that exist on the site. Matching plant to site is the simplest route to a thriving garden. In addition, it is an effective way to minimize maintenance and create a sustainable garden, since you will no longer have to fight the natural conditions of the site to keep plants healthy and growing well.

(overleaf) Studying the exposure and learning about the soil type and other conditions that characterize a site is the secret to creating a successful garden. To plan a garden that thrives while requiring minimal maintenance, select plants that thrive in those conditions. Photo by Neil Soderstrom; design by Oehme, van Sweden Landscape Architecture.

Even gifted gardeners who seem able to grow anything—and who seem able to pop plants in at random with great results—pay attention to site conditions, even if they do not express it quite that way. Their planting process is rarely as random as it seems because they know their garden and planting sites well—how much sun or shade each site receives and the type of soil that exists on their property. Site assessment gradually becomes second nature as gardeners gain experience, as does an almost instinctive understanding of growing conditions and what to look for when matching a plant to a site. Fortunately, every gardener can learn to pay attention to site conditions and discover what will grow well in his or her garden.

Reading the Landscape

Deciding what to grow and where to plant it is one of the great challenges of gardening. Learning to look closely at a site is not difficult, and it will prove helpful in guiding your choices. The plants already growing on a site speak volumes about other plants that will thrive there. Observing the growing conditions in a garden is a continual process: The longer you garden, the more you learn. With experience, more subtle gradations of sun and shade or moist and dry become apparent, and this knowledge will help you identify suitable spots for plants. Also watch garden performance. Some plants will grow nearly anywhere they are planted, while others need that perfect site. Experimenting to determine what grows best in your own garden is part of the fun and fascination of gardening.

Evaluate Existing Plants

Plants already growing on your property provide clues to what else might thrive. This is true of weeds, native plants, and non-native plants. For example, if

This planting consists of tough species that thrive in a wide range of soil types—eastern red cedar (*Juniperus virginiana*) and arrowwood viburnum (*Viburnum dentatum*), with white flowers. Suitable companions should be equally tough. Photo by Neil Soderstrom; Adkins Arboretum.

junipers (*Juniperus* spp.) and barberries (*Berberis thunbergii*) thrive in your foundation plantings but bigleaf hydrangeas (*Hydrangea macrophylla*) wilt and struggle, you probably have dry, well-drained soil. A bed where azaleas (*Rhododendron* spp.) are constantly plagued by lacebugs probably provides hot, dry conditions in summertime, since lacebugs are worst on plants exposed to heat and drought.

Plants that tolerate a wide range of conditions, like Norway maples (*Acer platanoides*) or forsythia (*Forsythia × intermedia*), do not disclose much about

🍃 Adaptable Plants

One option for creating a new garden is to start with plants that tolerate a wide range of conditions. The following natives are easy to grow and adaptable. All do fine in sun or shade, although they bloom best in sun. Full sun to part shade is best for the grasses, although they will survive in shade. All can manage in soil that ranges from moist and well drained to dry. Plants marked with an asterisk (*) need even soil moisture in order to tolerate full sun.

Perennials

Cup plant (*Silphium perfoliatum*)

Foamflower, heart-leaved or Allegheny (*Tiarella cordifolia*)*

Goldenrod, wreath (*Solidago caesia*)

Onion, nodding (*Allium cernuum*)

Shooting star (*Dodecatheon meadia*)

Sneezeweed (*Helenium autumnale*)

Spiderwort (*Tradescantia virginiana*)*

Stonecrop, Allegheny (*Hylotelephium telephioides*, formerly *Sedum telephioides*)

Grasses and Grasslike Plants

Bluestem, little (*Schizachyrium scoparium*)

Dropseed, prairie (*Sporobolus heterolepis*)

Indian grass (*Sorghastrum nutans*)

Muhly, pink (*Muhlenbergia capillaris*)

Panic grass or switchgrass (*Panicum virgatum*)

Purpletop tridens (*Tridens flavus*)

Sedges (*Carex* spp.). Appalachian sedge (*C. appalachica*); Pennsylvania sedge (*C. pensylvanica*)

Shrubs

Bayberry, southern or swamp (*Morella caroliniensis*, formerly *Myrica caroliniensis*)

Dogwood, gray (*Cornus racemosa*)

Inkberry (*Ilex glabra*)

Itea, Virginia sweetspire (*Itea virginica*)

Mountain laurel (*Kalmia latifolia*)

Viburnums (*Viburnum* spp.). Mapleleaf viburnum (*V. acerifolium*); southern arrowwood (*V. dentatum*); blackhaw viburnum (*V. prunifolium*)

Spiderwort (*Tradescantia virginiana*). Photo by Neil Soderstrom; Emily Dickinson Museum.

Eastern white pines (*Pinus strobus*) prefer moist, well-drained soil, although they tolerate a wider range of conditions once they are established. Purple-leaved ninebark (*Physocarpus opulifolius* 'Mindia'/Coppertina) and Canada goldenrod (*Solidago canadensis* 'Baby Gold') also are widely tolerant. Photo by Neil Soderstrom; design by Mary Streb.

growing conditions, but fussier species will. Healthy blueberries (*Vaccinium* spp.) signal acid soil, for example, and flowering dogwoods (*Cornus florida*) thrive in partial shade and soil that is well drained and rich in organic matter. (They are lovely dotted at a woods' edge.) Thriving dogwoods may indicate a healthy layer of natural mulch, since mulch keeps soil cool and moist. On the other hand, sickly dogwoods are likely growing in poorly drained soil or in open, exposed areas in full sun with too little water during the heat of summer. These conditions make them more prone to invasion by insects and diseases.

To identify what might thrive, look for plants that are already healthy and happy, including weeds and scrubby plants that appeared on their own. Have them identified by an expert, if necessary, and use field guides, garden books, or the Internet to determine the cultural conditions they need and what that tells you about your site.

Examine the Lawn

Under ideal conditions, a lawn should be a uniform carpet of green. Patches of lawn that do not conform to this ideal may provide clues to the underlying site conditions. (Insect infestations and urine spots from pets do not count.) A thin, scraggly carpet of grass near or under trees can indicate partial shade to shade (most lawn grass mixtures are best in full sun) and likely means that tree roots are out-competing the grass. Stick a spade or fork into the ground to find out. While it is fairly easy to find space for ground covers under trees like oaks (*Quercus* spp.), there is little soil space under trees that form a dense mat of shallow roots, such as maples (*Acer* spp.), including non-native Norway maple (*A. platanoides*). See "Planting under Trees" later in this chapter for suggestions for replacing lawn on shady sites.

Thin and/or yellowed grass in spots with full sun may indicate compacted soil (see the soil section in this chapter for remedies). Buried rocks, rock outcrops, concrete, or gravel may also create drier conditions than in the surrounding area. A higher spot in the lawn where the mower scalps the soil surface can also create a thin, yellowed patch of grass. To fix scalped spots, shave off the grass, remove some soil to level out the bump, and then replace the grass. If investigation reveals rocks, rock outcrops, or simply a higher, drier spot, consider replacing lawn in that area with a bed of drought-tolerant perennials, ground covers, or shrubs.

Lush, deep green grass that grows faster than the surrounding area indicates soil that is constantly moist to wet. While such spots may be good can-

To plan a lawn that thrives with minimal maintenance, identify where in the landscape it is needed and most useful, as well as where it will thrive. This lawn is on an easy-to-mow site, but aerating and amending the soil might encourage denser growth. Ground covers surrounding the lawn help catch stormwater runoff. Photo by Neil Soderstrom; design by Mary Jo Messenger.

didates for rain gardens, lush grass can also indicate a leak in a septic system or underground pipes, so investigation is in order. If the spot is naturally wet, amending the soil with organic matter may create the perfect spot for plants that need moist soil. Another option is to mulch and plant with ground covers or other plants that need average garden conditions.

Read Weeds

While the existence of a specific weed does not replace the need for a proper soil test, weeds can in-

dicate site conditions. The overall health of a weed patch speaks volumes. If the plants are large, lush, and growing vigorously, the soil is probably fairly rich and evenly moist. Thin, stunted patches of weeds signal poor soil and compacted conditions. The existence of some individual weeds can be useful for figuring out what else might grow there or the steps you will need to take to improve the site. Here are some examples:

Campion, white (*Silene latifolia* ssp. *alba*), is common in full sun on sites with rich, well-drained soils.

Cattails (*Typha* spp.) indicate constantly moist or wet soil as well as standing water.

Dandelions (*Taraxacum officinale*) tolerate a wide range of soils and soil conditions, but if you dig them up and they yield long, unbranched roots, you probably have fairly deep, loose soil. Short, branched roots indicate compaction or rocky obstructions in the soil.

Hawkweed, yellow (*Hieracium caespitosum*, formerly *H. pratense*), commonly grows in meadows and abandoned fields in poor, dry, acidic soils.

Moneywort, creeping Jenny (*Lysimachia nummularia*), is found in moist, shady spots.

Phragmites or common reed (*Phragmites australis*) indicates constantly moist soil or, at minimum, moist subsoil. It grows in ditches and other areas with standing water, either flowing or stagnant.

Queen Anne's lace (*Daucus carota*) is most common in well-drained to dry soils.

Toadflax, yellow or butter-and-eggs (*Linaria vulgaris*), is a pretty weed found in full sun and dry soil that is gravelly or sandy.

Cattails (*Typha* spp.) are a sure sign of wet or poorly drained soil. Photo by Neil Soderstrom; J. Kent McNew garden.

Consider Communities

If you have remnant woods on your property, even if the trees are now underplanted by struggling lawn or invasives like English ivy (*Hedera helix*), these communities indicate other plants that might thrive there. For example, oak-hickory forests typically include a variety of oaks (*Quercus* spp.) and hickories (*Carya* spp.) as canopy trees in addition to understory trees like redbuds (*Cercis canadensis*) and flowering dogwoods (*Cornus florida*). In areas with acid soil, shrubs include lowbush blueberry (*Vaccinium pallidum*), deerberry (*V. stamineum*), and maple-leaved viburnum (*Viburnum acerifolium*). Perennials and ground covers include plantain-leaf pussytoes (*Antennaria plantaginifolia*), Pennsylvania sedge (*Carex pensylvanica*), and Solomon's seal (*Polygonatum biflorum*). In less acid soil, perennials such as cut-leaved toothwort (*Cardamine concatenata*), spring beauties (*Claytonia virginica*), bottlebrush grass (*Elymus hystrix*), Solomon's plume or false lily-of-the-valley (*Maianthemum racemosum*), and wreath goldenrod (*Solidago caesia*) are typical.

Look at wild corners of your yard, where remaining plants may give you a clue to what once grew there. Canada goldenrod (*Solidago canadensis*) is a vigorous native wildflower that grows in a wide variety of conditions, but it is most common in evenly moist soils. A clump may suggest a spot for a meadowlike planting of ornamental grasses and coneflowers (*Rudbeckia* spp. and *Echinacea* spp.). Sassafras (*Sassafras albidum*) is a tough small tree that thrives in full sun or part shade and can tolerate soils from acid and rocky to loamy and rich. Combine it with other native trees and shrubs like gray dogwood (*Cornus racemosa*) and common serviceberry

A site with shade and rich, moist, well-drained, acid soil is ideal for flowering dogwood (*Cornus florida*) along with foamflowers (*Tiarella cordifolia*), bellworts (*Uvularia* spp.), wild blue phlox (*Phlox divaricata*), and Christmas ferns (*Polystichum acrostichoides*). Photo by Neil Soderstrom; design by Renee Kemmerer at Mt. Cuba Center.

(*Amelanchier arborea*) to re-create the framework of a hedgerow. See "Layered and Matrix Plantings" on p. 65 for information on building gardens based on plant communities.

Turn over Some Soil

Even a single shovel of soil can reveal a lot about a site. Pay attention to how difficult it is to stick a

spade or a garden fork into the soil. Is it hard as a rock or wet and sticky? Does the shovel strike a dense mass of roots just under the surface? The presence or absence of earthworms in a shovelful of soil helps determine soil health. In lawn and garden beds, if a single shovelful contains several earthworms, the soil is probably in good shape and contains a good measure of organic matter. If earthworms are absent, increasing soil organic matter by spreading compost and mulch is a good idea. For more information on evaluating soil, see "Start with the Soil," below.

Ask for Answers

Neighbors, especially those who garden, may have valuable advice about what grows well in addition to information about soil types and conditions you may encounter. (Be aware that they may or may not have sustainable gardens.) If you live in a fairly new development, ask older residents what they know about pre-construction plant communities. You may be able to unearth valuable insights by visiting the library and looking at local history sources, old zoning books, or old aerial photographs.

The local Cooperative Extension office will have valuable information on soil types in your area, along with other vital information on growing conditions. The Internet is a valuable resource as well.

Start with the Soil

Soil seldom receives any credit for a beautiful garden or landscape. Most people don't give much thought to what goes on underground, and even some gardeners assume soil is inert—not much more than a support structure for plants. Nothing could be further from the truth. Healthy soil is a complex, liv-

🍃 Sustainable Historic Gardens

Historic gardens and landscape designs inspired by history can be sustainable while keeping true to their ideals. While common boxwood (*Buxus sempervirens*), the signature plant of a great many historic landscapes in this part of the country, is not a native, there is no denying its important role in the region's gardens. Plants that traveled to the New World with the colonists are an essential part of Colonial-style gardens. The principles that guide sustainable landscapes provide plenty of options for creating a garden that is both sustainable *and* historically accurate.

A good place to start is reducing the size of the lawn. To accomplish this, combine native plants with non-natives such as those Thomas Jefferson planted at Monticello. Native trees such as sweetbay magnolia (*Magnolia virginiana*) and white fringetree (*Chionanthus virginicus*) are striking surrounded by beds of flowers grown in Colonial times. Both species are prized in this country and were sent to England as early as 1735 and 1736. For larger properties, native meadows make handsome replacements for high-maintenance lawn.

While non-natives that are unlikely to spread are fine in a garden that is both historic and sustainable, take steps to eliminate invasive plants such as English ivy (*Hedera helix*). Even if invasives are currently well controlled, eliminating them means that these plants will not be lying in wait, ready to spread, when you turn over the reins of your garden to its next owner.

Reducing runoff is another great way to introduce sustainability into a historic or historically inspired project. Rain barrels, of course, are not a new invention. They have been in use for centuries and, along with other features designed to reduce runoff, can fit nicely into a historic design.

By adjusting plant choices, materials, and installations, you can create a Bay-friendly landscape that satisfies the spirit of a historically inspired design.

Boxwood (*Buxus* spp.) is a traditional feature in historic gardens and landscapes. To include sustainable elements in a historic-style planting, consider using wildlife-friendly plants, especially natives, in conjunction with hedges. This knot garden features non-native annual salvias, which are attractive to pollinators. Photo by Neil Soderstrom; New York Botanical Garden.

Panic grass or switchgrass (*Panicum virgatum*) and button-bush (*Cephalanthus occidentalis*) can both grow in moist soil. Buttonbush also grows in wet soil or standing water but does not tolerate drier conditions. Panic grass also grows in dry soil and flops if conditions are too wet or too rich. Photo by Neil Soderstrom; U.S. Botanic Garden.

ing, breathing community. It is the engine that drives everything that grows aboveground. A basic under-standing of soil principles and processes is invaluable for keeping soil healthy and plants thriving.

Soil Texture

Soil is primarily composed of three types of par-ticles—sand, silt, and clay—that determine its texture. A soil's texture affects both its fertility and how quickly water drains through. Sand, silt, and clay make up the mineral portion of soil, which is determined by the parent materials from which the soil formed. Parent material can be bedrock that has broken down into smaller pieces over millennia or particles carried by wind or water. (Many soils also contain larger particles, from gravel to boulders.) Parent material is one reason soil type varies from site to site, but climate, soil organisms, and topogra-phy also affect soil formation.

Soils are classified into types by texture—loam, clay loam, silt loam, and sandy loam, for example. Each type has different characteristics and contains different percentages of sand, silt, and clay. Loam soil, for example, contains nearly equal parts of sand, silt, and clay. Because of the balance of soil particles, loam is perfect for gardening and farming. It drains well yet holds plenty of moisture and nutrients for plants. Soils that contain more sand, such as sandy or sandy loam soils, drain more quickly and dry out faster. (Maryland's and Virginia's state soils, Sas-safras and Pamunkey, respectively, are both sandy loams; the District of Columbia's and Delaware's state soils, Sunnyside and Greenwich, respectively, are loams.) Soils with a high percentage of clay do not drain well. They hold water, keeping much of it so tightly bound to soil particles that it is not readily available to plants. Texture affects how fertile a soil is because minerals and nutrients are dissolved in water that is present in the soil. Soils with small particles, like clay, hold more water and are more fertile than sandy soils.

For a general soil assessment, dig a 4- or 5-inch-deep hole and dig a teaspoon of soil from the bottom of the hole. Add a little bit of water to the sample and roll it into a ball. Sandy soil does not make a ball and feels gritty and coarse to the touch. Silty soil is less coarse than sandy soil and feels something like talcum powder. When moistened, silty soil can be rolled into a loose ball that is easy to break apart with pressure from a thumb or finger. Clay soil feels slick and slippery. It is easy to press into a ball or roll into a worm shape.

Soils and Sustainability

Healthy soil benefits plants, but it is also important in the fight against global warming. That is because a great deal of carbon is stored in soil. Plants remove carbon dioxide from the atmosphere and release oxygen for us to breathe. In the process, carbon is stored in plant tissues. That means every leaf that is composted or used as mulch contains carbon that is added to the soil. Microorganisms also store carbon in soil, so fostering a healthy, vigorous soil community helps sequester it as well. According to the Ecological Society of America, "Although oceans store most of the Earth's carbon, soils contain approximately 75 percent of the carbon pool on land—three times more than the amount stored in living plants and animals." So while planting trees is one way to help in the fight against global warming, increasing the amount of organic matter in the soil is another important way to help reduce your carbon footprint.

Carbon stored in soil can either remain there for millennia or be rereleased fairly quickly depending on the climate, gardening or agricultural practices used, soil texture, and plants that are growing on the site. In addition to planting trees and other long-lived plants, there are many ways to keep carbon in the soil and out of the atmosphere: Reducing the number of times a bed (or field) is tilled or dug, keeping the soil covered with mulch (itself a source of stored carbon), planting cover crops in vegetable gardens and agricultural fields, and incorporating organic matter such as compost into beds are just a few.

In addition to improving soil conditions for plants, building soil organic matter benefits water quality because it improves soil permeability, thus reducing runoff. This, in turn, improves the filtration of water through the soil. It reduces the amount of nutrients that wash off the land and into bays, rivers, and other bodies of water. Healthy soil covered with plants and leaf litter or mulch also decreases soil erosion. In the vegetable garden and farm field, soil organic matter increases crop production.

It is important to understand that improving soil by changing its texture is not practical. Adding a bucket or two of sand to a site with clay soil results in cement, not sandy loam. Changing texture means moving truckloads of materials, not just a few shovels. Fortunately, you can improve any soil structure by adding organic matter.

Soil Structure and Organic Matter

In healthy soil, the sand, silt, and clay component only comprises about 45 percent of the total volume. Another 5 percent is organic matter: living and dead organisms, including roots, bacteria, fungi, insects, nematodes, and much more. Because of soil structure, the rest of soil is actually open space. The open space in soil consists of soil pores, formed when individual sand, silt, and clay particles clump together and form soil aggregates. Good soil structure occurs when aggregates create both small and large pores. The small pores hold water in the soil, and they allow water to move around via capillary action. The large pores let water drain through during rainstorms. Once water drains away, these pores fill with air, a necessary component for plant roots and soil organisms to live. (Some plants and soil organisms have

Healthy soil is a complex, living, breathing community that supports plants and a diversity of life, from tiny microbes to insects, earthworms, and small mammals. The soil's organic matter holds water like a sponge. An important feature of healthy soil is its ability to store carbon, reducing your carbon footprint.

adapted to living in constantly wet soil or in standing water, but most plants and organisms cannot tolerate these conditions.) Soil structure is the reason why rich, well-tended soil is fluffy and easy to dig. Increasing soil organic matter improves the structure of any soil, from sandy to clay.

Healthy soil is a complex web of organisms, organic matter, and minerals. According to *Sustainable Landscape Construction* (Island Press, 2008), by J. William Thompson and Kim Sorvig, one pound of healthy soil contains more than 460 billion organisms. A cubic yard contains 740 trillion. In the process of living and dying, soil organisms release compounds that help aggregates form and create soil structure. They break down organic matter and release nutrients essential for plant growth. Plant roots and organisms such as bacteria and fungi decompose other organisms and contribute to the web by secreting substances that bind particles. Plant roots also form mutually beneficial relationships with mycorrhizal fungi that increase the surface area of roots,

thus improving nutrient availability and water uptake. The fungi take carbon from plants in exchange. Freeze and thaw cycles cause clumps to form. Earthworms, beetles, and other soil organisms pull organic matter down from the surface, such as decomposing mulch and leaf litter. Organisms from earthworms to voles tunnel through soil, creating space for air and mixing up the brew. Fungi, tiny plant roots, and root hairs help stabilize aggregates and hold them together. This is one reason soil organic matter is so important. As it decomposes, it feeds the fungi and plant roots that help maintain aggregates, thus helping retain the essential pores that hold air and water in the soil. Decomposition releases essential nutrients that are available to plants.

Eventually, organic matter—everything from leaves and bits of plants to dead insects and microbes—becomes humus, a combination of hard-to-digest materials such as waxes, lignins, gums, and starches. While the terms "organic matter" and "humus" are sometimes used interchangeably, true humus is an end product of the decomposition process and is relatively stable. While it does not break down further to release more nutrients, it does help to improve soil structure and is very effective at holding nutrients in the soil. In addition, humus can hold 80 to 90 percent of its weight in water, creating a reservoir of water in the soil that is available to plants.

A plentiful supply of organic matter is the secret to creating healthy soil. While most homeowners do not start out with great soil, adding organic matter such as compost will improve any soil. Adding too much organic matter is not a problem, since soil organisms—sometimes referred to as the soil's microherd—are constantly at work breaking it down. As the microherd break down soil, they release compounds that form more soil aggregates and pores. Decomposition also makes nutrients available to

Incorporating organic matter into the soil and continuing to add it by replenishing mulch improves plant growth and reduces runoff. This tiny garden features a pin oak (*Quercus palustris*), yucca (*Yucca* spp.), thread-leaved coreopsis (*Coreopsis verticillata*), and other plants. Photo by Neil Soderstrom; design by Pat Harrington.

plants. It is this process that gave rise to the organic gardener's favorite phrase, "Feed the soil, and let the soil feed the plants." Conventional chemical fertilizers do not fuel this process. The salts they contain drive away earthworms and the microherd, and the nutrients in chemical non-organic fertilizers dissolve quickly in water and then rapidly leach through soil or run off the soil surface into nearby waterways.

Adding organic matter, feeding the soil's microherd, and building up the humus content in the soil all contribute to the crumbly structure gardeners

refer to as good tilth. As a result, soil that is rich in organic matter is not just good for earthworms and plants; it is also beneficial for humans. Soil with good tilth is easy to dig and is great for gardening.

Keeping Soil Healthy

Adding organic matter helps to build structure, which improves drainage and increases biologic activity. Traditionally, gardeners add organic matter when they begin a flower bed or vegetable garden. They first clear the site and scrape off weeds or lawn grass, spread organic matter over the entire site, and then dig or till it into the soil. While this process is an option, tilling or digging is not necessarily good for soil, and there are other ways to prepare a site for planting. Tilling or digging breaks down soil aggregates, destroys pore space, and affects the balance of air and water in the soil. Tilling and digging speed up the decomposition of existing organic matter as well, so *never* dig or till soil without adding additional organic matter such as compost. Otherwise, the result is a net loss of this essential ingredient.

Repeated tilling results in powdery soil with little or no structure, since it breaks down aggregates. In clay soils, which have lots of small pores that hold water and not enough large ones for holding air, tilling destroys the large pores so the soil drains even less well. Sandy soils, on the other hand, have high metabolisms and burn through organic matter quickly. Tilling adds oxygen and speeds up the decomposition process even further.

Tilling or digging also disrupts the soil's microherd by destroying tunnels created by creatures such as earthworms that facilitate the movement of other organisms, water, and air. Tilling or digging also brings weed seeds to the surface, where they are much more likely to germinate.

One of the best ways to keep soil healthy and avoid disturbing the soil community is to keep it covered with plants. Northern sea oats (*Chasmanthium latifolium*) is the primary ground cover in this shady woodland planting. Photo © Roger Foley; design by Tom Mannion Landscape Design.

If you are growing vegetables or planting a traditional flower bed, digging or tilling may make sense as a starting point. However, there are other options for preparing a site for plants while still protecting the soil. Here, too, selecting plants that will grow in the soil conditions *as they currently exist* by matching plant to site is nearly always a more effective, lower-maintenance option, whether you are creating a native plant garden or growing a mix of natives and non-natives.

Use the tips and techniques below to protect and build healthy soil.

Protect existing cover. Prevent unnecessary clearing on new home sites or on construction sites at existing homes. Do not allow developers or construction crews to bulldoze the entire site just because that may be the easiest option for them. (Builders with a sustainable orientation do not pre-clear sites.) Saving established trees and even patches of weedy vegetation helps protect existing soil and prevents the loss of soil organic matter. Fence off trees, shrubs, and any other areas that can be saved. Keep bulldozers and other construction equipment out from under trees, and designate parking areas for construction vehicles to protect existing vegetation. Protecting existing cover not only saves trees and shrubs; it also protects the soil, the soil community, and wild patches that may support insects, birds, and other wildlife. Contracts with construction crews should specify which areas are to be strictly protected from vehicular traffic, trash, and other damage.

Do not improve soil unnecessarily. Contrary to traditional garden wisdom, all soil does not need to be improved. Sustainable gardeners think in terms of different types of soil fertility and not just whether soil is rich or poor. This is another opportunity to practice matching plants to the site: Learn about the native soil and pick plants that will thrive there. This not only results in a garden that thrives; it also helps avoid the endless treadmill of caring for plants that require continual soil improvement and fertilization. If your goal is a vegetable garden or a bed filled with flowers that demand rich conditions to perform at their peak, amending soil to increase fertility is probably necessary. When designing and planting beds, group specimens that need high-fertility soils to concentrate soil-improvement efforts.

In other areas of the landscape, either plant the soil as it is or provide an initial infusion of organic matter before planting. Compost is by far the best soil amendment, regardless of soil condition or type. A soil test will help determine precisely what conditions exist and is especially valuable for gardeners who face damaged urban soils or are gardening on sites with extremely degraded soil. According to *Sustainable Landscape Construction*, by J. William Thompson and Kim Sorvig, freshly made compost tea is valuable for building soil on degraded sites, since it helps replenish the soil community that is absent or lacking in damaged soils. Make it yourself by soaking finished compost in water for a few hours and apply it as soon after that as possible. (To be effective, compost tea should be used within 24 hours.) Manufactured soil is also an option for severely damaged sites.

Make beds with deep mulch. Patience is key to this effective, soil-saving technique, also called lasagna gardening, as it involves spreading layers of mulch one season and waiting 3 to 6 months before planting the finished bed. Deep mulching minimizes disruption of the soil, eliminates the need to dig beds, and prevents weed seeds from germinating. Use it to create new vegetable or flower beds, to replace lawn with ground covers, or to grow wildflowers or other plants. See "Deep Mulching" on p. 92 for more information.

Keep soil covered. Mulch protects the soil from erosion by wind and rain and prevents raindrops from beating down on the soil surface, which can destroy soil structure and create a crust on the surface. Mulching benefits plants by helping soil retain moisture and stay cool. A layer of mulch also provides a ready supply of organic matter to feed the soil's microherd.

Maintain natural mulch. Gardeners spend a great deal of time and money annually raking leaves to the curb and spreading bagged mulch or wood chips on their gardens. Natural cover, such as leaves that fall from overhead trees, is far more beneficial for native soils. Each type of soil has a unique soil community, and leaf litter and other natural cover is most suited to provide the fertility level and nutrients that community requires. Natural mulch typically consists of leaves and various plant parts, but it may contain twigs and rotting logs in a wooded area or grass and other plant parts in a meadow. Another advantage of retaining natural leaf litter is that many insects, including beautiful io, polyphemus, and other showy native moths, overwinter in leaf litter. This is another reason to return a bit of wildness to our home landscapes: Raking and removing the leaf litter destroys these beautiful creatures.

Mulch mixes. While natural leaf litter makes for ideal mulch, supplementing it is an option. Compost made from local ingredients makes excellent mulch and keeps the soil's microherd well fed. Mixing mulches is another fine idea. Supplement leaf litter with homemade compost, sheet compost by spreading chopped leaves and other ingredients in the garden as mulch, or spread purchased compost or organic matter. Mixing in bagged mulch is an option as well. Keep in mind, however, that bagged compost does not have the level of biological activity that homemade compost does.

Avoid Soil Compaction

While adding organic matter is one essential component of any soil care program, avoiding soil compaction is another. Walking or driving cars or lawn tractors on soil compresses the pores and affects the way water and air flow through soil. Compaction affects soil types differently. Clay soils can become so compressed that air and water cannot penetrate, which means the roots of most plants will be unable to survive. Water drains quickly through sandy soils that are walked or driven on, but the structure is still damaged. In this case, compaction destroys small, water-holding pores that have developed. Foot traffic and compaction also damage roots and can cause erosion.

To minimize soil compaction, try to walk around,

 Protect Topsoil

Although topsoil is typically sold by the bag or brought in by the truckload, you are far better off protecting existing soil on your property than bringing it from somewhere else. Whether it is spread on the ground or collected in a pile, soil is a living community. The best way to protect it is to leave it in place and care for it as outlined in this section. However, moving topsoil is sometimes necessary to accomplish a particular project or to prevent construction equipment from damaging it. To preserve it, follow these guidelines:

- Make several small piles, rather than one large one. Keep piles less than 6 feet tall for sandy soil and 4 feet for clay soil.
- Cover piles with breathable tarps to hold in moisture, reduce wind erosion, and keep out windblown seeds.
- Water as necessary to keep piles damp.
- Store soil for as short a time as possible and handle it as little as possible.

not through, garden beds. (It helps to remember that half the volume of healthy soil is pore space.) Plan pathways to direct foot traffic and prevent visitors from trampling planting areas. Use stepping-stones or planks (suitable for a vegetable garden) to make pathways. In beds that are too wide to reach from either side, install work paths either behind the shrubs or flowers or right through the center of the bed so plants or weeds are easy to reach. Cardboard or a thick layer of newspaper (10 or more sheets) topped with several inches of mulch is fine for work paths. It does not provide ideal protection, but it is better than walking on uncovered soil.

Also designate areas for working on cars or other equipment to minimize compaction to the lawn. Maintaining mulch or gravel on these areas makes more sense than trying to grow grass. Another option is to create work areas by installing hardscape such as grass block—pavers that provide a framework for supporting weight and have space in the center for growing grass or ground covers. Lawn is usually the best option for areas reserved for sports.

Ten Tips for Keeping Soil Healthy

Soil is a valuable resource that should be protected, whether in tiny city plots or on large properties with considerable acreage. Use the following tips to build and maintain healthy soil.

1. Have your soil tested. Contact the local Cooperative Extension Service office for a soil test kit, or look on the Internet for commercial soil labs that test chemical makeup as well as microbial activity. Specify that recommendations should be sustainable and organic.

2. Work with the soil on site. Instead of trying to amend soil or change its pH (how acid or alkaline the soil is), learn about natural soil types and their challenges. Restoring depleted soil is one thing—even fill dirt can be amended and made suitable for growing plants, since adding organic matter will improve any soil—but creating conditions that would not naturally exist is another. While it is possible to raise pH to make soil less acid or to accommodate plants that require rich soil or perfect drainage, such changes mean a long-term investment of time and effort that is best avoided. The most sustainable, lowest-maintenance option is to select native plants that thrive in the soil as it is.

3. Make adding organic matter easy. Keep a supply of compost, straw, chopped leaves, grass clippings, or other organic matter handy so you can easily add at least a shovelful of organic matter every time you dig a hole in the garden. Also add to the mulch layer every time it is disturbed. This is especially easy in vegetable gardens, where crops are routinely pulled up and replaced. A supply of compost or other organic matter kept out of sight behind shrubs or flower beds also provides a handy source.

4. Mulch. Maintain a layer of mulch on the soil surface. This helps control weeds and prevents the formation of a crust on the soil surface. Keep a supply of mulch on hand and replenish the covering on beds every time you plant. If you need to bring in mulch or soil amendments from elsewhere, try to stick to local, recycled materials.

5. Mulch with plants. Living plants make great mulch and are effective at protecting soil. Space perennials, ground covers, and other plants closely enough that they will cover the soil completely once they have become established. New plantings will need to be mulched initially, but once they have filled in, the leaves will cover the soil and create an effective, low-maintenance mulch.

6. Learn to love leaf litter—and compost. Leaves and other natural plant matter are the best mulch for maintaining healthy soil. If overhead trees produce enough leaves to bury the plants below them, add excess leaves to the compost pile or spread them in another area with insufficient cover.

7. Go organic. Homemade compost is an ideal source if plants do need added nutrition. If soil tests indicate that soil needs more than compost can provide, or if you simply do not have enough compost, look for slow-acting organic fertilizers that will feed plants and benefit the soil community.

8. Minimize tilling and digging. Tilling, along with digging unnecessarily, damages or destroys soil structure and affects the movement of air and water in the soil. If tilling or digging is necessary, first make sure the soil is not too wet or too dry (see "Is the Soil Ready?" on p. 86 for more information). Then spread 1 to 2 inches of organic matter such as compost over the site before tilling it under.

9. Control weeds with mulch, not tilling. In addition to damaging soil structure, tilling and digging bring weed seeds to the surface where they can germinate. Use newspaper under mulch to suppress weeds initially. If weeds come back, try raking back existing mulch, spreading newspaper 2 or 3 sheets thick, and then replacing the mulch.

10. Stay off the soil. Walking on soil compresses soil pores and destroys soil structure. Reach in from the sides of beds to weed and tend to plants. Add work paths or walkways to make plants accessible.

Planting Gardens and Landscapes

The planting process is simple. Dig a hole, loosen and spread out the roots, refill the hole, pat down the soil, and water deeply. While planting individual plants is easy, accomplishing ambitious planting operations leaves many gardeners overwhelmed. This section reviews planting basics, but it also contains information on low-maintenance techniques for eliminating lawn, strategies for creating large plantings that minimize digging, and methods for restoring sites where some native plants are still in evidence.

Planting Basics

Proper planting minimizes stress and can make all the difference between a plant that grows vigorously and one that simply dies. It is also one of the best ways to protect the money you have invested in plants for the garden. Whether you are digging a

Tree tubes protect tree seedlings from deer and other wildlife. They also create greenhouse-like conditions and speed growth. To prevent birds from falling inside, cover the tops of the tubes with wire mesh. Photo by Neil Soderstrom.

single hole or planting an entire bed—planting one plant or many—a few basic techniques apply. For tips on planting in soil that is either constantly or periodically wet, such as sites that are naturally boggy or are subject to tides or periodic flooding, see "Gardens in Wet Soil" on p. 257.

Handle with care. Gentle handling helps protect roots and crowns of all plants. Handle container-grown plants and balled-and-burlapped (B&B) trees and shrubs by grasping the container or root ball. This is especially important when handling

Regular watering is essential until new plantings are established. Run soaker hoses through beds to make regular watering easy. Various options are available for individual trees, such as the tree bag watering the redbud (*Cercis canadensis*). Photo by Neil Soderstrom; design by Pat Harrington.

B&B nursery stock, since moving plants by pulling at the trunk or top growth can permanently damage the connection between the upper growth and the roots.

Timing. In general, mail-order suppliers and local nurseries can recommend a planting time based on your zip code (the personnel in big box stores are not generally knowledgeable enough). While container-grown plants can be planted nearly any time of year in the Chesapeake Bay region, post-planting maintenance is easier if trees, shrubs, perennials, and other plants are set in the ground in early spring or in fall. That is because plants have a spell of cool weather to establish roots and start growing before they have to deal with summertime heat and humidity. Spring- and early-summer-blooming perennials are best planted in fall, and those that bloom in late summer or fall are best planted in spring. Bare-root plants are planted from late fall to very early spring, as soon as the soil can be worked, while they are completely dormant. Although planting in summertime is possible, it means committing to regular watering until your new charges resume growing.

🍃 Is the Soil Ready?

Before digging for any reason, take a few minutes to check the soil moisture level. Working soil (digging or tilling) when it is either too wet or too dry destroys soil structure. If the soil is too dry, soil aggregates will break apart, leaving dust. If it is too wet (especially in soils high in clay), digging or tilling results in a solid, sticky mess. In both cases, soil structure and the balance of large and small pores are destroyed.

Fortunately, it is not hard to tell if the soil is ready to dig. To check soil moisture, pick up a handful of soil and squeeze it in your palm. Then press your thumb into the soil. If your thumb makes a hole in the clump, as if you were handling clay, the soil is too wet to work. Wait a few days and test it again. On the other hand, if the sample instantly crumbles into dust when touched, it is too dry. (Sandy soil, whether wet or dry, will generally break apart this way unless it contains ample organic matter.) Water thoroughly, then test again in a day or so. If the sample crumbles into light, fluffy clumps, it is ready to work.

🍃 Planting Weather

Transplanting is stressful, so try to plant on a cloudy or overcast day, or even in light rain. This protects new transplants from being exposed to the full force of the sun and eases the transition. Whether they are planted in sun or shade, plants need to adapt to sun exposure, fluctuating temperatures, and wind, all of which can pull moisture from leaves faster than roots, stressed from transplanting, can take it up. This is especially important with container-grown plants because they are fully leafed out and growing actively. A spell of overcast weather gives roots, and the plants they support, a few days to adapt and resume growing. If overcast weather is not predicted or if the sun peeks out sooner than expected, cover plants with burlap suspended on wire frames or plastic laundry baskets, or protect them with cardboard boxes propped up on one side. Cut several holes in the boxes to let the heat escape. Leave covers in place for several days until plants resume growing.

Heeling in and holding over. Instead of planting in the garden when the timing is not right, set purchases in a protected spot in partial shade when you bring them home. Check on them daily and water as needed until it is time to plant. This is a great way to handle sale plants offered in late summer and early fall, as nursery managers set out specimens that have suffered over summer. Just place them in a protected spot, water regularly until cooler temperatures return, and then plant. To repot extremely pot-bound specimens, remove them from their pots, cut back damaged and dead top growth, rough up and/or prune the roots to eliminate circling, and then repot into a slightly larger container. Move plants held in this manner to the garden once cooler weather returns. Another temporary option is to grow plants in a holding bed for a year or so before planting out in the garden.

Aftercare. The planting process is not complete until plants are established and growing well. Check on newly planted specimens daily for a week, every few days for a month, and then weekly for the first season. Water and replenish mulch as necessary to be sure plants are off to a good start.

Planting Container-Grown Plants

Perennials, annuals, herbs, ground covers, and vines grown in containers all require the same basic treatment at planting time. Make sure they are well watered before transferring them to the garden. Dig a hole that is at least as deep as the root ball and twice as wide. Loosen the soil in the bottom and on the sides of the hole, since digging can compress the soil and make it hard for roots to spread. Add some organic matter such as compost—a handful or two when planting smaller pots (3 or 4 inches or less), a shovelful if the container is larger. Work it in to the edges of the hole while loosening the sides and mix a bit into the soil that was removed. Tip the plant out of its pot and set it in place to check planting depth. The objective is to set plants no deeper than they were growing in their containers. If necessary, use a tool handle or yardstick across the top of the hole to help visualize. Adjust the depth by digging farther down or adding more soil at the bottom to make the hole shallower.

Plants in biodegradable containers can be planted pot and all, but check to make sure they are not root-bound, then tear away the top of the pot when planting. That ensures that the remaining container is completely below the soil surface. Otherwise the container rim can wick water up and out of the soil, causing the pot to become a dry barrier that roots will not penetrate.

After teasing out or cutting roots, set the plant back in the hole, fill soil in around the roots, and gently firm it down to ensure good contact between roots and soil. Depending on the soil medium used by the grower, soil around the plant's roots may fall off. This is especially common with coarse bark mixes. Some experts recommend removing all potting media, essentially bare-rooting the plants, before setting them in the soil. Whatever method you use,

 The Kindest Cut

Check the root ball for circling roots before setting any plant in the ground. Plants that have been in their containers too long commonly have roots that wind around the outside of the container, especially at the bottom of the pot. Sometimes a plant develops a solid mass of roots around the outside of the root ball.

Cutting roots may seem harsh, but roughing them up at planting time is best for all container-grown plants. For smaller plants, fingers may suffice for teasing out roots, but do not hesitate to score the sides with a knife or other sharp gardening implement. Cut about 1 inch into the root ball on larger pots, about ¼ inch on small pots. On trees and shrubs, try to tease out circling roots so they can be spread out in the soil. Use pruning shears to trim off dead, damaged, or excessively long roots. Cut just beyond where another root branches off.

Rhododendron and azalea enthusiasts sometimes recommend a process called butterflying to keep the roots of these naturally shallow-rooted plants close to the soil surface. See "Gardens in Wet Soil" in Chapter 8 for more information.

be sure that the roots do not dry out before the plant is set into the soil. Cover the root ball with a wet cloth or, if many roots are visible, set it in a bucket of damp soil medium. As each plant is set in place, check again to make sure the soil level around the stem is still at the same depth it was in the container. If the soil is fluffy and well prepared, set plants *slightly* high, since they will settle with time. There should be no more than ½ inch of soil on top of the root ball, perhaps up to 1 inch for larger plants. When plants are set with the root ball too high, water flows around it, allowing the roots to dry out. When plants are set too low, the hole can fill with water and plants can drown. Covering the root ball *slightly*, as described above, is beneficial because the root ball tends to dry out more quickly than the surrounding soil.

Once the hole is full, form a wide, shallow saucer of soil around each plant to catch and direct water. Next, water each plant deeply—adjust the sides and edges of the soil saucer as necessary to make sure water flows toward the plant and not away from it. For best results and to minimize root damage from dry soil, water each plant as it is planted.

Finally, spread 1 to 2 inches of mulch around each new plant to control weeds, prevent soil crusting, and retain soil moisture. Reduce the thickness of the mulch layer as you spread toward the stem of each plant, feathering it out so mulch does not touch the stem. Keep mulch ½ to 2 inches away from plant stems, depending on the size of the plant, to avoid rot.

Planting Bare-Root Plants

As the name implies, these are plants sold without soil. A variety of trees, shrubs, roses, ground covers, and perennials are sold this way, especially via mail order. One advantage of bare-root plants is their affordability. The cost advantage stems in part from the fact that the soil and containers do not add to the cost of shipping. Bare-root plants can be planted in early spring or late fall and should be completely dormant, since shipping and planting are too stressful if plants are growing.

Bare-root plants do need special handling to become established and grow successfully. Whether you bring them home from the local garden center or order them by mail, be prepared to plant as soon as possible. Check the packing material (wood shavings, peat moss, and sawdust are typical) when they arrive to make sure it is barely moist, not wet. Store in a cool, dark place until you are ready to plant. A refrigerator or cool garage is fine. Or unpack them and heel them in by digging a shallow hole or trench on the north side of a building. Set plants at an angle so the roots can be completely covered with moist soil or a mix of moist soil, compost, chopped leaves, and/or mulch. You can also plant bare-root plants temporarily in containers.

At planting time, remove plants from the packing material or holding trench. Clip off damaged, moldy, or dead roots. Place plants in a bucket of water to rehydrate them. Soak perennials and ground covers for 5 to 10 minutes; soak woody plants like roses and trees for 8 to 10 hours. Carry bare-root plants to the garden in the bucket of water to make sure roots do not dry out before they are covered with soil. To plant, follow the steps below.

1. Dig a broad hole that is both deep and wide enough to accommodate the roots. Build up a cone of soil in the center. To determine the right depth, look closely at the plant to determine how deep it was growing before it was dug at the nursery. Place perennials with their crowns just at the soil surface. On all plants, but especially on trees, shrubs, and roses, look for a line between darker stems that were under the soil and lighter areas that were above it. Good-quality nurseries will enclose planting directions with each shipment. Read the directions and plant according to their recommendations.
2. Spread the roots over the cone of soil. Try to distribute them evenly in all directions.
3. Place a pole or a tool handle across the hole to make it easy to check if the plant is at the correct depth. For best results, set plants *slightly* higher

than they were growing in the nursery, since they will settle slightly after planting.

4. Refill the hole halfway with soil and then flood it with water. Once the water drains away, finish filling the hole with soil. Then flood the hole again.

5. Form a wide, shallow saucer of soil around the plant that will hold water while it soaks into the soil, instead of letting it drain off. Spread ½ to 2 inches of mulch around the plant, reducing the thickness of the mulch close to the plant. Keep mulch ½ inch to 2 inches away from plant stems to avoid rot. For bare-root roses, mulch the plants and then create a 6- to 8-inch-deep mound that buries the canes with loose soil or soil mixed with compost. This prevents the canes from drying out while allowing roots to start growing before the top growth does. Gently remove the mound when buds sprout— in about 2 weeks if you are planting in spring.

Planting Basics for Trees and Shrubs

Large trees and shrubs can be more difficult to handle, but they offer immediate benefits. Nurseries and landscaping companies will plant them for you, and this is often the best option for installing large plants. Professionals can handle large plants without damaging root balls. In addition, nurseries generally guarantee trees and shrubs they plant themselves, which means replacement at no charge if a plant dies within a given period of time. If you are planting yourself, use the following tips to plant trees and shrubs properly.

Dig the right hole. Make planting holes the same depth as the root ball and about three times as wide to encourage roots to spread into the surrounding soil. To encourage roots to spread, loosen the sides and bottom of the hole where digging has com-

 To Stake or Not to Stake

At one time every newly planted tree was staked in place. Small and medium-size trees that were either container grown or balled-and-burlapped (B&B) do not need staking unless they are planted in a windy spot or in a high-traffic location where visitors might knock against them. Stake bare-root trees that are over 8 feet tall as well as container-grown and B&B specimens that are over 6 feet tall or more than 1 inch in trunk diameter. Leave stakes in place for no more than one year.

pacted the soil. To ensure that the tree or shrub is set at the same depth it was growing in the nursery, measure the height and width of the root ball *before* transferring the plant into the hole, since large trees are heavy and difficult to move. If the tree will arrive on a trailer, dig the hole and measure before unloading it so it can be slid off the trailer and into the proper-size hole in one motion. If the hole is too deep, replace some soil and firm it in place so that the plant does not settle too much after planting. If in doubt, plant *slightly* higher to prevent the tree or shrub from settling too much.

Pick the position. Before sliding a new tree or shrub into its hole, look at it from all sides to determine the best position. It is fairly easy to spin a plant around on a trailer or on level ground to orient it properly, but repositioning once it is in the hole is difficult and can damage the roots.

Create planting beds. Instead of digging individual holes for trees and shrubs, consider making large planting beds that accommodate a number of plants. This encourages roots to spread more widely and creates a more natural growing situation. See "Deep Mulching" on p. 92 for a no-dig way to create planting beds.

Refill with unamended soil. Filling planting holes with rich topsoil mixed with compost seems like the best option, but it actually is not. Roots tend to stay in amended soil used to fill a planting hole and thus do not spread into the surrounding soil. This prevents trees from forming the wide-spreading root system they need at maturity to support them during windstorms. As a result, they blow over more easily. In addition, water can pool in a hole filled with amended soil, creating wet conditions that kill roots. Instead of amending, refill with the native soil and do not add fertilizer. Keeping the site mulched after planting encourages soil organisms such as earthworms to gradually move organic matter into the soil and improve it over time.

Check before you finish filling. When you have filled the hole about one-third of the way, step back and examine the plant from all angles to make sure it is straight and is sitting at the correct depth (the same depth it was growing in the nursery). Correct the position, if necessary, and then firm the soil in the hole to eliminate large air pockets before filling it the rest of the way.

Create a soil saucer, then mulch. Build a wide saucer with a 2- to 3-inch-tall edge of mounded soil around the edge to collect water and hold it as it seeps into the soil. The saucer should be at least as wide as the soil ball. Once the soil saucer is in place, cover the site with a ½- to 2-inch layer of mulch, reducing the thickness of the mulch layer closer to the plant. Keep mulch ½ inch to 2 inches away from the trunk or stems to avoid rot.

Water, water, water. Give your newly planted tree or shrub a deep, thorough watering as soon as the hole is filled. Adjust the soil saucer as necessary to ensure that water soaks into the soil and does not run off. Water weekly for the first year.

Handling B&B Stock

One of the best options for purchasing larger trees and shrubs is balled-and-burlapped, or B&B, stock. (Some nurseries and landscapers offer large trees that are dug and moved using truck-mounted transplanters.) B&B stock is grown in the ground in nurseries and is typically dug in fall or early winter, although early spring digging is possible. The soil and roots are wrapped in burlap. Some suppliers encase the root ball in a wire basket as well.

Like all plants, B&B trees and shrubs need to be set at the same depth they were growing in the nursery. Dig a hole that is *at least* 1 foot wider in diameter than the root ball; wider is better. Use these tips for handling B&B stock properly.

- At the nursery before buying, measure the root ball to make sure it is large enough to support the plant. It should measure 10 to 12 times the diameter of the trunk, measured 6 inches from the bottom.
- Make sure the root ball is not broken. A tree or shrub that feels loose in the root ball, as if they are separate, indicates that many of the roots have been broken off during the digging process.
- Plant B&B trees and shrubs as soon as possible. Water unplanted stock regularly so that the soil ball does not dry out. Protecting the soil ball with a tarp to prevent drying is helpful, but planting permanently is best.
- Keep the burlap on the root ball until the plant is in the hole. This keeps the soil ball intact.
- Handle the plant by the root ball, never by holding the trunk or top growth. Improper handling puts stress on the stem and roots, and especially

To prepare a bed by deep mulching, start by cutting grass and weeds down as close to the soil surface as possible. Then cover the site with a thick layer of newspaper topped by chopped leaves, compost, and/or bark. Wait at least six months to plant. Photo by Barbara Ellis.

This is the same garden, originally mulched in spring, a year later in the fall. Spot weeding is necessary because determined weeds will find their way to the surface. Where necessary, rake back the mulch, remove weeds, then add more newspaper and mulch. Photo by Barbara Ellis.

the connection between them, because the root ball is much heavier than the top growth.

- Water regularly to keep the soil around the roots evenly moist, both before and after planting.
- Once the tree or shrub is positioned in the hole, cut and remove all rope, twine, or straps (natural and synthetic) around the soil ball and the trunk.
- Loosen the burlap and fold it down into the hole. If the "burlap" is actually synthetic (typically polypropylene), remove it completely. If in doubt, use a match: Natural burlap burns; synthetic melts. If there is a wire basket, use wire cutters to cut away parts that are near the surface. The rest will rust away underground.
- Fill the hole, making sure that the burlap is completely buried. If it is near the surface, it can wick water away from the roots.

Finish by flooding the hole with water, building a saucer of soil, flooding it again, and mulching. If you plant in fall or winter, check the soil weekly until cold weather arrives to make sure it remains moist. Check during warm spells in winter and water weekly during the first summer, especially if you planted in spring.

Preparing Sites for Planting

Jobs that involve planting more than one plant easily become overwhelming. Traditionally, gardeners have tackled these tasks by stripping off grass and weeds, then tilling or digging before planting. While this tried-and-true approach does work, it demands a great deal of strength, time, and effort to prepare a site and plant it. In addition to disturbing the soil,

Before digging holes and planting individual plants, space containers out over the site, then step back to assess their positions. Try to visualize the plants at maturity and adjust them accordingly before digging. Photo by Barbara Ellis.

Mulching to Make Islands

Transforming a landscape from lawn scattered with a few trees and shrubs to a more varied, Bay- and wildlife-friendly configuration becomes a much more manageable objective when you use deep mulching as a planting strategy. Use the tips below to help make the transition. See "Beds, Borders, and Planting Islands" in Chapter 2 for information on visualizing and designing beds and islands.

Mulch in sections. Instead of mulching huge areas all at once, attack the task in sections to fit the time, energy, and budget available for the project. For example, start by deep mulching the area between two fairly closely spaced plants, or expand the mulched area around a tree or two. Enlarge the mulched areas at a later date.

Set a schedule. This helps set a rhythm that keeps a project moving ahead without letting frustration or budget worries derail it. Every year—or every spring and fall—mulch a new area and plant the one mulched the previous season. This spreads out the cost of plants and mulch along with the after-care new plantings require, making it easier to keep up with weeding and watering while newly planted areas become established.

Target hard-to-mow spots. Eliminating patches of lawn that are difficult or inconvenient to mow makes perfect sense in a deep mulching program. For example, mulch over patches of grass that can only be cut with several back-and-forth passes. Mulch stray patches that are away from the main lawn and eliminate stretches that cannot be mown cleanly with even passes of the mower. For example, a lawn mower with a 20-inch-wide deck takes two passes to cut a strip of grass that is 22 inches wide. Use deep mulching to make the strip 20 inches and eliminate the need for a second pass.

Plant now, create islands later. If you are starting out with a huge lawn and only a small tree or two, plant trees first. Plan the shape of eventual planting islands or beds that will surround them later. Even though these plants will be surrounded by lawn for the foreseeable future, this strategy gives the trees a chance to become established and start growing. Once the entire area is mulched and planted, well-established trees will make it look more mature.

Plan for shade. This is not necessary on properties graced with mature trees, but shade is at a premium around houses located on converted cornfields. Take time to study where and when trees planted in various locations will cast their shade. Metal fence posts make fine temporary stand-ins for trees and will cast a shadow that indicates where shade will fall. Trees on the west side of the house will create an area that is shady in the afternoon, but pay attention to time of year as well, since as the sun moves in the sky, the location of shade on the ground will shift accordingly. For shade in the short term, plant the largest trees you can afford, but also think about shady areas years down the road. A grove of small trees or even saplings can become a woodland in 20 years. Small trees need protection from deer, as well as rabbits and voles, from the day they are planted. Surround the trunks with cages made of poultry wire or other protection immediately after planting, since new plants in their habitat are especially appealing to deer.

Consider temporary ground covers. These are an option to cover ground on a budget or to cover an area for a single season before planting it permanently in fall. Ornamental sweet potatoes (*Ipomoea batatas*) are vigorous, sprawling ground covers grown for their handsome chartreuse or purple leaves. ('Margarita' is chartreuse; 'Blackie' is one purple-maroon-leaved cultivar.) Even pumpkins or gourds can be used to fill a spot with foliage for a summer. Combining annuals with perennials, shrubs, or permanent ground covers is an option.

Install permanent plantings at the proper spacing and then fill in between them with annuals for the first season or two.

Planting Slopes

Slopes present a special planting challenge, and the steeper the slope, the more difficult it is to plant. Not only does water run off quickly without soaking into the soil, making it hard to get plants established, but working on steep slopes also can be difficult because of the stress it puts on a gardener's knees and other joints. Tackle slopes in small sections and use the techniques below to install and help plants become established. See "Greenwalls" on p. 98 for another option for steep slopes. Drought-tolerant plants are the best choices for slopes. Once they are established, supplemental watering should not be necessary. See Chapter 5 for plant recommendations.

Manage existing lawn grass. Do not start a slope-planting project by stripping off existing lawn, weeds, or other ground cover, since this leaves the soil uncovered and prone to serious erosion. Mulching and using newspaper is only an option on very gentle slopes, although biodegradable landscape fabric topped by mulch is somewhat effective, provided the mulch is not washed away by a storm before plants become established. One option is to use an herbicide to kill the grass and then leave it in place to hold soil on the slope. When planting, dig through it enough to create level planting pockets. If appearance is not a huge concern, leave any existing plantings in place, including weeds, and add new ones planted in level planting pockets. Gradually remove grass, weeds, or other unwanted plants as their replacements become established.

Create level planting pockets. Anything that slows the flow of water down the slope is beneficial. Dig a small planting pocket for each plant. The surface

Temporary terraces are an effective, relatively inexpensive way to establish ground covers on a slope and give water a chance to soak into the soil. Cut level planting sites across the slope and stake pine or other untreated wood along the front of each terrace. This gives ground covers time to become established before the wood begins to rot.

Minimal soil disturbance was the goal for planting this hillside. Lawn grass on the site was treated with herbicide and left in place so that shrubs could be planted through the grass. Soaker hoses were arranged across the slope so the shrubs could be watered regularly. Once they were established, they were underplanted with various grasses, self-sowing wildflowers, and ground covers. Photo by Barbara Ellis.

This slope below a terrace wall is covered with a rich carpet of grasses, conventional perennials such as hostas, and wildflowers. Azaleas and redbuds (*Cercis canadensis*) complete the picture. Photo © Roger Foley; design by Tom Mannion Landscape Design.

of each pocket should slant back into the slope to catch water that would otherwise flow off the site. Mulch planting pockets or create mini-terraces by staking short pieces of wood in place to hold the outside edge of the slope. Wood (such as pine) that will eventually rot is fine because the plants will have enough time to become established before it disappears.

Plant a checkerboard. To cover the slope effectively, do not plant in straight rows across and down the slope. Instead, stagger the rows so plants in one row are located in the space between plants in the rows above and below.

Install terraces. Transforming a slope into a series of level planting spaces is another option. For permanent terraces, use stone or brick to hold the lower side of each terrace. Landscape ties are another option. Consult a professional if the terrace walls need to be more than a foot or so high or if the slope is very steep. Incorporate drains through the walls so water in the soil can drain away. Temporary terraces using pine or other untreated wood that will eventually rot away are fine for establishing ground covers on slopes. (Warped or other damaged boards are an economical choice.) To install them, dig level beds and hold them in place by pegging boards along the outside edge of each terrace. Although the wood will eventually rot, plants will have time to become established. In all cases, the soil surface in the terraces should be level or angled slightly back into the slope to catch the maximum amount of runoff.

Companion plant. For permanent, long-term cover, plan on covering a slope with a collection of different plants. For example, combine several different shrubs and underplant them with ground covers.

Mulch. While it is difficult to keep mulch on a slope, it does help retain moisture in the soil, so spread it and replace as needed. Installing burlap over the mulch and securing it with wooden pegs or wire landscape staples can help hold the mulch in place.

Water. Slow, gentle water delivery is the secret to watering plants on slopes. An overhead sprinkler will deliver water, but the best option is to install soaker hoses that water the plants at ground level. Position soaker hoses across the slope. Start watering at the top, by connecting the hose to the first soaker. Set it to seep water out very slowly, and let it run for at least 2 hours (check soil moisture by sticking a finger into the ground) before moving the hose down to the next row.

Planting under Trees

Lush plantings in the shade add appeal to any landscape, and shade-loving plants are far better suited to sites under trees than lawn grass. Not surprisingly, proper plant selection and technique are the secret to success.

 **Greenwalls**

This new building technology makes it possible to plant nearly vertical slopes. Greenwalls can be incorporated into new construction or used to re-engineer extremely steep slopes, and they are especially useful in urban sites where space is at a premium. There are several types of greenwalls, including walls constructed from special blocks that provide gaps for plants to grow through the wall, as well as flexible, honeycomb-like structures that allow plants to grow in individual cells. Troughs offer another option: These are soil-filled containers or tubs that are stacked to form the wall. Gabons, an option for large sites, consist of large wire baskets filled with stone that allow plants to grow up and through the basket and stones. Gabons and most types of greenwall have a decided advantage over conventional impervious walls because they allow water to seep through.

Minimizing damage to the roots of existing trees and shrubs is essential when planting. Contrary to popular belief, most tree roots generally spread out fairly near the soil surface. Even the roots of so-called deep-rooted trees such as oaks have fairly shallow roots. A tree's large support roots may delve one to several feet down into the earth to stabilize the plant, but it will have many smaller feeder roots that form a net near the surface. Feeder roots spread beyond the tree's canopy and are responsible for absorbing water, nutrients, and oxygen. Changing the grade around a tree by piling even an inch or two of topsoil on top of the roots affects the health of feeder roots and root hairs, compromising the tree's ability to take up these essential elements or even killing it.

Still, some species of tree are better for under-planting than others. While all trees have surface feeder roots, some, like native silver and red maples (*Acer saccharum* and *A. rubrum*), produce an exceptionally dense network. So-called deep-rooted trees such as oaks (*Quercus* spp.) tend to have spaces between roots and lack the dense mats of feeder roots. With maples and other shallow-rooted trees, mulching and planting outside the drip line (the line around the tree where rain drips to the ground from the outermost branches) often is the best option. There are few species that can compete with a dense mass of tree roots, and most that can are non-native invasive weeds such as English ivy (*Hedera helix*). Another option for adding color and interest under a maple or other tree with dense surface roots is to install and plant large containers under the canopy. To prevent tree roots from growing up into the containers, set the containers on landscape ties or other support to keep them off the soil surface.

Deep mulching is a good way to eliminate grass and weeds under trees. It is far easier and is less damaging to roots than trying to strip off existing grass. A couple inches of loose mulch will not damage a tree's feeder roots the way topsoil will, but using an inch or two of bark mulch topped with 3 or 4 inches of chopped leaves (chop them up using a mulching lawn mower) is equally effective and a more natural cover for the tree. Do not use the lasagna gardening technique under the canopy of a tree. As always, avoid piling mulch directly around the trunk of a tree, reduce the thickness of the mulch layer as it approaches the tree, and keep mulch ½ to 2 inches away from the trunk. While natural leaf litter is fine up against the trunk of a tree, damp bark mulch in contact with the trunk can lead to rot as well as insect and disease infestation. Read and follow label directions closely before using an herbicide to eliminate existing lawn or weeds under a tree prior to spreading mulch. Avoid spraying herbicide on the tree's trunk.

When the site is ready for planting, use a trowel to locate pockets of soil between larger roots that have few feeder roots. If all you encounter is an impenetrable mass of roots, the best option is to mulch, not plant, the site. If you can find pockets of soil under a tree, avoid cutting any roots that are larger than about 1½ inches in diameter. Smaller roots can regenerate fairly quickly, but larger ones generally cannot.

Restoring Wild Sites

On sites that support at least some existing wildflowers or other plants that are worth saving, widespread clearing and soil disturbance is not the best approach. Clearing actually favors invasive and weedy species, so minimizing disturbance is an important goal. Instead, consider the approaches described below. All use the makeup of natural plant communities to help establish or restore a site. They also minimize, but do not eliminate, maintenance.

Minimize disturbance. Regardless of the type of site, plants fill in areas that are disturbed, whether that means a site that was cleared with a bulldozer or by pulling weeds. An equally important fact is that lovely, delicate native wildflowers will not be first to the finish line without some help. Vigorous plants, meaning weeds and non-native invasives, fill in disturbed areas faster than anything else. That is why techniques like deep mulching are so effective: They minimize disturbance and avoid bringing weed seeds to the soil surface where they can germinate.

Typical clearing techniques that use front loaders and other gasoline-powered equipment are especially damaging because they cause soil compaction and disturbance. Even if the site is planted after clearing, invasive species like Japanese honeysuckle (*Lonicera*

To help an existing site that has some native plants on it, start by identifying the species that are already growing, including wildflowers, shrubs, and even small seedlings of native trees. This woodland already has a rich community of natives, and simply controlling unwanted invasives is a best first step. Photo by Neil Soderstrom; design by Alan Visintainer.

japonica) have the upper hand because they are so vigorous and so effective at filling in disturbed areas. New transplants generally have difficulty competing, partly because they have to overcome the stress of being moved, while pieces of weed roots are already in the soil and are ready to sprout.

Minimizing the amount of disturbed ground helps many native species compete. One way to keep disturbance to a minimum is to restore or renovate an area in manageable sections. Instead of clearing an entire area, tackle a square yard or two at a time. That way, it is relatively easy to keep an eye out for invasives and take steps to control them before they overwhelm new transplants or existing wildflowers.

Mother plant colonies. Pulling up weeds creates disturbance, which means that traditional weeding—pulling every plant not planted by the gardener—becomes a never-ending source of new weeds. In areas that still contain even a few native plants, mark the location of each native with a flag or other marker so each "mother clump" will be easy to find later. Then create a small disturbed area around each plant by pulling competing weeds. Replace natural mulch around each mother clump. Revisit the site regularly. Try to identify the new plants that fill in around it, and leave any seedlings of the mother clump that appear. Manage the weeds that crop up in the zone around the mother clump by cutting them off at the soil line. Do not pull them up, since pulling creates more disturbed ground, favoring weeds and invasives. As the mother plant spreads, enlarge the patch. In the process, keep an eye out for other native species that appear in the disturbed circle and leave them as well. Also watch for seedlings that appear elsewhere, and either enlarge the managed patch to include them or start new patches for each seedling.

Plant and maintain. Use a similar tactic to add new native species to a natural area. Clear a small area and plant, then treat the new addition as a mother plant by managing the weeds in a zone around it. This approach eliminates the need to manage weeds over the entire site and focuses attention on caring for individual plants. Gradually tend larger areas around each newly added plant as the spaces between them become smaller and smaller.

Deal with invasives. On a site dominated by invasive, non-native plants, try marking favored native species with caution tape or stakes. Then cut or kill the rest of the plants on the site. In this case, managing invasives that reappear will be a priority, but having marked the natives that are worth saving helps direct the overall effort to restore natives. See "Managing Invasive Plants" later in this chapter for more information on control measures.

Plant communities. In nature, different species of plants grow together in habitats. Plants that have evolved together are adapted to growing side by side. For this reason, communities of plants that grow together naturally perform better and provide better weed suppression than a mixture of plants from unrelated sites. Communities also generally are better at covering ground than monocultures (plantings that feature a single plant species such as a ground cover or lawn). This is another example of why learning about the growing conditions on a site and the plant community that originally occupied it can be beneficial.

Start with small plants. It can be difficult to find spots that are relatively free of roots under trees. It is easier to dig adequate holes for smaller plants than large ones. Regular watering is especially important in this case so that roots can penetrate the soil and obtain adequate moisture.

Plant in bold drifts. To create a natural-looking area while maintaining a gardenlike appearance with bold blocks of color, arrange plants in free-form-shaped drifts or groupings consisting of three or more individual plants. Grouping several plants of the same species together instead of arranging them singly emphasizes the natural way that plants grow and suggests the drifts have formed over time.

Essential Aftercare

The planting process is not over until plants are fully established and growing. That means regular watering and weed control. Plan on watering regularly for the first season—at least every week or ten days, depending on natural rainfall, but more often in areas with sandy soil or naturally dry spots on slopes. As a general rule, most plants thrive with one inch of water per week, although rainfall is rarely that regular. Monitor rainfall and supplement it whenever natural rainfall falls below that level. Even drought-tolerant species need regular watering while they are growing roots and becoming established in their new location.

Avoid sprinkling plants with a hose, since that seldom provides enough water to wet the soil down to the bottom of the root ball. Instead, water deeply, wetting the top 5 to 6 inches of soil. (Stick a finger into the soil to check for moisture.) Soaker hoses are ideal for delivering water to the root zone while keeping foliage dry. This also minimizes waste, since it cuts evaporation by putting water directly to the soil surface to seep into the ground. Once they are established, native plants that are matched to the conditions that exist naturally on the site should not need regular watering.

Plants do not need to be fertilized, especially if you spread compost and prepared the soil at planting time. In fact, research has shown that fertilizer benefits weeds: Decreasing fertility along with maintaining the natural pH of the surrounding soil will benefit native species. Amending the mulch layer annually keeps soil-dwelling organisms well fed and busy breaking down organic matter to release necessary nutrients. Mulch protects the soil, helps retain moisture, and makes weeds that do appear easier to pull.

New plantings need regular attention to remove any weeds that manage to find their way through the layers of newspaper and mulch. To keep weeding chores to a minimum, check new plantings weekly for at least a month so that weeds in need of pulling or cutting are still small. Use an asparagus fork or gardening knife to dig deep-rooted species like dandelions and eliminate the entire root the first time. Otherwise the plants will resprout from the remaining root fragments. Another option is to rake back the mulch around an emerging patch of weeds, cut them down, and cover them with new layers of newspaper (8 to 10 sheets). After that, re-cover the newspaper with mulch.

It pays to watch how quickly plants become established. Some will begin growing quickly, while others will seem to struggle. Keep notes—and keep plants labeled so you can identify them down the road. Not only will you probably want more of the vigorous ones, but they will give you clues to what you can add to your landscape.

Managing Invasive Plants

Non-native invasive plants are not just weeds like Canada thistle (*Cirsium arvense*), multiflora rose (*Rosa multiflora*), and tree of heaven (*Ailanthus altissima*) that show up unwanted in yards and gardens. Unfortunately, many are deliberately planted in home landscapes. Experts estimate that several thousand species of non-native plants have been introduced and become established in North America.

Dandelions (*Taraxacum officinale*) and a number of other species have been here since the 1600s. Out of the total number of introduced species, 10 percent, or about 400 species, are truly invasive. Scientists define non-native invasive species as those that were introduced by humans and are able to take over and damage significant portions of the natural habitat. Different species are invasive in different regions of the country.

Eliminating established non-native invasive plants is a long-term project, but taking steps to control them helps make a landscape more sustainable and provides huge benefits for wildlife and the environment. Regardless of how invasive plants came to your property, begin taking steps to eliminate them. A simple, positive choice is to use local and regional lists, such as the one in this book, to avoid purchasing non-native invasives at garden centers. Reject them if they are suggested in a landscape design. Reducing demand is one effective way to begin turning the tide against invasives. Another way is to identify non-native invasive plants on your own property and begin to eliminate them.

Gardeners can also help prevent invasives from spreading. Escapees move from one spot to another via roots and rhizomes that grow from season to season or via seeds spread by birds and other wildlife. Gardeners help them travel by dumping prunings and unwanted divisions on the edge of their property or along a wild area, allowing them to root and travel into wild landscapes. Dispose of invasive plants by placing them in plastic bags and putting them in the trash, not in compost. Be especially cautious with plants that have set seed, and seal the bags so seeds cannot escape. It is also possible to dispose of invasives by spreading them in the sun on a driveway or patio until they are crispy and thoroughly dead, then adding them to the trash.

Invasive Trees, Shrubs, and Vines

The list below includes some of the more serious invasive plants of concern in the Chesapeake Bay watershed. See Chapter 5 for a list of invasive, or potentially invasive, ground covers. In the list below, species still offered for sale by nurseries and garden centers are marked with an asterisk (*).

Invasive Trees

Ailanthus, tree of heaven (*Ailanthus altissima*)
Amur cork tree (*Phellodendron amurense*)*
Aralia, Japanese angelica tree (*Aralia elata*)*
Elaeagnus, autumn olive (*Elaeagnus umbellata*); Russian olive (*E. angustifolia*)*
Elm, Siberian (*Ulmus pumila*)
Locust, black (*Robinia pseudoacacia*)*
Maple, Norway (*Acer platanoides*)*
Mimosa (*Albizia julibrissin*)*
Mulberry, white (*Morus alba*); mulberry, paper (*Broussonetia papyrifera*)
Oak, sawtooth (*Quercus acutissima*)*
Paulownia, empress tree (*Paulownia tomentosa*)*
Pear, callery pear, Bradford pear (*Pyrus calleryana*)*
Poplar, white (*Populus alba*)*
Tamarix (*Tamarix parviflora*)*

Invasive Shrubs

Barberry, Japanese and European (*Berberis thunbergii, B. vulgaris*)*
Buckthorn, sea (*Hippophae rhamnoides*)*
Burning bush, winged euonymus (*Euonymus alatus*)*
Honeysuckles, bush (*Lonicera maackii, L. morrowii*)*
Jetbead, black (*Rhodotypos scandens*)*

Knotweed, Japanese (*Fallopia japonica*, formerly *Fatsia japonica*)
Privets (*Ligustrum* spp., *L. obtusifolium, L. ovalifolium, L. sinense, L. vulgare*)*
Rose, rugosa (*Rosa rugosa*)*
Spiraea, Japanese meadowsweet (*Spiraea japonica*)*
Viburnum, linden (*Viburnum dilatatum*)*
Vitex, beach (*Vitex rotundifolia*)*
Wineberry (*Rubus phoenicolasius*)

Invasive Vines

Akebia, five leaf or chocolate vine (*Akebia quinata*)*
Bittersweet, Oriental (*Celastrus orbiculatus*)*
Clematis, sweet autumn (*Clematis terniflora*)*
Honeysuckle, Japanese (*Lonicera japonica*)*
Hops, Japanese (*Humulus japonicus*)*
Ivy, English (*Hedera helix*)*
Kudzu (*Pueraria lobata*)
Porcelain berry (*Ampelopsis brevipedunculata*)*
Wintercreeper (*Euonymus fortunei*)*
Wisteria, Chinese and Japanese (*Wisteria sinensis, W. floribunda*)*

Control Measures

Techniques like pulling and spraying are worth the effort because invasive plants crowd out native species and do not play the same role in the environment or feed wildlife as natives do. Once established, vines like English ivy (*Hedera helix*) will completely smother cherished spring wildflowers and other undergrowth. Established plants can also pull down mature trees if they are allowed to climb. According to recent studies, scientists have discovered evidence that habitats with high concentrations of Japanese barberries (*Berberis thunbergii*) have much higher than normal populations of ticks infected with Lyme disease. Garlic mustard (*Alliaria petiolata*), another troublesome non-native invasive, not only crowds out vast areas of native wildflowers such as toothworts (*Cardamine* spp.) and spring beauties (*Claytonia virginica*), but it is also toxic to the larvae of native butterflies and has been shown to suppress the growth of native tree seedlings. Japanese stiltgrass (*Microstegium vimineum*) forms dense patches that replace native wildflowers and ground covers on disturbed sites. These plants represent just a small portion of invasives that can cause damage throughout the Chesapeake landscape.

Various techniques are suitable for eliminating invasives. The best one for your situation depends on the plants present, the size of the population, and how much dedication and effort you can bring to the attack. Since control measures are more effective on some species than on others, it helps to start by inventorying the invasives that have a foothold. Most people can identify plants like English ivy (*Hedera helix*) and common periwinkle (*Vinca minor*), but the guidebooks listed in Suggested Resources are helpful to have on hand for other species. See the online resources link in Suggested Resources to find websites with specific control information. Use the information below to start a management program.

Pulling and Cutting

Annuals such as Japanese stiltgrass (*Microstegium vimineum*), biennials like garlic mustard (*Alliaria petiolata*), and perennials such as purple loosestrife (*Lythrum salicaria*) can be controlled by pulling the plants. Where possible, cutting invasives down to the soil line is effective, reduces disturbance to the soil, and keeps weed seeds from being pulled to the soil surface. Cutting plants at the soil line is not as effective for species that have fleshy roots for food

storage, such as common daylily (*Hemerocallis fulva*). Work when the soil is moist and use a garden fork to loosen the soil around deep-rooted species before pulling them.

Repeated pulling or cutting over several seasons is generally necessary to eliminate a population, especially if you are dealing with perennials and self-sowing biennials such as garlic mustard. The good news is that each season there are fewer plants to eliminate. Timing can make all the difference: Try to pull or cut Japanese stiltgrass in late summer before it sets seed. If you pull after seeds appear, put the plants in a plastic bag to avoid spreading the seeds. Pull or cut garlic mustard before the flowers begin to set seed in late spring. Canada thistle (*Cirsium arvense*) has brittle roots that make it difficult to control by pulling. Some gardeners have been successful with repeated cutting or pulling, but it is necessary to attack populations every week or ten days for one or more seasons.

It is possible to control smaller woody vines by pulling as well. In fact, small populations of plants such as Japanese honeysuckle (*Lonicera japonica*) are fairly easy to manage in this manner. The best approach is to start work on the outside edge of a clump, where plants have not yet formed a dense cover. Begin pulling and winding up the vines as you go. English ivy can be managed in the same way, although established stands will take years of determined effort. Always check back a few weeks or months later and eliminate any plants that resprout.

It is possible to eliminate shrubs such as winter creeper (*Euonymus fortunei*), Japanese barberry (*Berberis thunbergii*), and armur honeysuckle (*Lonicera maackii*) by digging.

When pulling invasives, do not add them to the compost pile or dump them along the edges of your property where they could spread. Invasives are extremely vigorous, and unless the plants are completely brown, dried up, and dead, there is a good chance they will root wherever they are dumped and continue growing. Either collect the plants in bags (this is an option for recycling plastic mulch bags) and add them to the trash, or set them in the hot sun until they turn completely brown and die before disposing of them.

Using Harsher Measures

Herbicides can be a valuable tool in the arsenal against invasive plants, especially if the populations on your property are too large for you to manage by pulling and/or cutting. See the online resources link in Suggested Resources to find sites with recommendations for specific herbicides and application methods. Before applying any herbicide, read the entire label. Follow the directions carefully. Wear the proper clothing, including heavy rubber gloves, long pants, long sleeves, and eye protection. Note that spring and summer are not necessarily the best seasons to use herbicides: Some can be used in late fall and winter by painting them on the bark of invasives such as autumn olive (*Elaeagnus umbellata*), tree of heaven (*Ailanthus altissima*), and Oriental bittersweet (*Celastrus orbiculatus*). This technique, called basal barking, involves a higher concentration of herbicide, often mixed with oil, but it can be targeted very specifically to individual plants. When used with other controls, spraying in late summer and early fall makes it possible to manage invasives without affecting spring-blooming wildflowers that die back in summer.

Regardless of the method used, be prepared to check back on populations of invasive plants regularly over several years to make sure that they have been eliminated.

PART TWO *Recommended Plants and Gardens*

Whether you plan a little or a lot, designing a garden ultimately comes down to choosing plants. There are literally thousands of plants native to the Chesapeake Bay region, and deciding which ones to buy can be difficult. One reason is that every site is unique. There are subtle gradations of sun, shade, or other environmental conditions, and every gardener starts out with a site that already has different plants growing on it. Where one landscape may have nothing more than lawn and basic foundation plants, another may feature a mature garden. A third may have a natural area partially overrun with non-native invasives. The style of each garden, along with each gardener's objectives, also varies. Determining what to do in each situation can be challenging, but also fun.

While some gardeners may aim for a landscape planted entirely with native species, most homeowners will end up with a mix of native and non-native plants. A great many yards start out with very few native species, if any, and increasing the percentage of native plants in the landscape is a worthwhile goal.

Since many landscapes combine native and non-native species, it is important to know which plants in the landscape are or could become invasive. See "Managing Invasive Plants" on p. 102 for information on species to watch in the Chesapeake Bay region. The plant lists throughout Part 2 are designed to help gardeners select native species for all parts of their landscapes. Use them to increase the number of native plants you buy and grow, as well as to determine which non-native plants can stay and which need to go.

The best place to start, especially for fairly new gardeners, is by choosing plants that are easy to grow. That means looking in the chapters that follow for plants that are identified as tolerating a fairly wide range of conditions. There are lots of choices that grow in sunny to shady sites, for example, and many more that can grow in full sun to part shade, or part shade to full shade. Starting with plants that are tough and tolerant ensures a healthy framework for your garden. They can tolerate experimentation as you become familiar with the sites your landscape has to offer. Eventually, expand your plant choices to include species that may be more difficult to grow.

Learning about plant communities in your area is another way to determine what plants will thrive. Look for remnant wild areas and build similar areas by identifying and planting species from that community. Learn about plant communities in books such as field guides, on the Internet, and by taking classes or

(overleaf) This shade garden features a carpet of native wildflowers, including American alumroot (*Heuchera americana*), Gray's sedge (*Carex grayi*), Virginia bluebells (*Mertensia virginica*), Celandine poppy (*Stylophorum diphyllum*), and trillium (*Trillium cuneatum*). Photo by Neil Soderstrom; design by Jimmy Testa at Mt. Cuba Center.

participating in nature walks at a local botanical garden or nature preserve. See "Reading the Landscape" on p. 69 for more methods to help identify plants that will thrive.

Part 2 contains chapters on shrubs, trees, and vines; ground covers; flowers for sun; and plants for shade. The plants are sorted into lists to help make selection easier. Plants do not conform neatly to these lists, so read several to widen your search. They are generally divided into choices for sun to part shade and part shade to full shade. As a result, gardeners with part shade conditions may find the best flowers for their garden in Chapter 6, "Flowers for Chesapeake Gardens," or in Chapter 7, "Plants and Gardens for Shade," since both contain plants suitable for partial shade. Part 2 also contains a chapter on rain gardens and wet-soil plantings as well as one on gardening for wildlife.

This section of the book contains information on a great many native plants. For this book, the term "native" specifically refers to species that grow naturally within the Chesapeake Bay region, primarily in Maryland, Virginia, Delaware, and the District of Columbia. A few plants that grow naturally in nearby areas, and that are great choices for gardens in this area, are included and identified as "nearly native."

Plant Responsibly

Before buying any native plant, it is important to ask questions about where it came from. Thousands of plants are collected from the wild annually, and wild collection is not a sustainable practice that responsible gardeners or homeowners should support. When purchasing plants, look for those described as "nursery propagated," not "nursery grown." The latter may actually be plants that were dug from the wild and then potted and grown for a few months before sale. Nursery propagated plants may be grown from seed, or they may be propagated by division or by potting offsets of plants already in cultivation. Some natives are propagated by tissue culture. Reputable nurseries will be proud of their propagation program and will make the origin of their plants clear on signage, on websites, or in catalogs. If they do not, or if you get mixed signals, shop elsewhere.

Asking questions is a useful tactic when buying plants at a local nursery. If the nursery is selling wild-collected plants, shop elsewhere. If possible, politely let staff know that they have lost your business and why. Looking closely at the plants themselves may provide the necessary clues. Plants that have been wild

Native plant sales, such as this one at Adkins Arboretum, are an excellent source of responsibly propagated native plants. Photo by Ann S. Rohlfing; Adkins Arboretum.

collected and then potted for sale commonly have an uneven or lopsided habit caused when a mature plant is stuffed into a pot. Price provides another clue: Propagating and caring for plants until they reach selling size costs money. If the price is too good to be true, you are likely looking at wild-collected plants.

Native plant societies, botanical gardens, and arboreta are great sources of native plants. In addition to offering responsibly produced plants, they offer rare species often not widely available in the trade.

Digging plants from wild areas and moving them to your own garden is not a responsible activity and should not be construed as somehow "saving" the plants. Backyard gardens do not offer permanent protection the way that public gardens do. In addition, transplants frequently do not survive digging and replanting. (Some require specific mycorrhizal fungi in order to survive, making them difficult or impossible to transplant or grow in nurseries.) If you know of a site that is threatened with development, contact a local native plant society and then help them obtain the necessary permission to organize a rescue.

FOUR ❦ Shrubs, Trees, and Vines for Landscaping

Woody plants—shrubs, trees, and vines that do not die back to the ground in winter—are investments that will live for many years. Selecting whatever looks pretty or seems the right size at the nursery is easy, but that approach can lead to major headaches. Problems that commonly result include ending up with a plant that simply will not grow where it is planted or one that is entirely too large for the site once it reaches maturity. Well-chosen woody plants will look more beautiful every year without the need for harsh annual pruning or shearing.

Plants grown from locally collected seed are considered by many the best alternative for building genetic diversity and restoring native habitats, but for many landscape situations, cultivated forms—cultivars—offer advantages as well. Many tree and shrub cultivars feature smaller size at maturity than the species, so the cultivars are often better suited to smaller yards than their full-size counterparts. Compact forms can also be useful for foundation plantings and smaller or narrower shrub borders or hedgerows. Many cultivars have been selected for outstanding foliage and flower color, disease resistance, and extended bloom, as well as weeping or creeping habits that further extend the possibilities.

Use the design ideas and information in Part 1 together with the plant lists in this chapter to select new woody plants for the landscape. Also consult lists in Chapter 7, "Plants and Gardens for Shade,"

(overleaf) Shrubs, trees, and other woody plants can play many roles in a landscape. While they are typically used as foundation plants or single specimens, they are far more valuable when grouped in beds, borders, and other plantings. Hydrangeas figure prominently in this cityscape, where terraced beds overflow with wild hydrangea (*Hydrangea arborescens*). Photo © Roger Foley; design by Tom Mannion Landscape Design.

for more trees, shrubs, and vines that grow in partial shade to shade. For plants that tolerate wet soil, see Chapter 8, "Water, Rain Gardens, and Wet Soil."

Shrubs

Use native shrubs in foundation plantings, in shrub plantings or hedges, or as specimens, or combine them in mixed borders with perennials and trees. Unless otherwise noted below, the plants on this list grow in full sun to part shade and in average, well-drained soil.

Evergreen Shrubs

Both needle- and broad-leaved evergreens make excellent foundation shrubs and can be used in shrub borders, hedges, and privacy screens. Unless otherwise noted below, all plants in this list grow in full sun to partial shade and tolerate average, well-drained soil. Some of the species below are trees, but the list highlights compact cultivated forms that are suitable for foundations, island beds, mass plantings, and mixed borders.

Dwarf eastern arborvitae (*Thuja occidentalis* 'Umbraculifera'). Photo by Neil Soderstrom; Green Spring Gardens.

Arborvitae, eastern arborvitae (*Thuja occidentalis*). This native tree reaches 60 feet and will grow in wet

🍃 Native Trends

Native plants have not always had to struggle for respect. During the early part of the twentieth century a vital and active movement celebrated the use of native plants and plant ecology. Landscape design luminaries such as Jens Jensen, among others, promoted the use of natives and of native plant communities in designed landscapes. In 1929, Dr. Edith A. Roberts, professor of botany at Vassar College, and Elsa Rehmann, a landscape architect, writer, and lecturer, published *American Plants for American Gardens*, a book that promotes the use of native plants and highlights the value of using natural plant communities as design inspiration. Their ideas led to landscapes not only that were sustainable but that celebrated the unique characteristics that make a place special—its sense of place.

In the second half of the twentieth century, mainstream design and landscape architecture steered away from linking design with native plants and plant ecology. One reason for the change was that modernist style led to plants being selected and used as sculptural elements rather than as part of a natural community. Another part of the change of focus was due to suburban development, including increasingly large lawns, after World War II. The landscape industry grew to meet the demand and began producing and promoting tough, widely adapted plants that were not affected by pests. Most were not native but were easy to recommend and could withstand being planted nearly anywhere. These factors, and the development and marketing of chemical pesticides, herbicides, and fungicides, led to a new standard for what a cultivated or "developed" property should look like. The resulting landscapes look pretty much the same, regardless of where they are located, and are filled with non-native plants that are seldom planted in natural communities and do not support insects, birds, and other wildlife.

Fortunately, sustainable landscaping and native plant movements are working to shift the tide. By replacing even some non-native plants with natives, you can help shift the tide as well.

---

to dry soil. Many dwarf forms suitable for foundation plantings are available, including 'Little Gem', which grows to 3 feet and spreads to 6 feet. 'Little Giant' reaches 4 feet tall and wide. 'Pendula' has a weeping habit and reaches 15 feet. 'Holmstrup' forms a narrow pyramid, from 5 to 10 feet at maturity and 2 feet wide. Hardiness: Zones 3 to 8.

Bayberries (*Morella* spp., formerly *Myrica* spp.). Both species listed here feature aromatic leaves and berries that are attractive to birds. Southern, small, or swamp bayberry (*Morella caroliniensis*, formerly *Myrica caroliniensis*, *M. heterophylla*) ranges from 8 to 12 feet tall

Northern bayberry (*Morella pensylvanica*, formerly *Myrica pensylvanica*). Photo by Neil Soderstrom.

and wide. Plants grow in sun to shade and wet to dry soil. Hardiness: Zones 6 to 9. Northern bayberry (*Morella pensylvanica*, formerly *Myrica pensylvanica*)

🍃 Native Roses

Wild roses are an asset in informal shrub borders, on the edges of wild areas, and in mixed borders and hedgerows. Three species are native to the Chesapeake Bay area. All bear single, 2- to 2½-inch flowers in early to midsummer and are hardy in Zones 4 to 9. They grow in full sun and average soil and are excellent substitutions for non-native invasive multiflora rose (*Rosa multiflora*).

Carolina or pasture rose (*R. carolina*). This species bears fragrant pink flowers and bright red hips on 3- to 6-foot plants that sucker freely to form thickets or drifts. They thrive in average to wet soil but also tolerate dry conditions.

Prairie or climbing rose (*R. setigera*). This species has pink flowers that fade to white and red-brown hips. The canes can reach 15 feet in one season, and plants can be trained as climbers or used as ground covers.

Virginia rose (*R. virginiana*). Fragrant pink flowers, red hips, and disease-resistant foliage make this wild rose a garden asset. Plants range from 3 to 6 feet in height and spread freely by suckers to form broad thickets.

ranges from 5 to 10 feet tall and wide. Plants are not reliably evergreen, but they tolerate dry to wet soil and can grow in tidal and non-tidal marshes and wetlands, either brackish or fresh. Hardiness: Zones 3 to 7. Both species spread by suckers and form thickets or colonies with time.

Hollies, evergreen (*Ilex* spp.). American (*I. opaca*) reaches 40 or 50 feet, but 'Maryland Dwarf' is a spreading cultivar that reaches 3 to 5 feet in height and spreads from 6 to 8 feet. 'Clarendon Spreading' reaches 10 to 12 feet and spreads to 8 feet. It can be kept shorter with pruning. Use dwarf American hollies as ground covers, in informal shrub borders, and in the shade garden. Hardiness: Zones 6 to 9. Yaupon (*I. vomitoria*) is a tough, adaptable, 10- to 20-foot shrub or small tree that spreads by suckers to 10 or 12 feet. 'Nana' ranges from 3 to 5 feet tall and spreads to 6 feet. Hardiness: Zones 7 to 9. Inkberry (*I. glabra*) ranges from 6 to 8 feet tall and spreads by suckers to

(above) Dwarf American holly (*Ilex opaca* 'Maryland Dwarf'). Photo by Barbara Ellis.

(left) Inkberry (*Ilex glabra*). Photo by Neil Soderstrom; Adkins Arboretum.

form broad colonies if conditions suit. Plants feature small, rounded, evergreen leaves and black berries that are attractive to wildlife. They prefer rich, consistently moist soil but tolerate somewhat drier conditions. Plants grow in full sun to full shade. 'Shamrock' is a compact selection that ranges from 3 to 4 feet tall and wide. Hardiness: Zones 4 to 9. Use hollies in shrub borders, hedges, bird gardens, and windbreaks and as accents. Both male and female plants are required for fruit set. If there are other hollies of the same species growing nearby, it may not be necessary to plant both males and females. One male plant can provide pollen for five or more females.

Hypericum, Kalm's (*Hypericum kalmianum*). Also called Kalm's St. John's wort, this nearly native species grows naturally in states north and west of the Chesapeake Bay area. Plants range from 2 to 3 feet tall and wide. Their evergreen leaves are blue-green and narrow, and plants bear yellow, 1½-inch-wide flowers in mid- to late summer. Plants are native to rocky, sandy soils and tolerate some drought but perform best in moist, well-drained soil. Hardiness: Zones 4 to 7.

Junipers (*Juniperus* spp.). Common juniper (*J. communis*) reaches 50 to 60 feet at maturity, but many more compact cultivars are available, including 'Pfitzeriana', which reaches 5 feet tall and 10 feet wide at maturity; slightly smaller 'Pfitzeriana Aurea', with gold-tipped branches; and 'Pfitzeriana Compacta', which grows to about 1½ feet tall and 6 feet wide. Common junipers struggle with summertime heat and humidity. Light, dappled shade during the hottest part of the day may help them with summer heat, but they are best used in the cooler parts of Zone 7 and north. Hardiness: Zones 2 to 7a. Creeping juniper (*J. horizontalis*) is native from New York State

Dwarf eastern red cedar (*Juniperus virginiana* 'Grey Owl'). Photo by Barbara Ellis.

north, not in the Chesapeake Bay region. A handsome ground cover that grows in a wide range of soil conditions, it is much more tolerant of summertime heat and humidity. See "Junipers" on p. 154 for more information. Hardiness: Zones 4 to 9. Eastern red cedar (*J. virginiana*) is a tough, 50-foot native, but dwarf cultivars are available. Plants will grow in poor soil and acid to alkaline pH, although they grow best with rich, moist, well-drained soil. 'Grey Owl' is 2 to 3 feet tall and 4 to 6 feet wide at maturity. 'Brodie' is 20 to 25 feet tall and 4 to 6 feet wide. 'Emerald Sentinel' is 15 to 20 feet tall and 6 to 8 feet wide at maturity. Use compact forms for foundation plantings and larger forms for windbreaks, hedges, and shrub borders. Hardiness: Zones 3 to 9.

Pine, eastern white (*Pinus strobus*). While this species is a large 50- to 80-foot tree, homeowners with limited space do have options. 'Nana' is a catchall term for compact selections that grow very slowly and normally reach 3 to 7 feet in height and up to 12 feet in width. Individual specimens can grow larger. 'Haird's Broom' is a dwarf cultivar that reaches 1 foot tall at maturity and spreads to 3 feet. 'Merimack' ranges from 2 to 3 feet tall and spreads to 4 feet or more. Plants are best in average, well-drained soil but tolerate dry soil as well once established. Use compact forms as specimen plants or in hedges and shrub borders in place of non-native conifers. They provide a nice backdrop for flowering shrubs and small trees. Hardiness: Zones 3 to 9.

Southern wax myrtle (*Morella cerifera*). Photo by Neil Soderstrom; Environmental Concern, Inc.

Wax myrtle, southern (*Morella cerifera*, formerly *Myrica cerifera*). This large shrub, 10 to 15 feet tall and wide at maturity, features aromatic leaves and berries that are attractive to birds. Compact forms are available. Although plants are native to tidal and non-tidal marshes, brackish or fresh, they tolerate wet to dry soil. Wax myrtles can be limbed up to form a small tree or used as shrubs in foundation plantings and mixed borders. Hardiness: Zones 6 to 9. The leaves are damaged when temperatures drop below 0°F.

White cedar, Atlantic (*Chamaecyparis thyoides*). This native tree ranges from 50 to 70 feet at maturity, but compact cultivars are available. White cedar naturally grows in wet, acid, organic soils, but established plants tolerate drier conditions. Plants are best in part shade to shade but grow in full sun with moist soil. Compact cultivars include 'Top Pont', to 5 feet tall and 2 feet wide at maturity; 'Rubicom'/Red Star, 15 to 25 feet at maturity; and 'Compacta Glauca', which reaches 15 feet and features bluish foliage. Hardiness: Zones 4 to 8.

Atlantic white cedar (*Chamaecyparis thyoides*). Photo by Neil Soderstrom; J. Kent McNew garden.

Shrubs for Foundations and Beds

The following list includes shrubs of all sizes with a variety of features, including flowers, fruit, and fall foliage. Unless otherwise noted, all grow in full sun to part shade and need average, well-drained soil.

American beautyberry (*Callicarpa americana*). Photo by Neil Soderstrom; U.S. Botanic Garden.

Beautyberry, American (*Callicarpa americana*). This mounding shrub, 3 to 6 feet tall and wide at maturity, bears lavender-pink flowers in summer followed by showy clusters of violet- to magenta-purple berries. Plants grow in rich, moist soil as well as in dry soil. Cut them to the ground in spring if they become overgrown or to encourage denser growth. Hardiness: Zones 6 to 10.

Blueberries (*Vaccinium* spp.). Provided they are planted in soil with an acid pH, blueberries make excellent additions to shrub borders and other plantings. Most need full to part sun and will grow in soil that ranges from dry to moist. They bear white flowers followed by blue-black fruit and feature showy orange, bronze, or red fall foliage. The genus contains many species, but highbush blueberry (*V. corymbosum*) is an excellent, commonly available shrub with tasty, edible fruit. It grows from 6 to 12 feet tall and wide at maturity and tolerates dry or average to wet soil. Plant several different cultivars for maximum fruit production, plus extra plants to feed the birds. Hardiness: Zones 3 to 7. Deerberry (*V. stamineum*) is 6 to 12 feet tall and bears sour, but edible, berries. Hardiness: Zones 5 to 9.

Bush honeysuckle, northern (*Diervilla lonicera*). This tough, drought-tolerant, summer-blooming native bears yellow flowers in early summer on 2- to 3-foot plants that spread by suckers and rhizomes to 4 feet or more. Plants grow in sun to shade and in poor, dry soil as well as in moist conditions. Fall foliage is yellow to orange, and the seed capsules attract birds. Use this species for massing or naturalizing, as well as for controlling erosion on slopes. The plants are determined spreaders: Give them a large site or deep edging so they do not spread beyond their bounds. Plants can be sheared or cut back hard to promote dense, compact growth. Hardiness: Zones 3 to 8. Southern bush honeysuckle (*D. sessilifolia*), native

from the Carolinas south but not in the Chesapeake Bay region, is 3 to 5 feet tall and 5 or more feet wide. Hardiness: Zones 5 to 8.

Buttonbush (*Cephalanthus occidentalis*). Photo by Neil Soderstrom; U.S. Botanic Garden.

Buttonbush (*Cephalanthus occidentalis*). This large shrub ranges from 5 to 12 feet tall and spreads to about 8 feet. Plants bear round, pincushion-like clusters of small, fragrant, white flowers in early summer that attract butterflies and other pollinators. The seeds that follow are attractive to birds, including ducks. In nature, buttonbush is a plant of wet soil and even shallow standing water. Plants will grow in any rich, moist soil. Cut them to within 8 or 12 inches of the ground in late winter or early spring if they become too large. Hardiness: Zones 5 to 9.

Chokeberries (*Photinia* spp., formerly *Aronia* spp.) These tough, handsome natives bear white flowers in spring followed by attractive berries. Prune them to encourage denser, more compact growth. They grow in dry to wet soils and are found growing in bogs as well as on rock outcrops. Black chokeberry (*P. melanocarpa*, formerly *A. melanocarpa*) bears blackish purple fruit and wine red fall foliage and ranges from 3 to 5 feet tall. Plants spread by suckers and can form broad clumps. 'Morton'/Iroquois Beauty is 2 to 3

Purple chokeberry (*Photinia floribunda*). Photo by Neil Soderstrom; Innisfree Garden.

Clethra or sweet pepperbush (*Clethra alnifolia*). Photo by Neil Soderstrom; Duncan Brine Garden.

feet tall and spreads to 4 feet. 'Viking' features brilliant red fall foliage and large edible fruit. Hardiness: Zones 3 to 8. Red chokeberry (*P. pyrifolia*, formerly *A. arbutifolia*) features astringent, bright red fruit that stays on the shrubs into winter. Plants are 6 to 10 feet tall and spread by suckers to 5 or more feet. Fall foliage is red to red-purple. 'Brilliantissima' features scarlet fall foliage and ranges from 6 to 8 feet. Hardiness: Zones 4 to 9. Use chokeberries in hedgerows, bird gardens, massed plantings, and naturalized areas.

Cinquefoil, shrubby (*Dasiphora fruticosa*, formerly *Potentilla fruticosa*). This tough, easy-to-grow, nearly native shrub is better known by its former name, potentilla. Plants have lacy, deeply cut leaves and are covered with cup-shaped, 1½-inch-wide, bright yellow flowers from summer to early fall. They range from 2 to 4 feet tall and spread from 3 to 5 feet, so they are suitable for shrub borders as well as ground covers. Plants grow in full sun to part shade but bloom best in sun. They prefer average moist, well-drained soil but can tolerate poor and/or dry soil. A site that receives shade during the hottest part of the day is beneficial throughout the hotter parts of the Chesapeake Bay region. Many cultivars are available. Hardiness: Zones 3 to 7.

Clethra, sweet pepperbush (*Clethra alnifolia*). Also called summersweet, this handsome native bears fragrant white flowers in mid- to late summer, when few other shrubs are in bloom. Plants range from 4 to 8 feet tall and wide and spread by suckers to form broad clumps. They need moist soil for best growth and tolerate shade but bloom less. Use them in mixed borders and as ground covers. Many cultivars are available, including 'Ruby Spice', with pink flowers, and low-growing cultivars such as 'Hummingbird', 2½ to 3½ feet tall and spreading from 3 to 4 feet, and 'Sixteen Candles', 2½ feet tall and spreading to 3½ feet. Hardiness: Zones 4 or 5 to 9, depending on the cultivar.

Dogwoods (*Cornus* spp.). Gray dogwood (*C. racemosa*) is a large shrub that ranges from 10 to 15 feet tall and wide and spreads by suckers. Plants grow in dry to wet soil and sun to shade. They bear clusters of white flowers in spring followed by white or bluish white berries that are extremely attractive to birds. Fall foliage is purple-red. Hardiness: Zones 4 to 8. Silky dogwood (*C. amomum*), from 6 to 12 feet tall and wide, bears white flowers and berries that attract

Silky dogwood (*Cornus amomum*). Photo by Neil Soderstrom; Owen Brown Interfaith Center.

birds. Plants thrive in moist to wet soil but tolerate average well-drained garden soil. They grow in sun to nearly full shade and will form thickets with time. Use both species in bird and wildlife gardens, against large buildings, on slopes, and for shrub borders. Hardiness: Zones 5 to 8.

Hybrid fothergilla (*Fothergilla gardenii* × *F. major*). Photo by Neil Soderstrom; Mt. Cuba Center.

Fothergillas (*Fothergilla* spp.). Two nearly native fothergillas—both from the Southeast—are well worth including in shrub plantings. Both bear white, bottlebrush-like flowers in spring and handsome rounded foliage that turns brilliant shades of yellow, orange, and red-purple in fall. Dwarf fothergilla (*F. gardenii*), also called dwarf witch-alder, ranges from 1½ to 3 feet tall and spreads to 4 feet. Hardiness: Zones 5 to 8. Large fothergilla (*F. major*), also

called mountain witch-alder, ranges from 6 to 10 feet tall and spreads from 5 to 9 feet. Hardiness: Zones 4 to 8. Both grow in rich, moist, well-drained acid soil. They bloom best in full sun but grow in part shade. Soil moisture needs to be consistent in full sun sites.

Dwarf winterberry holly (*I. verticillata* 'Nana'/Red Sprite). Photo by Neil Soderstrom; Green Spring Gardens.

Holly, deciduous (*Ilex* spp.). Winterberry holly (*I. verticillata*). A handsome shrub that grows in average to wet soil, winterberry ranges from 6 to 10 feet tall and wide. Greenish flowers are followed by masses of showy red berries on female plants. Plant one male per three females to ensure adequate pollination. Many cultivars are available, and it is important to match female plants to appropriate male pollinators. 'Southern Gentleman', 'Jim Dandy', 'Apollo', and 'Raritan Chief' are three male cultivars. 'Winter Red' ('Southern Gentleman' is a suitable pollinator) reaches 9 feet and is an outstanding selection. 'Red Sprite' ('Jim Dandy' and 'Apollo' are suitable pollinators) is 3 to 5 feet tall. Use winterberry holly for massing, in shrub borders, and in wet areas. Hardiness: Zones 3 to 9. Possumhaw (*I. decidua*) is a large shrub that ranges from 6 to 20 feet tall and wide. The spring flowers are inconspicuous but are followed by showy orange-red berries that are very attractive to wildlife.

The glossy, dark green leaves turn purplish to yellow in fall. In the wild, this is a plant of wet soils. Plants are happiest in rich, moist soil but tolerate average moist, well-drained conditions. Use possumhaw in shrub borders, in hedge plantings, along streams or ponds, or in rain gardens. Hardiness: Zones 5 to 9.

Oakleaf hydrangea (*Hydrangea quercifolia*). Photo by Neil Soderstrom; James van Sweden home.

Hydrangeas (*Hydrangea* spp.). Wild hydrangea (*H. arborescens*) is a handsome native with rounded white flower clusters in summer. Plants tolerate full sun, provided the soil remains moist, but otherwise are best in partial shade. See p. 222 for more information. Oakleaf (*H. quercifolia*) is a popular, nearly native species from the southeastern United States that is prized for its huge, rounded, 4- to 10-inch-long clusters of white flowers that appear in early to midsummer when few other shrubs are blooming. The flowers, which age to pinkish, then tan, are set against large lobed leaves that turn brilliant shades of bronze, red, and purple in fall. Plants range from 6 to 8 feet tall and spread as far. They grow in rich, moist, well-drained soil; do not tolerate drought; and thrive in full sun to part shade. Hardiness: Zones 5 to 9.

Hypericums (*Hypericum* spp.). Also called St. John's worts, these tough, tolerant natives bring brilliant yellow summer flowers to the garden. The plants listed here will grow in soil that ranges from dry to moist. They need full sun for best bloom. Prune them in early spring, as needed, to encourage branching and bushy growth. Bushy St. John's wort (*H. densiflorum*) is 4 to 6 feet tall and spreads to about 4 feet. Plants bloom from midsummer to early fall. Hardiness: Zones 5 to 8. Golden or cedar glade St. John's wort (*H. frondosum*) blooms from early to midsummer and is 3 to 4 feet tall and wide. Hardiness: Zones: 5 to 8. Shrubby St. John's wort (*H. prolificum*) blooms from mid- to late summer and ranges from 1 to 4 feet tall and wide. Hardiness: Zones 4 to 8.

Itea, Virginia sweetspire (*Itea virginica*). Also called Virginia willow, this adaptable shrub produces cylindrical, arching clusters of tiny, white, lightly fragrant flowers in summer and showy yellow, orange, red, and red-purple fall foliage. Plants range from 3 to 6 or more feet in height. They sucker to form clumps 10 or more feet across, especially in moist soil. Plants tolerate wet to dry conditions and sun to shade. Prune immediately after flowering to encourage dense branching and compact habit. 'Henry's Garnet' has red-purple fall foliage and larger flowers than the species. 'Sprich'/Little Henry is 3 to 4 feet tall and bears shorter flower clusters. Hardiness: Zones 5 to 9.

Itea or Virginia sweetspire (*Itea virginica* 'Henry's Garnet'). Photo by Barbara Ellis.

Ninebark (*Physocarpus opulifolius* 'Seward'/Summer Wine). Photo by Neil Soderstrom; U.S. Botanic Garden.

New Jersey tea (*Ceanothus americanus*). This native bears clusters of white flowers in summer that attract butterflies and pollinators followed by dry, non-showy fruit that is attractive to birds. Plants are 3 to 4 feet tall and spread to about 5 feet. They grow in sun or shade in average to dry soil. Plants fix atmospheric nitrogen and can survive in poor soil. Use New Jersey tea in shrub borders and foundation plantings as well as on slopes or in other tough locations. Hardiness: Zones 4 to 8.

Ninebark (*Physocarpus opulifolius*). While this tough species bears round clusters of small, white to pinkish flowers in spring to early summer, it is primarily grown for the colorful foliage produced by some of the cultivars. Plants are 5 to 10 feet tall and wide but can be cut back or cut to the ground in late winter to encourage branching and reduce size. 'Diablo' bears leaves that are red-purple in spring and into summer. 'Dart's Gold' is 4 to 5 feet tall and wide and has yellow foliage in spring that fades to lime green. Ninebark is an excellent substitute for large shrubs such as forsythia (*Forsythia* spp.) and winged euonymus (*Euonymus alatus*). Hardiness: Zones 2 to 7.

Staghorn sumac (*Rhus typhina*). Photo by Neil Soderstrom; J. Kent McNew garden.

Sumacs (*Rhus* spp.). These large shrubs or small trees spread by root suckers to form clumps. They are best suited for hedgerows, informal beds, and wild areas. Sumacs bear compound leaves, meaning each leaf is divided into separate leaflets, as well as fruit that is attractive to birds and other wildlife. Give all the species listed here a site with average, well-drained, dry to somewhat moist soil in full sun or part shade. They are valuable for covering tough sites with dry, poor, rocky, or sandy soil. Fragrant sumac (*R. aromatica*) is a 6- to 12-foot-tall shrub that spreads to 8 or more feet. Plants bear yellowish flowers and 3-leaflet leaves that may turn yellow, orange, or red in fall. 'Gro-low' is a ground cover selection ranging from

1½ to 3 feet tall and spreading to 8 or more feet. Hardiness: Zones 3 to 9. Shining or winged sumac (*R. copallinum*, formerly *R. copallina*) ranges from 7 to 15 or more feet and spreads from 10 to 20 feet. Plants bear large, compound leaves that turn scarlet in fall. Clusters of greenish flowers appear in late spring or early summer, followed by showy red, conelike clusters of berries. Hardiness: Zones 4 to 9. Sweet or smooth sumac (*R. glabra*) is similar but generally only reaches 15 feet tall and wide. Plants bear red fall fruit and large compound leaves with up to 27 leaflets that turn orange or red in fall. Hardiness: Zones 3 to 9. Staghorn sumac (*R. typhina*) ranges from 15 to 25 feet tall and spreads to 30 feet. Plants bear red fall fruit and 2-foot-long compound leaves that turn yellow, orange, and red in fall. 'Balitiger'/Tiger Eyes features chartreuse leaves. 'Laciniata' bears leaves with deeply cut leaflets. Hardiness: Zones 3 to 8.

Sweetshrub or Carolina allspice (*Calycanthus floridus* 'Michael Lindsay'). Photo by Barbara Ellis.

Sweetshrub, Carolina allspice (*Calycanthus floridus*). Grown for its fragrant, red-brown flowers that have a subtle, fruity aroma, this is a tough shrub that grows in sun or shade and ranges from 6 to 9 feet tall, spreading to 12 feet. Plants are happiest in moist, well-drained soil but adapt to a range of conditions. Prune immediately after flowering to encourage branching and dense growth. Fragrance varies from plant to plant, so smell the flowers before making a purchase, or buy a cultivar like 'Michael Lindsay', which features fragrant blooms and a slightly more compact habit. Site sweetshrub near sitting areas to enjoy the fragrance. Hardiness: Zones 4 to 9.

Viburnums (*Viburnum* spp.). Every native plant garden should include at least a couple of these handsome shrubs. Viburnums bear white spring or early summer flowers, attractive summer foliage, fall berries, and colorful autumn foliage. American cranberry bush (*V. opulus* var. *americanum*, formerly *V. trilobum*) is native to nearby states north and west of the Chesapeake Bay region. (European cranberry bush viburnum [*V. opulus* var. *opulus*] is a non-native relative found in the region.) American cranberry bush is 8 to 12 feet tall and wide at maturity; 'Bailey Compact' is about 6 feet tall and wide. Flowers are followed by clusters of red fruit and yellow to purple-red foliage in fall. Hardiness: Zones 2 to 8, but plants need protection from afternoon heat in Zone 8. Arrowwood viburnum or southern arrowwood (*V. dentatum*) is 6 to 15 feet tall and wide. Plants bear flat-topped clusters of flowers in spring followed by blue-black fruit and yellow, red, or red-purple fall foliage. They tolerate a range of well-drained soils and spread by suckers. Hardiness: Zones 3 to 8. Nannyberry viburnum (*V. lentago*) is 15 to as much as 30 feet tall and wide. Flat-topped clusters of flowers are followed by blue-black berries. Fall color is purplered. Hardiness: Zones 3 to 7. Possumhaw viburnum (*V. nudum*) and withe-rod viburnum (*V. nudum* var. *cassinoides*) average 5 to 10 feet tall and wide, but they can reach 20 feet and can be trained as small ornamental trees. Both bear flat-topped clusters of flowers followed by fruit that turns from pink to red, then

Small Ornamental Trees, below, for more information. Viburnums are excellent for screening, shrub borders, naturalizing, and mass plantings. Use them to attract birds and other wildlife. Many viburnums need a pollinator for best fruit production, and for this reason they are best planted with more than one specimen or cultivar of the same species.

American or common witch hazel (*Hamamelis virginiana*). Photo by Neil Soderstrom; Brooklyn Botanic Garden.

Witch hazel, American or common (*Hamamelis virginiana*). This is a huge shrub at maturity that reaches 20 to 30 feet tall and wide. Plants can be trained as small trees. Fragrant yellow flowers with strap-shaped petals appear in fall, and fall foliage is yellow. Plants grow in full sun to shade and prefer moist soil. Use common witch hazel in shrub borders, for naturalizing, and against buildings. Hardiness: Zones 3 to 8.

Trees

Small Ornamental Trees

Unless otherwise noted, the trees listed here will grow in average, well-drained soil and full sun to partial shade. Use ornamental trees as specimens, include them in foundation plantings as vertical accents, and add them to shrub borders, island beds, and mixed borders.

(above) Arrowwood viburnum or southern arrowwood (*Viburnum dentatum*). Photo by Neil Soderstrom; Adkins Arboretum.

(left) American cranberry bush (*Viburnum opulus* var. *americanum*). Photo by Neil Soderstrom; Owen Brown Interfaith Center.

purple. Fall foliage is red-purple, and plants grow in average to wet soil and tolerate drought. 'Winterthur' features shiny foliage and a compact habit. 'Brandywine' is compact, ranging from 5 to 6 feet tall and wide. Hardiness: Zones 3 to 8. Blackhaw viburnum (*V. prunifolium*) is a large shrub or small tree. See

Amelanchier, serviceberries (*Amelanchier* spp.). Native serviceberries are typically 15 to about 25 feet in height and can be used as large shrubs or multi-stemmed small trees. Spread varies but is about 20 feet, since the plants sucker. All feature white flowers in very early spring, edible red to purplish fruit that birds eat before humans find it, and excellent yellow to red fall foliage. Three species make handsome ornamental trees: downy serviceberry (*A. arborea*), also called juneberry and shadbush; shadblow serviceberry (*A. canadensis*); and Allegheny serviceberry (*A. laevis*). A number of cultivars of *A. arborea* are available, with either improved fruit production or outstanding fall foliage. *A. canadensis* has a more shrubby, multistemmed habit than the other two species. In addition to the uses mentioned above, plant serviceberries along woodland edges and stream banks. Hardiness: Zones 3 or 4 to 8 or 9, depending on the species.

Red buckeye (*Aesculus pavia*). Photo by Neil Soderstrom; George Fenn garden.

Buckeye, red (*Aesculus pavia*). A multistemmed, clump-forming tree, red buckeye normally ranges from 15 to 20 or more feet high and wide at maturity. Plants produce erect, 4- to 8-inch panicles of brilliant red flowers in spring. They tolerate dry spells but are happiest with even soil moisture, and they appreciate some afternoon shade in hot climates. Red buckeyes bloom in time to attract returning ruby-throated hummingbirds. The nuts are poisonous and are avoided by many types of wildlife. Hardiness: Zones 4 to 8.

Flowering dogwood (*Cornus florida*). Photo by Neil Soderstrom; Leslie and Art Jacoby garden.

Dogwoods (*Cornus* spp.). Few trees are as beloved as flowering dogwood (*C. florida*), which ranges from 20 to 30 feet tall and wide. Plants are best known for the masses of white or pink flowers they bear in spring. The flowers are followed by red fruit in fall that is attractive to birds and other wildlife, and the foliage turns stunning shades of red to red-purple in fall. The horizontally spreading branches and attractive gray bark add winter appeal. For best growth, flowering dogwoods require rich, moist, well-drained, acid soil and a consistent layer of mulch to keep the soil cool and moist. Although plants survive in full sun, partial shade is best. Good culture is the best defense against insects, such as borers, and the various diseases that plague flowering dogwoods. They will languish in hot, sunny, dry sites as well as in sites that are constantly wet. To protect the trunk from damage by lawn mowers, surround them with ground covers or use flowering dogwoods in island beds. Also plant them along woodland edges or in naturalized landscapes. Hardiness: Zones 5 to 9. Pagoda dogwood (*C. alternifolia*) is a tree or large shrub with similar cultural needs. Plants reach 20 to 25 feet and spread from 25 to 35 feet. They bear fragrant, yellowish white flowers in late spring or early summer followed by blue-black fruit. Fall foliage is reddish purple. 'Golden Showers' features leaves edged in yellow; 'Argentea' bears leaves variegated with white. Hardiness: Zones 3 to 7.

White fringetree (*Chionanthus virginicus*). Photo by Barbara Ellis.

Fringetree, white (*Chionanthus virginicus*). Prized for its frothy white flowers in spring, this 20- to 30-foot native is a large multistemmed shrub or small tree. Fringetree bears male and female flowers on separate plants, along with some perfect flowers (with both male and female organs). Male flowers are showier than female. Ideally, plant one of each, since the dark blue fruit is attractive to birds. Happiest with moist, acid soil, fringetree adapts to drier conditions and withstands brief flooding. Hardiness: Zones 4 to 9.

Hawthorns (*Crataegus* spp.) These small trees are grown for their white spring flowers and red fall fruit. The species listed here have orange, red, or red-purple fall foliage. Cockspur hawthorn (*C. crus-galli*), Washington hawthorn (*C. phaenopyrum*), and green hawthorn (*C. viridis*) are all roughly 20 to 30 feet at maturity with a spread of about 35 feet. All have thorns, making them ideal for nesting birds but unsuitable for high-traffic areas or places where children play. A thornless variety of cockspur hawthorn is available, *C. crus-galli* var. *inermis* 'Princeton Sentry'. Washington hawthorn is nearly thornless. 'Winter King' is an outstanding cultivar of green hawthorn with large, handsome fruit. Use hawthorns in barrier plantings, hedgerows, shrub borders, bird gardens, and hedges. Thornless forms can be used as street trees. Hardiness: Zones 4 to 7 or 8, depending on the species.

American holly (*Ilex opaca* 'Miss Helen'). Photo by Neil Soderstrom; New York Botanical Garden.

Holly, American (*Ilex opaca*). Although American hollies can reach 50 feet at maturity, most are considerably smaller, and they make excellent small ornamental trees. Glossy evergreen foliage and colorful berries that are attractive to birds and other wildlife are two outstanding features. Plants need full sun to partial shade with evenly moist, well-drained soil. Avoid dry soil conditions and windy sites. Unless American hollies are common in your area, plant one male plant for every three females to achieve berry production. A great many cultivars with improved foliage and/or fruit are available. 'Jersey Princess' and 'Old Heavy Berry' are two female cultivars. 'Jersey Delight' is compact, to 30 feet in 30 years. 'Jersey Knight' is a good male cultivar. In addition to the uses listed above, plant hollies along woodland edges, as screening, and in bird gardens. Hardiness: Zones 5 to 9.

(left) Sweetbay magnolia (*Magnolia virginiana*). Photo by Neil Soderstrom; Adkins Arboretum.

(right) Southern magnolia (*Magnolia grandiflora*) with northern sea oats (*Chasmanthium latifolium*). Photo by Neil Soderstrom; design by Oehme, van Sweden Landscape Architecture.

American hop hornbeam (*Ostrya virginiana*). Photo by Neil Soderstrom; U.S. Botanic Garden.

Hop hornbeam, American (*Ostrya virginiana*). This small tree normally grows in the understory, beneath larger shade trees. Plants reach 25 to 40 feet tall and spread to about 30 feet. They grow in sun or part shade but are happiest with cool, moist, well-drained soil. Try hop hornbeam as a specimen in shade or woodland gardens, as a street tree, or as a small shade tree. Hardiness: Zones 3 to 9.

Magnolias (*Magnolia* spp.). Sweetbay magnolia (*M. virginiana*) is a semi-evergreen to evergreen species that ranges from 10 to 60 feet and spreads to about 20 feet. Plants have dark green leaves that are silver underneath. They bear fragrant, creamy white, 2- to 3-inch-wide flowers in late spring and summer. Plants, which grow in sun or shade, are generally multistemmed and thrive in average, well-drained soil as well as moist and wet conditions. A number

of cultivars are available, including 'Henry Hicks' and 'Northern Belle', which were selected for consistently evergreen foliage and/or larger flowers. Hardiness: Zones 5 to 9. Southern magnolia (*M. grandiflora*) is normally a 60- to 80-foot tree, but compact cultivars fit into many smaller gardens. Give plants rich, well-drained soil. They bear glossy evergreen leaves and fragrant, 8- to 12-inch-wide flowers in late spring and early summer. 'Little Gem' and 'Baby Doll' reach about 20 feet tall and wide at maturity and bear smaller flowers than the species. 'Edith Brogue' reaches about 30 feet at maturity. Hardiness: Zones 6 or 7 to 9, depending on the cultivar selected. Large-leaved cucumber tree (*M. macrophylla*) is a 30- to 40-foot tree with fragrant, 8- to 10-inch-wide white flowers and huge, 30-inch-long, tropical-looking leaves. Plants require rich, moist, well-drained soil and do not tolerate wet or dry soil extremes. Hardiness: Zones 5 to 8.

Pawpaw (*Asimina triloba*). Photo by Neil Soderstrom; Adkins Arboretum.

Pawpaw (*Asimina triloba*). This 15- to 30-foot tree bears clusters of small, dark, blackish maroon flowers in spring followed by edible, yellow-green fruit. The leaves are large, from 6 to 12 inches long, and turn an attractive shade of pale yellow in fall. Plants spread by rhizomes and can form clumps 30 or more feet wide. Give them moist to wet, well-drained soil and sun to part shade or shade. Plant two different plants or cultivars (there are several) for fruit production, and be prepared to share the fruit with wildlife! Hardiness: Zones 5 to 9.

Redbud (*Cercis canadensis*). Photo by Neil Soderstrom; New York Botanical Garden.

Redbud (*Cercis canadensis*). These handsome trees range from 20 to 30 feet tall at maturity and spread to about 30 or 35 feet. They produce clouds of tiny pink flowers along branches, stems, and trunk in early spring. The attractive heart-shaped leaves turn yellow or yellow-green in fall. Cultivars with outstanding foliage color are available, including purple-leaved 'Forest Pansy' and chartreuse-leaved 'Hearts of Gold'. 'Covey'/Lavender Twist is a weeping form. Plants grow in sun or light shade and in moist, well-drained to dry soil. They are often found as understory plants in woodlands. Plant redbuds in shade gardens, along woodland edges, and in naturalized areas. Hardiness: Zones 4 to 9.

Sassafras (*Sassafras albidum*). Photo by Neil Soderstrom; Adkins Arboretum.

Sassafras (*Sassafras albidum*). Long overlooked as an ornamental, this native tree is worth growing because its dark blue fruit is extremely attractive to birds and wildlife and its aromatic leaves bring shades of rich red, orange, yellow, and purple to the fall landscape. Plants reach 30 to 60 feet tall at maturity. They spread by suckers and can form wide thickets. Ideally, select a spot with rich, well-drained, acid soil, but sassafras trees can easily grow on rocky sites. Plant sassafras in naturalistic shrub borders, hedgerows, and wild gardens. Plants can be trained as single-trunked specimen trees. Hardiness: Zones 4 to 9.

Smoketree, American (*Cotinus obovatus*). This is a tree or very large, nearly native shrub from the Southeast that ranges from 20 to 30 feet tall and wide. It bears rounded, blue-green leaves that turn shades of yellow, red, red-purple, and orange in fall. Plants produce airy, 8- to 10-inch clusters of tiny, insignificant

🍃 Crab Apples

Many hybrid crab apples are available in the nursery trade, but species are another matter. Two native species, both ranging from 25 to 30 feet tall and wide at maturity, are occasionally available. Both bear fragrant pink flowers and yellow or yellow-green fall fruit that is consumed by a variety of birds and wildlife. Neither exhibits the disease resistance of hybrid crabs. Southern crab apple (*Malus angustifolia*) is hardy in Zones 5 to 9, while sweet or American crab apple (*M. coronaria*) is hardy in Zones 3 to 8. Both need full sun and average soil. Use them along meadows and other wild areas, as well as in hedgerows, wildlife gardens, and woodland or shade garden edges.

flowers in early summer that are followed by hairs that turn pink or purple-pink and give the plant a smoky appearance. Moist, well-drained soil is best, but the plants tolerate poor and rocky conditions. Hardiness: Zones 4 to 8.

Sourwood (*Oxydendrum arboreum*). Prized for its lacy, delicate-looking, 4- to 10-inch-long clusters of small, fragrant flowers, sourwood blooms in early summer. Plants range from 25 to 30 feet. In fall, the leaves turn yellow, purple, and red. Give sourwood acid, moist, well-drained soil that is rich in organic matter. Unless they are well established, plants do not tolerate drought: Water regularly and watch them carefully after planting. Hardiness: Zones 5 to 9.

Viburnum, blackhaw (*Viburnum prunifolium*). A large, multistemmed shrub or small tree, this species produces flat-topped clusters of white flowers in spring followed by berries that turn from pink-

ish to blue-black. The fruit is edible and attractive to birds and other wildlife. Fall foliage is purple to red-purple. Blackhaw viburnums grow in sun or shade and in average to dry soil. They range from 12 to 20 feet tall and spread to about 12 feet. Use them as small, multistemmed specimen trees by removing lower branches, or grow them as shrubs and include them in shrub borders, hedgerows, and other mass plantings. Hardiness: Zones 3 to 9.

Large Trees

Trees add a stately presence to your landscape and are a long-term investment. They cast more shade every year, they contribute to real estate estimates, and their value increases annually as they grow. As with all woody plants, select planting sites carefully: Trees are difficult or impossible to move once they are in the ground. Visualizing can help determine the right spot. See "Planning on the Ground" on p. 63 for a simple way to evaluate sites. Be sure to carefully consider where the tree's shade will fall.

The list that follows includes some of the best native shade trees. Some will be easy to find, and others may take some searching. To find them, ask your local nursery to search their suppliers, shop at native plant sales and nurseries, or use the online resources link in Suggested Resources to find sources. Some species are only available as very young plants, since they need to be transplanted while still small because of deep taproots. This is especially true of hickories (*Carya* spp.) and rarer oaks (*Quercus* spp.). One option is to plant a good-size specimen or two for immediate results and also plant some smaller, less common trees as an investment in shade and to add diversity down the road. Unless otherwise noted below, all of these trees thrive in sun or partial shade and tolerate a wide range of soils.

American Elms

The stately, adaptable American elm (*Ulmus americana*) was all but wiped out during the last century due to Dutch elm disease. Since then, horticulturists have worked hard to identify and release disease-resistant cultivars. Some very promising cultivars are now available. Gardeners with space to experiment and a desire to grow one of these handsome trees should try 'American Liberty', 'Delaware', 'Independence', 'New Harmony', or 'Valley Forge'. Hybridizers also have released various cultivars that are the result of crosses between American elm and non-native species.

American beech (*Fagus grandiflora*). Photo by Neil Soderstrom; Green Spring Gardens.

Bald cypress (*Taxodium distichum*). Although not a typical shade tree, this species adds a stately presence to large sites that can accommodate it. Mature trees have a pyramidal shape, range from 50 to 70 feet tall, and spread to about 45 feet. This is a deciduous conifer, or cone-bearing, tree related to evergreen species like pines (*Pinus* spp.). The foliage is green in summer and turns orange to red-brown in fall. In nature, this is a species of wet soils, and it will grow in standing water. It also tolerates average well-drained soil as well as drought. Consider planting bald cypress trees along ponds, lakes, creeks, swamps, and rain gardens. The roots produce woody, upright projections, called knees, especially when growing in moist soil. For this reason, it is best to underplant these trees with ground covers or other plants, since the knees make mowing difficult. Hardiness: Zones 4 to 9.

Beech, American (*Fagus grandiflora*). Ranging from 50 to 100 feet tall and wide at maturity, this species bears handsome, smooth gray bark and features beautiful gold fall foliage. The edible nuts are valu-

able for wildlife. Plants have very shallow, wide-spreading roots, and they do not tolerate wet or compacted soil, so give them plenty of room and a spot well away from foot traffic. The roots also are easily damaged by lawn mowers. Beech trees grow in sun or shade and need moist, well-drained, acid soil. Hardiness: Zones 4 to 9.

Birch, river (*Betula nigra*). This species ranges from 40 to 70 or more feet at maturity and spreads to about 50 feet. Plants are best in moist to wet soil but will withstand drier conditions. The species has handsome exfoliating bark, and while the exact colors vary from plant to plant, they include gray, brown, cinnamon, and red-brown. Fall foliage is yellow. 'Cully'/ Heritage is an outstanding cultivar with ornamental, creamy brown bark. 'Tecumseh Compact' and 'Little King'/Fox Valley are small, compact selections. Prune birches, if necessary, in summer, as they bleed sap if pruned in spring. Hardiness: Zones 4 to 9.

Buckeye, yellow (*Aesculus flava*). The largest of the native buckeyes, this species bears panicles of showy yellow flowers in mid spring. Mature trees range from 50 to 75 feet in height and are nearly as wide. The dark green, compound leaves consist of 5 leaflets arranged like fingers on a hand and turn yellow-orange in fall. The nuts are poisonous and are avoided by most wildlife. Yellow buckeye thrives in rich, moist, well-drained soil. Plants are taprooted and are difficult to move once established. Hardiness: Zones 4 to 8.

Hickories (*Carya* spp.). These large trees, over 60 feet at maturity, are taprooted and must be transplanted when very young. They are difficult to find in commerce but are worth the search. Unless otherwise noted below, they grow in full sun to part shade. New transplants take several years to establish deep, wide-ranging roots and then begin growing 1 or 2 feet per year. Plant them as an investment in the future. Fall foliage is yellow to gold. The nuts are very valuable for wildlife. Hardiness: Zones 4 or 5 to 9, depending on the species. Hickories to consider include mockernut hickory (*C. alba*, formerly *C. tomentosa*), which grows in part shade to shade and in dry to average soil; bitternut hickory (*C. glabra*), which grows in dry to wet sites; shellbark hickory (*C. laciniosa*), a native of flood plains and spots with poor drainage that tolerates dry to wet soil; and shagbark hickory (*C. ovata*), which thrives in average moist, well-drained soil but tolerates dry conditions. Pecan (*C. illinoinensis*) is a well-known member of

this genus. A native of flood plains, it tolerates occasional flooding and is best in moist, well-drained soil.

Honeylocust (*Gleditsia triacanthos*). Photo by Neil Soderstrom; Arnold Arboretum.

Honeylocust, thornless (*Gleditsia triacanthos* var. *inermis*). This thornless form of common honeylocust lacks the long, sharp, branching thorns of the species. Plants usually range from 30 to 70 feet tall and wide, and they bear lacy-textured leaves with 20 to 30 small leaflets. Fall foliage is yellow. Many cultivars are available, including ones with chartreuse foliage. Hardiness: Zones 4 to 9.

Linden or basswood, American (*Tilia americana*). This 60- to 100-foot tree spreads to about 60 feet at maturity and produces fragrant, pale yellow flowers in early summer that are extremely attractive to bees. Fall foliage is yellow, but it is not consistent or outstanding. Plants prefer rich, moist soil but tolerate drier conditions. Hardiness: Zones 4 to 8.

Maples (*Acer* spp.). Of the maples, red maple (*A. rubrum*) is one of the most commonly planted natives. Plants range from 40 to 60 feet tall and wide at maturity and grow in average to wet soil. They tolerate occasional standing water. Fall foliage is yellow, orange-red, or red. All red maples feature handsome fall foliage, but for outstanding color, select a cultivar such as 'October Glory' or 'Red Sunset'. There also are compact cultivars for small sites. Hardiness: Zones 3 to 9. Silver maple (*A. saccharinum*) is a very fast-growing tree that ranges from 50 to over 100 feet in height and spreads to about 60 feet. Fall foliage is an unremarkable yellow-green. Plants thrive in moist soil but tolerate very poor soil and survive flooding for several weeks at a time. Fast growth causes weak wood that breaks during windstorms, and shallow roots will heave up sidewalks and paved areas. Still, silver maples are good choices for tough conditions, fast shade, limited budgets, and sites away from houses and hardscape. Hardiness: Zones 3 to 9. Sugar maple (*A. saccharum*) is another large maple with a height and spread similar to that of silver maple. Fall color—yellow, orange, and red—is outstanding, and many cultivars have been selected for their striking display. Sugar maples need rich, moist, well-drained soil and tolerate shade, but they do not tolerate pollution or soil compaction. They need large sites where their roots can spread widely. Hardiness: Zones 4 to 8.

Oaks (*Quercus* spp.). The Chesapeake Bay region is home to an incredible array of oaks that range from huge majestic trees to smaller, shrubbier plants. Some tolerate a wide range of conditions, while others are more fussy. To determine which species may work for your garden, see "Oaks for the Bay Region" on p. 133. Note that the commonly sold sawtooth oak (*Q. acutissima*) is a non-native species, originally from Asia, that has been deemed an invasive. Native species are far better choices.

Common persimmon (*Diospyros virginiana*). Photo by Neil Soderstrom; U.S. Botanic Garden.

Persimmon, common (*Diospyros virginiana*). This 35- to 60-foot tree spreads to about 35 feet. Plants bear white to greenish yellow flowers in spring, followed by edible orange to red-purple fruit that is attractive to a variety of wildlife. Humans use the fruit for jelly, pudding, ice cream, and other treats: Harvest after fall frost or the fruit will be extremely astringent. Foliage is deep green and glossy, and fall color is orange to red-purple. Plants prefer moist, well-drained, somewhat sandy soil, but they tolerate seasonal flooding and grow in dry to average well-drained garden soil. Hardiness: Zones 4 to 9.

Pines (*Pinus* spp.). While deciduous trees are most often thought of as shade trees, three native pines make good shade trees and fine landscape specimens. White pine (*P. strobus*) reaches 50 to 80 feet at maturity and spreads to about 40 feet. As trees age, the lower branches die out or break off during windstorms, leaving a wide crown toward the top of the trunk. Plants prefer average to rich soil that is

Plants have a spreading crown with mostly horizontal branches at maturity and tolerate a range of soils. They are especially happy in moist to wet soils. Hardiness: Zones 6 to 9. Virginia pine (*P. virginiana*) is a small pine, comparatively speaking, averaging from 15 to 40 feet in height at maturity and spreading to 30 feet. Plants grow fairly slowly and develop horizontal, outstretched branches. They grow well in poor, dry soil and are fine in heavy clay soil. Hardiness: Zones 4 to 8.

Sweetgum (*Liquidambar styraciflua*). This handsome tree ranges from 60 to 100 feet at maturity with a spread of 50 to 60 feet. Give plants full sun. They prefer deep, rich, moist, well-drained, slightly acid soil but tolerate wet soil and extended flooding. Plants generally take time to adjust to transplanting and may not grow for up to a year. The spiny round fruit can be messy and hard to manage ('Rotundiloba' is a cultivar that does not bear fruit), but it attracts birds and other wildlife. For this reason, sweetgums are best planted in naturalized areas or informal landscapes, where the fruit will not be a problem. Fall foliage is excellent, from yellow to red and purple, and cultivars have been selected for outstanding foliage color. Hardiness: Zones 5 to 9.

Tulip tree, tulip poplar (*Liriodendron tulipifera*). This large, fast-growing tree averages from 70 to 90 feet at maturity with a spread of about 50 feet. Trees bear greenish and orange, tuliplike flowers in late spring, but the flowers are generally borne above eye level. Fall foliage is yellow to gold. Give tulip trees rich, moist, well-drained soil. They need considerable space to grow and tend to be weak wooded. 'Ardis' and 'Compactum' are compact cultivars about half the size of the species. Birds and other wildlife are attracted to the seeds. Hardiness: Zones 4 to 9.

(top) Loblolly pine (*Pinus taeda*). Photo by Neil Soderstrom; J. Kent McNew garden.

(bottom) Virginia pine (*Pinus virginiana*). Photo by Neil Soderstrom; U.S. Botanic Garden.

deep, moist, and well drained, but they will grow in dry or moist to wet conditions. They do not tolerate air pollution or salt. Hardiness: Zones 3 to 8. Loblolly pine (*P. taeda*) is a fast-growing pine that ranges from 60 to 90 feet tall and spreads to 40 or 50 feet.

Tupelo, black (*Nyssa sylvatica*). Also known as black or sour gum, this species ranges from 30 to 50 feet at maturity and spreads to about 30 feet. Plants have dark green leaves in summer that turn brilliant shades of yellow, orange, scarlet, and purple. Insignificant flowers yield blue-black berries that are very attractive to birds and other wildlife. Plants prefer moist, well-drained, acid soil, but tolerate wet and clay soil. In the wild, tupelos are found in dry soil. Hardiness: Zones 4 to 9.

Willow oak (*Quercus phellos*). Photo by Neil Soderstrom; Phantom Gardener.

Oaks for the Bay Region

Nurseries routinely offer very few species of these outstanding trees for sale, but the list below reflects a portion of the oaks native to the Chesapeake Bay watershed. As with all plants, oaks (*Quercus* spp.) are not one-size-fits-all: Different species are adapted to different types of sites. For best results, match the plant to the site.

Unless otherwise noted below, oaks grow in full sun or part shade and are fairly slow growing. Fall foliage ranges from yellow or yellow-green to burgundy, wine-red, red, and red-brown. The color generally is long lasting. Acorns are a valuable food source for native wildlife, and oaks are essential for native butterflies, moths, and other insects.

Most of the oaks listed here are large, stately trees that reach more than 50 feet tall and wide—often considerably more—at maturity. Most are pyramidal when young and mature to a broad, rounded oval with spreading branches. Oaks generally grow slowly, especially for the first 20 to 30 years. With time, they become great specimen and shade trees: Planting an oak is an investment that is worth the wait. All of the species listed are hardy in our region. Unless otherwise noted below, hardiness ranges from Zones 3 or 4 to 8 or 9.

One of the challenges of adding native oaks to your landscape is that some species are much more difficult to find than others. Part of the problem is that many are hard to transplant unless they are still very small. Searching for rare species can be an adventure, and asking for these plants at local nurseries will eventually help to increase availability. Local nurseries may have sources they can investigate for you, but inquire at local native plant sales, or see the online resources link in Suggested Resources to get started.

The species below are listed in two groups: white oaks and red oaks. White oaks have entire, toothed, or lobed leaves that have rounded tips and produce acorns on the current year's growth. Red oaks have entire, toothed, or lobed leaves with bristle-like tips, and most bear their acorns on the previous year's growth.

White Oaks

Bur oak (*Q. macrocarpa*). Also called blue or mossy-cup oak, this drought-tolerant species grows in dry to wet, acid or alkaline soil and can grow in sandy soil or dry clay. Bur oaks tolerate urban conditions better than most oaks.

Post oak (*Quercus stellata*), a white oak. Photo by Neil Soderstrom; Adkins Arboretum.

Chestnut oak (*Q. prinus*). Also called basket, rock, and rock chestnut oak, this species grows on rocky ridges and slopes where the soil is well drained. Plants tolerate a range of soils, from average moist, well-drained to dry. They are very drought tolerant.

Chinkapin oak (*Q. muehlenbergii*). Another oak that tolerates dry soils, this species grows naturally on outcrops and dry bluffs, although plants thrive in rich, moist, well-drained conditions as well. Plants are often found on high pH (alkaline) soils. Hardiness: Zones 5 to 7.

Overcup oak (*Q. lyrata*). Named for its acorns, which have caps that cover nearly the entire acorn, this species grows in dry to wet soil and tolerates periodic standing water. Plants have handsome and relatively uniform branching habits, with lower branches that sweep upward, unlike those of pin oak (*Q. palustris*), which sweep downward. Hardiness: Zones 5 to 9.

Post oak (*Q. stellata*). This smaller oak, typically 40 to 50 feet tall and wide at maturity, is found naturally on dry upland ridges and tolerates average, well-drained soil to dry conditions and also gravelly or sandy soil. Hardiness: Zones 5 to 9.

Swamp chestnut oak (*Q. michauxii*). Also called basket oak and very similar to chestnut oak (*Q. prinus*), this native grows along rivers and swamps. Plants thrive in moist to wet soil as well as average, moist, well-drained conditions. They survive periodic flooding. Hardiness: Zones 5 to 8.

Swamp white oak (*Q. bicolor*). This native of swamps and bottomlands requires acid soil and tolerates occasional standing water. Plants can grow in dry soil. Once established, they are quite drought tolerant.

White oak (*Q. alba*) prefers rich, well-drained, acid soil and is magnificent in woods, meadows, parks, and large landscapes. Plants do not tolerate encroaching development because it causes compaction and other changes in the soil, which lead to gradual death and decline.

Red Oaks

Bear oak (*Q. ilicifolia*). Also called scrub or black scrub oak, this small, shrubby species reaches about 20 feet. Plants grow on dry, poor, sandy, or rocky soil and do not tolerate poor soil drainage. Hardiness: Zones 3 to 7.

Blackjack oak (*Q. marilandica*). This shrubby species ranges from 20 to 40 feet in height and spread. Plants grow in dry, very poor soils, including sandy soil. Hardiness: Zones 6 to 9.

Black oak (*Q. velutina*). This is a 50- to 60-foot-tall oak that spreads about as far. Plants are happiest growing on rich, moist, well-drained acid soil, but they tolerate poor, dry sandy or clay soil.

Cherrybark oak (*Q. pagoda*, formerly *Q. falcata* var. *pagodifolia*). This species thrives in rich, moist, well-

Black oak (*Quercus velutina*), a red oak. Photo by Neil Soderstrom; Adkins Arboretum.

drained soils. The dark, scaly bark resembles that of black cherry (*Prunus serotina*). Hardiness: Zones 6 to 9.

Northern red oak (*Q. rubra*). This fast-growing oak is common in the nursery trade. Plants prefer well-drained, sandy loams and an acid pH. Southern red oak (*Q. falcata*) is more tolerant of heat, drought, and wet soils than northern red oak, and other species are better for tough, dry conditions. Hardiness: Zones 4 to 8.

Pin oak (*Q. palustris*). This fast-growing oak has a pyramidal shape and branches that sweep downward. Plants grow in moist to wet soil—another common name is swamp oak—and they tolerate shallow standing water for short periods, along with drought once established. The leaves become chlorotic (turn yellow) in alkaline soil.

Scarlet or red oak (*Q. coccinea*). This species, another oak common in the nursery trade, grows in average to dry soil and is found naturally on uplands and slopes as well as in sandy soil. Established plants are very drought tolerant.

Shingle or laurel oak (*Q. imbricaria*). Unlike most oaks, this species bears oblong or lanceolate, not lobed, leaves. They turn yellow or yellow-brown in fall and often remain on the plant into winter. Plants thrive in rich, moist, well-drained acid soil but can tolerate dry soils as well. Plants tolerate pruning and can be used in hedges or large shrub borders.

Shumard's oak (*Q. shumardii*). This is typically a smaller species, normally ranging from 40 to 60 feet tall and wide, although plants are considerably larger in the wild. Plants thrive in rich, moist, well-drained soil and grow along streams and near swampy areas in the wild. Hardiness: Zones 5 to 9.

Southern red oak (*Q. falcata*). This is a relatively fast-growing species that primarily grows on uplands and ridges in the drier soils of the Piedmont region. Hardiness: Zones 7 to 9.

Water oak (*Q. nigra*). This species prefers part to full shade and moist or wet sites, although plants will also grow in moist, well-drained soil. Plants tolerate flooding in winter and have been used successfully as street trees. They tend to be more weak wooded than most oaks. Hardiness: Zones 6 to 9.

Willow oak (*Q. phellos*). Narrow, willow-like leaves characterize this species, which grows in average to wet soils. Plants tolerate shallow standing water for short periods as well as dry soil once established. Hardiness: Zones 5 to 9.

Vines

There are many ways to incorporate vines into a garden. Traditionally, smaller vines have been trained up trellises, fence posts, lamp posts, and screens. Larger, more vigorous vines have been used to cover arbors to create shady sitting areas or are allowed to scramble up trees and cover fences as well as sheds and other structures. Some vines can do double duty as ground covers, covering level spots or slopes as well as hiding spoil areas or rock piles.

Use these native vines to replace non-native invasive species such as five-leaf akebia (*Akebia quinata*), porcelain berry or Amur peppervine (*Ampelopsis brevipedunculata*), oriental bittersweet (*Celastrus orbiculatus*), and Japanese honeysuckle (*Lonicera japonica*). Unless otherwise noted below, the vines listed grow in full sun to part shade.

Bittersweet, American (*Celastrus scandens*). This vigorous, twining climber can easily exceed 20 feet in height. Plants are grown for their fall clusters of showy red berries, each produced in a pale orange capsule that opens when ripe. Male and female flowers are borne on separate plants, so having one of each is essential. Grow American bittersweet in place of its rampantly invasive Asian cousin, oriental bittersweet (*C. orbiculatus*). It can be allowed to climb or used to cover rock piles and spoil areas. Both species can girdle and kill trees. Hardiness: Zones 3 to 8.

Carolina jessamine (*Gelsemium sempervirens*). Also called evening trumpet flower, this species ranges from 10 to 20 feet and climbs via twining stems. Plants have evergreen leaves and produce yellow, trumpet-shaped flowers in spring. They flower best in sun but tolerate shade. Rich, moist, well-drained soil is ideal, but they survive in nearly pure sand. Use Carolina jessamine on fences, trellises, arbors, and other structures, or train it as a ground cover. Hardiness: Zones 6 to 9.

White-leaf leather flower (*Clematis glaucophylla*). Photo by Neil Soderstrom; Mt. Cuba Center.

Clematis (*Clematis* spp.). Native clematis species have smaller flowers than the hybrids typically grown in gardens today, but they make charming additions to shrub and flower borders. Let plants climb up and over shrubs or along a fence, or provide a trellis or other support. Most clematis attach via twining leafstalks. Virginia clematis, or devil's darning needles (*C. virginiana*), is a 10- to 20-foot vine with clouds of small white flowers in early fall. Use it instead of sweet autumn clematis (*C. terniflora*), a widely planted non-native species. Hardiness: Zones 3 to 8. Vasevine or leather flower (*C. viorna*) bears small, red-purple bells with curved cream to green edges all summer on 8- to 12-foot plants. Hardiness: Zones 5 to 8. Swamp leather flower (*C. crispa*), also called curly clematis or blue jasmine, is a 3- to 6-foot vine that bears white bells with curved blue-purple edges in early summer. Hardiness: Zones 6 to 9. White-leaf leather flower (*C. glaucophylla*) bears hot pink bells with curved, creamy green edges in summer on 10- to 15-foot plants. Hardiness: Zones 6 to 11. In addition to flowers, all of the clematis above bear showy seedheads that add interesting texture and appeal to the garden.

🍃 How Vines Climb

The method that each species of vine uses to climb affects what type of support it needs.

Twining stems: Many vines have stems that can wrap around supports, both large and small. Twining stems can be thin and delicate or very large and woody.

Clinging roots: These can look like roots or may have discs on the tips. Either way, they allow plants to attach directly to buildings or other supports. Keep these vines off surfaces that must be painted periodically.

Tendrils: Crossvines, passionflowers, and other species use these to cling to wires or small-diameter supports. Virginia creeper has tendrils with discs at the tips that attach to buildings.

Twining leafstalks: Clematis have leafstalks that act like tendrils by wrapping around wires and wire trellises.

Crossvine (*Bignonia capreolata*). A large, vigorous native, crossvine has semi-evergreen or evergreen leaves and attaches to supports by tendrils with adhesive disks that cling to trees and walls, allowing plants to climb to 50 or more feet. It is less vigorous than trumpet vine (*Campsis radicans*), another native plant. Crossvines bear masses of fragrant, trumpet-shaped flowers—attractive to humming-birds—in spring in shades of brownish red or orange with yellow or red-brown inside. A number of cultivars selected for showier flower color are available. Crossvines tolerate full shade but bloom best with sun. Give plants rich, moist, well-drained soil. They tolerate periodic flooding. Flowers appear on the previous season's wood, so prune immediately after flowering. Train plants up trees, on screens or other supports, and over rock piles or uneven spots as ground covers. Hardiness: Zones 6 to 9.

Dutchman's pipe (*Aristolochia macrophylla*). A twining climber with large, heart-shaped leaves, Dutchman's pipe ranges from 20 to 30 feet tall and grows in any moist, well-drained soil. Plants are useful for creating dense cover on shade structures such as arbors, screens, and even awning frameworks over porches. The vines bear small, unusual-looking pipe-shaped flowers in late spring, and they are an important larval host for pipevine swallowtail butterflies. Hardiness: Zones 4 to 8.

Trumpet honeysuckle (*Lonicera sempervirens* 'Major Wheeler'). Photo by Barbara Ellis.

Honeysuckle, trumpet (*Lonicera sempervirens*). A twining climber, trumpet honeysuckle bears clusters of small, trumpet-shaped red, orange-red, or yellow flowers in spring and sporadically through the summer and fall. The flowers are attractive to hummingbirds, and plants climb to 20 or more feet, depending on the size of their support. They grow in moist, well-drained soil and tolerate shade but bloom best in sun. Flowers are primarily borne on last year's wood, so prune immediately after the main flush of flowers in spring. A number of cultivars are available, including ones with red, scarlet, or yellow flowers. There also are reblooming, or remontant, selections, including red-flowered 'Alabama Scarlet' and 'Major Wheeler' as well as yellow-flowered 'John Clayton'. Grow this species on fences, lamp posts, and trellises and up and over established shrubs. Hardiness: Zones 4 to 9.

Hydrangea, climbing (*Decumaria barbara*). Also called woodvamp and wild hydrangea vine, this native attaches itself by rootlets to trees and other supports. Plants climb to 20 or more feet and bear flat-topped clusters of fragrant white flowers in early summer. Fall foliage is pale yellow. Give plants rich, moist soil and part shade or shade. Grow climbing hydrangea on trees or other sturdy supports. Hardiness: Zones 5 to 9.

Passionflower, purple (*Passiflora incarnata*). Also called maypop, this exotic-looking vine climbs by tendrils to about 8 or more feet, and it also can be trained to produce a wide, ground-covering mound. Plants bear 2- to 4-inch-wide purple flowers with fringed, hairlike petals. The egg-shaped fruits that follow the flowers are edible. Train this vigorous species on screens, arbors, or trellises, or use it as a ground cover. Hardiness: Zones 5 to 9.

Trumpet vine (*Campsis radicans*). This tough, vigorous native grows in any soil and reaches 30 to 40 or more feet in height and spread. Plants have compound leaves with 9 to 11 leaflets and feature trumpet-shaped orange, red, apricot, or yellow flowers that attract hummingbirds from early summer to early fall. The vines cling to supports with roots and spread by

Trumpet vine (*Campsis radicans*). Photo by Neil Soderstrom; New York Botanical Garden.

rooting wherever they touch the earth. Train them up poles or trellises, or use them to cover rock piles or spoil areas. Cut plants back to a few buds in spring to keep them in check. Removing seed pods in summer lengthens the bloom season. Hardiness: Zones 4 to 9.

Virginia creeper (*Parthenocissus quinquefolia*). This species climbs from 30 to 50 or more feet and produces branched tendrils with holdfasts that cling to buildings and other supports. The flowers are insignificant, but birds and other wildlife relish the blue-black berries. Fall color is outstanding: Leaves turn scarlet, crimson, and purple-red. Plants grow in sun or shade and in any soil, from sand to clay. Train Virginia creeper on buildings, let it climb trees, or use it as a ground cover over rock piles or spoil areas. Plants also tolerate considerable shade and can be used under trees. Hardiness: 4 to 9.

Wisteria, American (*Wisteria frutescens*). This handsome, native twining climber grows 20 to 30 feet in height and bears fragrant lilac-purple flowers in late spring, after non-native invasive Japanese and Chinese wisterias (*W. floribunda* and *W. sinensis*) have finished blooming. Much more easily controlled than its rampant Asian cousins, American wisteria also blooms sporadically through the summer. Prune hard in late winter to keep plants in bounds. 'Amethyst Falls' features lavender-blue flowers. Give plants average to moist soil. They tolerate wet soil. Hardiness: Zones 5 to 9.

Plants for Hedgerows and Windbreaks

Whether you want a privacy screen, a mix of plants to block prevailing winds, or a naturalistic hedgerow to attract birds and other wildlife, the following trees and shrubs are good candidates. Planting a variety of shrubs and trees, both evergreen and deciduous, brings rich texture, color, and variety to the landscape. Look for compact forms of the various species if you do not have room for full-size plants. The plants here all thrive in full sun to part shade and in a range of soil types. Plants marked with an asterisk (*) are evergreen.

Arborvitae, eastern arborvitae (*Thuja occidentalis*)*
Bayberries (*Morella* spp., formerly *Myrica* spp.). Southern, small, or swamp bayberry (*Morella caroliniensis*, formerly *Myrica caroliniensis*, *M. heterophylla*)*; northern bayberry (*Morella pensylvanica*, formerly *Myrica pensylvanica*)*
Cherries (*Prunus* spp.). American wild plum (*P. americana*); pin cherry (*P. pensylvanica*); black cherry, chokecherry (*P. serotina* and *P. virginiana*)
Crab apples (*Malus* spp.)
Dogwoods (*Cornus* spp.). Pagoda or alternate-leaf dogwood (*C. alternifolia*); red-osier dogwood (*C. sericea*); gray dogwood (*C. racemosa*)
Hawthornes (*Crataegus* spp.). Cockspur hawthorn (*C. crus-galli*); Washington hawthorn (*C. phaenopyrum*); green hawthorn (*C. viridis*)
Hollies (*Ilex* spp.). American holly (*I. opaca*)*; common winterberry (*I. verticillata*)
Juniper, common (*Juniperus communis*)*

Osage orange (*Maclura pomifera*)

Pines (*Pinus* spp.). Eastern white pine
(*P. strobus*)*; loblolly pine (*P. taeda*)*;
Virginia pine (*P. virginiana*)*

Redbud (*Cercis canadensis*)

Red cedar, eastern (*Juniperus virginiana*)*

Red elderberry, scarlet elder (*Sambucus
racemosa* ssp. *racemosa*).

Sassafras (*Sassafras albidum*)

Serviceberries (*Amelanchier* spp.)

Sumacs (*Rhus* spp.)

Viburnums (*Viburnum* spp.). Blackhaw
viburnum (*V. prunifolium*); nannyberry
(*V. lentago*); southern arrowwood
(*V. dentatum*)

White cedar, Atlantic (*Chamaecyparis
thyoides*)*

Witch hazel, American or common
(*Hamamelis virginiana*)

Salt-Tolerant Trees and Shrubs

Windblown salt is a challenge in seaside gardens, but salt that runs off roads in the winter
is equally problematic. The plants listed below
tolerate salt.

Trees

American sycamore (*Platanus occidentalis*)

Arborvitae, eastern (*Thuja occidentalis*)

Ashes (*Fraxinus* spp.). White ash
(*F. americana*); green ash (*F. pennsylvanica*)

Bald cypress (*Taxodium distichum*)

Birches (*Betula* spp.). Gray birch
(*B. populifolia*); river birch (*B. nigra*)

Boxelder (*Acer negundo*)

Buckeyes (*Aesculus* spp.). Yellow buckeye
(*A. flava*, formerly *A. octandra*); red
buckeye (*A. pavia*)

Cherries and plums (*Prunus* spp.). Chickasaw
plum (*P. angustifolia*); black cherry,
chokecherry (*P. serotina*)

Fringetree, white (*Chionanthus virginicus*)

Hackberry (*Celtis occidentalis*)

Holly, American (*Ilex opaca*)

Honeylocust (*Gleditsia triacanthos*)

Kentucky coffeetree (*Gymnocladus dioicus*)

Magnolias (*Magnolia* spp.). Southern
magnolia (*M. grandiflora*); sweetbay
magnolia (*Magnolia virginiana*)

Oaks (*Quercus* spp.). White oak (*Q. alba*);
bur oak (*Q. macrocarpa*); pin oak
(*Q. palustris*); willow oak (*Q. phellos*);
blackjack oak (*Q. marilandica*); northern
red oak (*Q. rubra*); Shumard's oak
(*Q. shumardii*)

Persimmon, common (*Diospyros virginiana*)

Pitch pine (*Pinus rigida*)

Red cedar, eastern (*Juniperus virginiana*)

Sugarberry (*Celtis laevigata*)

Sweetgum (*Liquidambar styraciflua*)

Tupelo, black (*Nyssa sylvatica*)

Walnut, black (*Juglans nigra*)

Shrubs

Baccharis, eastern (*Baccharis halimifolia*)

Bayberry, northern (*Morella pensylvanica*,
formerly *Myrica pensylvanica*)

Beautyberry, American (*Callicarpa americana*)

Blueberry, highbush (*Vaccinium corymbosum*)

Buckeye, bottlebrush (*Aesculus parviflora*)

Chokeberry, red (*Photinia pyrifolia*)

Dogwood, red-osier (*Cornus sericea*)

Elderberry, American black or common
(*Sambucus nigra* ssp. *canadensis*)

Hazelnut or filbert, American (*Corylus
americana*)

Hollies (*Ilex* spp.). Inkberry (*I. glabra*); yaupon (*I. vomitoria*)

Itea, Virginia sweetspire (*Itea virginica*)

Junipers (*Juniperus* spp.). Common juniper (*J. communis*); creeping juniper (*J. horizontalis*)

Plum, beach (*Prunus maritima*)

Rose, Virginia and swamp (*Rosa virginiana* and *R. palustris*)

Snowberry, common (*Symphoricarpos albus*)

Sumacs (*Rhus* spp.). Staghorn sumac (*R. typhina*)

Summersweet, sweet pepperbush (*Clethra alnifolia*)

Sweet fern (*Comptonia peregrina*)

Viburnum, southern arrowwood (*Viburnum dentatum*)

Wax myrtle (*Morella cerifera*, formerly *Myrica cerifera*)

Vines

Honeysuckle, trumpet (*Lonicera sempervirens*)

Jessamine, Carolina (*Gelsemium sempervirens*)

Trumpet vine (*Campsis radicans*)

Virginia creeper (*Parthenocissus quinquefolia*)

FIVE ❧ Ground Covers for Chesapeake Landscapes

Ground covers are the go-to plants for reducing lawn, covering slopes, and minimizing maintenance. Although non-native plants fill most of the ground cover display area in nurseries, there are many natives that make excellent choices for covering ground in the landscape.

When selecting ground covers, use the site evaluation details you gathered in Chapter 2. Knowing site conditions is critical, since matching plant to site is essential for creating plantings that will require minimal maintenance. Local botanical gardens or other gardens that feature native plants offer another way to evaluate suitable ground covers. Many have demonstration gardens that exhibit some of the choices

(overleaf) Consider ground covers for a shady hillside where lawn would be difficult to mow and grass would struggle to survive. Here, Christmas ferns (*Polystichum acrostichoides*) and ostrich ferns (*Matteuccia struthiopteris*) thrive despite the tough conditions. Photo by Neil Soderstrom; design by Mary Streb.

available. These organizations often hold plant sales that offer natives, including those not yet commonly sold. One option for finding plants that look attractive throughout the year is to visit these sites during droughts, excessively rainy periods, or other tough climatic conditions. If wintertime appearance is most important, that is the best time to visit and observe demonstration plantings.

Ground covers may be tough, adaptable plants, but they do need basic care at planting time and for the first season they are in the ground. To provide the best start possible, review and follow the soil preparation and planting techniques in Chapter 3. Once plants are in the ground and mulched (use the deep mulching technique of spreading newspaper under mulch before planting to discourage weeds), plan on watering daily for a week. If the weather is sunny, shading new ground cover plantings with burlap for a few days after planting can help plants adjust. (Rainy or overcast weather is ideal for planting, since it helps plants cope with transplant stress.) Water weekly for

To add interest and diversity to ground cover plantings, combine plants that grow at similar rates and thrive in the same conditions. Here, Allegheny pachysandra (*Pachysandra procumbens*) surrounds marginal wood fern (*Dryopteris marginalis*) and maidenhair fern (*Adiantum pedatum*). Photo by Neil Soderstrom; design by Jimmy Testa at Mt. Cuba Center.

the first season unless the ground covers have been planted in fall. In that case, water until cool weather sets in and growth slows. Then watch plants the following spring—check them every few days if the weather is warm—and water as necessary until they are growing strongly. Also weed weekly for the first season. Pulling any weeds that appear while they are still small keeps this job easy and manageable.

This chapter features selections suitable for sites in both sun and shade.

Designing with Ground Covers

Creativity is not a word normally associated with ground covers. Traditionally, they are meant to provide a soothing, fairly uniform carpet, but that does not mean they have to be boring. There are more creative options for using them than the typical single-species mat. Planting a variety of ground covers is an effective way to create attractive, low-

maintenance plantings. Having several plants on a single site makes plantings more resilient. If one does not grow as well as expected, others are nearby to fill in and cover the site. The same is true if one species does far too well and begins overwhelming a less-enthusiastic neighbor. In this case, the gardener can step in and move the slower spreader to another location. Ground cover combinations also increase plant diversity, which is good for wildlife. Use the following design ideas to incorporate ground covers effectively in the landscape.

Formal and informal. Native ground covers can be used in both an informal, naturalistic style and a formal design. For an informal display, set them out in drifts of several species arranged in a pleasing pattern. A minimum of five to seven plants of each species makes an effective drift, but use more to make larger drifts to suit the space. Create drifts of different ground covers that feature contrasting foliage sizes, colors, and textures. For a uniform, lawnlike cover, choose plants for each drift that are

Underplant vigorous perennials with shorter ground covers to carpet the soil and keep down weeds. This combination also features contrasting foliage textures between feathery-leaved eastern blue star flower (*Amsonia tabernaemontana*) and the heart-shaped leaves of native violets (*Viola* spp.). Photo © Roger Foley; design by Tom Mannion Landscape Design.

all about the same height. Or select ground covers of several different heights and arrange them with the shorter ones toward the edges of the planting and taller ones in the center. While prostrate selections are best planted along walkways or near the front edge of woodland plantings—otherwise they may be impossible to see—mix up the heights a bit when planting taller selections. Planting shorter selections next to ones slightly taller creates an interesting rhythm.

An alternative is a natural-style planting, with plants arranged as they might be in the wild. In this case, plant them singly or set them out in small drifts (three or five plants). Let plants grow together and mix as they will. Consider including some taller native perennials that spread by seed—like white wood aster (*Eurybia divaricata*, formerly *Aster divaricatus*) or columbine (*Aquilegia canadensis*).

For a formal design, arrange ground covers in square, rectangular, or oval beds. Plant solid beds of one species, or edge with one ground cover and then plant the rest in a second plant with contrasting foliage color, size, or texture. Evergreen ground covers are especially suitable for formal designs because they emphasize the garden's framework year-round. Planting concentric rectangles, squares, or other shapes is another effective way to use ground covers in a formal design. In this case, each concentric block of plants could be a different species, with a single specimen in the center. Here, too, select plants with similar heights to create a lawnlike appearance, or combine different heights as well as colors and textures for a more gardenlike feel.

Plan for foliage interest. For the best-looking ground cover plantings, consider foliage first. While many of the natives listed here have nice flowers and/or attractive berries, ground covers need foliage that looks attractive all season long—or all year round in the case of evergreen species. Day in and day out, it is foliage that keeps the ground covered and your garden looking attractive. When selecting ground covers for a particular area, look for foliage

Drifts of various ground covers, vigorous perennials, and spreading shrubs combine to cover this hillside front yard. This complex planting adds color and diversity to a site that would typically be covered with lawn grass. Photo © Roger Foley; design by Florence Everts & Associates.

colors and textures that contrast or compliment one another. The amount of contrast is up to you. Mix chartreuse and deep green, for example, or look for feathery-shaped leaves to pair with bolder foliage.

Make ground cover gardens. While ground cover beds are typically designed simply to be low maintenance and attractive, they can also add creative flair to a landscape. Large drifts with at least five to seven plants per drift will create an attractive planting that looks like a traditional ground cover planting. For a planting that looks more like a garden, cover a site with a mixture of single ground covers or plants arranged in small drifts consisting of fewer than five plants. Provided the plants have been matched to

the site, such plantings look more like flower beds, but ground covers used in this fashion require far less maintenance once they are established because they will fill in and are easy to grow. Plantings that combine both perennials and woody plants are fine. This type of garden is easiest to manage if the plants are allowed to intermingle and create their own interesting combinations.

Mix plants that grow at similar speeds. To avoid having one plant completely overwhelm the others in a ground cover planting, try to select species that all grow at about the same rate. To determine how vigorous various species are, try to observe them in other people's gardens or in public plantings.

Planting ground covers around and under shrubs helps prevent weeds and lessens the need to keep the soil covered with mulch. Here thickly planted plantain-leaved sedge (*Carex plantaginea*) covers ground around wild hydrangeas (*Hydrangea arborescens*). Photo by Nancy Ondra.

Or plant them and just watch closely to make sure one species is not dominating. If growing rates are out of balance, either move the slower-growing species and replace it with something more vigorous or replace a vigorous species with one that grows more slowly.

Try taller ground covers. While most popular ground covers grow no taller than 1 to 2 feet, there is no rule that says these plants cannot be taller. To cover large areas, consider using taller plants, es-

pecially spreading shrubs. Almost any shrub that is wider than it is tall at maturity is a candidate: A variety of them are listed in this chapter.

Mulch with plants. Let low-growing ground covers take over the soil-protection chores that mulch ordinarily handles. In shrub borders, in mixed plantings, or along hedges, fill the area under the shrubs with ground covers that will take the place of grass, crowd out weeds, and eventually eliminate the need to mulch. (Use the deep mulching technique described in Chapter 3 to control weeds and get them established.) Before deciding what to plant, study the sun and shade patterns around shrubs, since exposure will vary. Sites on the south side of a shrub border may be dry and sunny, while those on the north side may be moister and quite shady. Planting ground cover mulches under perennials in flower beds is also effective and eliminates the need to mulch while helping to control weeds. Regular applications of mulch such as chopped leaves also replenish soil organic matter. Work them in around plants to avoid smothering.

Lawn alternatives. While nearly any ground cover can be used to cover ground, and some can handle foot traffic, lawn grass is best for areas that need to withstand regular foot traffic. To increase sustainability and reduce maintenance, while retaining lawn areas for sports or other activities, either stop fertilizing or switch to organic fertilizers. Also stop herbicide applications and let clover and other weeds come into the lawn. The end result will still look like a lawn, but it will require far fewer chemicals to maintain. There also are seed mixes for planting more sustainable lawns, including Ecolawn, a mixture of fine fescues. Another option is to substitute low-growing plants that create a uniform texture similar to lawn but that do not require weekly mowing. These tend to be taller than

Creeping junipers (*Juniperus horizontalis*) create an effective, permanent ground cover that resembles lawn but requires far less maintenance. Plantings such as this one do require regular weeding, especially at first, but the plants thrive in full sun, tolerate most soil types, and never need mowing. Photo by Barbara Ellis; Longwood Gardens.

 Start Small

Instead of trying to replace a lawn by planting masses of ground covers all at once, plan a series of smaller, more manageable plantings. This not only spreads out digging and planting; it makes aftercare chores such as watering and weeding more manageable. Smaller planting sessions spread out the cost, too, and safeguard the initial investment in plants because it is easier to keep up with basic care. Established plants also offer the opportunity to experiment with propagation and save some money. Ground covers generally are easy to propagate. See "How Ground Covers Spread" on p. 150 for more information.

traditional lawn grass but offer a similar texture. They tolerate very limited foot traffic. Many sedges (*Carex* spp.), including Pennsylvania sedge (*C. pensylvanica*), Texas or low-lawn sedge (*C. texensis*), and shaved sedge (*C. tonsa*), can be mass planted and used as lawn substitutes. Other options include red fescue (*Festuca rubra*), three-toothed potentilla 'Nuuk' (*Sibbaldiopsis tridentata*, formerly *Potentilla tridentata*), and plantain-leaved pussytoes (*Antennaria plantaginifolia*), which all can be mass planted as a lawn substitute. In addition, prostrate forms of creeping juniper (*Juniperus horizontalis*), such as 1-foot-tall 'Bar Harbor', 8- to 10-inch-tall 'Blue Chip', or 4- to 6-inch-tall 'Wiltonii', can be used to create a lawnlike planting. All spread from 6 to 8 feet.

Invasive Ground Covers

Unfortunately, the most widely offered and popular ground covers are non-native invasive plants that are far too effective at their appointed roles. They are problematic, both in cultivated landscapes and in wild areas, because they do not stop when they reach the boundary of their assigned spot in the garden. Instead, they keep spreading, leaving gardeners fighting to keep walkways from being engulfed and nearby plants from being smothered. Non-native invasives eventually escape into wild areas, traveling by wandering stems, wildlife-sown seed, or trimmings and divisions dumped by gardeners. Once they reach parks and wild areas, these plants are free to smother nearly everything in their path, except perhaps other non-native invasives. In addition to out-competing native species, non-native invasive ground covers eliminate essential food that native species provide to wildlife.

🍃 How Ground Covers Spread

Every ground cover worth its salt spreads by suckers, rhizomes, runners, or stolons, although the speed of spread varies from plant to plant and site to site. Some spread far and wide, while others reach only as far as they are tall. To use the latter as ground covers, mass them by arranging plants just slightly closer than their width at maturity. In addition to affecting spread, structures such as suckers, rhizomes, runners, and stolons all are important for propagating ground covers.

Suckers. These are short shoots produced by both shrubs and perennials that arise from the roots of a plant or from the crown. They can grow next to the clump or quite a distance away. To use them for propagation, make sure suckers have formed roots before severing and potting them up. Or sever the root that connects the sucker to the parent plant and leave it in place for several months while it forms an effective root system.

Rhizomes. These specialized stems run either along the surface of the soil or underground. Rhizomes and runners look quite similar. Rhizomes range from long, thin stems to thick and fleshy ones. All have nodes and inter-nodes along their length. Roots and sometimes shoots form at the nodes. Rhizomatous plants can have short, slow-growing rhizomes that creep and fill a space slowly, or they can produce very long, wide-ranging rhizomes that spread very quickly. To propagate plants that spread by rhizomes, use a sharp spade to dig and divide the clump or a gardening knife to sever a portion of the clump. Replant divisions immediately, or pot them up. Discard portions of the clump that appear to be unhealthy, using the healthiest, most vigorous sections for propagation.

Runners and stolons. While gardeners often use these terms interchangeably, a runner is a long, horizontal, aboveground stem that extends along the soil surface and produces roots and small plantlets at the tip and at leaf nodes. True stolons only produce roots and plantlets at the tip of the stolon. Sever and pot up or replant rooted plantlets to propagate either runners or stolons.

Not all of the plants listed below have been designated as invasive, but all are non-native plants that spread rampantly and are difficult to control in a garden. Nearly all of them are commonly offered for sale in nurseries and garden centers.

Archangel, yellow (*Lamiastrum galeobdolon*, formerly *Lamium galeobdolon*)
Bishop's weed (*Aegopodium podagraria*, includes variegated form, 'Variegata')
Crown vetch (*Coronilla varia*)
Deadnettles or henbits (*Lamium album*, *L. maculatum*, *L. purpureum*)
Honeysuckle, Japanese (*Lonicera japonica*)
Ivy, English (*Hedera helix*)
Moneywort, creeping Jenny (*Lysimachia nummularia*)
Ribbon grass, variegated (*Phalaris arundinacea* 'Variegated' or 'Feesy')
Spurge, cypress (*Euphorbia cyparissias*)
Strawberry, mock or Indian (*Duchesnea indica*)
Vinca, periwinkle (*Vinca* spp.). Common or lesser periwinkle (*V. minor*); big-leaved periwinkle (*V. major*)
Wintercreeper (*Euonymus fortunei*)

Ground Covers for Sun

Use sun-loving ground covers for replacing lawn, creating beds in sunny spots, and filling in along the sunny edge of foundation shrubs or other plantings.

Perennials

Unless otherwise noted below, all of the plants in this list thrive in full sun to part shade. They grow best in rich, well-drained soil. For good cover, space plants slightly closer than their spread at maturity. Propagate perennials by division or by taking cuttings.

Orange coneflower (*Rudbeckia fulgida* var. *sulvantii* 'Goldsturm'). Photo by Neil Soderstrom; Institute of Ecosystems Studies.

Coneflower, orange (*Rudbeckia fulgida*). Prized in flower gardens and as a cut flower, this species bears 2½- to 3-inch-wide orange-yellow daisy flowers with brown centers from late summer to mid fall. The 2- to 2½-foot-tall plants spread to 3 or more feet via rhizomes and self-sowing. 'Goldsturm' (*R. fulgida* var. *sulvantii* 'Goldsturm'), more commonly grown than the species, is somewhat more compact and bears 3½- to 5-inch-wide flowers on 2-foot-tall stems. Both tolerate drought and grow in any soil but are happiest and spread fastest in average to rich, moist, well-drained soil. Hardiness: Zones 3 to 9.

Coreopsis (*Coreopsis* spp.). Thread-leaved coreopsis (*C. verticillata*) is a popular, long-blooming species that forms 1½- to 2-foot mounds that spread by short rhizomes to about 3 feet. Plants have narrow leaves and are covered with 2-inch-wide, daisylike flowers in summer. Shear them after the main flush of flowers, and they will produce a second flush of bloom in fall. Established plants tolerate dry soil and drought. 'Moonbeam' bears soft yellow blooms, and 'Zagreb' has golden yellow flowers. Lobed or mouse-ear tickseed (*C. auriculata*) ranges from 6 to 9 inches tall and spreads by creeping rhizomes to 2 feet. Plants, which are happiest in partial shade or with morning sun and afternoon shade, bear oval leaves and orange-yellow flowers from summer through fall, especially if they are sheared back after the main flush of bloom. They grow in any well-drained soil. Hardiness: Zones 3 or 4 to 9.

Moss or creeping phlox (*Phlox subulata* 'Candy Stripe'). Photo by Barbara Ellis.

Phlox, creeping (*Phlox* spp.). Moss or creeping phlox (*P. subulata*) is a popular spring-blooming ground cover with white, pink, lavender, or purple flowers. Leaves are needlelike and evergreen. The plants are 4 to 6 inches tall and spread to 2 or more feet. They need well-drained soil and tolerate heat, drought, and sandy soil. Dappled shade is best in hot, dry sites. Hardiness: Zones 3 to 8. Mountain phlox (*P. latifolia*) and trailing phlox (*P. nivalis*) are similar species.

Potentilla, three-toothed (*Sibbaldiopsis tridentata*, formerly *Potentilla tridentata*). Also called shrubby five-fingers and three-toothed cinquefoil, this is a 3- to 6-inch-tall species that spreads from 1 to 1½ feet. Plants, which are actually subshrubs, feature glossy, three-leaflet, evergreen leaves and white flowers from early to midsummer. The foliage turns dark red in fall. Plants are best in well-drained soils and

are drought tolerant once established. Hardiness: Zones 2 to 8.

Pussytoes (*Antennaria* spp.). While common pussytoes (*A. dioica*) is widely available at garden centers, it is native to cool, temperate regions of Europe, Asia, and Alaska, making it a poor choice for the Chesapeake Bay region's hot, humid summers. Three native species make fine ground covers: plantain-leaved pussytoes or woman's tobacco (*A. plantaginifolia*), field pussytoes (*A. neglecta*), and shale barren pussytoes (*A. virginica*). All form ground-hugging, 1- to 3-inch-tall mats of spoon-shaped green or silver leaves that spread from 1 to 2 feet. Flowers are white, borne in spring, and held above the semi-evergreen to evergreen leaves. All three species thrive in dry, sandy, or gravelly soil. They grow in sun to part shade, although light, dappled shade during the hottest part of the day is best in the hottest parts of the Chesapeake Bay region. The first three species are hardy in Zones 3 to 8 or 9. Shale-barren pussytoes is hardy in Zones 4 to 7.

Virginia strawberry (*Fragaria virginiana*). Photo by Neil Soderstrom; National Arboretum.

Strawberry, Virginia (*Fragaria virginiana*). Although not as dense as many ground covers, Virginia strawberry produces white, five-petaled flowers in late spring and early summer, followed by sweet, edible berries. Plants range from 3 to 4 inches tall and spread by runners to about 2 feet. Birds and other wildlife also spread the seeds. Foliage turns rich red in fall and is semi-deciduous. Hardiness: Zones 3 to 9.

Common sundrops (*Oenothera fruticosa*). Photo by Neil Soderstrom; U.S. Botanic Garden.

Rose verbena or rose vervain (*Glandularia canadensis*). Photo by Neil Soderstrom; U.S. Botanic Garden.

stead Purple' is an especially vigorous selection with deep purple flowers from late spring to fall. Hardiness: Zones 5 to 9.

Shrubs

Unless otherwise noted below, the shrubs listed here all thrive in full sun to part shade and rich, moist, well-drained soil.

Bearberry (*Arctostaphylos uva-ursi*). Also called kinnikinnick, this low-growing subshrub or shrub grows to about 1 foot and spreads from 3 to 6 feet. Plants feature glossy, rounded, evergreen leaves and bear small clusters of pale pink to white flowers in summer. The flowers are followed by round red berries. Plants grow in dry or average well-drained soil and do not tolerate poor drainage. They are best for poor, acidic soils, grow well in sandy soil, and tolerate salt. An exposed site with good air circulation is best, and shade during the hottest part of the day is beneficial throughout the hotter parts of the Chesapeake Bay region. A number of cultivars are available, including 'Massachusetts' and 'Vancouver Jade'. Plants spread by sprawling stems that can root at the nodes. To propagate, sever rooted pieces and pot them up. Hardiness: Zones 3 to 7.

Sundrops, common (*Oenothera fruticosa*). Showy yellow, 1- to 2-inch-wide flowers are the most outstanding feature of this native species. Plants bloom from late spring to late summer and are 1½ to 2 feet tall and spread to 2 or more feet. Cut plants back in midsummer to renew flowering. Leaves turn red in fall. Plants thrive in dry and sandy soil. 'Summer Solstice'/'Sonnenwende' has red leaves that turn maroon in fall. 'Fireworks'/'Fyrverkeri' has bronze foliage, red buds that open to yellow, and a more compact habit than the species. Hardiness: Zones 4 to 9.

Verbena, rose (*Glandularia canadensis*, formerly *Verbena canadensis*). Also known as rose vervain, this is a creeping plant that also can be used as an edging plant. This species bears rounded, 2-inch-wide clusters of pink, lavender, or sometimes white flowers from late spring to late summer. Plants have sprawling stems that may root at the leaf nodes and range from ½ to 1½ feet tall and spread to about 2 feet. Rose verbena can be grown as an annual, and plants will self-sow when conditions suit. Plants grow in dry to average soil, provided it is well drained. 'Home-

Lowbush blueberry (*Vaccinium angustifolium*). Photo by Ann S. Rohlfing; Adkins Arboretum.

Blueberries (*Vaccinium* spp.). Blue Ridge or hillside blueberry (*V. pallidum*, formerly *V. vacillans*) is a 2- to 3-foot-tall shrub that spreads by rhizomes to 5 or more feet. Plants bear white flowers in spring, followed by sweet, edible, blue-black berries in summer. In fall, the leaves turn scarlet or crimson. Blue Ridge blueberries grow in dry, gravelly or sandy acid soil, but they tolerate heavy clay and have been found growing on the edges of swamps. Plants will grow in sun or shade. Hardiness: Zones 3 to 7. Lowbush blueberry (*V. angustifolium*) is a 6-inch- to 2-foot-tall species that spreads to 2 or 3 feet. It is similar to Blue Ridge blueberry but is less heat tolerant. Hardiness: Zones 2 to 5 or 6.

Bush honeysuckle, northern (*Diervilla lonicera*). See "Bush honeysuckle, northern" on p. 117 for more information.

Cinquefoil, shrubby (*Dasiphora fruticosa*, formerly *Potentilla fruticosa*). See "Cinquefoil, shrubby" on p. 118 for more information.

Coralberry (*Symphoricarpos* spp.). One of the best ground covers in this genus is 'Hancock' coralberry (*S.* × *chenaultii* 'Hancock'). This is a hybrid selection, the result of crossing native coralberry (*S. orbiculatus*) with pink snowberry (*S. microphyllus*), a species that is native to New Mexico. The result is a spreading shrub that most often stays about 2 feet tall and spreads by suckers to 12 feet. Plants bear small leaves and white or pale pink flowers in late summer that are followed by pink fruit. Hardiness: Zones 4 to 7. Indiancurrant coralberry (*S. orbiculatus*) also spreads by suckers. Plants range from 2 to 5 feet and spread to 6 or 8 feet. They bear yellowish white flowers and purple-red berries. Hardiness: Zones 2 to 7. Both species grow in any soil and are drought tolerant once established.

Holly, American (*Ilex opaca*). Dwarf, spreading American hollies such as 'Maryland Dwarf' make fine ground covers. See "American" under "Hollies" on p. 114 for more information.

Golden creeping juniper (*Juniperus horizontalis* 'Mother Lode'). Photo by Barbara Ellis; Pinkham garden.

Junipers (*Juniperus* spp.). Common juniper (*J. communis*) is a 50- to 60-foot-tall tree, but low-growing cultivars make good ground covers in the right situation. This species struggles with summertime heat and humidity and is best used in the cooler parts of Zone 7 and north. Compact cultivars include 8-inch-tall 'Mondap'/Alpine Carpet, which spreads to 3 feet. 'Pfitzeriana Compacta' is about 1½ feet tall and spreads to 6 feet. 'Blue Stripe' reaches 2 feet tall and spreads to 5 or more feet. 'Effusa' is a 1½-foot selection that spreads to 4 or 6 feet. 'Green Carpet' is only 6 inches tall and spreads from 2 to 3 feet. Give common junipers a site with well-drained to dry soil. Light, dappled shade during the hottest part of the day may help them with summer heat. Hardiness: Zones 2 to 7a. Creeping juniper (*J. horizontalis*) is native from New York State north but is far more tolerant of summertime heat and humidity. This tough, tolerant species is a ground cover by nature. Plants of the species are only 1 to 2 feet tall at maturity and spread 8 or more feet. They grow in moist, well-drained soil as well as in poor sandy or rocky soil. They tolerate clay soil and acid to alkaline pH. 'Bar Harbor' is 1 foot tall and spreads from 6 to 8 feet. 'Blue Chip', 8 to 10 inches tall, spreads to 10 feet. Hardiness: Zones 4 to 9.

Paxistima, Canby's (*Paxistima canbyi*). Also called Canby's ratstripper and Canby's mountain lover, this 1-foot-tall evergreen species spreads from 3 to 5 feet. Plants grow in rich, well-drained soil but tolerate dry conditions once established. As the common name "mountain lover" suggests, this species grows naturally in higher elevations along the Appalachian mountains. A spot that is shaded during the hottest part of the day may help plants cope with summertime heat, which can be a problem in the warmer parts of Zone 7. Hardiness: Zones 3 to 7.

Red cedar, eastern (*Juniperus virginiana*). This species is best known as a tree, but 'Grey Owl' is a dwarf cultivar suitable for covering ground. See "eastern red cedar" under "Junipers" on p. 115.

Fragrant sumac (*Rhus aromatica* 'Gro-low'). Photo by Barbara Ellis; J. Kent McNew garden.

Sumac, fragrant (*Rhus aromatica*). This low-growing, suckering shrub has insignificant yellowish flowers, ranges from 2 to 6 feet in height, and spreads to 10 feet. The cultivar 'Gro-low' is 2 to 3 feet tall and spreads to 6 or 8 feet. Both the species and 'Gro-low' are vigorous spreaders that will overwhelm smaller shrubs and perennials. The branches root where they touch the soil, making both suitable for covering slopes or other tough spots. Fall foliage is orange to red-purple. Plants grow in sun to considerable shade and tolerate salt, drought, and soil that ranges from dry to average moist and well drained. Hardiness: Zones 3 to 9.

Sweet fern (*Comptonia peregrina*). Despite the common name, this is not a fern but a rhizomatous, suckering shrub that ranges from 2 to 4 feet tall and spreads from 4 to 8 or more feet. Plants bear aromatic, deeply cut, fernlike leaves and insignificant

best. The species grows naturally along stream banks and ponds. Established plants have good drought tolerance. Hardiness: Zones 3 to 9.

Ground Covers for Shade

Ground covers are ideal for filling in under trees, but also consider the plants listed here for beds on the north or east side of the house as well as in shade and woodland gardens. Sites on the north or east side of shrub borders or other plantings also tend to be shady. On shady sites where the rain is blocked by the eaves of your house, installing soaker hoses may be the best option for keeping plants watered.

Perennials

All of the plants listed below will grow in part shade to full shade. Some tolerate sun, provided the soil is consistently moist.

Appalachian barren strawberry (*Waldsteinia fragarioides*). Photo by Barbara Ellis.

yellow-green flowers. They grow in any acid soil, including sandy, and tolerate salt and drought. One reason they are good for poor soil is that they can fix nitrogen. A site with shade during the hottest part of the day is best in the warmer parts of our area. Hardiness: Zones 2 to 7.

Yellowroot (*Xanthorhiza simplicissima*). Photo by Barbara Ellis; Brookside Gardens.

Yellowroot (*Xanthorhiza simplicissima*). This handsome, low-growing shrub ranges from 2 to 3 feet tall and spreads via suckers to 5 feet. Established specimens can form dense thickets. Plants bear brownish purple flowers in spring and featherlike leaves that turn yellow and red-purple in fall. Plants tolerate most soils, but moist, well-drained conditions are

Barren strawberry, Appalachian (*Waldsteinia fragarioides*, also listed as *Geum fragarioides*). A 6-inch-tall species that spreads by underground rhizomes to 1 foot or more, Appalachian barren strawberry pro-

🍂 Shrubs for Bold Ground Cover

There is no rule that says ground covers need to be a certain height, and as long as they are wider than they are tall at maturity, many shrubs can be used very effectively as ground covers. Plant one specimen and surround it with smaller ground covers, or mass several plants to cover a large area. Most of the plants in the list below are described in more detail in Chapter 4. Bottlebrush buckeye, mapleleaf viburnum, and Canadian hemlock are described in Chapter 7.

Bayberry (*Morella* spp., formerly *Myrica* spp.)

Buckeye, bottlebrush (*Aesculus parviflora*)

Chokeberries (*Photinia* spp., formerly *Aronia* spp.)

Hemlock, Canadian (*Tsuga canadensis*), 'Cole's Prostrate' and other spreading cultivars

Holly, winterberry (*Ilex verticillata*)

Itea, Virginia sweetspire (*Itea virginica*)

New Jersey tea (*Ceanothus americanus*)

Ninebark (*Physocarpus opulifolius*)

Pine, eastern white (*Pinus strobus*), dwarf or weeping cultivars

St. John's wort, golden (*Hypericum frondosum*)

Sweetshrub, Carolina allspice (*Calycanthus floridus*)

Viburnum, mapleleaf (*Viburnum acerifolium*)

Ninebark (*Physocarpus opulifolius*). Photo by Barbara Ellis.

duces yellow flowers in spring above a mat of handsome, three-leaflet, evergreen to semi-evergreen leaves. The fruit is not edible. While suitable for full-sun sites in the north, partial shade, especially during the hottest part of the day, is best in most of the Chesapeake Bay region to help plants cope with summertime heat and humidity. Hardiness: Zones 5 to 9.

Celandine poppy (*Stylophorum diphyllum*). Photo by Barbara Ellis; Mt. Cuba Center.

and leaves have orange sap. Plants spread indefinitely and bear showy, 1-inch-wide, poppylike flowers from spring to early summer. Select a spot in light shade to shade with any moist soil. They do not tolerate drought. They are especially effective for filling in around shrubs and larger perennials. Hardiness: Zones 4 to 8.

Large-flowered bellwort (*Uvularia grandiflora*). Photo by Barbara Ellis.

Bellwort, large-flowered (*Uvularia grandiflora*). Also called great merrybells, this handsome native ranges from 1 to 2 feet tall and spreads to 2 or more feet. The leaves remain attractive throughout the summer months. Rich yellow, bell-shaped flowers appear in spring, hanging singly or in pairs from the stem tips. Plants spread slowly but steadily by rhizomes to form broad clumps of arching stems with oval leaves. They also self-sow. See "Bellworts" on p. 225 for information on other species. Hardiness: Zones 4 to 9.

Celandine poppy (*Stylophorum diphyllum*). This is not a typical ground cover because it spreads by enthusiastic self-sowing rather than spreading roots. Nevertheless, celandine poppies can be used to cover large shady areas, either alone or in combination with larger ground covers. The 1- to 1½-foot-tall plants produce rosettes of deeply cut leaves. Stems

Foamflower, Allegheny (*Tiarella cordifolia*). This species, also called heart-leaved foamflower, is a popular shade-garden plant that produces clumps of lobed, heart-shaped leaves that are evergreen to semi-evergreen. The leaves turn maroon to bronze in fall. Clumps are topped by wands of tiny white flowers in spring. Plants range from 4 to 12 inches in height and spread by stolons from 1½ to 2 or more feet. They are happiest in partial to full shade and in rich, moist, well-drained soil, although they tolerate average soil once established. Numerous cultivars are available, but not all are good for covering ground, as many are crossed with West Coast native Wherry's foamflower (*T. wherryi*), which is clump-forming, not rhizomatous. For covering ground, plant the species, or look for spreading cultivars such as 'Elizabeth Oliver', 'Jeepers Creepers', 'Running Tapestry', 'Susquehanna', 'Slick Rock', and 'Tiger Stripe'.

See "Foamflowers" on p. 226 for more information. Hardiness: Zones 3 to 8.

Spotted or wild geranium (*Geranium maculatum*). Photo by Neil Soderstrom; Hannelore Soderstrom garden.

Geranium, spotted (*Geranium maculatum*). Also called spotted cranesbill and wild or spotted geranium, this 1- to 2-foot-tall species bears deeply cut leaves with narrow, toothed lobes and loose clusters of lavender-pink or pink flowers from late spring to midsummer. Clumps expand gradually, eventually spreading from 2 to 3 feet. Plants also spread by self-sown seeds. Select a spot in partial or full shade with moist, well-drained soil. They are able to tolerate dry shade but are shallow-rooted and do not have much tolerance for real drought. Hardiness: Zones 3 to 8.

Green-and-gold (*Chrysogonum virginianum*). Photo by Neil Soderstrom; U.S. Botanic Garden.

Green-and-gold (*Chrysogonum virginianum*). Also called goldenstar, this native wildflower spreads by rhizomes and produces 6- to 9-inch mounds of rounded, semi-evergreen leaves topped by starry golden yellow flowers from mid spring to early summer, then intermittently through midsummer and into the fall. Plants need partial shade to shade and spread via rhizomes to 2 or more feet. They need rich, evenly moist, well-drained soil but tolerate wet soil and can be used in rain gardens. They also grow in full sun, provided the soil remains moist. Hardiness: Zones 5 to 9.

Hairy alumroot (*Heuchera villosa* 'Autumn Bride'). Photo by Barbara Ellis.

Heucheras, alumroots (*Heuchera* spp.). This genus contains coral bells, which are grown for their flowers, along with plants commonly called heucheras or alumroots, prized primarily for their foliage. Two species are native to the Chesapeake Bay region: American alumroot (*H. americana*) and hairy alumroot (*H. villosa*). Hybrids of these two species and West Coast native crevice alumroot (*H. micrantha*) are widely available. (Coral bells are hybrids of several species native in the western United States.) Heucheras are grown for their 1- to 2-foot-tall mounds of foliage that spread to 2 feet. They bear loose panicles of tiny flowers in summer. The species primarily have green leaves, but hybrids have been developed that display leaves mottled with silver, maroon, black-purple, chartreuse, and caramel as well as foliage with silver veins or mottled with contrasting colors. Heucheras need rich, evenly moist, well-drained soil. They grow in full shade, but the leaves are more colorful in light to partial shade. A site with morning sun and afternoon shade is ideal, since it helps plants cope with heat. These plants must be massed if they are used as ground covers—the clumps grow larger every year, but they are not rhizomatous. Divide clumps every 3 to 4 years. Cultivars, which have lobed, sometimes maplelike leaves, include 'Dale's Strain', with green leaves blotched in silver; 'Frosted Violet', deep purple; 'Plum Pudding', purple-red frosted with silver; 'Cajun Fire', purple fading to maroon; 'Silver Scrolls', silver with maroon-purple veins; 'Spellbound', silver with dark veins and a purple flush; and 'Citronelle', with chartreuse leaves. Hardiness: Zones 4 to 8.

Crested iris (*Iris cristata*). Photo by Neil Soderstrom; Mt. Cuba Center.

Iris, crested (*Iris cristata*). This spring-blooming charmer produces broad clumps of arching, sword-shaped leaves topped by lilac-blue flowers. Clumps are 4 to 8 inches tall and spread to 3 or more feet. Give plants rich, well-drained, evenly moist soil for best performance. They grow in part to nearly full shade but tolerate full sun, provided the soil remains moist. Plants tolerate drought once established. 'Alba' bears white flowers. Hardiness: Zones 4 to 8.

Knotweed, Virginia (*Persicaria virginiana*, formerly *P. filiformis*, *P. filiforme*, and *Tovara virginiana*). Wild

Variegated Virginia knotweed (*Persicaria virginiana* 'Painter's Palette'). Photo by Barbara Ellis.

patches of this common species, also called jumpseed, bear green leaves, but gardeners have selected cultivated forms that feature striking foliage color. Green leaves with a maroon-brown chevron are common, but the cultivar 'Painter's Palette' features leaves marked with green, white, yellow, and red-brown. Individual leaves are 3 to 10 inches long, and clusters of tiny, deep pink flowers appear in late summer and fall. The plant spreads by seed, and seedlings "come true," meaning most of them feature the colorful foliage of their parents. Pull and discard all-green seedlings. While Virginia knotweed spreads by rhizomes as well as self-sown seed, it is not invasive like its non-native relative, Japanese knotweed (*Fallopia japonica*, formerly *P. cuspidatum*), a fast-spreading weedy shrub. Give Virginia knotweed light shade to shade and average to moist soil. Plants range from 2 to 4 feet tall and spread from 5 to 6 feet. Keep this species away from less vigorous perennials. It is ideal as a ground cover under and around trees and shrubs. Hardiness: Zones 4 to 8.

Mint, Meehan's (*Meehania cordata*). Also called creeping mint and heart-leaved meehania, this species is not a true mint (*Mentha* spp.). Plants range from 3 to 6 inches tall and spread by long, trailing stems to 3 or more feet. Leaves are toothed, triangular, and borne in pairs. Clusters of two-lipped purple flowers with white lips appear in spring. Meehan's mint spreads best with rich, moist soil, but plants can tolerate dry shade. Hardiness: Zones 5 to 8.

Allegheny pachysandra (*Pachysandra procumbens*). Photo by Neil Soderstrom; Mt. Cuba Center.

Pachysandra, Allegheny (*Pachysandra procumbens*). Native to the Appalachian region from Pennsylvania south, this is a handsome and under-used relative of Japanese pachysandra (*P. terminalis*). Plants are about 1 foot tall and spread by rhizomelike stems to form broad, dense clumps to 2 or more feet across. They produce spikes of small, fragrant white flowers in spring. New leaves emerge green in the spring, but by fall the semi-evergreen foliage is heavily mottled with maroon-brown and silver. Give plants moist, acid soil in partial to full shade. Established plants can withstand some drought. Hardiness: Zones 5 to 9.

Partridge berry (*Mitchella repens*). Sometimes called running box, this evergreen native bears rounded, white-veined leaves on trailing stems that root at the nodes. Plants are only 1 to 2 inches tall and spread from 1 to 2 feet. Pairs of white, ½-inch-long flowers appear in early summer, and blooms are followed by

Partridge berry (*Mitchella repens*). Photo by Neil Soderstrom; Mary Streb garden.

round red berries. Give partridge berry partial shade and rich, moist, well-drained acid soil. Keep it away from more vigorous perennials that will out-compete it. Hardiness: Zones 4 to 9.

Creeping phlox (*Phlox stolonifera*). Photo by Neil Soderstrom; Mt. Cuba Center.

Phlox (*Phlox* spp.). Two native species of shade-loving phlox can be used to cover ground. Wild blue phlox (*P. divaricata*) bears purple, lilac, or white flowers from late spring into early summer. Plants are 8 to 12 inches tall and spread from 2 to 3 feet. They also self-sow, and this species is handsome when allowed to fill in around other ground covers. Hardiness: Zones 3 to 9. Creeping phlox (*P. stolonifera*) is stoloniferous and produces purple-blue, pink, or white flowers on 4- to 6-inch-tall plants that spread to 1 foot or more. Hardiness: Zones 4 to 8.

Plantain, robin's (*Erigeron pulchellus*). This species deserves to be better known, since plants attract butterflies and tolerate dry shade and drought. They also grow in sun, provided the soil remains moist. The leaves produce a dense, 6-inch-tall mat, and white, daisylike flowers with yellow centers appear on 1-foot stems in late spring. 'Lynnhaven Carpet' bears larger leaves than the species and makes an especially nice ground cover. Hardiness: Zones 5 to 9.

Giant Solomon's seal (*Polygonatum biflorum* var. *commutatum*). Photo by Barbara Ellis.

Woodland sedum (*Sedum ternatum*). Photo by Neil Soderstrom; Mt. Cuba Center.

Sedum, woodland (*Sedum ternatum*). Also called whorled or three-leaved stonecrop, this species ranges from 4 to 6 inches tall and spreads from 1 to 1½ feet via creeping stems that root at the leaf nodes. Plants bear rounded, succulent leaves and showy, upright clusters of tiny white flowers from spring to early summer. They thrive in partial shade to full sun and moist, well-drained soil, and they also tolerate drought, heat, dry shade, moist shade, humidity, and competition from tree roots. In the wild, plants are found growing on mossy boulders, on ledges, and along streams. Hardiness: Zones 4 to 9.

Solomon's seal, small (*Polygonatum biflorum*). The erect, featherlike leaves of small Solomon's seal add handsome contrast to shade gardens. Plants are 1 to 3 feet tall and spread by rhizomes to form broad clumps 3 or more feet across. They bear small clusters of bell-shaped, greenish white flowers under the leaves in spring. Blooms are followed by black, berrylike fruit. Giant Solomon's seal (*P. biflorum* var. *commutatum*, formerly *P. commutatum*) is 3 to 5 feet tall—even taller in rich, moist soil—and spreads as far. Give Solomon's seals a site with rich, moist, well-drained soil. Hardiness: Zones 3 to 7.

Prostrate blue violet (*Viola walteri*). Photo by Neil Soderstrom; Mt. Cuba Center.

Violets (*Viola* spp.). Some of the best violets for covering ground are common wildflowers that have simply been pushed out of gardens because they are enthusiastic spreaders and not considered "refined" enough for flower gardens. They also are not plants commonly sold at nurseries. The secret to using them successfully is to pair them with shrubs or larger, vigorous perennials and give them ample space to spread. The species listed here will form mats several feet across, bear heart-shaped leaves, and, unless otherwise noted, grow in average to moist, well-drained soil. All are larval food for great spangled, meadow, variegated, regal, and silver-bordered fritillary butterflies. Canada violet (*V. canadensis*) bears white flowers on 1- to 1½-foot plants from early summer to fall. Plants spread by self-sowing. Common blue violet (*V. sororia*) is another species that self-sows with enthusiasm. Plants bear lavender-blue flowers on 6- to 8-inch plants from spring to summer. Sweet white violet (*V. blanda*) bears white flowers on 6-inch plants in spring. Plants spread primarily by runners. Downy yellow violet (*V. pubescens*) is a more reserved spreader than the other three species listed here. Plants bear yellow flowers in spring and self-sow, but not as widely. Labrador violet (*V. labradorica*) is found for sale in garden centers and makes an excellent ground cover. Plants are 3 to 4 inches tall and bear dark green leaves flushed with purple. Pale purple flowers appear in spring and summer. Plants spread by rhizomes and self-sowing. Prostrate blue violet (*V. walteri*) is another excellent native violet for covering ground. Its cultivar 'Silver Gem' is commercially available and features silver foliage with darker veins on 3- to 5-inch plants. Lavender flowers appear in early spring, and plants continue blooming intermittently until fall. Plants spread by trailing stems and are quite drought tolerant. Hardiness for *V. walteri* is Zones 5 to 8; for all other species listed here, Zones 2 or 3 to 8.

Wild gingers (*Asarum* spp. and *Hexastylis* spp.). These handsome ground covers were once all classified as species of *Asarum*. As a result, plants are

Canadian wild ginger (*Asarum canadense*). Photo by Neil Soderstrom; Alan Visintainer garden.

Mottled wild ginger (*Hexastylis shuttleworthii* 'Velvet Queen'). Photo by Barbara Ellis; Mt. Cuba Center.

listed by old or new botanical names as well as a variety of common names. They bear attractive, heart-shaped leaves and spread by creeping rhizomes to form broad mounds. Urn-shaped flowers, which are usually brown or maroon-brown, are borne in spring under the leaves. The flowers are pollinated by flies, wasps, ants, thrips, and beetles. Give wild gingers average to rich, moist, well-drained soil and shade to part shade. Canadian wild ginger (*A. canadense*) is most widespread and is the fastest spreader of the species listed here. Plants bear 6-inch-wide heart- or kidney-shaped deciduous leaves. They range from 6 to 10 inches in height and easily spread to 2 or more feet. Hardiness: Zones 2 to 8. Little brown jug

🍃 Vines for Covering Ground in Shade

Vines are especially useful for covering tough spots such as slopes and spoil areas. Another site where it is difficult to grow plants is under shallow-rooted trees like maples (*Acer* spp.), since surface roots make growing anything nearly impossible. Even if you find a pocket of soil in which to plant, it is likely the tree's roots will quickly fill the space and crowd out the plant. Spreading soil on top of the roots leads to a similar problem: Not only is it bad for the tree, but the tree's roots inevitably grow upward and infiltrate, again crowding out the ground covers.

Vines are one of the best choices for covering ground under trees. Plant vines away from the crowded soil under the tree, outside the drip line, and train the stems back over the roots. Ideally, plant on the north side, since the vines naturally grow toward the sun. See "Planting under Trees" on p. 98 for more information on growing plants under these conditions. Carolina jessamine (*Gelsemium sempervirens*), crossvine (*Bignonia capreolata*), climbing hydrangea (*Decumaria barbara*), and Virginia creeper (*Parthenocissus quinquefolia*) all tolerate shade and can be used in this manner. For more information on these and other vines, see "Vines" on p. 135.

Virginia creeper (*Parthenocissus quinquefolia*). Photo by Neil Soderstrom; Hannelore Soderstrom garden.

(*H. arifolia*, formerly *A. canadense*) features shiny evergreen leaves that emerge green but are mottled with silver later in the season. Plants are 3 to 4 inches tall and spread to 12 inches. Hardiness: Zones 5 to 9. Mottled wild ginger (*H. shuttleworthii*, formerly *A. shuttleworthii*) is also commonly called large-flower heartleaf. Plants bear stunning 4-inch-long evergreen leaves that are dark green and marked with silver or cream. Plants are 4 to 6 inches tall and spread to 2 feet. Hardiness: Zones 6 to 8. Virginia heartleaf

(*H. virginica*, formerly *A. memmingeri, A. virginicum,* and *H. memmingeri*) bears dark green leaves mottled with silver. Leaves are evergreen and 2 to 3 inches long. Plants are 6 to 8 inches tall and spread from 1½ to 2 feet. Hardiness: Zones 5 to 9.

Wintergreen (*Gaultheria procumbens*). Also commonly called winterberry, checkerberry, and eastern teaberry, this is a 3- to 6-inch evergreen subshrub with leathery, dark green leaves that smell of winter-

Ostrich ferns (*Matteuccia struthiopteris*) and sensitive ferns (*Onoclea sensibilis*) combine with hostas, azaleas, and a weeping Japanese maple to cover ground in a shady garden. Photo by Neil Soderstrom; design by Mary Jo Messenger.

green when crushed. White or pale pink urn-shaped flowers appear in summer followed by round red berries. Plants spread slowly to about 3 feet by creeping underground stems. Give wintergreen rich, moist, acid, well-drained soil. With sufficient moisture, plants grow in sandy soil. Hardiness: Zones 3 to 8.

Ferns

Woodland gardens seem incomplete without ferns, and many native species make excellent ground covers for shade. While they can be planted in drifts and used alone, they are handsome combined with other species—both native and not. For handsome textural contrast, combine them with a mixture of broad- and grassy-leaved plants that contrast with the lush, lacy texture of the fronds. Unless otherwise noted below, the ferns here are deciduous and prefer rich, moist, well-drained soil and partial to full shade. All can be propagated by dividing the clumps in spring or fall.

Beech fern, broad (*Phegopteris hexagonoptera*, formerly *Dryopteris hexagonoptera* and *Thelypteris hexagonoptera*). This vigorous species is 1½ to 2 feet tall

A bed of royal ferns (*Osmunda regalis*) fills the space in front of southern magnolias (*Magnolia grandiflora*). Photo © Roger Foley; design by Scott Brinitzer Design Associates.

and spreads to 3 or more feet. Plants spread by creeping rhizomes and travel fastest in rich, evenly moist soil. They grow in drier conditions, provided they are in full shade. Hardiness: Zones 3 to 8.

Bracken fern (*Pteridium aquilinum*). This tough, even weedy, fern has large triangular fronds and deep rhizomes. It can be used to stabilize banks in shade and is only suitable for large sites because the rhizomes spread widely. Plants, which are toxic to livestock, range from 1 to 4 feet tall and tolerate dry or wet soil and sun or shade. Hardiness: Zones 3 to 10.

Christmas fern (*Polystichum acrostichoides*). This evergreen species is 1 to 2 feet tall and spreads from 2 to 3 feet. Plants have rhizomes but spread very slowly

Christmas ferns (*Polystichum acrostichoides*), shown here on a hillside with hostas, are evergreen and tolerate dry soil once established. Photo by Barbara Ellis; London Town and Gardens.

to form broad clumps. They are happiest in rich, moist soil but tolerate dry soil and drought. Hardiness: Zones 3 to 8.

Hayscented fern, eastern (*Dennstaedtia punctilobula*). Sometimes called boulder fern, this vigorous species

Eastern hayscented fern (*Dennstaedtia punctilobula*). Photo by Barbara Ellis.

spreads quickly by creeping rhizomes. Plants are 1½ feet tall and spread indefinitely. While the species is too vigorous for small gardens, it is useful for informal areas under trees and shrubs, for covering slopes, and for filling in around rocks or other obstacles where a lawn mower is difficult to maneuver. Plants have yellow-green fronds that are fragrant when handled; but the fronds are brittle, and plants can be ragged looking by the end of the season. While a site in partial shade to shade is ideal, plants tolerate light shade and full sun, provided the soil remains moist. They grow in poor, acid soil and can withstand drought and dry shade. Hardiness: Zones 3 to 8.

Lady fern, common (*Athyrium filix-femina*). Prized for its lacy, deeply cut leaves, this fern is happiest in part shade or shade and moist to wet soil. Plants tolerate fairly dry shade along with full sun, provided the soil remains moist. The clumps range from 2 to 4 feet tall and spread to 3 feet. Many cultivars with crested and finely dissected fronds are available. Hardiness: Zones 4 to 9.

New York fern (*Thelypteris noveboracensis*, formerly *Dryopteris noveboracensis*, *Polypodium noveboracense*, and *T. thelypterioides*). This 1- to 2-foot-tall species

spreads vigorously and indefinitely by rhizomes. Plants are happiest in rich, well-drained soil, but they tolerate dry shade, moist shade, short periods of drought, and some sun, provided the soil remains moist. Hardiness: Zones 2 to 8.

Ostrich fern (*Matteuccia struthiopteris*, formerly *M. pensylvanica*). This easy-to-grow fern is 3 to 5 feet tall and spreads to 8 or more feet via vigorous rhizomes. Plants form lush clumps of plumelike fronds in moist to wet soil. They tolerate average soil but are smaller and not as vigorous. Hardiness: Zones 2 to 7.

Sensitive fern (*Onoclea sensibilis*). Photo by Barbara Ellis.

Sensitive fern (*Onoclea sensibilis*). This species has dense, well-branched roots that are good for binding soil. The plants have coarsely divided fronds that turn yellow and die at the first hint of frost. They range from 1 to 2 feet tall and spread to 3 or more feet. Plants thrive in rich, moist soil, but they tolerate average, well-drained conditions as well as wet soil. Hardiness: Zones 4 to 9.

Shrubs

Shrubs can be effective ground covers for shade gardens, woodlands, and even the shady north side of a house or other buildings. The following species, and in some cases dwarf forms of larger species, are all suitable choices for covering ground in shade, since they spread farther than they are tall. Most can be used in shrub borders and as foundation plants. Use them in masses of a single species or combine several shrubs to create a shady border. Consider combining them with perennial ground covers, ferns, or sedges. Either underplant shrubs with herbaceous ground covers or arrange them as an edging. Unless otherwise noted below, all thrive in partial shade to shade and in average moist, well-drained soil.

Azaleas (*Rhododendron* spp.). Coast azalea (*R. atlanticum*) is a stoloniferous species that is usually 3 to 4 feet tall but spreads to 6 or more feet if conditions suit it. Plants bear blue-green leaves and fragrant white to pinkish flowers in spring before the leaves emerge. Coast azalea plants prefer sandy, moist, acid soil but tolerate heavier soil, provided it is well drained. In the wild, they are found growing in sandy pine barrens, in moist woods, and along stream banks. Hardiness: Zones 5 to 8. Pinxterbloom azalea (*R. periclymenoides*, formerly *R. nudiflorum*) is another stoloniferous species. It bears white, pale pink, or purplish flowers in spring before the leaves appear. Flowers usually are fragrant. Plants range from 2 to as much as 10 feet in height and spread from 6 to 12 feet. They grow in sun or shade and tolerate dry sandy or rocky soil as well as moist to wet conditions. Hardiness: Zones 4 to 8. Choptank Hybrid azaleas are especially well suited to Chesapeake Bay landscapes. These include 'Marydel', an *R. atlanticum* selection with fragrant pink flowers, and 'Choptank Rose', an *R. atlanticum* × *R. periclymenoides* cross with fragrant white and rose-pink flowers.

Fothergilla (*Fothergilla* species). Both dwarf fothergilla (*F. gardenii*) and large fothergilla (*F. major*) can be used as ground covers. See "Fothergillas" on p. 119 for more information on these species.

Huckleberries (*Gaylussacia* spp.). Black huckleberry (*G. baccata*) features pink to nearly red spring flowers, edible summer fruit, and brilliant red fall foliage. Plants are 1 to 3 feet tall and spread by suckers to 4 or more feet. They require well-drained, dry to average acid soil and are a good choice for part shade in rocky woods. Part shade is best for flowering and fall foliage color. Plants grow in moist, well-drained soil. Hardiness: Zones 3 to 7. Box huckleberry (*G. brachycera*) requires part shade and moist, well-drained, acidic soil. Plants bear pale pink flowers, black edible berries, and evergreen leaves. They are 6 to 12 inches tall. Provided the conditions are to their satisfaction, they spread to several feet. Hardiness: Zones 4 to 7. Both species are excellent companions for blueberries (*Vaccinium* spp.), as well as azaleas and rhododendrons (*Rhododendron* spp.), which also thrive in moist, acid, well-drained soil.

Smooth hydrangea (*Hydrangea arborescens* 'Annabelle'). Photo by Neil Soderstrom; New York Botanical Garden.

Hydrangea, smooth (*Hydrangea arborescens*). This native hydrangea bears 4- to 6-inch-wide clusters of white flowers from summer to fall. Plants range from 3 to 5 feet in height and spread by suckers to 5 or more feet. They spread quite quickly in rich, moist, well-drained soil. Partial shade is best, although they will grow in full sun, provided the soil remains moist. Flowers appear on new wood, and the clumps can be cut to the ground in late winter. 'Annabelle' bears flower clusters up to 1 foot across. Hardiness: Zones 4 to 9.

Coastal leucothoe (*Leucothoe axillaris*). Photo by Neil Soderstrom; U.S. Botanic Garden.

Leucothoes (*Leucothoe* spp.). Also commonly called doghobbles, two species in this genus make fine ground covers because they spread by suckers. Both are evergreen with arching racemes of urn-shaped flowers in spring. The leathery leaves change from green to bronze or maroon-purple in winter. They need part shade and average to rich soil that is moist but well drained. Plants can grow in full sun with adequate moisture but do not tolerate drought or windy sites well. Coastal leucothoe (*L. axillaris*), sometimes called swamp doghobble, grows from 2 to 4 feet tall and spreads from 5 to 10 feet. Hardiness: Zones 6 to 9. Drooping leucothoe (*L. fontanesiana*), also called fetterbush and doghobble, is a 3- to 5-foot-tall species that spreads by suckers to 5 or more feet. Hardiness: Zones 5 to 9.

Summersweet (*Clethra alnifolia*). Dwarf cultivars of this popular native are especially effective for cov-

ering ground in shade. See "Clethra, sweet pepperbush" on p. 118 for more information.

Yew, Canada (*Taxus canadensis*). This wide-spreading evergreen species bears glossy needles that often turn bronze in winter. Plants are 3 to 6 feet tall and spread 6 to 10 feet at maturity. Give them rich, moist, well-drained soil in partial shade to shade. Plants do not tolerate heat and drought well, so shade during the hottest part of the day is essential in the warmer parts of the Chesapeake Bay region. Look for a site with protection from winter sun as well. Hardiness: Zones 2 to 6 or 7, with good site selection.

Moss Gardens for Acid Shade

For a shady site with moist, acid soil, a velvety carpet of moss makes a handsome ground cover. Often considered to be a lawn weed by gardeners trying to tend grass on shady sites, moss tolerates light foot traffic and is ideal for covering ground under trees, in woodland gardens, and along walkways. Moss is a fine choice for covering shady slopes; north- or east-facing ones are ideal.

Once established, moss is a very forgiving evergreen ground cover. Plants need part shade to shade and poor, moist, very acid soil—ideally, the pH should be between 5.0 and 5.5, although moss will grow in slightly less acid conditions. Existing moss provides a clue that the pH is suitable, but if in doubt, test the pH before deciding to plant moss. If the pH is slightly higher than it should be, you can take steps to lower it, at least while moss becomes established. Keep in mind, though, that trying to maintain pH at an artificial level is not a sustainable practice and violates the principle of right plant, right place.

Unlike conventional garden plants, moss requires

(top) This shade garden features a moss lawn sprinkled with tiny bluets (*Houstonia caerulea*) surrounded by informal clumps of wildflowers and woods. Photo by Barbara Ellis; Burnet moss garden.

(bottom) Moss can thrive on moist paving stones. Photo by Neil Soderstrom; Leslie and Art Jacoby garden.

firmly packed soil, rather than the loose, well-aerated conditions most conventional plants prefer. Established plantings of moss tolerate drought by simply going dormant until the weather changes.

One easy way to identify a suitable location for a moss garden is to look for patches of moss already growing in the yard. Moss often coexists with struggling lawn grass. In this case, one easy way to establish a moss lawn is to reduce the pH of the soil to favor the moss and eliminate some of its competition. (Or simply stop applying lime, which raises the pH.) Adjusting pH instead of digging and pulling weeds is best, since digging loosens the soil and eliminates the packed soil consistency that moss prefers. If pulling some weeds is necessary, press the soil and moss back down firmly. Or cut weeds off at the soil surface with scissors.

Moss also is an effective ground cover under azaleas and other shrubs such as huckleberries (*Gaylussacia* spp.) and blueberries (*Vaccinium* spp.). Consider combining it with low-growing wildflowers that demand acid soil, such as partridge berry (*Mitchella repens*) and wintergreen (*Gaultheria procumbens*).

Moss can be purchased from suppliers, but do not buy from sellers who simply collect from the wild. Reputable companies grow their own, collect on a sustainable basis from their own property, and/or work with developers to collect moss that would otherwise be destroyed. Use the online resources link in Suggested Resources to find local suppliers to be sure you start with moss species that grow well in the Chesapeake Bay region. Carefully follow planting directions sent with shipments, and after plant-

 Moss Milkshakes

A blender, locally collected moss, buttermilk, and water are the ingredients in this useful concoction. To start a moss planting, collect some moss from a spot in your yard or the yard of a friend or neighbor. (Do not collect from the wild.) Crumble it into a blender and add equal parts buttermilk and water. Blend until the concoction is a little less thick than pancake mix or cream of potato soup. If in doubt, thicker is better, as the moss plants use the fat and acid of the buttermilk to grow. Thin, runny mix has more water and less buttermilk, and thus fewer nutrients. Pour the mix where you want to establish moss as a ground cover. Keep the area moist until the bits of moss begin to grow. Be sure to mist, but not water, since a heavy stream of water will wash away the bits of moss before they are established.

ing, keep the site moist with regular misting until the moss is established—this will probably take several weeks. Once moss is growing, it needs little regular care. One important chore is to keep leaves and other debris from smothering the moss. Gently brush away leaves and other debris with a broom—it takes practice to brush away leaves without uprooting the moss. Another option is to spread out lightweight plastic netting (the kind used to cover blueberry bushes) before leaves fall and simply pick up the netting to carry away the leaves.

six ❦ Flowers for Chesapeake Gardens

Whether grown in conventional beds and borders, combined with shrubs in mixed plantings, or used in wild gardens and meadows, native perennials contribute color and interest to the landscape. While their foliage and flowers are attractive, the element of change they add throughout the year is a compelling reason to add perennials to the garden. Over the course of a growing season, herbaceous perennials—plants that live for more than two years but die back to the ground each winter—sprout, unfold their leaves, produce buds, display their flowers, and then produce seed. Fill a garden with perennials, and change through the seasons becomes an integral part of the design as every clump blooms on its own schedule. The garden looks different every day as flowers come in and out of bloom. While they add color to the garden, native flowers also attract birds, butterflies, and a host of other wildlife, making change a moment-to-moment occurrence.

Well-designed perennial gardens are also appealing because they are diverse, a characteristic gardens can share with meadows and other wild areas. Diversity bolsters the appeal of a landscape by helping it support a wider variety of butterflies and other wildlife. In addition, it introduces the challenge of experimenting with many different colors, textures, plant habits, and bloom times—one of the reasons garden design is so fascinating. Sustainable garden design combines art, craft, and science. For a garden to be sustainable, we have to let the plants tell us where they will be most successful.

Determining what to plant where, so that something will be in bloom throughout the season, can be a challenge, whether you are a novice or an experienced gardener experimenting with a new site or an unfamiliar, more naturalistic style of garden. In the interest of helping readers sort through the options, I list the perennials in this chapter by bloom season. Plants are separated into the following sections: Spring, Late Spring to Early Summer, Summer, and Late Summer to Fall. In addition, from summer onward, the plants are further divided by soil preference: Dry to Average and Moist to Wet.

Sorting plants this way is challenging for a variety of reasons, but mainly because plants do not always fall neatly into bloom times, even if the lists that follow imply that they do. Many are widely tolerant as well and can be grown in a wide range of conditions. Still, this chapter should help gardeners understand the options, consider matching plants to available sites, and select plants that will thrive, while also planning a garden that has something in bloom for most of the season. The lists here focus on plants suitable for full sun to partial shade. See Chapter 7 for information on plants for partial shade to shade.

Using Native Perennials

What to plant is only part of the equation. How the perennials will be used in the landscape is also a factor. Chapter 5 lists many that make excellent ground covers, and Chapter 9 highlights perennials that attract butterflies, insects, and other wildlife. Here are a few more suggestions:

(overleaf) A mix of annuals and native perennials fills this narrow border, which screens the vegetable garden behind it. Perennials, including hybrid agastache (*Agastache* 'Blue Fortune'), Joe-Pye weed (*Eutrochium dubium* 'Little Joe'), and New York ironweed (*Vernonia noveboracensis*), share space with annual zinnias (*Zinnia* spp.) and spider flowers (*Cleome hassleriana*). Photo by Neil Soderstrom; Hannelore Soderstrom garden.

Flower gardens are ever changing, and each gardener's creation is unique. These borders include a mixture of shrubs and perennials at their height in fall, including non-native frost grass (*Spodiopogon sibiricus*) on the left, clouds of pink bloom from native panic grass (*Panicum virgatum* 'Cloud Nine'), yellow-leaved common elderberry (*Sambucus nigra* 'Aurea'), and pink New England asters (*Symphyotrichum novae-angliae* 'Harrington's Pink'). Photo by Nancy Ondra.

Spiderworts (*Tradescantia virginiana*) surround a bold clump of shrub-size baptisia (*Baptisia alba*) in a late spring to early summer combination. Photo by Barbara Ellis; Clarke garden.

Native beebalm (*Monarda didyma*) with Russian sage (*Perovskia atriplicifolia*), a shrubby, non-native perennial that seldom spreads. Photo by Barbara Ellis; Grotsky garden.

Plant popular perennials. Many of the most popular garden perennials are actually native plants that were collected, grown, selected, and hybridized by English and German horticulturists and then reintroduced to the U.S. market. See "Ten Tips for Growing More Native Plants" on p. 21 for a list of popular garden plants that are also native wildflowers.

Grow natives with non-invasive, non-native flowers. Do not be afraid to grow native perennials in conventional beds and borders with classic, non-native flowers that do not spread invasively. These include peonies (*Paeonia* spp.), balloon flowers (*Platycodon grandiflorus*), Siberian iris (*Iris sibirica*), lavender (*Lavandula angustifolia*), Russian sage (*Perovskia atriplicifolia*), and pinks (*Dianthus* spp.).

Combine bold perennials with shrubs. Add color to shrub borders or foundation plantings with bold, shrub-size native perennials that have attractive flowers and interesting foliage. These include baptisias (*Baptisia* spp.), blue stars or amsonias (*Amsonia* spp.), coreopsis (*Coreopsis* spp.), rattlesnake master (*Eryngium yuccifolium*), Maryland senna (*Senna marilandica*, formerly *Cassia marilandica*), yucca (*Yucca filamentosa*, especially variegated forms), and sunflowers (*Helianthus* spp.)

Plant specimen plants. These are useful for highlighting the entrance to a path, accenting a sitting area, or complementing a piece of garden sculpture. In addition to bold, clump-forming perennials such as common rose mallow (*Hibiscus moscheutos*)

🍃 Sun or Shade?

While it is easy to determine if a site is in full sun, which means no shade whatsoever, or full shade, which means no sun, the gradations in between can cause problems for gardeners. Not only does sun or shade exposure change throughout the day and from season to season, but a bed or border can be sunny at one end and shady at the other, with varying amounts of sun or shade on different sections in between. Soil also plays an important role in what thrives where. A great many plants grow well in sun with rich, well-drained loam but need shade if the soil is sandy and therefore drier. While many plants are not troubled by subtle gradations of sun and shade, experimentation is in order when planting a fussier species or a difficult site. Experienced gardeners often say they have to kill a plant three times before deciding they cannot grow it. One way to experiment is to buy several specimens of the same plant and then plant them in different sites that seem suitable. Watch them carefully to see what works. If your budget is limited, stick to widely adaptable natives, especially until you have a good idea of the conditions your garden has to offer—knowledge that will increase every year you garden.

The following are some general guidelines to keep in mind. For more information, see "Sun and Shade Terms" on p. 45. Plants that thrive in hot, sunny sites but tolerate some shade typically grow best in full sun to part sun, meaning they need to receive a minimum of 4 to 6 hours of sun and varying amounts of shade the rest of the day. In most cases, afternoon sun is best, since such sites are typically hotter than those that are sunny in the morning.

Plants that grow in part shade to full shade generally do better in a spot that receives shade in the afternoon. That is especially true for gardeners who live in the city but are trying to grow a species native to the mountains, as sites that are shady in the afternoon and receive sun (if any) in the morning are cooler than those that are shady in the morning and sunny in the afternoon. Dappled, daylong shade is another great option for shade plants and is yet another reason to plant and nurture shade-casting trees.

Most sites have gradations of sun or shade. In this garden shaded by a red oak (*Quercus rubra*), plants in the foreground receive sun from midday into the afternoon, while those toward the back receive dappled shade for most of the day. Photo by Barbara Ellis.

Self-sowing annuals such as brilliant blue larkspur (*Consolida ajacas*) and native yellow-and-maroon plains coreopsis (*Coreopsis tinctoria*) are great for filling spaces between plants and adding long-lasting color to gardens. Photo by Barbara Ellis; Grotsky garden.

and yucca (*Yucca filamentosa*, especially variegated forms), ornamental grasses such as pink muhly (*Muhlenbergia capillaris*) and panic grass or switchgrass (*Panicum virgatum*) make excellent specimens. See "Grasses for Gardens" on p. 201 for more information on native ornamental grasses.

Let plants sow and spread. Self-sowers such as blue-eyed grass (*Sisyrinchium* spp.) and wild petunias (*Ruellia* spp.) are especially effective in cottage gardens or informal beds and borders. This is also the case with hardy ageratum (*Conoclinium coelestinum*) and plants that have sprawling stems, such as purple poppy mallow (*Callirhoe involucrata*) and gaura (*Gaura lindheimeri*), nearly native species from the central United States.

Grow a meadow or meadow garden. Wildflower meadows or informal gardens that feature meadow plants are another way to use native perennials successfully. See "Meadows and Meadow Gardens" on p. 205 for more information.

Basic Care for Flowering Perennials

Once they become established in a site that suits them, the flowers in this chapter require little maintenance. Prepare both soil and plants using the guidelines provided in Chapter 3. Good post-planting care is vital: All need regular watering to help them become established and mulching to keep weeds at bay. The care techniques below are optional. Experiment and decide for yourself whether the rewards are worth the extra effort.

Cut back to reduce height and increase bloom. Tall perennials benefit from a buzz cut in midseason. Cutting them back hard—by half or two-thirds—results in shorter, more compact plants with sturdy stems that are less likely to need staking. Plants that have been cut back also branch more and produce more flowers. To use this method with plants that bloom in early to midsummer—including purple coneflowers (*Echinacea* spp.), yellow coneflowers (*Ratibida* spp.), tall coreopsis (*Coreopsis tripteris*), oxeye (*Heliopsis helianthoides*), and Culver's root (*Veronicastrum virginicum*)—cut back once or twice before the end of May. This will delay flowering but will result in more flowers and shorter stems. For plants that bloom from late summer to fall, cut back by the end of June. Try this with agastaches (*Agastache* spp.), asters (*Symphyotrichum, Doellingeria,* and *Ionactis* spp., formerly *Aster* spp.), boltonia (*Boltonia asteroides*), goldenrods (*Solidago* spp.), heleniums (*Helenium autumnale*), tall rudbeckias (*Rudbeckia* spp.), ironweeds (*Vernonia* spp.), Joe-Pye weeds (*Eutrochium* and *Eupatoriadelphus* spp., formerly *Eupatorium* spp.), and sunflowers (*Helianthus* spp.). Do not postpone the operation further, since the process delays bud formation, and cutting back too late in the season can mean that plants do not have enough time to bloom before fall frost.

Cutting back plants in early summer helps prevent many fall-blooming perennials from flopping and also increases the number of flowers produced. Shearing plants after flowers are finished can encourage repeat bloom. Photo by Neil Soderstrom; design by Leigh Sands.

Pinching. Pinching out the tips of stems is another way to encourage branching, sturdier stems, and more flowers. Try it with beebalms (*Monarda* spp.), shorter species of coreopsis such as lance-leaved tickseed (*Coreopsis lanceolata*) and thread-leaved coreopsis (*C. verticillata*), purple and yellow coneflowers (*Echinacea* spp. and *Ratibida* spp.), Allegheny stonecrop (*Hylotelephium telephioides*, formerly *Sedum telephioides*), and wild petunias (*Ruellia* spp.).

Shearing and cutting back. There are two reasons to shear or cut back perennials. Some will rebloom if the plants are sheared after the main flush of flowers has faded. Thread-leaved coreopsis (*Coreopsis verticillata*) is an excellent candidate for shearing, but also try this technique with purple coneflowers (*Echinacea purpurea*) and rudbeckias or orange coneflowers (*Rudbeckia* spp.). Shearing off spent flowers will also neaten the clumps. Try this with spring-blooming moss phlox (*Phlox subulata*), for example. Cutting back plants close to the ground after they have finished flowering is another useful technique for encouraging fresh, new leaves and more compact, non-flopping growth to form, even if the plant will not rebloom. Spiderworts (*Tradescantia* spp.), beebalms (*Monarda* spp.), and queen of the prairie (*Filipendula rubra*) will all respond with new foliage when sheared.

Deadheading. Removing flowers as they fade is an effective way to lengthen the bloom season, as it prevents seeds from forming and encourages the formation of new buds and flowers. Deadheading works with coneflowers (*Echinacea* and *Rudbeckia*

Many perennials and grasses benefit from being divided regularly. If the growth in the center of the clump dies out altogether or looks weak and unhealthy, that is a sign that a plant needs dividing. In this case, dig the clump, discard the unhealthy growth at the center, and then replant the sections of healthy growth on the outside. In general, the best time to dig and divide perennials is when they are growing vegetatively. That means dividing spring-blooming perennials from late summer to fall. Dig and divide plants that bloom from midsummer to frost in spring.

Do not dig or otherwise disturb taprooted perennials such as butterfly weed (*Asclepias tuberosa*), as taprooted plants generally resent disturbance once they are established. One way to propagate any flower is to move self-sown seedlings when they are still quite small. They are easy to dig and replant with a trowel and can generally be moved without difficulty. Another option is to slice off a section from the edge of a clump.

spp.), coreopsis (*Coreopsis* spp.), Stokes' aster (*Stokesia laevis*), and many other species. Balance deadheading with leaving seedheads on the plants, though, since seeds are an important source of food for overwintering birds and other animals. Drifts of seedheads also are attractive in the winter garden.

Color from Spring to Fall

Having flowers every day of the growing season is the goal of nearly everyone who gardens. It is also one of the reasons why long-blooming annuals such as impatiens and marigolds are so popular. With perennials, the secret is selection. To plant a garden that features flowers to enjoy all season long, start by selecting two or three perennials from each of the seasonal sections that follow. Again, keep in mind that bloom times are approximate. It also pays to experiment with sites. Sometimes giving a plant a little more sun or shade, adding extra organic matter, or even planting on a high spot that provides better drainage can make all the difference.

Spring: March to May

The species listed here bloom soon after the soil begins to warm up. Unless otherwise noted, all grow in average moist, well-drained soil and full sun to partial shade.

Eastern blue star flower (*Amsonia tabernaemontana*). Photo by Neil Soderstrom; U.S. Botanic Garden.

Amsonias (*Amsonia* spp.). Eastern blue star flower (*A. tabernaemontana*) bears clusters of star-shaped blue flowers on dense, mounding, 1- to 3-foot plants that spread as far. The leaves turn yellow in fall. Plants are best in moist soil, tolerate wet conditions, endure some drought, and are suitable for rain gardens. Har-

🍃 Spring Ephemerals

Many spring wildflowers produce flowers and foliage, set seed, and then die back very early in the season, generally by early summer. Collectively called spring ephemerals, plants such as Virginia bluebells (*Mertensia virginica*), bloodroot (*Sanguinaria canadensis*), and spring beauties (*Claytonia virginica*) are typically thought of as shade plants because they are often found growing in wooded areas. Many spring ephemerals also grow in full sun, especially if the soil is rich and moist, since even in shade gardens they do most of their growing in full sun, before overhead trees leaf out. See "Wildflowers for Spring" on p. 236 for more information on native spring ephemerals.

White-flowered moss phlox (*Phlox subulata* 'Snowflake'). Photo by Barbara Ellis.

diness: Zones 3 to 9. Thread-leaved blue star (*A. hubrectii*), native to Arkansas and Oklahoma, bears very pale blue flowers on 3-foot plants and features stunning gold fall foliage. Hardiness: Zones 6 to 9.

Iris, zigzag (*Iris brevicaulis*). This species thrives in wet soil but also grows in rich, moist, well-drained conditions. Plants bear showy violet-blue flowers in spring among clumps of arching, strap-shaped, 1- to 1½-foot leaves. Zigzag iris is one of the Louisiana irises, five closely related species crossed to create a large group of hybrids that thrive in wet to constantly moist soil. *I. brevicaulis* is one of the hardiest parents of the Louisianas. Hardiness: Zones 4 to 8.

Phlox (*Phlox* spp.). Popular moss phlox (*P. subulata*) forms rounded, 4- to 6-inch-tall mounds of needle-like evergreen leaves topped by pink, blue, lavender, purple, or white flowers. Plants spread 2 or more feet. They require well-drained soil, tolerate drought, and

remain most compact and bloom best with full sun. Hardiness: Zones 3 to 9. Downy or prairie phlox (*P. pilosa*) bears fragrant clusters of pale pink to lavender flowers on 1- to 2-foot plants that also prefer dry sandy or rocky to average well-drained soil. Hardiness: Zones 5 to 8.

Sage, lyre-leaf (*Salvia lyrata*). This spring-blooming salvia bears white, pale blue, or pale purple flowers above lobed leaves. Plants are 18 inches tall in bloom and spread to 1 foot. They also self-sow to form a dense ground cover. A site in average to moist soil is ideal, but plants also tolerate drought. 'Knockout' features burgundy foliage. Hardiness: Zones 6 to 9.

Sisyrinchium (*Sisyrinchium* spp.). Commonly known as blue-eyed grasses, these lovely spring flowers actually belong to the iris family. Narrow-leaved blue-eyed grass (*S. angustifolium*) produces clumps of grassy leaves that are usually 12 inches tall but can reach 20 inches. Clumps spread to about 1 foot, and the plants self-sow if conditions suit. Plants produce clusters of small, blue, six-petaled flowers with yellow

Narrow-leaved blue-eyed grass (*Sisyrinchium angusti-folium*). Photo by Neil Soderstrom; Adkins Arboretum.

Blue wild indigo (*Baptisia australis*). Photo by Neil Soderstrom; Kathleen Nelson garden.

centers. Give them consistently moist, well-drained soil. They can survive periodic flooding and are suitable for rain gardens; established plants tolerate some drought. Hardiness: Zones 4 to 9. Coastal or eastern blue-eyed grass (*S. atlanticum*) is similar but requires moist to wet soil. Hardiness: Zones 5 to 9.

Late Spring to Early Summer: May to June or Early July

As days lengthen and the soil warms, more and more natives come into bloom. The plants listed here thrive in soil that ranges from dry to moist but well drained. All need full sun to part sun.

Baptisias, wild indigos (*Baptisia* spp.). Blue wild indigo (*B. australis*) produces handsome clumps of blue-green leaves and showy spikes of purplish blue to blue flowers that are followed by blue-black seed pods. Plants are 3 to 4 feet tall and with time form clumps that are as wide. They tolerate drought as well as brief flooding, making them suitable for rain gardens. Wild indigo (*B. tinctoria*), also called horsefly weed and rattleweed, bears yellow flowers and blooms slightly after blue wild indigo on similar-size plants. Several species native to the Southeast, although not necessarily to the Chesapeake Bay watershed, are great garden plants, including white-flowered *B. alba*, yellow-flowered *B. sphaerocarpa* (including the cultivar 'Screaming Yellow'), and pale yellow *B.* × 'Carolina Moonlight', a hybrid of these two species. All baptisias have taproots and dislike being dug after planting. Hardiness: Zones 3 or 4 to 8 or 9 for all.

False lupine, Carolina (*Thermopsis villosa*, formerly *T. caroliniana*). This handsome native bears dense spikes of showy pea-shaped flowers in shades from rich to pale creamy yellow. Plants range from 3 to 6 feet and form good-size 2- to 3-foot-wide clumps with time. They need rich, well-drained soil. Hardiness: Zones 3 to 9.

Iris, blue flag (*Iris versicolor*). Also called harlequin blue flag, this native iris forms clumps of strap-shaped leaves that are 2 to 2½ feet tall and wide. Plants produce violet-blue flowers in late spring or early summer. Normally this is a species for wet soils, and it will grow along pond edges in 2 to 4 inches of standing water. It also grows in rich, consistently moist soil in garden beds. Hardiness: Zones 3 to 9. Southern blue flag (*I. virginica*) is a similar species that needs boggy to wet soil and can be grown in ponds and water gardens. Hardiness: Zones 5 to 9.

Lupine, sundial (*Lupinus perennis*). Spikes of lavender-blue, pealike flowers characterize this 2- to 3-foot native that spreads to about 1 foot. Plants have palmate leaves divided into 7 to 9 leaflets arranged like the fingers on a hand. They thrive in dry to average soil and self-sow with enthusiasm in sandy soil. Hardiness: Zones 4 to 9.

Foxglove beardtongue (*Penstemon digitalis*). Photo by Nancy Ondra.

Penstemons (*Penstemon* spp.). Also called beardtongues, these snapdragon relatives are grown for their erect racemes or panicles of tube- or funnel-shaped, two-lipped flowers. Foxglove beardtongue (*P. digitalis*) bears erect panicles of white flowers above semi-evergreen leaves. Plants are 3 to 5 feet tall and form 1½-foot-wide clumps. 'Husker Red' features white flowers with deep-maroon-colored leaves. They self-sow and also tolerate drought. Hardiness: Zones 3 to 8. Eastern smooth beardtongue (*P. laevigatus*) is a similar species with white to purplish pink flowers that thrives in moist soil. Hardiness: Zones 5 to 8 or 9. Hairy beardtongue (*P. hirsutus*) bears lavender to white flowers on 1- to 3-foot

stems. Plants thrive in dry, poor soil. Dwarf hairy beardtongue (*P. hirsutus* var. *pygmaeus*) is only 4 inches tall and comes true from seed. Hardiness: Zones 3 to 9.

Ohio spiderwort (*Tradescantia ohiensis*). Photo by Barbara Ellis.

Spiderwort, Ohio (*Tradescantia ohiensis*). Also called blue jacket, this species produces grassy, 2- to 3-foot-tall clumps of blue-gray leaves that spread to about 1½ feet. Plants are topped by blue flowers from late spring into summer. The species and the tough, popular cultivar 'Mrs Loewer' thrive in full sun to light shade and dry to average soils. Many hybrids with native midwestern species are available. Cut plants to the ground when the main flush of flowers has finished. Hardiness: Zones 4 to 9.

Stokes' aster (*Stokesia laevis*). Native from North Carolina through Louisiana, this nearly native garden perennial thrives in the heat and humidity characteristic of southeastern summers. Plants bear showy, 4-inch-wide, daisylike flowers with petals that are ragged on the outer tips in shades of lavender-blue to purple. They are 1 to 2 feet tall and form 1½-foot clumps. Plants tolerate some drought and can be used in rain gardens, but well-drained soil is essential in winter. Hardiness: Zones 5 to 9.

Thimbleweed, tall or eastern (*Anemone virginiana*). This dainty wildflower bears 1-inch-wide, white

Tall or eastern thimbleweed (*Anemone virginiana*). Photo by Neil Soderstrom; Kathleen Nelson garden.

Spotted beebalm (*Monarda punctata*). Photo by Neil Soderstrom; Owen Brown Interfaith Center.

flowers with yellow centers on 1- to 2-foot-tall stems. Clumps spread to about 1½ feet. Plants grow in dry to moist soil and are not as aggressive as most other herbaceous anemones. Hardiness: Zones 2 to 8.

Summer: June to September

By early summer, the landscape is alive with flowers. Areas with wet soil typically lag behind drier sites because the soil remains cold later in the season. (This also is true when clay soil is compared with sandy soil. Clay warms up more slowly in spring, and flowers lag as a result.) By early summer, though, there are plenty of wildflowers that prefer soppy sites. In this section plants that thrive in average soil are listed separately from those that need wet conditions.

Dry to Average Soil
Unless noted otherwise in the individual entries, the plants in this section thrive in a range of conditions, from dry to average garden soil that is moist but well drained. All need full sun to part sun.

Beebalm, spotted (*Monarda punctata*). Also called spotted horsemint and dotted beebalm, this relative of popular scarlet beebalm (*M. didyma*) is a 2-foot-tall biennial or short-lived perennial that bears clusters of two-lipped yellow flowers at the tops of the stems along with showy pinkish or purplish bracts. Plants spread to 1 foot, prefer dry soil, and self-sow best in sandy conditions. Wild beebalm or bergamot (*M. fistulosa*) is a 2- to 4-foot-tall species that spreads to 2 or 3 feet. This species bears pink or lavender flowers and also prefers poor, somewhat dry soil. Both species have aromatic foliage that can be used in tea, and flowers are very popular with butterflies. Hardiness: Zones 3 to 8 or 9.

Butterfly weed (*Asclepias tuberosa*). This taprooted perennial produces clusters of brilliant orange flowers in mid- to late summer on 2-foot-tall plants that form 2-foot-wide clumps. Plants need well-drained soil and full sun to part sun. They resent being moved once they are planted. Like other milkweeds (*Asclepias* spp.), butterfly weed is an important food

Butterfly weed (*Asclepias tuberosa*). Photo by Neil Soderstrom; Adkins Arboretum.

plant of monarch butterfly larvae. The flowers also attract many other species of butterflies and insects. Yellow-flowered forms, including 'Hello Yellow', also are available. Hardiness: Zones 3 to 9.

Purple coneflowers (*Echinacea* spp.). Photo by Neil Soderstrom; New York Botanical Garden.

Coneflowers, purple (*Echinacea* spp.). Also simply called echinaceas, these tough, drought-tolerant natives attract butterflies, birds, and beneficial insects to the garden. (Hybrids, especially double-flowered forms, may be less attractive to pollinating insects and birds.) Goldfinches are among the birds that feed on the seedheads during winter. All tolerate heat, humidity, and poor soil. Eastern purple cone-

flower (*E. purpurea*) is best known. Plants range from 2 to 5 feet tall, spread to about 2 feet, and produce showy, daisylike flowers with drooping pink, purplish pink, or white petals surrounding orange-brown cones. The Mt. Cuba Center in Delaware has evaluated many of the available cultivars. Some of the best for the Chesapeake Bay watershed include 'Pica Bella', 'Elton Knight', and 'Fatal Attraction', all with pink petals and orange cones on plants ranging from 2 to 3 feet tall and 2 to 2½ feet wide. The center also recommended 'White Fragrant Angel', with white petals and orange cones, and 'CBG Cone 2'/Pixie Meadowbrite, a compact selection that reaches 22 inches tall and spreads to 24 inches. Mt. Cuba also evaluated hybrids featuring new, non-standard colors and recommended yellow-flowered 'Sunrise', orange-petaled 'Tiki Torch', and 'Coconut Lime', with double, creamy green flowers. While all echinaceas thrive in well-drained soil, hybrids are especially demanding of very well-drained conditions in winter. For best results, plant coneflowers, especially hybrids, in late spring or early summer. Look for plants that are not yet flowering, or cut all bloom stalks down to the crown of the plant before planting. This encourages the plant's taproots to become established, which is essential for winter survival. Note that seeds sown by hybrids will not resemble the parent plants. Hardiness: Zones 4 to 9. Pale purple coneflower (*Echinacea pallida*) ranges from 2 to 3 feet tall, spreads to 1½ feet, and bears flowers with very long, narrow, spidery pink petals around a darker cone. Hardiness: Zones 3 to 10. Yellow purple coneflower (*E. paradoxa*), native to the south central United States, bears flowers with yellow petals and dark brown centers on 2- to 3-foot plants that spread 1½ feet. This nearly native species has been used to produce many of the new hybrids. Like other coneflowers, it requires good soil drainage. Hardiness: Zones 5 to 9.

Coneflowers, yellow (*Ratibida* spp.). Prairie or yellow coneflower (*R. pinnata*) is also commonly called gray-headed or prairie-pinnate coneflower. Plants bear showy, daisylike flowers with yellow petals that curve downward surrounding a rounded brown to grayish disk. Plants are 3 to 6 feet tall and spread to about 2 feet. They tolerate drought as well as poor soil in addition to average garden soil. Upright prairie coneflower (*R. columnifera*), a nearly native species found in states surrounding the Chesapeake Bay region, is also called Mexican hat. It bears flowers with tall, columnar centers surrounded by yellow petals or dark maroon petals edged in yellow. Hardiness: Zones 4 to 9.

(left) Tall coreopsis (*Coreopsis tripteris*). Photo by Neil Soderstrom; U.S. Botanic Garden.

(right) Common or large-flower tickseed (*Coreopsis grandiflora*). Photo by Neil Soderstrom; Gilbertie's Nursery.

Coreopsis (*Coreopsis* spp.). Also called tickseeds, these long-blooming perennials tolerate a wide range of conditions in the garden. Common or large-flower tickseed (*C. grandiflora*), a short-lived perennial often grown as an annual, bears showy single, semidouble, or double daisylike flowers with ragged petal tips. Plants grow to 2 feet tall and wide and self-sow freely. Plants tolerate heat, humidity, and drought. Many cultivars are available, including 'Early Sunrise', with double flowers. Hardiness: Zones 4 to 9. Lance-leaved tickseed (*C. lanceolata*), also called sand tickseed, is similar and thrives in dry or sandy soil. Hardiness: Zones 4 to 9. Tall coreopsis (*C. tripteris*), also called tall tickseed, is a robust species, ranging from 2 to 8 feet tall and wide at maturity. Plants bear yellow daisies with rounded petal edges. In dry soil, plants are best with light shade, but they grow in full sun with adequate soil moisture. They also tolerate damp soil. Hardiness: Zones 3 to 8. Thread-leaved coreopsis (*C. verticillata*) is a popular, long-blooming, 1- to 2-foot-tall species that spreads as far. Plants produce an abundance of small yellow daisylike flowers over mounding plants with fine-textured leaves. 'Moonbeam' bears pale yellow flowers. 'Zagreb' produces bright golden yellow flowers on 1½-foot plants. All coreopsis rebloom when deadheaded, but this technique is especially effective with thread-leaved coreopsis: Shear the plants after the first flush of bloom begins to fade, and they will rebloom from late summer into fall. Hardiness: Zones 3 to 9. Lobed tickseed (*C. auriculata*) is a low-growing species that ranges from 6 to 8 inches and spreads as far. It produces golden yellow daisy flowers in early summer. The plants are best in rich, moist, well-drained soil and do not tolerate drought as well as most coreopsis. Hardiness: Zones 4 to 9.

Showy evening primrose (*Oenothera speciosa*). Photo by Neil Soderstrom; New York Botanical Garden.

Evening primroses (*Oenothera* spp.). Sundrops or narrow-leaved evening primrose (*O. fruticosa*) bring showy, cup-shaped yellow flowers to the garden on tough, reliable plants that easily tolerate hot, dry sites as well as average garden soil. Plants are approximately 18 to 24 inches tall and wide. 'Fireworks' features bronze foliage and red stems and flower buds. Foliage is burgundy in winter. Showy evening primrose (*O. speciosa*), also called pink ladies, is a 1- to 2-foot-tall species that bears pink, cup-shaped flowers. Plants can spread very aggressively by rhizomes and self-sowing to form large drifts. It can be used as a ground cover. Hardiness: Both species, Zones 4 to 9.

Goldenrods (*Solidago* spp.) While most goldenrods do not show color until late summer, two species begin blooming in midsummer: early goldenrod (*S. juncea*) and showy goldenrod (*S. speciosa*). Both bear plumelike, golden yellow flowerheads. Plants are 3 to 4 feet tall and spread to about 3 feet. Hardiness: Zones 3 to 8. For more information, see "Goldenrods" under "Late Summer to Fall" on p. 195.

Liatris (*Liatris* spp.). Commonly called blazing stars or gayfeathers, these perennials are native to eastern and central North America. Several species are native to the Chesapeake Bay watershed, two of which commonly bloom in summer. Liatris plants bear spikes or racemes of pink, purple-pink, or white flowers that are attractive to butterflies. The tiny flowers are arranged in buttonlike flowerheads borne along a central stem. Spike liatris (*L. spicata*), the most common species available in garden centers, is also called dense blazing star. It bears fuzzy, 2- to 5-foot wands of pinkish purple flowers and spreads to about 2 feet. It is more tolerant of moist to wet soil than other *Liatris* species, and it generally is the first to bloom. Plants grow best in average moist, well-drained soil but also tolerate drought. While moist soil is fine during the growing season, wet soil in winter is generally fatal. *L. squarrosa* (scaly blazing star) is a 1- to 3-foot-tall

species with pinkish purple flowers. It is also suited for dry rocky or sandy soil. Hardiness: Zones 3 to 8 or 9 for both species. See "Liatris" under "Late Summer to Fall" for information on later-blooming species.

Milkweed, horsetail (*Asclepias verticillata*). Also called whorled milkweed, this relative of butterfly weed (*A. tuberosa*) is a tough, taprooted plant that tolerates drought, although it grows in any well-drained soil. The 1- to 3-foot plants, which are an important host to monarch butterfly larvae, produce clusters of tiny white flowers and spread to 2 or more feet by runners, which can be pulled up or left to wander. All parts are poisonous to livestock, so do not allow this plant in pastures. Hardiness: Zones 4 to 8.

Clustered mountain mint (*Pycnanthemum muticum*). Photo by Neil Soderstrom; design by Kathleen Nelson.

Mountain mints (*Pycnanthemum* spp.). Essential plants for butterfly gardeners, mountain mints also attract beneficial insects. The plants feature aromatic leaves that smell of peppermint and spicier herbs like oregano. The two-lipped flowers are carried in rounded clusters above silvery green leaves. Hoary mountain mint (*P. incanum*) bears white flowers mottled with purple and grows in moist to dry soil. Clustered mountain mint (*P. muticum*), also 3 to 4 feet tall, bears white to violet flowers with silvery bracts beneath the clusters. Clustered mountain mint is less drought tolerant than other mountain mints. Both species spread to 4 or more feet and are hardy in Zones 3 to 9. Other species native to the Chesapeake Bay watershed include southern mountain mint (*P. pycnanthemoides*), narrow-leaved mountain mint (*P. tenuifolium*), and Virginia mountain mint (*P. virginianum*).

Onion, nodding (*Allium cernuum*). This is an ornamental onion with delicate, rounded clusters of small pink or lavender-pink flowers in early summer. Flowers are borne on individual 12- to 15-inch-tall stems that arch downward at the tips, and plants form 6-inch-wide clumps of grassy leaves that smell of onions when bruised. They thrive in sun to part shade. Established clumps tolerate drought. Hardiness: Zones 3 to 9.

Sunflower or smooth oxeye (*Heliopsis helianthoides*) with wild beebalm (*Monarda fistulosa*). Photo by Barbara Ellis.

Oxeye, smooth (*Heliopsis helianthoides*). Also called sunflower oxeye, this is a shrub-size, 3- to 6-foot-tall perennial that spreads from 3 to 4 feet. The blooms resemble true sunflowers (*Helianthus* spp.). Plants produce an abundance of golden yellow, daisy flowers with darker gold centers on stems above the foliage. They are happiest in average moist, well-drained garden soil but also tolerate some drought. 'Ballerina'

and 'Summer Sun' bear semi-double flowers. Hardiness: Zones 4 to 9.

Poppy mallow, purple (*Callirhoe involucrata*). This sprawling, nearly native species is from the central and western United States. Plants have deeply lobed leaves and reach about 1 foot in height. They spread to 3 feet and can clamber over the ground or up through nearby shrubs and perennials. Cup-shaped, magenta pink flowers with white centers appear over a long season in summer. Leaves are deeply lobed. Hardiness: Zones 4 to 8.

Wild quinine (*Parthenium integrifolium*). Photo by Neil Soderstrom; U.S. Botanic Garden.

Quinine, wild (*Parthenium integrifolium*). Also called American feverfew, this 2- to 4-foot-tall perennial spreads 1 to 2 feet. Plants bear flat-topped clusters of small, white, buttonlike flowers in summer. The leaves are aromatic when crushed. Hardiness: Zones 4 to 8.

Rattlesnake master (*Eryngium yuccifolium*). Also called button eryngo, this architectural-looking perennial produces 2-foot-wide clumps of strappy, slightly spiny leaves that resemble yuccas (*Yucca* spp.). Round, white to pale blue, thistlelike flowers are borne in branched clusters atop erect 4- to

Rattlesnake master (*Eryngium yuccifolium*). Photo by Neil Soderstrom; design by Kathleen Nelson.

5-foot-tall stems. Plants thrive in dry, sandy soil and are taprooted and drought tolerant. While they also grow in average to rich well-drained soil, the clumps tend to flop over if the soil is too rich or too moist. Hardiness: Zones 5 to 9.

American senna (*Senna hebecarpa*). Photo by Neil Soderstrom; Owen Brown Interfaith Center.

Senna, Maryland (*Senna marilandica*, formerly *Cassia marilandica*). A plant for meadow gardens or the back of the border, Maryland or wild senna bears clusters of yellow, pealike flowers followed by black seed pods that feed quail and other wildlife. Plants have delicate-looking, ferny leaves but are tough and strong-stemmed. They range from 3 to 6 or more feet tall and form shrubby, 3- to 4-foot-wide clumps. They thrive in ordinary moist, well-drained garden soil and self-sow where happy. American senna (*S. hebecarpa*, formerly *C. hebecarpa*) is a similar native with slightly

larger leaves and more flowers. The main difference between the two is the seedpods: Pods of Maryland senna remain closed when ripe, while those of American senna open to release the seeds. Both species are hardy in Zones 4 to 9.

Spurge, flowering (*Euphorbia corollata*). This native wildflower produces masses of small, white flowerheads with yellow centers atop ½- to 3-foot-tall stems. The plants have narrow leaves and resemble baby's breath (*Gypsophila paniculata*). They grow in almost any type of soil, are quite drought tolerant, and prefer dry, poor, rocky conditions. Plants grow from taproots and gradually form small clumps. Hardiness: Zones 3 to 10.

Stonecrop, Allegheny (*Hylotelephium telephioides*, formerly *Sedum telephioides*). Also called Allegheny sedum, this easy-to-grow perennial bears flat-topped clusters of pale pink flowers from midsummer to fall. The blooms attract butterflies and bees galore. Plants are about 2 feet tall and nearly as wide. They grow in sun to part shade and ordinary well-drained garden soil, but they are best in dry soil. Clumps tend to flop if the soil is too rich. Hardiness: Zones 4 to 9.

Wild petunias (*Ruellia* spp.) These heat-loving perennials with trumpet-shaped flowers resemble annual petunias (*Petunia* spp.). Each flower opens for only a day. Carolina wild petunia (*R. caroliniensis*) bears light blue flowers on sprawling, 1- to 2-foot-tall plants. Plants grow in sun to light shade, in average well-drained soil. Hardiness: Zones 6 to 9. Fringe-leaved wild petunia (*R. humilis*) is very similar. Hardiness: Zones 5 to 9.

Yucca (*Yucca filamentosa*). Also called Adam's needle, this is a tough, evergreen shrub that resembles

Variegated yucca (*Yucca filamentosa* 'Golden Sword'). Photo by Barbara Ellis.

Beebalm (*Monarda didyma*). Photo by Neil Soderstrom; Emily Dickinson Museum.

a perennial. Plants produce clumps of strap-shaped leaves that are 3 feet tall and wide. In summer, branched, 8-foot-tall flower stalks appear above the foliage with hundreds of nodding, bell-shaped, creamy white flowers. Plants thrive in average, well-drained soil but have deep, fleshy taproots and are extremely drought tolerant. The species has green leaves, but attractive variegated forms are available, including 'Color Guard', 'Golden Sword', and 'Bright Edge'. Hardiness: Zones 4 to 9.

Moist to Wet Soil

Unless otherwise noted, these plants thrive in soil that ranges from moist but well-drained to wet. All need full sun to part sun.

Beebalm (*Monarda didyma*). Also called Oswego tea and red bergamot, this is a popular mint-family plant with the characteristic square stems, aromatic mint-scented leaves, and rounded clusters of two-lipped flowers that are hummingbird magnets. Plants are typically 3 to 4 feet tall and spread to several feet via creeping rhizomes, especially in rich, moist soil. Red is the typical color, but pink-flowered cultivars are available, as are dwarf forms, including 20-inch-tall 'ACrade'/Grand Parade, which spreads to 2 feet.

'Jacob Cline' bears red flowers and resists powdery mildew. Hardiness: Zones 4 to 9.

Culver's root (*Veronicastrum virginicum*). Photo by Neil Soderstrom; New York Botanical Garden.

Culver's root (*Veronicastrum virginicum*). This tough, stately perennial ranges from 4 to 7 feet tall, spreading to 4 feet, and is suitable for a meadow or the back of a border. Plants bear erect spikes of small, densely packed flowers in shades of white to pale blue from mid- to late summer. They thrive in moist, well-drained to wet soil. Plants also will grow in partial shade, although inadequate sun leaves them more prone to flopping. Hardiness: Zones 3 to 9.

Cup plant (*Silphium perfoliatum*). This robust, somewhat coarsely textured perennial ranges from 4 to 8 feet tall and forms robust, 3-foot-wide clumps. The common name refers to the fact that leaves form a cup where they are attached to the square stem.

Cup plant (*Silphium perfoliatum*). Photo by Neil Soderstrom; Green Spring Gardens.

Cardinal flower *(Lobelia cardinalis)*. Photo by Neil Soderstrom; Owen Brown Interfaith Center.

Plants thrive in average moist to wet soil but tolerate some drought once established. They are quite large for the average perennial garden and are more suited to meadows, pond edges, and other wild areas. Hardiness: Zones 3 to 9.

Canada lily (*Lilium canadense*). Photo by Neil Soderstrom.

Lilies (*Lilium* spp.). While hybrid lilies are available nearly everywhere plants are sold, native species are harder to find. Canada lily (*L. canadense*) bears branched clusters of downward-pointing, widely trumpet-shaped yellow flowers with maroon spots. Hardiness: Zones 3 to 8. Turk's cap lily (*L. superbum*) produces racemes of 3-inch-wide orange flowers spotted with maroon. Hardiness: Zones 5 to 8. Both species require rich, consistently moist but well-drained soil. Full sun is best, but afternoon shade may help plants cope with heat. Both species are 3 to 5 feet tall. They have rhizomatous bulbs and will spread in the right site.

Lobelia (*Lobelia* spp.). These are relatives of popular edging lobelia (*L. erinus*), a perennial grown as an annual. Cardinal flower (*L. cardinalis*) is an eye-catching, 2- to 4-foot perennial with showy racemes of densely packed, brilliant red, two-lipped flowers from summer into early fall. Where happy, plants spread by short rhizomes to 2 feet. Great blue lobelia (*L. siphilitica*) bears racemes of brilliant blue flowers on 2- to 3-foot plants that spread to 1½ feet. Pale-spike lobelia (*L. spicata*) bears pale lavender to white flowers on 2-foot plants. This last species grows in moist and wet soil but also tolerates drier conditions than the other two. All are short lived but do self-sow in ideal conditions. The flowers attract butterflies and hummingbirds. Plants of all three species tolerate moist shade, and they also are suitable for planting in bogs and wetlands. In much of the Chesapeake Bay region, a site with high dappled shade or afternoon shade may help plants cope with heat. Hardiness: Zones 3 to 8 for all species listed.

Milkweed, swamp (*Asclepias incarnata*). Another essential plant for butterfly lovers, swamp milkweed supports monarch butterfly larvae and attracts a wide variety of butterflies to its showy, rounded clusters of pink, mauve, or white flowers. The plants, which are taprooted and are best not moved once planted in the garden, are 4 to 5 feet tall and spread from 2 to 3

Swamp milkweed (*Asclepias incarnata*). Photo by Nancy Ondra.

Garden or summer phlox (*Phlox paniculata* 'Bright Eyes'). Photo by Neil Soderstrom; Brooklyn Botanic Garden.

feet. They thrive in wet soil but also tolerate average moist, well-drained garden conditions. Hardiness: Zones 5 to 8.

Obedient plant (*Physostegia virginiana*). Photo by Neil Soderstrom; Hannelore Soderstrom garden.

Obedient plant (*Physostegia virginiana*). This fast-spreading summer bloomer is best planted in moist to wet soil and given room to spread. Plants, which also grow in average well-drained soil, bear spikes of two-lipped pink, purple-pink, or white flowers. The common name refers to the fact that each individual flower can be repositioned, as if hinged, around the central stalk. Plants range from 3 to 4 feet tall and need dividing every few years to keep them from taking over the garden. 'Miss Manners' is a slow-spreading, white-flowered, 2-foot-tall selection. 'Vivid', another clump-former, bears pink flowers on 2- to 3-foot plants. Hardiness: Zones 2 to 9.

Phlox (*Phlox* spp.). These beloved perennials are among the highlights of summer flower borders. Many of the garden hybrids—especially the mildew-resistant ones—are the result of crosses among three native species. Thick-leaved or Carolina phlox (*P. carolina*) bears loose clusters of pink to purple flowers on 2- to 3-foot plants that are resistant to powdery mildew and grow in dry to wet soil in sun or partial sun. 'Miss Lingard' bears white flowers. Hardiness: Zones 3 to 8. Meadow phlox or wild sweet William (*P. maculata*) bears rounded clusters of fragrant, pinkish purple flowers on 2- to 3-foot plants. The plants thrive in average moist, well-drained soil and are resistant to powdery mildew. They bloom best in sun but also tolerate some shade. Garden or summer phlox (*P. paniculata*) bears rounded clusters of pink, lavender, or white flowers on 3- to 4-foot plants that spread from 2 to 3 feet. Pink-flowered 'Jenna' and white-flowered 'David' are two cultivars that resist powdery mildew. Plants need rich, moist, well-drained soil; will survive brief flooding; and bloom best in full sun to light shade. Hardiness: Zones 3 to 8.

Queen of the prairie (*Filipendula rubra*). Grown for its frothy pink flowers that resemble cotton candy, queen of the prairie ranges from 6 to 8 feet tall and spreads to 3 or 4 feet. Plants thrive in constantly moist to wet soil and full sun, although they tolerate some shade. Shade during the hottest part of the day is best in southern zones. If the soil dries out, the leaves scorch. If this happens, cut the plants back hard to encourage new growth. Plants will self-sow if conditions suit. Hardiness: Zones 3 to 8.

Late Summer to Fall: August to October

As nights become longer, late-season natives begin to decorate roadsides, meadows, and fall gardens.

Dry to Average, Moist but Well-Drained Soil

Unless noted otherwise, these plants thrive in a range of conditions, from dry to average garden soil that is moist but well drained. All need full sun to part sun.

Blue giant hyssop
(*Agastache foeniculum*).
Photo by Neil Soderstrom;
Brooklyn Botanic Garden.

Agastache (*Agastache* spp.). Also called giant hyssops, these perennials in the mint family have the characteristic square stems and leaves that are aromatic when crushed. Agastaches bear small, two-lipped flowers from midsummer into early fall. Purple giant hyssop (*A. scrophulariifolia*) bears spikes of rose-purple to purple flowers on 3- to 6-foot-tall plants that spread 2 to 3 feet. Blue giant hyssop (*A. foeniculum*) bears spikes of blue flowers on 2- to

4-foot plants that spread to 3 feet. Both species thrive in average moist but well-drained soil. Blue giant hyssop tolerates drier soil than purple giant hyssop. Hardiness: Zones 4 to 8 or 9 for both species listed.

Asters (*Symphyotrichum* and *Ionactis* spp., formerly *Aster* spp.). Asters are prized plants for meadows and flower borders. Their daisylike blooms attract butterflies and a host of beneficial insects, and their seedheads help feed birds over winter. Most also self-sow. White heath aster (*S. ericoides*, formerly *A. ericoides*) bears clouds of tiny, ½-inch-wide white daisies with yellow centers on 1- to 3-foot plants that self-sow

(top) Smooth blue aster (*Symphyotrichum laeve*). Photo by Neil Soderstrom; New York Botanical Garden.

(bottom) Aromatic aster (*Symphyotrichum oblongifolium* 'October Skies'). Photo by Barbara Ellis; Longwood Gardens.

that tolerates a wide range of soil conditions. Hardiness: Zones 4 to 8. Aromatic aster (*S. oblongifolium*, formerly *A. oblongifolius*) bears masses of 1¼- to 1½-inch daisies with purple to violet-blue petals and yellow centers. The foliage is aromatic when crushed, and plants form rounded mounds that range from 2 to 4 feet tall and spread to 3 feet. Plants bloom from mid to late fall, after most asters have finished flowering. They thrive in dry to average soil and tolerate drought. 'Raydon's Favorite' bears 2-inch flowers on 2- to 3-foot plants. 'October Skies' is a more compact selection, to 18 inches. Hardiness: Zones 5 to 8.

Boltonia (*Boltonia asteroides*) with firecracker bush (*Bouvardia ternifolia*), a native of the Southwest. Photo by Neil Soderstrom; New York Botanical Garden.

and easily spread to several feet by rhizomes. Plants thrive in sandy dry soil as well as in average garden loam. Hardiness: Zones 3 to 10. Calico aster (*S. lateriflorum*, formerly *A. lateriflorus*) is a 3-foot-tall species that spreads as far. Plants bear masses of white or pale purple flowers and tolerate a wide range of well-drained soils as well as drought. 'Lady in Black' features purplish leaves and daisylike flowers with white petals and rose-purple centers. Hardiness: Zones 3 to 8. Hairy white oldfield aster (*S. pilosum*, formerly *A. pilosum*) is a similar white-flowered species. Smooth blue aster (*S. laeve*, formerly *A. laevis*) is another species that tolerates drought and dry, rocky soil but also thrives in average garden soil. Plants bear showy, 1-inch-wide violet-blue flowers with yellow centers on 3- to 4-foot plants that spread from 2 to 3 feet. 'Bluebird' is an especially handsome selection

Boltonia (*Boltonia asteroides*). Also called white doll's daisy and false aster, this robust, clump-forming perennial ranges from 4 to 6 feet and spreads to 4 feet. Plants bear masses of small, white, daisy flowers with yellow centers. They are best with moist, well-drained soil but tolerate dry soil as well as periodic flooding. Cut the plants back by half by the end of June to keep them compact and to reduce flopping. 'Snowbank' is a popular white-flowered selection. 'Pink Beauty' bears pink flowers with yellow centers. Hardiness: Zones 4 to 8.

Gaura (*Gaura lindheimeri*). Also called Lindheimer's beeblossom, this species is native to Texas and Oklahoma but is well suited for the Chesapeake Bay region. Plants produce sprawling clumps of wiry stems decorated with four-petaled, orchidlike flowers. They range from 2 to 5 feet tall and spread to 3 feet. Some selections bloom from late spring to fall, while others begin in late summer. Plants are taprooted, thrive in poor, dry soil, and also tolerate heat and humidity. They can be short lived. Perfect drainage in winter is essential, and a site with sandy soil or along the edge of a wall or raised bed is best. 'Whirling Butterflies' bears pink buds and white flowers. It is more compact than the species. 'Siskiyou Pink' is a popular pink-flowered selection, and 'Benso'/Blushing Butterflies is a compact pink-flowered form. Hardiness: Zones 5 to 9.

Goldenaster, Maryland (*Chrysopsis mariana*). This drought-tolerant native produces loose clusters of showy, yellow, daisy flowers on 2-foot-tall plants that spread to 3 feet. Plants thrive in dry, sandy soils and also grow in average, moist, well-drained conditions. Full sun is best, but plants will grow in partial shade. While individual plants are short lived, they produce colonies of self-sown seedlings if given the right conditions. Hardiness: Zones 4 to 7.

Goldenrods (*Solidago* spp.). A number of goldenrods make handsome additions to fall borders and meadows that offer dry to average, well-drained garden soil. All bear showy, dense clusters of tiny golden yellow flowers that are very attractive to butterflies and a wide range of insects. Gray goldenrod (*S. nemoralis*), also called field or dwarf goldenrod, is a 1-foot-tall species that spreads as far and blooms from midsummer to fall. Plants grow in very poor soil, where few other things survive, and may only reach 6 inches in height. Hardiness: Zones 2 to 9. Anise-scented goldenrod (*S. odora*) is a clump-forming, 2- to 5-foot-tall

Autumn goldenrod (*Solidago sphacelata* 'Golden Fleece'). Photo by Neil Soderstrom; J. Kent McNew garden.

species that spreads to 2 feet. Its leaves smell of licorice when crushed. Plants tolerate partial shade, although they bloom better in sun. They also tolerate drought as well as average moist, well-drained soil. Hardiness: Zones 5 to 9. Seaside goldenrod (*S. sempervirens*) grows in dry to average soil, including sandy dunes, and also tolerates salt spray. Plants are typically 3 feet tall, spreading as far, but they can reach 6 feet in rich, moist, well-drained soil. They bloom from midsummer to fall. Hardiness: Zones 4 to 9. Autumn goldenrod (*S. sphacelata*) is a handsome, 2- to 4-foot-tall species best known in gardens by its cultivar 'Golden Fleece', which features narrow, arching sprays of golden flowers above semievergreen leaves. 'Golden Fleece' is 1 to 2 feet tall and spreads as far. Plants tolerate dry as well as average moist, well-drained soil. Hardiness: Zones 4 to 9. Elm-leaved goldenrod (*S. ulmifolia*) is another relatively low-growing species that is about 3 feet tall and wide and thrives in a variety of well-drained to dry soils. Plants spread by rhizomes to form colonies with time and also tolerate partial shade. Hardiness: Zones 3 to 8.

Helenium (*Helenium autumnale*). Perhaps best known by the unattractive common name sneezeweed, this is a robust 2- to 5-foot-tall perennial that

Helenium (*Helenium autumnale* 'Mardi Gras'). Photo by Barbara Ellis.

bears daisylike flowers with fan-shaped petals that have sharply lobed outer edges. Flowers may be yellow or feature combinations of orange, dark red, copper, soft yellow, and red-bronze. Many cultivars are available. Plants, which spread to 3 feet, thrive in average, well-drained soil, although consistent moisture is best. They also tolerate some drought. Hardiness: Zones 3 to 8. Purplehead sneezeweed (*H. flexuosum*) bears yellow flowers with round brown centers on 1- to 3-foot plants that spread to about 2 feet. Give plants average moist, well-drained soil or somewhat wetter conditions. Hardiness: Zones 5 to 9.

Ironweeds (*Vernonia* spp.). While New York ironweed (*V. noveboracensis*) is a plant of moist to wet soils, one native and one nearly native species grow in average, well-drained garden soil. Both also tolerate drought. Broad-leaved ironweed (*V. glauca*) ranges from 3 to 5 feet and spreads to 4 feet. Plants produce flat-topped clusters of purple flowers in late summer and early fall. Hardiness: Zones 6 to 8. Narrow-leaved ironweed (*V. lettermannii*) is native to rocky flood plains in Oklahoma and Arkansas. In their native habitat, plants need to be able to survive both drought and periodic inundation. They do not survive constantly moist soil. The species and its cul-

tivar 'Iron Butterfly' have very narrow, fine-textured leaves and bear flat-topped clusters of purple flowers on 2- to 3-foot plants that spread as far. Hardiness: Zones 4 to 9.

Joe-Pye weed (*Eupatorium* spp.). Best known as plants of wet soils, a few Joe-Pye weeds grow in average moist but well-drained soil. All are extremely attractive to butterflies and other insects. Hyssop-leaved thoroughwort (*E. hyssopifolium*) bears broad, flat-topped clusters of white flowers that have a texture similar to baby's breath (*Gypsophila paniculata*). Plants are 2 to 3 feet tall and spread to about 1 foot. They thrive in dry, sandy soil but also grow in average well-drained garden conditions. Hardiness: Zones 4 to 8. Sweet-scented Joe-Pye (*E. purpureum*) blooms from midsummer on and bears large, rounded clusters of pinkish purple flowers on 5- to 7-foot-tall plants that spread to 4 or more feet. 'Gateway' is a somewhat compact selection that ranges from 4 to 6 feet, spreads to 5 feet, and bears pink flowers. Hardiness: Zones 4 to 8.

Liatris (*Liatris* spp.). Commonly called blazing stars or gayfeathers, several species of liatris are native to eastern and central North America, including the Chesapeake Bay watershed. Plants bear spikes or racemes of pink, purple-pink, or white flowers that are attractive to butterflies. The tiny flowers are arranged in buttonlike flowerheads borne along a central stem. Eastern blazing star (*L. scariosa* var. *scariosa*), also called tall gayfeather, produces wands of pinkish purple flowers on 2- to 4-foot plants that spread from 1 to 2 feet. They tolerate dry as well as sandy soil and also can survive drought. In addition, they will grow in average well-drained garden soil. Tall or rough blazing star (*L. aspera*) also bears pinkish purple flowers and thrives in poor, sandy soil. Plants are 3 to 5 feet tall,

Grass-leaved blazing star (*Liatris pilosa* var. *pilosa*). Photo by Neil Soderstrom; U.S. Botanic Garden.

(left) Brown-eyed Susan (*Rudbeckia triloba*). Photo by Neil Soderstrom; design by Kathleen Nelson.

(right) Gloriosa daisies, developed from black-eyed Susans (*Rudbeckia hirta*). Photo by Neil Soderstrom; Shore Acres Gardens.

spreading to 2 or 3 feet, and tend to flop in average moist garden soil. Grass-leaved blazing star (*L. pilosa* var. *pilosa*, formerly *L. graminifolia*) is found along the coastal plain and bears pinkish purple flowers on 2- to 3-foot plants that spread about 1 foot. Hardiness: Zones 3 to 8 or 9 for all species listed. See "Liatris" under "Summer" for information on earlier-blooming species.

Rudbeckias (*Rudbeckia* spp.). Also collectively called orange coneflowers, rudbeckias are dependable, easy-to-grow perennials with daisylike flowers that are attractive to butterflies and other insects. Orange coneflower (*R. fulgida*), perhaps the best known, has golden yellow petals with brown centers. Plants are 2 to 3 feet tall and spread to 2 or more feet via rhizomes or self-sowing. 'Goldsturm' is a cultivar of this species. *R. fulgida* var. *fulgida* is a native form that has a longer, later bloom season. All grow in nearly any dry to average soil and also tolerate brief flooding. Black-eyed Susan (*R. hirta*) is a biennial or short-lived perennial with dainty golden yellow daisies that have dark brown centers. It, too, grows in dry to average soil. Gloriosa daisies, grown as annuals or biennials, were hybridized using this species. They produce showy, 5- to 6-inch-wide blooms that feature

petals marked with gold, yellow, maroon, bronze, and brown. Cut-leaved coneflower (*R. laciniata*) has yellow petals with green centers and ranges from 2 to 9 feet tall. Plants can spread 3 to 4 feet. Unlike other rudbeckias, this species prefers average moist or moist, well-drained soil. 'Goldquelle' has double flowers on 3- to 4-foot plants. Brown-eyed Susan (*R. triloba*) is a short-lived, 2- to 3-foot-tall perennial that spreads to about 1½ feet and bears golden yellow daisies with chocolate brown centers. Plants self-sow and need average well-drained, moist soil. Hardiness: Zones 3 to 9 for all species listed.

Sunflowers (*Helianthus* spp.). Best known of these, of course, is annual or common sunflower (*H. annuus*), native to the prairie states but naturalized in the East as well. The species bears 3- to 6-inch-wide flowerheads and heart-shaped leaves. Perennial relatives are ideal for adding late-season color to the garden, and all feed bees, butterflies, and birds. Maximilian sunflower (*H. maximiliani*) is a tough, adaptable plant that ranges from 3 to 10 or more feet and spreads to at least 4 feet. Plants bear masses of 2-

Dwarf willow-leaved sunflower (*H. salicifolius* 'First Light'). Photo by Nancy Ondra.

Hardy ageratum (*Conoclinium coelestinum*) with sedum 'Autumn Joy'. Photo by Neil Soderstrom; design by Andie Phillips.

to 3-inch yellow flowers with yellow centers. Few-leaf sunflower (*H. occidentalis*) is an excellent addition to borders and meadows. Despite also being commonly called western sunflower, this species is native to eastern and central North America. Plants range from 2 to 3 or 4 feet tall and spread to about 4 feet. They bear 2-inch daisylike flowers with golden yellow petals and darker centers on stiff, nearly leafless stems. Willow-leaved sunflower (*H. salicifolius*) is primarily native to the central United States but also has been found in the Chesapeake Bay watershed. Plants range from 6 to 10 feet tall and spread to 3 feet. They bear yellow, 2- to 3-inch, daisylike flowers atop stems with handsome, willowy leaves. 'Low Down' is 20 inches tall and spreads to 30 inches. 'First Light' produces masses of flowers on plants that are only 4 to 5 feet tall. The species listed here all tolerate a wide range of well-drained to dry soils. Cut Maximilian and willow-leaved sunflowers back once or twice before the end of June to encourage branching and control height. Hardiness: Zones 4 to 8 or 9 for all species listed.

Moist to Wet Soil

Unless otherwise noted, these plants thrive in soil that ranges from moist but well drained to wet. All thrive in full sun to part shade.

Ageratum, hardy (*Conoclinium coelestinum*, formerly *Eupatorium coelestinum*). Also called blue mist flower, this hardy perennial resembles annual ageratum or floss flower (*Ageratum houstonianuma*). Plants bear rounded clusters of fuzzy, bluish purple flowers on 2- to 3-foot-tall plants that spread to 3 or more feet. They thrive and spread quickly in moist to wet soil and sun to part shade. Hardiness: Zones 5 to 9.

Asters (*Symphyotrichum* and *Doellingeria* spp., formerly *Aster* spp.). Asters are classic fall flowers, and these species thrive in rich, moist to wet, well-drained soil. All are especially important as late-season food sources for butterflies, including migrating monarchs. New England aster (*S. novae-angliae*, formerly *A. novae-angliae*) is a popular garden perennial that blooms from late summer to after the first frost of fall. Plants bear purple, violet, lavender-blue, and pinkish purple flowers with orange centers on 2- to 5-foot plants that spread 3 feet. Many cultivars are available, including violet-flowered 'Purple Dome' and hot pink 'Vibrant Dome', both of which are 2 feet tall and wide, and classic, brilliant reddish pink 'Alma Pötschke', which reaches 3 to 4 feet tall. Hardiness:

Common boneset (*Eupatorium perfoliatum*). Photo by Neil Soderstrom; Duncan Brine Garden.

New England aster (*Symphyotrichum novae-angliae*) with wrinkle-leaved goldenrod (*Solidago rugosa* 'Fireworks'). Photo by Neil Soderstrom; design by Leigh Sands.

Zones 3 to 8. New York Asters (*S. novi-belgii*, formerly *A. novi-belgii*), also called Michaelmas daisies, are similar but have smooth rather than rough and hairy stems. They also are generally shorter. Plants bear blue-violet, purple, pink, and white flowers on 3- to 4-foot plants that spread to 3 feet, although many shorter cultivars are available. 'Professor Kippenburg' bears purple flowers on 18-inch plants. Hardiness: Zones 3 to 7. Both New England and New York asters thrive in rich, moist, well-drained soil. Flat-top white aster (*D. umbellata*, formerly *A. umbellatus*) bears white flowers earlier in the season than most asters. Plants range from 3 to 6 feet tall and spread to 3 feet. Although they are best in moist soil, they also tolerate drought. Hardiness: Zones 3 to 8. Cut taller asters back once or twice by July 4 to encourage branching, shorter, sturdier stems and more flowers.

Boneset, common (*Eupatorium perfoliatum*). This 3- to 6-foot-tall member of the aster family bears flat-topped clusters of closely packed, fuzzy white flowerheads from midsummer to fall. Plants form 3- to 4-foot-wide clumps and thrive in a wide range of soils, from moist to wet. Hardiness: Zones 3 to 8.

Wrinkle-leaved goldenrod (*Solidago rugosa* 'Fireworks'). Photo by Barbara Ellis.

Goldenrods (*Solidago* spp.). There are goldenrods for nearly every part of the garden, and sites with moist to wet soil are no exception. All the species listed here thrive in moist, well-drained to wet soil and bear clusters of tiny, densely packed, yellow flowers that attract a rich array of butterflies and insects. Wrinkle-leaved goldenrod (*S. rugosa*) produces branched clusters of flowers atop 2- to 5-foot stems, and plants spread to 3 or more feet. 'Fireworks' produces graceful, arching clusters of flowers on 3- to 4-foot plants and spreads to 3 or more feet. Plants also tolerate both drought and extended flooding. Hardiness: Zones 4 to 8.

Common rose mallow (*Hibiscus moscheutos*). Photo by Neil Soderstrom; New York Botanical Garden.

New York ironweed (*Vernonia noveboracensis*). Photo by Neil Soderstrom; Hannelore Soderstrom garden.

Hibiscus (*Hibiscus* spp.). Also called rose mallows, these are large, sturdy perennials that thrive in moist to wet soil. Both tolerate extended flooding and are suitable for planting along streams and ponds as well as in ordinary moist garden soil. They bear huge, tropical-looking flowers. Scarlet rose mallow (*H. coccineus*) ranges from 3 to 6 feet tall and spreads to about 3 feet. Plants bear scarlet, 3- to 5-inch-wide flowers beginning in midsummer. Common rose mallow (*H. moscheutos*), also called crimson-eyed rose mallow, is a shrubby perennial ranging from 3 to 8 feet tall and 3 or 4 feet wide. Plants bear 8- to 10-inch-wide flowers in shades of pink, red, and white. Many cultivars are available, including 3- to 4-foot-tall 'Kopper King', a hybrid with both *H. coccineus* and *H. moscheutos*, with maroon foliage and light pink flowers with red eyes. The Disco Belle series features pink-, white-, and red-flowered selections on 2½-foot plants. Hardiness: Zones 4 to 9.

Ironweed (*Vernonia* spp.). These bear rounded clusters of fuzzy, buttonlike flowerheads in rich purple. New York ironweed (*V. noveboracensis*) is a common sight along ditches and damp meadows in fall. The plants are 4 to 6 feet tall and spread to 4 feet. Giant ironweed (*V. gigantea*) ranges from 3 to 9 or more feet and spreads from 4 to 6 feet. Plants of both species thrive in rich, moist to wet soil and survive extended flooding. They are tallest in moist soil but also tolerate average garden soil, which yields more compact growth. The flowerheads are attractive to butterflies and other insects. Hardiness: Zones 5 to 8.

Joe-Pye weeds (*Eutrochium* and *Eupatoriadelphus* spp., formerly *Eupatorium* spp.). These robust perennials are a common sight in roadside ditches. All are magnets for butterflies and other insects and make wonderful additions to borders and meadows with soil that ranges from moist well drained to wet. All form robust clumps, ranging from 3 to 4 feet with time. Eastern or coastal plain Joe-Pye weed (*Eutrochium dubium*, formerly *Eupatorium dubium*) is a 5- to 7-foot-tall species that bears huge, rounded clusters of mauve-pink flowers. 'Little Joe' is a compact cultivar that ranges from 3 to 4 feet and spreads to 1 foot. Plants tolerate periodic drought in heavy clay soil and also grow in moist, well-drained soil. Hardiness: Zones 4 to 8. Spotted Joe-Pye weed (*Eupatoriadelphus maculatus*, formerly *Eupatorium maculatum*), also called spotted trumpetweed, is a 5- to 7-foot-tall species that features large, domed clusters of pinkish purple flowers and purple-spotted stems. Hardiness: Zones 3 to 7. Hollow-stemmed Joe-Pye weed (*Eutrochium fistulosum*, formerly *Eupatorium fistulosum*),

Joe-Pye weed (*Eutrochium dubium* 'Little Joe') with New York ironweed (*Vernonia noveboracensis*) and hybrid agastache (*Agastache* 'Blue Fortune'). Photo by Neil Soderstrom; Hannelore Soderstrom garden.

also called trumpetweed, is a 4- to 7-foot-tall species with dusky pink flowers. Hardiness: Zones 4 to 8.

Lady's tresses, nodding (*Spiranthes cernua*). This native orchid is fairly easy to establish in a moist to wet spot with rich soil in sun to part shade. Grow them in boggy areas or along the edges of ponds and water gardens with other emergent plants. Plants bear grassy leaves and erect, 1- to 2-foot-tall spikes of small, white, fragrant flowers. *S. cernua* var. *odorata* 'Chadds Ford' is especially fragrant. Hardiness: Zones 5 to 9.

Sunflowers (*Helianthus* spp.). Three species of sunflowers are ideal choices for adding late-season color to damp spots. All bear yellow, daisylike flowers with darker centers that attract butterflies. They thrive in moist to wet soil and form robust, 3- to 5-foot-wide clumps. Cut sunflowers back once or twice before the end of June to encourage branching and more flowers and to curtail height. Giant sunflower (*H. giganteus*) ranges from 4 to 10 feet tall and needs staking to keep stems erect. Plants bear an abundance of fairly small, 2- to 2½-inch-wide flowers. Swamp sunflower (*H. angustifolius*) thrives in bogs and other wet-soil sites but also tolerates average, consistently moist, well-drained soil, which helps slow down spreading. Plants bear masses of bright yellow, 3-inch-wide flowers in mid to late fall on 8- to 10-foot plants. 'Mellow Yellow' bears pale yellow blooms. 'First Light' features bright yellow flowers on 4-foot-tall plants. Thin-leaved sunflower (*H. decapetalus*) is a 2- to 5-foot-tall species that grows along woodland edges and tolerates full sun to nearly full shade, although it blooms best with sun. Plants grow in average well-drained to moist soil. Hardiness: Zones 5 to 9 for all species listed.

Vervain, blue (*Verbena hastata*). Also called simpler's joy, this 2- to 6-foot-tall species spreads to about 3 feet. Plants bear erect, branched clusters of purple-blue flowers that are attractive to butterflies. They thrive in moist to wet soil and are ideal for planting along marshes and other wet spots. Hardiness: Zones 3 to 9.

Grasses for Gardens

Grasses and grasslike plants such as sedges (*Carex* spp.) add texture, movement, and subtle color to beds, borders, and other plantings. This list includes some of the more ornamental species for both sun and shade. Unless otherwise noted, plants are hardy throughout the Chesapeake Bay region (in Zones 3 or 4 to 8 or 9) and thrive in sun to part shade in average moist but well-drained garden soil.

Little bluestem (*Schizachyrium scoparium*) with purple coneflowers (*Echinacea purpurea*). Photo by Nancy Ondra.

Bluestem, little (*Schizachyrium scoparium*). Suitable for both gardens and meadows, little bluestem ranges from 1 to 4 feet tall and spreads to 2 or more feet. Plants form attractive clumps of fine-textured, upright green or blue-green leaves, sometimes tipped with red, that turn shades of orange and red in fall. A number of cultivars are available, including 'The Blues', which was selected for handsome blue-green foliage. Plants grow in moist to dry soil.

Eastern bottlebrush grass (*Elymus hystrix*). Photo by Neil Soderstrom; Owen Brown Interfaith Center.

Bottlebrush grass, eastern (*Elymus hystrix*, formerly *Hystrix patula*). This grass ranges from 2 to 4 feet tall and has bluish green leaves. Clumps spread to about 2 feet. Plants bear bristly seedheads that fade to tan in summer and grow in sun or shade.

 Sweet Flag

Grown for its robust clumps of grassy foliage rather than its insignificant, greenish yellow flowers, sweet flag (*Acorus americanus*, formerly *A. calamus* var. *americanus*) ranges from 2 to 3 feet tall and grows in full sun or part shade. Plants produce clumps of strap-shaped, 1-inch-wide leaves that spread indefinitely via fleshy rhizomes. The rhizomes are used as herbs and are dried as a potpourri fixative. The leaves are fragrant when crushed. Although best in wet soil or standing water up to 6 inches deep, sweet flag can also grow in average consistently moist garden soil. The leaf tips turn brown if the soil dries out too much. Hardiness: Zones 4 to 10. Use sweet flag along ponds, in water gardens, or in low-lying areas that remain moist or wet. Note that European sweet flag (*A. calamus*), which has one distinct midrib rather than several indistinct ones, has naturalized over much of our area.

Prairie dropseed (*Sporobolus heterolepis*). Photo by Neil Soderstrom; design by Dave Korbonitz at Mt. Cuba Center.

Dropseeds (*Sporobolus* spp.). Sand dropseed (*S. cryptandrus*) is a fine-textured grass that ranges from 1 to 3 feet in height and spreads to about 2 feet. Plants produce purplish red to tan seedheads in summer. They thrive in dry, sandy, well-drained soil. Prairie dropseed (*S. heterolepis*) forms handsome, 1- to 3-foot-tall mounds of very narrow leaves that spread to 2 feet. Fluffy clusters of seedheads emerge in summer. Both seedheads and leaves turn from green to orange and apricot in fall. Plants grow in moist, well-drained to dry soil.

Panic grass or switch-grass (*Panicum virgatum* 'Northwind'). Photo by Neil Soderstrom; U.S. Botanic Garden.

Pink muhly (*Muhlenbergia capillaris*). Photo by Barbara Ellis.

Muhly, pink (*Muhlenbergia capillaris*). Also called hairawn muhly, this is a 2- to 3-foot-tall grass prized for its billowing, fine-textured clusters of mauve-pink seedheads in fall. Plants spread to about 3 feet and grow in sun to part shade and well-drained average soil. Hardiness: Zones 5 to 9.

Panic grass or switchgrass (*Panicum virgatum*). This handsome, upright species produces dense clumps of narrow leaves topped by loose, wispy seedheads that turn from green to tan. Plants grow in moist to dry soil and reach 3 to 6 feet tall with a spread of 2 to 5 feet. Excessively rich soil causes flopping. 'Dallas Blues' and 'Heavy Metal' feature silver-blue leaves, while 'Northwind' foliage is greenish gray. 'Shenandoah' features green leaves tipped in red. The clumps benefit from being divided every 4 or 5 years. In ad-

dition to using this species as a background plant in perennial gardens, consider it for screening, meadows, and mass plantings.

Northern sea oats (*Chasmanthium latifolium*). Photo by Neil Soderstrom; Longwood Gardens.

Sea oats, northern (*Chasmanthium latifolium*). This handsome grass bears flattened, nodding seedheads on 3- to 4-foot-tall plants. Clumps spread to 3 feet, but this grass also self-sows with enthusiasm. Use it in sun to light shade as a ground cover under shrubs and trees, or combine it with robust perennials. Plants tolerate drought and extended flooding.

Sedges (*Carex* spp.). Use these handsome, grasslike plants as accents in beds and borders, in wild gardens, as edgings, or in mass plantings as ground cov-

Flowers for Edgings and Rock Gardens

Low-growing flowers are a pretty addition along paths and walkways, at the front of a bed or border, and in rock gardens. Unless otherwise noted, the plants listed here require full sun to partial shade and average moist, well-drained soil. Some are suitable for bright patches in shade gardens.

Asters (*Ionactis* and *Symphyotrichum* spp., formerly *Aster* spp.). Stiff aster (*I. linariifolius*, formerly *A. linariifolius*), also called flax-leaved whitetop aster, has needlelike leaves and bears 1-inch-wide daisies in shades of lavender, blue-violet, or white from late summer to fall. Plants are 12 to 20 inches tall and wide. Hardiness: Zones 3 to 9. 'Snow Flurry' white heath aster (*S. ericoides*, formerly *A. ericoides*) is a dwarf form that is 4 to 6 inches tall and spreads to 2 feet. Hardiness: Zones 5 to 8, slightly less hardy than the species. Both species prefer poor, sandy soil and full sun, but they also grow in average moist, well-drained soil.

Catchflies, fire pinks (*Silene* spp.). Relatives of garden pinks (*Dianthus* spp.), catchflies grow in sun to shade and dry to average well-drained soil, although plants bloom best in sun. Sticky catchfly or wild pinks (*S. caroliniana*) bears pink flowers on 6- to 8-inch plants. Hardiness: Zones 4 to 7. Fire pink (*S. virginica*) produces brilliant red flowers on 1½-foot plants that spread as far. Fire pink plants are short lived, but they self-sow with enthusiasm. Hardiness: Zones 4 to 9. Both species require excellent drainage and are suitable for rock gardens or edging in a cottage garden.

Coneflower, dwarf purple (*Echinacea purpurea*). While most coneflowers are too tall to use as edging plants, the cultivar 'CBG Cone 2'/Pixie Meadowbrite reaches 22 inches tall and spreads to 24 inches. Plants are shorter in dry soil. See "Coneflowers, purple" under "Summer: June to September" earlier in this chapter for more information.

Green-and-gold (*Chrysogonum virginianum*). Also called goldenstar, this adaptable native wildflower can be used as a ground cover or edging. For more information on green-and-gold, see p. 159.

Penstemon, dwarf hairy (*Penstemon hirsutus* var. *pygmaeus*). This tiny native is only 4 inches tall and produces clusters of trumpet-shaped white or mauve-purple flowers. For more information, see Penstemons on p. 183.

Phlox, moss (*Phlox subulata*). A ground cover, edging, or rock garden plant, moss phlox is 4 to 6 inches tall and spreads to 2 or more feet. For more information, see Phlox on p. 181.

Prickly pear, eastern (*Opuntia humifusa*, formerly *O. compressa*). Also called devil's-tongue, this is a hardy cactus with flat, fleshy leaves and showy 2½- to 3½-inch yellow flowers in early summer. Some forms feature flowers with red centers. Plants are 1 foot tall and spread to 3 or more feet. As one might expect of a cactus, dry rocky or sandy well-drained soil is ideal. The leaf pads are armed with minute barbed bristles. Hardiness: Zones 4 to 10.

Verbena, rose (*Glandularia canadensis*, formerly *Verbena canadensis*). This is a creeping plant that can be used as a ground cover or grown as an annual. Plants self-sow where happy. See Verbena on p. 153 for more information.

Violet, birdfoot (*Viola pedata*). This native violet is more difficult to grow than other violets, but it is worth trying if the right spot is available. Plants bear purple, lilac-blue, or lavender-purple flowers with lighter eyes in spring and deeply lobed leaves. They are 4 to 6 inches tall and wide, spread slowly by rhizomes, and also self-sow if conditions suit. Give birdfoot violets a site with sandy or gravelly soil in full sun to light shade. Good soil drainage is crucial. Hardiness: Zones 4 to 8.

Large perennials such as Joe-Pye weeds (*Eutrochium* and *Eupatoriadelphus* spp.) can be scattered in a meadow or arranged in bold drifts to create a more intentional, designed look. Photo © Roger Foley; design by Oehme, van Sweden Landscape Architecture.

ers. Appalachian sedge (*C. appalachica*) forms 1-foot-tall fountain-like clumps of narrow leaves that spread to 1½ feet. Plants grow in sun to light shade and moist to dry soil. Blue sedge (*C. glaucodea*) forms attractive, ½- to 1½-foot-tall clumps of ½-inch-wide, blue-gray leaves that spread as far. Plants grow in sun to shade. Spreading sedge (*C. laxiculmis*) and its cultivar 'Bunny Blue' feature similar clumps of blue-green leaves and thrive in moist to wet shade. Pennsylvania sedge (*C. pensylvanica*), a good ground cover and lawn substitute, forms 10-inch-tall clumps that spread slowly to 20 inches. Plants are easy to grow in sun or shade.

Wood rush, hairy (*Luzula acuminata*). This species bears arching, 1-inch-wide leaves and forms mounds that are 6 to 16 inches tall and wide. Hairy wood rush makes a nice ground cover for shade or part shade.

Meadows and Meadow Gardens

Wildflower meadows are a very effective way to use sun-loving native perennials. Once established, the flowers and grasses in a meadow will be in bloom for much of the growing season and attract a constant parade of butterflies, insects, birds, and other wildlife, making them a source of constant activity and fascination.

Meadows are more than just beautiful wildlife habitats, though. Although they do not fit the conventional definition of ground covers—for one thing, they are far taller than typical ground covers—they are an excellent substitute for conventional lawn and are ideal for replacing it with useful habitat. They also can be used over septic fields, which are normally covered with grass. Once the plants are established and allowed to knit together the way they would in the wild, a meadow forms dense, weed-suppressing ground cover that needs very minimal maintenance. While planting a meadow and helping it become established takes work, meadows are very low-maintenance landscape features once established. Because they do not require the mowing, watering, and fertilizing required by lawn, established meadows also save time and money.

A meadow garden is more suitable for sites where space is an issue. It is an informal bed or border planted with native meadow species and managed more like a meadow than a conventional garden. Meadow gardens also can be planted with cultivated forms of native plants in order to establish a planting that is even more like a conventional garden. The goal is to create a flower garden that resembles a larger wild meadow. That means plants are allowed to spread a bit and are allowed to mix together and lean on one another as plants in a meadow do. Depending on your taste and the garden's location, either let plants grow as they will or employ some of the management techniques mentioned earlier in this chapter, such as cutting back to control height. Consider dividing clumps every few years to ensure that the plant community remains diverse and interesting. As with a wildflower meadow, the entire garden is cut down once a year in late winter. In both meadows and meadow gardens, it is necessary to weed out woody plants and other unwanted volunteers.

Meadow gardens also may be more acceptable to nearby neighbors who are uncomfortable with plantings that do not conform to typical suburban landscaping. Use a meadow garden as a teaching tool to demonstrate the value and aesthetic appeal of native flowers. Butterfly-watching is a great activity that will appeal to many visitors and excite them about the possibilities. In addition, there are ways to make meadows and meadow gardens more acceptable to neighbors and family members who prefer the look of a conventional lawn. When creating them, plan on a natural shape that fits with the existing plantings and the site's topography. One way to create a pleasing shape is to think of water pooling on the lawn. Mowing all the way around the meadow to reinforce a unified shape also helps make it look more purposeful.

Planting Meadows and Meadow Gardens

Meadows and meadow gardens are low maintenance in the long run, but they do take work to plant and establish. Scattering seeds and then waiting for a meadow to magically appear simply does not work. In the Chesapeake Bay area, fall is a good time for sowing or planting, as seedlings have a chance to germinate and become established during the winter and early spring before hot weather arrives. In addition, watering generally is not necessary until temperatures warm up in late spring.

Site evaluation is the first step in creating a meadow or meadow garden. It is important to select plants suitable for the soil conditions that exist on the chosen site. The soil can be wet or dry, sandy or clayey. A site that receives a minimum of 6 hours of direct sun per day is ideal. Have a soil test done to answer any questions about the conditions that exist. Most of the plants listed in "Color from Spring to Fall," especially the sections for summer and late summer to fall, are suitable for either meadows or meadow gardens. While it is possible to establish a meadow without supplemental watering, having a site with access to water is beneficial in case dry weather occurs just as seeds are germinating, or if the garden will be started using small plants, or plugs, instead of seeds.

While wildflower meadows are often grown from seed, meadow gardens can be planted much like any other flower garden. For quick results, select the species you want to grow and purchase plants. This garden features blue wild indigo (*Baptisia australis*) along with other native and non-native perennials. Photo by Barbara Ellis; Noble garden.

If the site has a steep slope, make a plan to control erosion. Even if the rest of the site can be planted by sowing seeds, use plants for covering sloping areas and install temporary terraces to protect the soil and prevent erosion. Burlap or hydroseeding with annual grasses will also help hold soil on sloping sites. For a disturbed site or for sites where erosion already is a problem, consult a professional for help in stabilizing the soil and ensuring that plants become well established.

Starting from seed is the easiest, least expensive option for planting a meadow. (Seeds are also an option for a meadow garden, although starting with plants offers quicker results and more control over the final design of the garden.) Investing in a good-quality seed mix is essential. Do not waste money on so-called meadow mixes that contain lots of showy, non-native annuals like cosmos (*Cosmos* spp.). Instead, buy a wildflower mix designed for the Chesapeake Bay region. Look for one developed for the type of soil, the moisture level, and the exposure that exists on the site. (Meadows are generally planted in full sun, but seed mixes are available that will thrive in partial shade.) A good meadow mix includes both native perennials and grasses. Experienced suppliers will have several different seed mixes available, not just one. Most also contain some fast-germinating annuals, grasses, or short-lived perennials to keep the soil covered and protected while slower-growing perennials become established. Another option is to create your own custom mix by ordering the seeds separately and then mixing them together for sowing.

Starting from plugs or small plants is another option for either a wildflower meadow or a meadow garden, although meadows are normally started from seeds because plugs or small plants are much more expensive. While plugs produce a mature planting more quickly than does seed, they also are more labor intensive to plant. Plugs need to be planted the same way that other garden plants are, although their root balls are much smaller and subsequently dry out much more quickly. As a result, regular watering is essential until plants are established. To make a decision, evaluate the cost difference between seeds and plants.

Proper site preparation and weed control are essential first steps for any meadow. Photo by Barbara Ellis.

Another option for creating a meadow is to use both seed and plugs. Start by sowing seeds and later add drifts of selected perennials using plugs or small plants. This is also an option if an area does not conform to the conditions on the rest of the site, such as a particularly wet or dry spot. It is also ideal for adding an element of design, such as drifts of specific colors, to a meadow or meadow garden.

Site Preparation

Meadow plants, especially when they are planted from seed sown directly on the site, cannot compete against established grasses and other plants. To create a site that is ready for planting or sowing in fall, devote the summer beforehand to eliminating vegetation on the site. Small sites can be prepared by spreading newspaper and mulch and then sowing seeds into the mulch. Stripping off lawn grass is another option, but you must also eliminate the weeds that inevitably germinate after the lawn has been removed. Digging up the entire site and removing existing vegetation is yet another possibility, but it is extremely labor intensive. Digging also brings to the surface more seeds that germinate and then need to be weeded, hoed, or otherwise removed before sowing new seed.

Herbicide, black-plastic mulch, and repeated tilling are the options most gardeners select. Glyphosate-based herbicides such as Roundup are effective and break down fairly quickly, although they are not an option for properties where only organic products are used. When using herbicides, read and follow label directions carefully. Mow the site two weeks before spraying to encourage weeds to grow new leaves that will be more susceptible to the herbicide. Plan on respraying once or twice to completely eliminate competing plants. To use black-plastic mulch, cover the site in spring and leave the plastic in place through the summer months. Make sure the plastic overlaps so that light and water are excluded. Another way to kill existing vegetation is to repeatedly till the site every two or three weeks throughout the growing season.

Once the site has been sprayed, the plastic has been removed, or several rounds of tilling have been completed, water the site and wait a few weeks to ensure that weeds and remaining lawn grass have been eradicated. Eliminate any that appear during this waiting period. Then till the soil lightly, just enough to break up the surface so that seeds can work their way into it and germinate. Do not fertilize or spread lime to adjust the pH: The plants should be happy in the conditions that exist naturally.

Sowing or Planting

Once weeds are under control, it is time to sow seeds. Suppliers can help calculate how much seed to order. Have enough weed-free straw on hand to scatter over the site after sowing and to help hide the seeds from birds and other hungry wildlife. Spread seed by hand or use a mechanical seeder. Before spreading, mix

Three years after sowing, this meadow features many natives grown from seeds plus some that were added by planting small container-grown specimens. Photo by Barbara Ellis.

seeds with an equal amount of white play sand so you can easily see where seed has already been scattered. Divide the seed-and-sand mix into batches and then walk over the site scattering it in rows, first horizontally and then vertically across the site to ensure even coverage. Once the seed has been spread, rake the site lightly and cover it with straw. There is no need to water sites sown in fall: Winter rains will generally give seedlings all the water they need. If seed is sown in spring, water regularly until seeds have germinated and seedlings are up and established.

Starting a meadow or meadow garden from plugs or small plants is best done in rainy or overcast weather because these plants dry out very quickly and are then susceptible to root damage. When determining where to plant, either distribute the plants over the site at random or create drifts of a single species for a more designed look with a bold color pat-

tern. In a meadow, plants are allowed to grow into one another more than in conventional perennial plantings. You can use the spacing guidelines on plant labels or estimate spacing based on the ultimate height of a particular species. Establishing a grid over the entire site and spacing all plants equally is fine as well: Draw grid lines in the soil with a hoe or a stick.

On planting day, if there is any chance that the plugs will dry out before they are set in the soil, keep them in a shady spot and take only a few plugs at a time to the planting site so they can be planted quickly with minimal exposure to sun and wind. If the soil is at all dry, water each plant as it goes into the ground. Once all plants are in place, spread weed-free straw over the site to help protect them and the soil surface. It is okay if the plants are lightly covered. Water the site, and then water again whenever the soil surface begins to dry out.

Meadow Management

While meadows take effort to plant, they also demand an element of patience. Annuals and short-lived grasses will predominate the first season or two, and it takes three years for longer-lived perennials to begin to bloom from seed. If too many weedy annuals appear the first year, consider mowing in late spring to reduce competition with perennials, which fill in more gradually and establish the character of the meadow. Be sure to take pictures frequently as the meadow matures and changes, and watch as different plants begin to bloom. Some species will thrive; others will not. It is important to have a light hand when intervening, though, since doing too much selecting will affect the overall amount of maintenance your meadow will require. Keep an eye out for weeds and remove them promptly. To add a particular color or species, consider buying plants and adding them as the meadow develops. It is best not to make a special effort to coddle individual plants that appear.

Meadow Grasses

The following native grasses are suitable for meadows and are found in many meadow seed mixes. All are hardy in the Chesapeake Bay region and, unless otherwise noted, grow in full sun to part sun and dry to average moist but well-drained soil.

Bluestems (*Andropogon* and *Schizachyrium* spp.). Big bluestem (*A. gerardii*) is a robust, 4- to 6-foot grass that spreads to 3 or more feet and features excellent red-bronze fall foliage. Plants spread by rhizomes and self-sown seed. They prefer dry to average soil, tolerate drought, and are good for preventing erosion. Plants also grow in moist garden soil but are more likely to flop over. Bushy bluestem (*A. glomeratus*) is a similar-size grass that grows in moist to

wet soil. Fall foliage is copper-orange. Little bluestem (*S. scoparium*) is about 4 feet tall and spreads to 2 feet. Plants feature purple-bronze foliage that ripens to bronze-orange in fall.

Dropseed, prairie (*Sporobolus heterolepis*). This clump-forming species is 2 to 3 feet tall and wide. Plants have fine-textured leaves that turn gold to orange in fall and billowy seedheads. Plants grow in a wide range of soils but are best in dry conditions. They are also used in rain gardens.

Gama grass, eastern (*Tripsacum dactyloides*). This is a robust, 4- to 8-foot-tall species that spreads to 6 feet via thick rhizomes and self-sowing. Plants bear arching leaves and grow in average soil in either full sun or partial shade.

Grama grass, side-oats (*Bouteloua curtipendula*). This is a 2- to 2½-foot grass that spreads as far. Plants have bluish green leaves and attractive purple-tinged, wheatlike seedheads that have seeds hanging only on one side. They grow in a wide range of soils and also can be mown like a lawn grass.

Hair grass, tufted (*Deschampsia cespitosa*). A handsome grass that forms clumps of fine-textured, semi-evergreen leaves, this species grows 2 to 3 feet tall and spreads to about 2 feet. Plants thrive in average to moist garden soil and also tolerate part shade as well as full sun. Crinkled hair grass (*D. flexuosa*) grows in sun to part shade and well-drained sandy or dry soil.

Indian grass (*Sorghastrum nutans*). A 3- to 5-foot-tall species that spreads to 2 feet, this species of grass grows in a wide range of soils, although plants tend to flop in rich, moist conditions. They tolerate brief flooding as well as drought and are suitable for rain gardens. Plants feature blue-green leaves, feathery seedheads, and orange-yellow fall foliage.

Love grass, purple (*Eragrostis spectabilis*). This species forms unassuming clumps of foliage, from 1 foot tall and wide, that produce fluffy, cloudlike, rosy purple seedheads that reach 2 feet. Plants grow in poor, dry soil and spread slowly by seeds and stems that root where they touch the ground.

Purpletop tridens (*Tridens flavus*). A 2- to 7-foot-tall perennial, this native grass produces fine-textured purple seedheads above arching leaves. Plants grow in moist to dry soil in sun but also tolerate part shade.

Wild ryes (*Elymus* spp.). These bear arching, wheat-like seedheads that turn tan and remain attractive in winter. Canada wild rye (*E. canadensis*) is 2 to 5 feet tall and spreads to 3 feet. Plants have blue-green leaves and tolerate a wide range of soils. Virginia wild rye (*E. virginicus*), 2 to 4 feet tall, grows in part shade and is useful for planting on shady hillsides or along shady streams.

SEVEN ❧ Plants and Gardens for Shade

Every property has room for shade plants. The lucky few have large trees that cast delightful patches of dappled shade, but shade gardens can begin as a remnant woodland where non-native invasives predominate, a spot where lawn is removed under a tree, or a site just large enough to tuck a bed against the sunless north side of the house. As landscapes mature, the amount of available space for shade plants increases as trees grow and extend their branches. Plant trees to capture more carbon dioxide, increase wildlife habitat, cool the air, shelter a home from wind, add beautiful foliage, or all of the above, and space for shade plants increases exponentially.

There are many reasons to value shade and shade gardens. For one, working in a shady garden bed on a hot summer day has decided advantages when compared with tending a garden in full sun. Early bloom is another advantage: While gardens in sun tend toward flashier colors, shade gardens produce some of the earliest flowers of the season. And while most shade plants bloom in spring, careful selection—both of plants and of the sites where they are planted—can ensure that flowers, showy foliage, interesting textures, and colorful berries will keep a shade garden attractive and interesting all season. A shady outdoor living space surrounded by shade-loving shrubs offers a wonderful, private, and restorative place to spend time outdoors. Once established, shade gardens also tend to require less maintenance than sun gardens.

(overleaf) A shade garden carpeted with wildflowers is hard to resist. This planting includes Allegheny foamflower (*Tiarella cordifolia*), mayapples (*Podophyllum peltatum*), wild blue phlox (*Phlox divaricata*), and Christmas ferns (*Polystichum acrostichoides*). Photo by Neil Soderstrom; design by Jimmy Testa at Mt. Cuba Center.

Creating a Shade Garden

Like sun gardens, successful shade gardens start with an honest site assessment. Careful site observation is crucial, as there are many gradations between full sun and full shade. In addition, shade is not static. Shady patches move, and shade density changes as the sun moves in the sky. To fully evaluate the amount and density of shade in a particular spot, observe it throughout the course of a day, and ideally throughout an entire year.

Other factors affect what will grow well. For example, a site may feature daylong, dappled patches of shade and sun, and if the overhead trees are oaks (*Quercus* spp.) or tulip poplars (*Liriodendron tulipifera*), the site may present a perfect opportunity for a woodland garden. On the other hand, if the trees are maples (*Acer* spp.) or beeches (*Fagus* spp.), both native trees with a multitude of surface roots, the best solution for the site may be a simple layer of mulch, with other plants sited outside the drip line of the trees. See "Sun and Shade Patterns" on p. 44 for more information on assessing the amount of light a site receives, and use the techniques in "Reading the Landscape" on p. 69 to learn about soil and other conditions that affect what plants will grow well there.

For gardeners who have planted trees that are still relatively small, starting with plants that grow in part or even full sun is a reasonable approach, even though the site will eventually be shady. As trees grow and shade deepens, these first choices can be moved to sunnier spots and replaced with plants that grow in partial to full shade. With observation, you can also predict which sites will become shadier as trees reach maturity. This process highlights another essential gardening truth: Matching plants to the site is not something that is done just once. As sites change, the parameters for plants that will succeed change as

Native trees predominate in this informal woodland garden that features a moss lawn and a variety of plants that thrive in moist soil and daylong shade, including native ferns, non-native azaleas, and hostas. Photo by Barbara Ellis; Liesfeld garden.

well. In a mature garden, plants do a portion of site selection themselves. Not only do they fill sites that suit them with lush growth—or die out if conditions do not provide what they need—they also migrate to sites that provide ideal conditions. While stepping in and moving or rearranging makes sense if one plant is overwhelming its bed mates, try not to be too rigid, even if plants are violating the initial design. Allowing plants to adapt and to do some of the site selection greatly increases the likelihood that a garden will succeed and that plants will thrive. Allowing plants to select sites that suit them helps ensure vigorous, healthy growth. Watching what happens is part of the fun of having a garden.

Building a garden on a shady site overgrown by non-native invasive plants poses a special challenge. Widespread clearing and soil disturbance actually favors invasives and weeds, so minimizing disturbance is an important goal. See "Restoring Wild Sites" on p. 99 and "Managing Invasive Plants" on p. 102 for information on preserving existing patches of native plants and eliminating weeds.

Ten Tips for Great Shade Gardens

Observing sun and shade patterns and then selecting plants that suit the site are the first steps in building a shade garden. Use the following tips to create great shade gardens.

1. Plant handsome foliage. Flowers come and go, but great foliage is there for the long haul and will keep plantings attractive regardless of whether they are in bloom. This is especially true in shade gardens. Fortunately, there are plenty of options for plants that bring long-lasting and colorful foliage to the shade. Select a mixture of plants that feature large and small leaves as well as deciduous and evergreen foliage to create a garden that is handsome throughout the season.

2. Start with easy plants. Some of the most popular, commonly available native species are easy to grow, and these are the best plants to select when starting a garden. Rare, finicky plants or the first variegated form of this or that are always tempting, but vigorous, easy-to-grow species form a more effective backbone for a garden. Dependable plants also tend to be less expensive and ensure a higher success rate per plant.

3. Check and double-check plant sources. When buying native shade plants, ask questions—lots of them—about origin. Buy only nursery-propagated plants, not those labeled "nursery grown," since these typically are collected in the wild and then grown in a nursery for a year or more. See "Plant Responsibly" on p. 109 for more information on buying plants that have not been wild collected.

4. Mix textures, forms, and colors. Add texture and contrast to shade gardens by combining plants with ferny, deeply cut leaves; large bold species; or plants such as sedges (*Carex* spp.) that produce clumps of strappy, grassy foliage. Including plants with different

Handsome foliage carpets this easy-care bed, including Ostrich ferns (*Matteuccia struthiopteris*), variegated Virginia knotweed (*Persicaria virginiana* 'Painter's Palette'), and self-sown asters (*Symphyotrichum* spp.). Photo by Barbara Ellis.

forms or habits, from mounding to erect, also helps add interest to a shade garden. Finally, look for different foliage colors. Green can vary, from dark green to gray- or blue-green to chartreuse. Plants with maroon, purple, purple-black, silver, and green with cream or white foliage also are available.

5. Continue improving the soil. It is nearly impossible to add too much organic matter to garden soil. Adding organic matter also increases the amount of carbon stored in the soil, thus decreasing your carbon footprint. Spread compost, incorporate organic matter at planting time, and keep the garden mulched with chopped leaves, compost bark, pine needles, or whatever organic mulch is available.

6. Layer plants. Plants are layered in meadows and sun gardens as well, but layers are especially evident in a woodland. Try to re-create the feel of a woodland in your design by including a canopy layer, understory trees, shrubs, large perennials, and lower-growing species as ground cover. See "Layered and Matrix Plantings" on p. 65 for more ideas on creating layers of plants in the garden.

7. Add accents once the garden matures. Wait to add spring ephemerals and fussier natives until after the

White-flowered crested iris (*Iris cristata* f. *alba*), wild blue phlox (*Phlox divaricata*), and white-flowered shooting stars (*Dodecatheon meadia*), natives all, surround a clump of hostas to create an interesting carpet for a shady spot. Photo by Barbara Ellis.

To cover ground in a naturalistic manner, layer plants by combining taller perennials with even lower-growing companions. This combination includes mayapples (*Podophyllum peltatum*) underplanted with Canadian wild ginger (*Asarum canadense*), rue anemone (*Thalictrum thalictroides*), and non-native creeping mazus (*Mazus reptans*). Photo by Neil Soderstrom; design by Marcie Weigelt at Mt. Cuba Center.

garden is established—once basic framework plants are thriving and it is clear what growing conditions exist and what plants grow well there. Always check sources before adding either ephemerals or fussier species, since these are frequently wild collected.

8. Remember ground covers. Fill shaded spots with drifts of shade-loving ground covers to reduce maintenance and create a uniform green carpet. Drifts of ground covers are especially useful for replacing lawn under trees. They can be used to connect and create a smooth transition between plantings of shrubs or perennials or added to the front of an existing planting as edging. For more information on shade ground covers, see Chapter 5.

9. Create communities. If your shade garden is located on a remnant woodland, try to identify the plants that once grew there. Use native trees and shrubs on the site as clues, but also look for similar sites at nearby gardens, both public and private. Identifying even three or four species that might once have grown there can prove helpful when selecting new species to plant. Growing plants in a community leads to a sustainable, low-maintenance planting.

10. Watch and learn. Native plants that move around in the landscape or in a particular garden bed are effectively matched to the site. Plants that are thriving produce seedlings that pop up near established clumps, and the clumps themselves expand. Before stepping in and digging up a plant that has appeared on its own, identify it. Eliminate it if it is a non-native invasive species, but if it is native, ask yourself, "What would happen if I did nothing?" The results may surprise you.

Flowering dogwood (*Cornus florida*). Photo by Neil Soderstrom; Mt. Cuba Center.

Understory Trees for Shade

Adding trees to a spot that is already shady may seem redundant, but small trees or large shrubs lend a more natural look to a shady site. Understory plants also add cover for birds and other wild creatures. Many of the trees described in Chapter 4 can be used in this manner, including flowering dogwood (*Cornus florida*), redbud (*Cercis canadensis*), American hop hornbeam (*Ostrya virginiana*), shadblow serviceberry (*Amelanchier canadensis*), and pawpaw (*Asimina triloba*). American holly (*Ilex opaca*) makes an attractive evergreen on shady sites, as does eastern or Canadian hemlock (*Tsuga canadensis*), another popular conifer that tolerates sun but is happiest in partial shade. Plant hemlocks in a cool site with afternoon shade and average to moist well-drained soil. They do not tolerate wind or road salt. In addition to the species, which can reach 80 feet, many cultivars are available, including 'Cole's Prostrate', which is 2 feet tall and spreads to 4 or more feet.

Other trees to consider for planting in part shade are listed below. Unless otherwise noted, all grow in partial shade and average to moist, well-drained soil.

Hop tree (*Ptelea trifoliata*). A large shrub or small tree that reaches 15 to 20 feet tall and wide, this species has greenish white flowers, aromatic foliage (one

common name is stinking ash), and tolerates dry soil in part to full shade. Hardiness: Zones 4 to 9.

Hornbeam, American (*Carpinus caroliniana*). Also called musclewood and ironwood, this species ranges from 20 to 35 feet tall. Plants feature attractive gray bark and good orange, red, or yellow fall foliage. They grow in part shade to shade and tolerate both wet and dry soil. Hardiness: Zones 3 to 9.

Maple, striped (*Acer pensylvanicum*). Grown for its handsome striped bark, this species needs cool, moist, well-drained soil and part shade. Hardiness: Zones 3 to 7.

Silverbell, Carolina (*Halesia tetraptera*, formerly *H. carolina*). Also called mountain silverbell, this species features white, bell-shaped flowers in spring and yellow fall foliage. In cultivation, plants normally mature at 30 feet and spread about as far. They need rich, moist, well-drained, acid soil. A site with afternoon shade is best in warmer parts of the Chesapeake Bay region. Hardiness: Zones 5 to 8.

Snowbell (*Styrax* spp.). Two species, both large shrubs or small trees, can be grown as understory

Dwarf eastern or Canadian hemlock (*Tsuga canadensis* 'Cole's Prostrate'). Photo by Neil Soderstrom; New York Botanical Garden.

American hornbeam (*Carpinus caroliniana*). Photo by Neil Soderstrom; Adkins Arboretum.

trees in shady sites. Both produce white, bell-shaped flowers in spring to early summer. American snowbell (*S. americanus*) ranges from 8 to 15 feet tall. Plants require a spot in part shade to shade with cool, acidic soil that is moist to wet. Hardiness: Zones 5 to 9. Bigleaf snowbell (*S. grandifolius*) grows in average moist, well-drained soil. Hardiness: Zones 7 to 9.

Stewartia (*Stewartia* spp.). Two species of stewartia, also called camellias, are native to the Chesapeake Bay region. Both are large shrubs or small trees that range from 10 to 15 feet tall and wide. Both bear showy, white, 2- to 3-inch-wide flowers in early to midsummer and need rich, moist, acid soil and shade during the hottest part of the day. Mountain camellia (*S. ovata*) features attractive orange and red

fall foliage. Hardiness: Zones 5 to 9. Silky camellia (*S. malacodendron*) grows primarily on the coastal plain. Hardiness: Zones 7 to 9.

Shrubs for Shade

Add structure to shade gardens by planting shrubs along property boundaries to add privacy, or add an understory layer to the shade garden by planting groups of shrubs throughout.

Azaleas (*Rhododendron* spp.). Both azaleas and rhododendrons are prized landscape plants. While hybrids prevail in most gardens, native species have much to offer. The azaleas listed here are deciduous

Pinxterbloom azalea (*Rhododendron periclymenoides*). Photo by Neil Soderstrom; Alan Visintainer garden.

Plumleaf azalea (*Rhododendron prunifolium*). Photo by Barbara Ellis; Mt. Cuba Center.

shrubs with clusters of showy, trumpet-shaped flowers that appear from spring to summer, depending on the species. Nearly all are best grown in partial shade in the Chesapeake Bay region. With a few exceptions, noted below, give these plants a site with acidic soil, rich in organic matter, that is moist and well drained but not wet. They have shallow, fibrous root systems, and wet feet or heavy clay soil are fatal for most species and hybrids. A layer of mulch helps keep the roots cool and moist.

Sweet or smooth azalea (*R. arborescens*) bears sweetly fragrant white flowers in late spring or early summer, after the leaves have appeared. Plants range from 4 to 10 feet tall and spread about as far. They also can be trained as small trees. Fall foliage is orange, yellow, and red. Although consistently moist, well-drained soil is best, sweet azalea tolerates a wider range of sites than some species and can grow in moist to dry soil, as well as in sun to shade. Hardiness: Zones 4 to 7. Dwarf or coast azalea (*R. atlanticum*) bears very fragrant flowers that are white or white flushed with pink and open as the leaves appear. Plants range from 3 to 7 feet tall and spread by rhizomes to form thickets 5 or more feet across. Hardiness: Zones 5 to 8. Flame azalea (*R. calendulaceum*) bears showy yellow, orange, or orange-red flowers in late spring, after the leaves appear. Plants range from 4 to 8 or more feet and spread to 10 feet. Give them average moist but well-drained to dry soil and par-

tial shade. Hardiness: Zones 5 to 7. Mountain azalea (*R. canescens*), also called Piedmont or hoary azalea, bears lightly fragrant flowers that appear before or with the leaves and are deep pink or white with a pink tube. Plants range from 3 to 10 feet and spread by root suckers about as far. Give them part shade and average well-drained, moist soil. Hardiness: Zones 5 to 7. Pinxterbloom azalea (*R. periclymenoides*, formerly *R. nudiflorum*), also called pink azalea, bears flowers that appear before or as the leaves emerge. Blooms, which are slightly fragrant, may be deep pink to white with pink tubes. Plants are 3 to 6 feet tall and spread by suckers to 7 or more feet. They grow naturally on dry cliffs as well as on the edges of swamps, but they still require good soil drainage. Give them partial shade and dry to moist, well-drained soil. Hardiness: Zones 4 to 9. Early or roseshell azalea (*R. prinophyllum*, formerly *R. roseum*) bears clove-scented pink flowers in spring, before or as the leaves appear. Plants range from 2 to 8 feet and spread about as far. They tolerate slightly dry soil but are best in average, moist but well-drained conditions. Hardiness: Zones 4 to 7. Swamp azalea (*R. viscosum*) produces fragrant white or pink-tinged flowers in early summer after the leaves have emerged. Plants are 3 to as much as 15 feet tall and spread by rhizomes to about 12 feet. They grow naturally in moist to wet woods and along stream banks and swamp edges. Give them partial shade and soil that is very rich in organic matter. Hardiness: Zones 4 to 7.

Among hybrid azaleas, a number of natural hybrids have been selected, including 'Marydel', a 4- by 6-foot plant with fragrant pink flowers that is thought to be a selection of dwarf or coast azalea (*R. atlanticum*). A group of azaleas called the Choptank Hybrids are excellent choices for the Chesapeake Bay region. They are the result of crosses between dwarf azalea and pinxterbloom azalea (*R. periclymenoides*). 'Marydel' is listed as a Choptank Hybrid. 'Choptank Rose', with fragrant pink flowers in spring on 5- to 6-foot plants, is another proven selection. Hardiness: Zones 5 to 9 for these hybrids. Plumleaf azalea hybrids, which were created by crossing Southeast native plumleaf azalea (*R. prunifolium*) and sweet azalea (*R. arborescens* var. *georgiana*), bear yellow, orange, or orange-red flowers from July to August on 8- to 12-foot plants. They need partial shade and moist, well-drained soil. Hardiness: Zones 5 to 7.

Bladdernut (*Staphylea trifolia*). This large shrub or small tree ranges from 10 to 15 feet tall and spreads by suckers to form thickets that are 20 feet across. Plants bear showy clusters of drooping, bell-shaped white flowers in spring followed by unusual 1- to 2-inch papery, egg-shaped fruits. They grow in part to full shade and also tolerate wet or dry soil. Because of their adaptability, they are suitable for rain gardens. Hardiness: Zones 3 to 8.

Blueberries (*Vaccinium* spp.). While popular highbush blueberry (*V. corymbosum*) is best in sun, other blueberry relatives are ideal for partial shade. All blueberries require acid soil. Farkleberry (*V. arboreum*) is a shrub or small tree that ranges from 10 to 20 feet tall and about 10 feet wide. Plants bear white flowers in spring followed by black berries that attract birds and red foliage in fall. They require well-drained soil and shade and tolerate drought once established. Hardiness: Zones 7 to 9. Deerberry (*V. stamineum*) is a 6- to 12-foot shrub that spreads as far and grows in dry to moist soil in partial shade or shade. Flowers are greenish white. The sour but edible fruit is green to blue-black when ripe. Fall foliage is red. Hardiness: Zones 3 to 7. Blue Ridge or hillside blueberry (*V. pallidum*, formerly *V. vacillans*), covered in Chapter 5, also grows in shade.

Buckeye, bottlebrush (*Aesculus parviflora*). This handsome native bears lacy, upright, 8- to 12-inch panicles of white flowers in summer when few shrubs

Bottlebrush buckeye (*Aesculus parviflora*). Photo © Roger Foley.

are blooming. Plants normally grow 8 to 12 feet tall and up to 15 feet wide, but they spread by suckers and can be much larger. Provide a site with moist, well-drained soil rich in organic matter. Use bottlebrush buckeye as a specimen or in shrub borders. It also is suitable for planting beneath shade trees. Hardiness: Zones 4 to 8.

Dogwoods (*Cornus* spp.). Both gray dogwood (*C. racemosa*) and silky dogwood (*C. amomum*) grow in partial shade or shade, although they bloom best with good light. See "Dogwoods" on p. 124 for more information.

Strawberry bush (*Euonymus americanus*). Photo by Barbara Ellis.

Euonymus (*Euonymus* spp.). This genus includes a fun, ornamental shrub and a woodland ground cover. Strawberry bush (*E. americanus*), also called bursting-heart and hearts-a-bustin', bears yellow-green flowers in spring followed by showy orange seed capsules that burst open to reveal red berries. This sprawling, almost vinelike shrub ranges from 4 to 6 feet tall and spreads to about 4 feet. Plants grow in part shade and moist to dry soil. Hardiness: Zones 6 to 9. Running strawberry bush (*E. obovatus*) is a spreading, 1-foot-tall shrub suitable for use as a ground cover. Plants have scarlet fall foliage and

cream flowers that ripen to red fruit. Hardiness: Zones 4 to 7. Eastern wahoo (*E. atropurpureus*), also called burning bush because of its scarlet fall berries and foliage, ranges from 12 to 20 feet and spreads about as far. Plants grow in sun to shade and tolerate a wide range of soils. Hardiness: Zones 3 to 7.

Huckleberries (*Gaylussacia* spp.). Shrubs for acid soil in the shade garden, huckleberries produce spring flowers followed by blue-black, edible, but very seedy berries in fall that are attractive to birds and other wildlife. Black huckleberry (*G. baccata*) is a 1- to 3-foot-tall shrub that spreads to 3 or more feet. Plants bear white to pink flowers and orange to red-purple fall foliage. They thrive in partial sun to shade and in dry to wet soil. Hardiness: Zones 4 to 9. Blue huckleberry or dangleberry (*G. frondosa*) ranges from 2 to 4 feet tall and wide. Plants bear greenish to purple flowers followed by blue berries and feature red-purple fall foliage. This species also grows in sun to shade and in dry to wet soil. Hardiness: Zones 3 to 9. Box huckleberry (*G. brachycera*) is a 1-foot-tall species that spreads to 2 or more feet and is suitable for use as a ground cover. Plants need moist, well-drained, acidic soil and partial shade to part sun. They bear pale pink flowers and nearly black berries. Box huckleberry is more difficult to grow than the other two species. Hardiness: Zones 4 to 7.

Hydrangeas (*Hydrangea* spp.). Two species of hydrangea, one native and one nearly so, are handsome additions to the shade garden. Wild hydrangea (*H. arborescens*) is a 3- to 10-foot-tall shrub with large, rounded, 4- to 6-inch-wide flower clusters from summer to early fall that start out white, fade to green, then turn tan. Plants spread steadily by root suckers to form 5- or 6-foot-wide drifts. In the garden, they are typically cut back hard in late winter and reach

Wild hydrangea (*Hydrangea arborescens*). Photo by Barbara Ellis; Nancy and Pierre Moitrier garden, Designs for Greener Gardens.

5 feet during the season. They thrive in part shade to shade and in average moist but well-drained soil. Plants can tolerate full sun provided the soil remains consistently moist to wet. A number of cultivars are available, including 'Annabelle', with 10-inch-wide blooms on sturdy stems. Hardiness: Zones 3 to 9. Oakleaf hydrangea (*H. quercifolia*) is nearly native and is found in the Carolinas, Tennessee, and south. It is an excellent plant for gardens in part shade to part sun. Plants range from 6 to 8 feet tall and wide and feature attractive, oak-leaf-shaped foliage that turns shades of burgundy, red, and purple in fall. White flowers appear in early summer and gradually fade to pink, then tan. They prefer moist, well-drained soil but also tolerate damp soil and some drought. Many cultivars are available, including 'Snow Queen'. Hardiness: Zones 5 to 9.

Itea, Virginia sweetspire (*Itea virginica*). Sweetspire is an excellent addition to gardens in sun or shade. See "Itea" on p. 120 for more information.

Leucothoe (*Leucothoe* spp.). Both coastal leucothoe (*L. axillaris*) and drooping leucothoe (*L. fontanesiana*) make excellent evergreen additions to shade gardens, whether used as shrubs or as ground covers. See "Leucothoes" on p. 169 for more information.

Lyonias (*Lyonia* spp.). Relatives of blueberries (*Vaccinium* spp.) and members of the heath family, lyonias bear white flowers in spring. They are not widely available in the nursery trade but are well worth looking for at native plant sales and nurseries. Male-berry (*L. ligustrina*) is a 6- to 12-foot shrub that spreads to form 12- to 20-foot-wide thickets. White spring flowers are followed by brown, berrylike fruit. Give plants a site in part shade to shade with moist to wet acid soil. They can tolerate permanently wet sites. Hardiness: Zones 4 to 8. Piedmont stagger-bush (*L. mariana*) is a 6-foot-tall shrub that grows in partial shade and prefers moist, well-drained sandy soil. Hardiness: Zones 5 to 9.

Mock orange, scentless (*Philadelphus inodorus*). This native shrub bears white, 2-inch-wide, cup-shaped flowers on arching branches in late spring. Plants are 6 to 10 feet tall and wide. They are best grown in partial shade with average moist, well-drained soil, although they tolerate a wider range of conditions. Hardiness: Zones 5 to 9.

Mountain laurel (*Kalmia angustifolia*). A handsome, broad-leaved evergreen, mountain laurel bears showy, rounded, 4- to 6-inch-wide clusters of bell-shaped flowers in shades of pink, red, and white. Blooms appear in late spring. Plants range from 3 to 15 feet tall and spread about as far. They grow in full sun to shade but are easiest in partial shade and require moist, well-drained, acidic soil. Plants can be difficult to establish, and good soil drainage is vital—

Mountain laurel (*Kalmia angustifolia*). Photo by
Barbara Ellis.

Northern spicebush (*Lindera benzoin*). Photo by
Neil Soderstrom; Hannelore Soderstrom garden.

plants do not grow well in heavy clay soil. Established plants tolerate drought. Hardiness: Zones 4 to 9.

New Jersey tea (*Ceanothus americanus*). White summer flowers and a relatively low, broad-spreading habit make this species an attractive addition to shade gardens. See "New Jersey tea" on p. 121 for more information.

Rhododendron, rosebay (*Rhododendron maximum*). Also called great laurel, this is a broad-leaved, evergreen shrub that ranges from 10 to 12 feet tall and wide. Plants bear showy, 5-inch-wide clusters, called trusses, of white or pink trumpet-shaped flowers in late spring or early summer. Like azaleas (*Rhododendron* spp.), they need part shade to shade and rich, acidic, moist but well-drained soil in order to thrive. Keeping plants mulched and planting them in a spot with afternoon shade helps them cope with heat. Hardiness: Zones 5 to 7.

Spicebush, northern (*Lindera benzoin*). Among the earliest plants to bloom, spicebush bears greenish yellow leaves in very early spring. Leaves are aromatic

when crushed and turn a nice yellow in fall. Plants range from 6 to 12 feet tall and wide. They grow in sun to shade, but they bloom best and develop the most outstanding fall color on sites where they receive at least a few hours of sun per day. Plants grow in moist to wet soil and tolerate drought as well as periodic flooding, making them useful additions to rain gardens. Hardiness: Zones 4 to 9.

Viburnums (*Viburnum* spp.). These outstanding plants bring flowers, fruit, and brilliant fall color to the garden. The viburnums listed in Chapter 4 grow in full sun to partial shade, but southern arrowwood (*V. dentatum*) and blackhaw viburnum (*V. prunifolium*), a large shrub or small tree, are most suited for the shade garden. Mapleleaf viburnum (*V. acerifolium*) is another species that is very shade tolerant. Plants bear flat-topped clusters of white flowers in early summer followed by black berries. Fall foliage ranges from pink to purple. Plants are 3 to 6 feet tall and can spread widely by suckers. They thrive in shade to part sun in average moist, well-drained soil and also tolerate some drought. Hardiness: Zones 3 to 8.

Many of the vines described in Chapter 4, including pipevine (*Aristolochia macrophylla*), crossvine (*Bignonia capreolata*), and Carolina jessamine (*Gelsemium sempervirens*), will grow in partial shade, although they will bloom less than they would in sun. Woodvamp or climbing hydrangea (*Decumaria barbara*) actually requires part shade to shade and rich, moist to wet soil. Virginia creeper (*Parthenocissus quinquefolia*) thrives in sun to shade.

Witch hazel, American or common (*Hamamelis virginiana*). This fall-blooming native is suitable for shade gardens. See "Witch hazel" on p. 123 for more information.

Foliage and Flowers for Shade

Great gardens develop over time, and the same is true of sustainable plantings. Use the plant lists that follow to build gardens slowly, selecting several plants from one list and a few from another. Included below is a list of wildflowers with long-lasting foliage. These help to create a framework that remains attractive all season long. Also included are lists of natives grown primarily for flowers, ferns for shade, and ephemeral spring wildflowers that bloom and then go dormant in early summer.

When planting the garden, use the site and soil preparation guidelines in Chapter 3 to minimize soil disturbance. Keep shade gardens mulched with chopped leaves or other mulch to keep the soil—and roots—cool, shaded, and moist.

Foliage First

The perennials listed below feature handsome foliage. While most of the plants listed also bear attractive flowers, their foliage makes them especially useful for keeping shade gardens looking their best all season. Unless otherwise noted, all are relatively easy to grow in part to full shade and average to rich, moist, well-drained soil. You will find references back to Chapter 5 after the names of the most popular shade-loving ground covers, but the list below contains information on additional species and cultivars that are not necessarily used to cover ground. Use any of these plants to create a gardenlike ground cover planting by arranging them singly or in very small drifts instead of in larger masses.

If your garden contains both native and non-native plants, several popular, non-native species contribute outstanding foliage to shady sites without spreading invasively, including epimediums (*Epimedium* spp.), pulmonarias (*Pulmonaria* spp.), and hostas (*Hosta* spp.).

Barren strawberry, Appalachian (*Waldsteinia fragarioides*, also listed as *Geum fragarioides*). See "Barren strawberry, Appalachian" on p. 156 for more information.

Bellworts (*Uvularia* spp.). In addition to large-flowered bellwort (*U. grandiflora*), discussed in Chapter 5, this genus contains two other outstanding plants for shade gardens. Perfoliate-leaved bellwort (*U. perfoliata*) bears pale yellow flowers on 6- to 18-inch plants that spread about as far with time. Hardiness: Zones 3 to 8. Large-flowered and perfoliate bellworts are very similar. The former has slightly larger flowers, and the undersides of the leaves are slightly hairy. Both have perfoliate leaves, meaning the lobes at the base of the leaf are united and the stem appears to travel through the leaf. Sessile-leaved bellwort (*U. sessilifolia*), also called straw lily and wild oats, has creamy yellow flowers. This species is slightly smaller than the other two and ranges from 6 to 13 inches tall and wide. As the name implies, the leaves are sessile, meaning attached directly to the stems. Bellworts prefer rich, moist soil and part shade but also tolerate drier conditions. Hardiness: Zones 3 to 8.

Fringed bleeding heart (*Dicentra eximia*). Photo by Neil Soderstrom; design by Leigh Sands.

Bleeding heart, fringed (*Dicentra eximia*). This species bears stems of dainty, dangling, heart-shaped flowers in shades of pink or white, primarily from late spring to early summer. Flowers are held atop mounds of fernlike leaves that have a delicate texture. Plants are 1 to 2 feet tall and spread about as far if conditions suit. When planted in rich, consistently moist, well-drained soil, they will continue flowering for much of the summer. In the right spot, the foliage will remain attractive all summer. Give them shade or part shade. Wet soil in winter is fatal. A number of cultivars are available, including 'Luxuriant', which is a hybrid between *D. eximia* and western bleeding heart (*D. formosa*). Hardiness: Zones 4 to 8.

Fairy bells (*Prosartes* spp., formerly *Disporum* spp.). These bring branched stems of rounded leaves with deep veins to the garden. Yellow fairy bells (*P. lanuginosa*, formerly *D. lanuginosum*), also called yellow mandarin, is about 2 feet tall and spreads as far with time. Plants bear yellow flowers that are partially hidden among the leaves in spring and orange to yellow berries in fall. Spotted fairy bells (*P. maculata*, formerly *D. maculata*) is similar but bears white flowers with purple spots and yellow fruit. Hardiness: Zones 4 or 5 to 7.

Foamflower (*Tiarella* 'Spring Symphony') with Dutchman's breeches (*Dicentra cucullaria*). Photo by Barbara Ellis; Mt. Cuba Center.

Foamflowers (*Tiarella* spp.). East Coast native Allegheny foamflower (*T. cordifolia*) is a spreader used as a ground cover, but a number of hybrids between various North American native species make excellent additions to any shade garden. 'Brandywine' and 'Oakleaf' tend to be more clump-forming than the selections listed in Chapter 5. 'Spring Symphony' is another excellent clump-former. All can be massed for use as ground covers as well. Hardiness: Zones 3 to 8.

Geranium, spotted (*Geranium maculatum*). See "Geranium, spotted" on p. 159 for more information.

Green-and-gold (*Chrysogonum virginianum*). See "Green-and-gold" on p. 159 for more information.

Indian pink (*Spigelia marilandica*). Photo by Barbara Ellis.

Heucheras, alumroots (*Heuchera* spp.). See "Heucheras, alumroots" on p. 159 for more information.

Indian pink (*Spigelia marilandica*). Also called woodland pinkroot, this mounding species is grown for its clusters of tubular, 2-inch-long red flowers with yellow throats. Plants are 12 to 18 inches tall and spread about as far. The oval, glossy green leaves form an attractive mound after flowers fade. Give Indian pink soil that is rich in organic matter and a site in part to full shade. Rich, moist soil is best. Once established, plants are drought tolerant. They are best not disturbed once they are planted. Hardiness: Zones 5 to 9.

Iris, crested (*Iris cristata*). See "Iris, crested" on p. 160 for more information.

Knotweed, Virginia (*Persicaria virginiana*, formerly *P. filiformis*, *P. filiforme*, and *Tovara virginiana*). See "Knotweed, Virginia" on p. 160 for more information.

Mint, Meehan's (*Meehania cordata*). See "Mint, Meehan's" on p. 160 for more information.

Pachysandra, Allegheny (*Pachysandra procumbens*). See "Pachysandra, Allegheny" on p. 161 for more information.

Wild blue phlox (*Phlox divaricata*). Photo by Barbara Ellis.

Partridge berry (*Mitchella repens*). See "Partridge berry" on p. 161 for more information.

Phlox, wild blue (*Phlox divaricata*) thrives in shade and blooms from late spring into early summer. The plants self-sow with enthusiasm, and their purple, lilac, or white flowers fill in around other shade-loving perennials. Hardiness: Zones 3 to 9. See "Phlox" on p. 161 for more information.

Sedum, woodland (*Sedum ternatum*). See "Sedum, woodland" on p. 162 for more information.

Solomon's plume (*Maianthemum racemosum*). Photo by Neil Soderstrom.

Solomon's plume (*Maianthemum racemosum*, formerly *Smilacina racemosa*). Also called false Solomon's seal, feathery false lily-of-the-valley, and false spikenard, this 2- to 3-foot-tall perennial slowly spreads by rhizomes to about 2 feet. Plants produce arching stems of oval leaves that turn yellow in fall. Stems are topped by a plume of small, creamy white flowers in spring, followed by red berries. Plants thrive in average to moist soil and are best not disturbed once planted. Hardiness: Zones 3 to 8. Canada mayflower (*M. canadense*) or wild lily-of-the-valley is a 3- to 6-inch relative that thrives in moist to wet soil throughout our area.

Spiderwort (*Tradescantia* 'Sweet Kate'). Photo by Barbara Ellis.

Solomon's seal, small (*Polygonatum biflorum*). See "Solomon's seal, small" on p. 162 for more information.

Spiderworts (*Tradescantia* spp.). These popular perennials produce 1- to 2-foot-tall clumps of arching, lance-shaped, blue-green leaves that add textural contrast to the shade garden. Clumps spread to 3 or more feet. Clusters of three-petaled flowers appear from early to midsummer. Plants tolerate light to full shade and poor soil but bloom best in partial shade in rich, moist, well-drained soil. Virginia spiderwort (*T. virginiana*), with violet-blue flowers, is the most common species. Many cultivars are also available, including 'Sweet Kate', with blue flowers and chartreuse foliage; rosy-purple 'Concord Grape'; and violet-blue 'Purple Profusion'. Cut plants to the ground in midsummer after the main flush of flowers fades to encourage new flowers and fresh, new foliage. Plants spread by self-sowing, although seedlings from cultivated forms will not necessarily resemble the parent plants. Hardiness: Zones 4 to 9.

Violets (*Viola* spp.). See "Violets" on p. 162 for more information.

Wild gingers (*Asarum* spp. and *Hexastylis* spp.). See "Wild gingers" on p. 163 for more information.

Wintergreen (*Gaultheria procumbens*). See "Wintergreen" on p. 164 for more information.

Flowers for Shade

Once a selection of plants that feature outstanding foliage is established, begin adding natives that are grown primarily for their flowers. The wildflowers listed below are dependable, attractive natives that are easy to grow in part or full shade. Soil needs vary, but unless otherwise noted, they will grow in average moist but well-drained soil.

Canadian or meadow anemone (*Anemone canadensis*). Photo by Neil Soderstrom.

Anemone, Canadian or meadow (*Anemone canadensis*). This vigorous, 1- to 2-foot-tall species spreads to 2 or 3 feet. Plants are grown for their cup-shaped white flowers with a showy central cluster of yellow stamens. They form dense drifts in partial shade with rich, moist to wet soil and grow in nearly full sun in consistently wet soil. Plant them under shrubs, along streams, and in other moist-soil sites where they have room to spread. Hardiness: Zones 4 to 8.

Common blue wood aster (*Symphyotrichum cordifolium*). Photo by Barbara Ellis.

Asters (*Eurybia* and *Symphyotrichum* spp., formerly *Aster* spp.). While the best-known asters are plants for sunny borders and meadows, shade gardeners can grow three outstanding species. White wood aster (*E. divaricatus*, formerly *A. divaricata*) produces airy mounds of tiny, white, daisy flowers with gold centers from late summer to early fall. Plants are 1 to 2½ feet tall and spread about as far. They thrive in partial to full shade. Common blue wood aster (*S. cordifolium*, formerly *A. cordifolius*) bears masses of tiny, pale to deep blue, daisy flowers with gold centers, also from late summer to early fall. Plants, which are best in part sun to part shade, range from 2 to 5 feet tall and spread to about 2 feet. Both species grow in soil that ranges from dry to average moist but well

drained. Bigleaf or large-leaved aster (*E. macrophylla*) produces clusters of violet to pale blue, daisy flowers above large leaves that range from 4 to 8 inches across. Plants are 2 to 4 feet tall and spread to 4 or more feet via rhizomes. Give bigleaf aster average moist but well-drained soil. All three species can be cut back hard (by half or two-thirds) once or twice before the end of June to encourage branching, more flowers, and lower height at bloom time. Hardiness: Zones 3 to 8 for all species.

Beardtongue, long-sepal (*Penstemon calycosus*). While most beardtongues are plants for sun, this species thrives in moist to dry woods and along woodland edges. Plants bear showy upright panicles of two-lipped, purple-pink or violet flowers in late spring and early summer. The blooms provide valuable early season nectar for hummingbirds. Plants range from 1 to 3 feet tall and spread to about 2 feet. They prefer partial filtered sun or part shade. The more sun plants receive, the more soil moisture they require. Hardiness: Zones 5 to 9.

Bowman's root (*Gillenia trifoliata*, also listed as *Porteranthus trifoliatus*). Also called Indian physic or American ipecac, Bowman's root bears masses of small, five-petaled, white flowers in late spring to midsummer on plants that range from 2 to 3 feet and spread about as far. The leaves, which turn red in fall, are narrow and fine-textured as well, and the overall effect is lacy and delightful. Plants bloom best in bright partial shade or part sun. A spot with shade in the afternoon is best. Once established, plants are drought tolerant. Hardiness: Zones 4 to 8.

Bugbanes (*Actaea* spp., formerly *Cimicifuga* spp.). These large, eye-catching perennials produce a handsome, shrub-size mound of ferny, deeply cut

Black or common bugbane (*Actaea racemosa*). Photo by Neil Soderstrom; design by Diana Bristol.

leaves. Bottlebrush-like stems of tiny white flowers appear from late summer to early fall above the foliage. Mountain or American bugbane (*A. podocarpa*, formerly *A. cordifolia*, *C. americana*, and *C. cordifolia*) is a 5- to 6-foot-tall plant that spreads to about 4 feet. Hardiness: Zones 3 to 7. Black or common bugbane (*A. racemosa*, formerly *C. racemosa*) is very similar but blooms in midsummer. Both species thrive in soil that is rich in organic matter and consistently moist. Plants are slow to establish and should not be disturbed once they are planted. Hardiness: Zones 4 to 6.

Columbine (*Aquilegia canadensis*). Also called eastern red and Canadian columbine, this species produces nodding, red-and-yellow flowers from late spring to early summer. The blooms are especially attractive to hummingbirds and are borne on erect

Columbine (*Aquilegia canadensis*). Photo by Neil Soderstrom; Innisfree Garden.

stalks above attractive blue-green foliage. Plants are 2 to 3 feet tall and spread to about 1½ feet. They also self-sow freely. Because they are taprooted, plants do not transplant well, but seedlings can easily be moved when they are still small. Plants prefer a wide range of soils, from sandy and poor to average moist garden loam, provided they are well drained. Dwarf cultivars, including 'Little Lanterns', with red-and-yellow flowers, and 'Corbett', with yellow flowers, are available. Both are about 1 foot tall. Hardiness: Zones 3 to 8.

Dwarf larkspur (*Delphinium tricorne*). Photo by Neil Soderstrom; Mt. Cuba Center.

Delphiniums (*Delphinium* spp.). Native delphiniums have long been overlooked in favor of the showy garden hybrids bred for the cool summer weather in the British Isles and Pacific Northwest. Two species that are native to the Chesapeake Bay region are much better choices for gardens in our area. Tall larkspur (*D. exaltatum*) bears racemes of deep, rich blue flowers in midsummer. Plants are 4 to 6 feet tall and spread from 1 to 2 feet. They need very rich, moist, well-drained soil and partial shade to full sun. A site with high dappled shade or with shade during the afternoon hours helps them cope with heat. Hardiness: Zones 5 to 7. Dwarf larkspur (*D. tricorne*) bears loose clusters of violet-blue flowers on 1- to 2-foot plants that spread to about 1 foot. They grow best in partial or dappled shade and spread if conditions suit. Hardiness: Zones 5 to 8. Both species need moist, well-drained soil that is rich in organic matter. They prefer neutral to alkaline pH.

Goat's beard (*Aruncus dioicus*). Photo by Neil Soderstrom; New York Botanical Garden.

Goat's beard (*Aruncus dioicus*). This large, robust wildflower ranges from 4 to 6 feet tall and spreads to 4 or more feet. Plants produce large clumps of foliage topped by branched, plumelike clusters of tiny, creamy white flowers in spring that resemble astilbe (*Astilbe* spp.) blooms. Give goat's beard partial shade and consistently moist to wet, well-drained soil. Established plants tolerate drought, but their foliage will turn brown around the edges. Hardiness: Zones 3 to 7.

Wreath goldenrod (*Solidago caesia*). Photo by Barbara Ellis.

Goldenrods (*Solidago* spp.). Two species of goldenrods bring golden yellow flowers to shade gardens late in the season. Goldenrods are very attractive to butterflies and pollinators. Wreath goldenrod (*S. caesia*) is a clump-forming goldenrod that bears arching stems dotted with fuzzy, buttonlike clusters of golden flowers on 1½- to 3-foot plants that spread as far. Plants bloom from late summer to fall. They grow in full sun to partial shade and tolerate dry to average soil. In sun, they need consistent moisture. Zigzag goldenrod (*S. flexicaulis*) bears loose clusters of tightly packed, golden flowers on 1- to 3-foot stems from midsummer to fall. Plants form clumps that are about 3 feet across. They grow in partial shade to shade and in dry to average moist but well-drained soil. Hardiness: Zones 3 or 4 to 8 for both species.

Golden groundsel (*Packera aurea*) with purple-leaved white snakeroot (*Ageratina altissima* 'Chocolate'). Photo by Barbara Ellis; Lang garden.

Groundsel, golden (*Packera aurea*, formerly *Senecio aureus*). Also called golden ragwort, this cheerful perennial brings clusters of small, golden yellow, daisy flowers to the shade garden in late spring and early summer. Plants are 12 inches tall and wide and have shiny green leaves. They are happiest in moist, well-drained soil and shade but tolerate full sun with consistent moisture. Plants self-sow where conditions suit. Hardiness: Zones 4 to 9.

Jacob's ladder (*Polemonium reptans*). Photo by Neil Soderstrom; Mt. Cuba Center.

Jacob's ladder (*Polemonium reptans*). Also called Greek valerian, this native wildflower forms a mound of sprawling stems with oval leaflets topped by loose clusters of small, bell-shaped blue flowers in mid to late spring. Plants are best in rich, moist soil and will self-sow if conditions suit. Hardiness: Zones 3 to 8.

Meadow rue, early (*Thalictrum dioicum*). This species ranges from 1 to 2 feet tall and wide, and plants feature gray-green leaves that are divided into many rounded leaflets. The tiny, greenish white flowers are borne in clusters in spring. Plants are best in partial shade with moist soil that is rich in humus and other organic matter. Hardiness: Zones 4 to 7.

Miterwort, two-leaved (*Mitella diphylla*). A little-known native related to foamflower (*Tiarella cordifolia*), in spring miterwort bears upright stalks of tiny white flowers with fringed petal edges that make them look like tiny snowflakes. The leaves resemble maple leaves. Plants are 6 to 18 inches tall and spread

Two-leaved miterwort (*Mitella diphylla*). Photo by Neil Soderstrom.

to about 1 foot. They thrive in rich, moist, well-drained soil and part shade. Hardiness: Zones 4 to 8.

Plantain, Robin's (*Erigeron pulchellus*). This native species brings white, daisylike flowers with yellow centers to the garden. Each flower has a multitude of threadlike petals, unlike those of asters and other perennials with daisylike blooms. Plants, which range from 12 to 15 inches in bloom and spread about as far, grow in a range of soil types, from poor, dry conditions to average garden soil. They bloom in part shade and need consistently moist soil if they are in sun. 'Lynnhaven Carpet' is an excellent cultivar being sold as a ground cover. Hardiness: Zones 5 to 9.

Skullcaps (*Scutellaria* spp.). These underappreciated natives belong to the mint family and bring two-lipped, lavender to bluish purple flowers to the garden from summer to early fall. Most grow in dry to average well-drained soil and spread by rhizomes as well as by self-sowing if conditions suit. Hoary skullcap (*S. incana*) bears blue-purple flowers from midsummer to early fall on 2- to 3-foot plants that spread to about 2 feet. Helmet flower (*S. integrifolia*) bears lavender-blue flowers from early to midsummer on 1- to 2-foot plants that spread about as far. Plants tolerate dry as well as wet soils. Heart-leaved skullcap (*S. ovata*) bears violet-blue flowers in summer on 1- to 2-foot plants that spread about as far. Plants are happiest in dry to average moist, well-drained soil and tolerate drought once established. In hot, dry weather, they may go dormant after flowering. Showy skullcap (*S. serrata*) is an 18-inch-tall species that spreads about as far and bears lavender- to violet-blue flowers in late spring. Hardiness: Zones 4 or 5 to 8 or 9 for all species listed.

White snakeroot (*Ageratina altissima*). Photo by Neil Soderstrom.

Snakeroot, white (*Ageratina altissima*, formerly *Eupatorium rugosum*). This species bears rounded clusters of fuzzy, white, buttonlike flowerheads in fall that are attractive to butterflies. In gardens, it is most often represented by the cultivar 'Chocolate', which has leaves flushed with maroon-brown and ranges from 3 to 5 feet tall. Plants grow in average to wet soil and in part shade to full sun. Clumps that are deadheaded before seeds form spread to about 3 feet, but plants can spread rapidly by self-sowing ('Chocolate' does not come true from seeds), especially in rich, moist soil. Hardiness: Zones 4 to 8.

Sunflower, woodland (*Helianthus divaricatus*). Sunflowers are typically plants for full sun, but this native species brings yellow, 2-inch-wide, daisy flowers with gold centers to sites with bright or dappled shade from mid- to late summer. Plants range from 2 to 6 feet tall and spread to about 3 feet. They grow in moist or dry shade. Try them along the edges of

Woodland sunflower (*Helianthus divaricatus*). Photo by Neil Soderstrom; Howard Country Conservancy.

shade gardens or in bright, partially shaded spots. Hardiness: Zones 5 to 9.

Twinleaf (*Jeffersonia diphylla*). A plant of rich, cool, consistently moist soil, twinleaf bears handsome blue-green leaves. Each leaf is so deeply lobed it appears to be a pair of leaves. Plants are about 8 inches tall when they flower in spring, but they reach 18 inches later in the season. They spread to about 10 inches. Flowers are white and 1 inch wide. Be sure to locate plants on sites where the soil does not dry out. Hardiness: Zones 5 to 7.

Golden zizia (*Zizia aurea*). Photo by Barbara Ellis.

Zizia, golden (*Zizia aurea*). This carrot-family plant is also called golden alexanders. Plants bear flat-topped clusters of yellow flowers in late spring to early summer that attract butterflies. The foliage

🍃 Bulbs for Shade

The best-known spring bulbs are not native plants, although daffodils (*Narcissus* spp.), crocuses (*Crocus* spp.), snowdrops (*Galanthus* spp.), tulips (*Tulipa* spp.), and winter aconites (*Eranthis hyemalis*) all are species that do not spread widely or invasively. The commonly sold stars of Bethlehem (*Ornithogalum umbellatum* and *O. nutans*), on the other hand, are invasive and quite difficult to eliminate once established. Siberian squill (*Scilla sibirica*) has jumped the bounds of gardens and is identified as problematic in some nearby states.

Bulbs are useful for adding early flowers to the garden. Very early pollinators can be seen visiting the flowers whenever temperatures are warm enough. Many spring ephemerals also grow from bulbs, corms, tubers, or tuberous roots, including dogtooth violet (*Erythronium americanum*), spring beauties (*Claytonia* spp.), and Virginia bluebells (*Mertensia virginica*). See "Wildflowers for Spring" on p. 236 for more information on ephemerals. Here are a few other native bulbs to consider:

Atamasco lily (*Zephyranthes atamasca*). This 12- to 18-inch bulb produces white, lilylike flowers above grassy leaves in mid to late spring. Plants thrive in partial shade and average to moist, well-drained soil. Hardiness: Zones 7 to 10.

Atlantic camas (*Camassia scilloides*). Also called wild hyacinth, this native bears clusters of sweetly scented, pale violet-blue flowers on 1- to 2-foot plants in late spring. Plants grow in part shade to shade and need well-drained moist soil when in bloom. Drier conditions are fine after the clumps go dormant in midsummer. Plants return and increase faithfully over the years. Give them rich, partially moist soil and full sun or partial shade. Hardiness: Zones 4 to 8. Other *Camassia* species, more common in the trade, are native to the western United States.

Wood sorrel, violet (*Oxalis violacea*). This 6- to 8-inch native grows from a bulb and spreads quickly by runners to form large colonies. Plants bear cloverlike leaves and five-petaled pink or lavender blooms in spring. They grow in full sun to part shade and in average well-drained soil. Hardiness: Zones 5 to 9.

feeds swallowtail butterfly larvae. Plants need consistently moist soil to survive in sun but will grow in average, well-drained conditions with part shade, especially afternoon shade. Hardiness: Zones 4 to 9.

Ferns for Shade

No shade garden is complete without ferns. Their feathery fronds add lush texture and rich green color to plantings, creating an easy elegance that is incredibly appealing. The ferns listed below all are relatively easy to grow. Most thrive in average moist, well-drained garden soil in part to full shade. In general, the more soil organic matter, the better. Use ferns singly, in drifts, or as ground covers. You will find references back to Chapter 5 after the names of ferns that can be used as ground covers.

Beech fern, broad (*Phegopteris hexagonoptera*, formerly *Dryopteris hexagonoptera* and *Thelypteris hexagonoptera*). See "Beech fern, broad" on p. 165 for more information.

Bracken fern (*Pteridium aquilinum*). See "Bracken fern" on p. 166 for more information.

Bulblet bladder fern (*Cystopteris bulbifera*). Also known as berry fern, this species produces feathery, 1- to 3-foot fronds. Plants spread by short rhizomes but also by pealike bulblets that form on the fronds and then fall off and roll away to sprout. Hardiness: Zones 3 to 8.

Chain ferns (*Woodwardia* spp.). Netted chain fern (*W. areolata*) is a 1- to 2-foot-tall fern that resembles sensitive fern (*Onoclea sensibilis*) but has toothed leaf margins. Plants spread fairly quickly if conditions suit and form drifts to about 2 feet. They thrive in average moist, well-drained to wet soil. In wet conditions, they can tolerate considerable sun. Hardiness: Zones 3 to 9. Virginia chain fern (*W. virginica*) is 2 feet tall and spreads to 3 feet. Plants are native to wet soil and form a thick, weed-suppressing ground cover in wet, shady sites. They also grow in average moist, well-drained soil, where they are less assertive. Hardiness: Zones 3 to 10.

Christmas fern (*Polystichum acrostichoides*). See "Christmas fern" on p. 166 for more information.

Cinnamon fern (*Osmunda cinnamomea*). This handsome species ranges from 2½ to 5 feet tall. The plants form vase-shaped clumps that spread from 2 to 3 or more feet. They are tallest and most vigorous in rich, moist to wet soil that is high in organic matter, but they tolerate drier, less ideal conditions. Hardiness: Zones 3 to 9.

Glade fern (*Diplazium pycnocarpon*, formerly *Asplenium pycnocarpon*). Also called narrow-leaved spleenwort, this vigorous, easy-to-grow fern ranges from 2

to 3 feet and spreads as far. Plants bear tall, narrow fronds and are best in rich, moist, well-drained soil. Hardiness: Zones 4 to 9.

Interrupted fern (*Osmunda claytoniana*). Photo by Barbara Ellis, Mt. Cuba Center.

Hayscented fern, eastern (*Dennstaedtia punctilobula*). See "Hayscented fern, eastern" on p. 166 for more information.

Interrupted fern (*Osmunda claytoniana*). A close relative of cinnamon and royal ferns, this species ranges from 2 to 4 feet tall and spreads to 2 or more feet. Plants are best in moist, but not boggy, soil. Hardiness: Zones 2 to 8.

Lady fern, common (*Athyrium filix-femina*). See "Lady fern, common" on p. 167 for more information.

Maidenhair fern (*Adiantum pedatum*). Also called five-finger fern, this species bears branched, 1- to 2½-foot-tall fronds with wiry black stems. Plants spread steadily by rhizomes to form 2-foot-wide clumps with time if conditions suit. Give plants a site with moist, well-drained soil that is rich in organic matter. Hardiness: Zones 2 to 8.

Male fern (*Dryopteris felix-mas*). Although native from Pennsylvania northward, this fern is a good choice for gardens in the Chesapeake Bay region.

Plants are 2 to 4 feet tall and spread to 3 feet. They are semi-evergreen in the north and evergreen in warm climates. Plants prefer rich, moist soil but tolerate poor, sandy, and dry soil and can grow in at least part-day sun, provided they have enough moisture. Many cultivars with crested and finely dissected fronds are available. Hardiness: Zones 4 to 8.

New York fern (*Thelypteris noveboracensis*, formerly *Dryopteris noveboracensis*, *Polypodium noveboracense*, and *Thelypteris thelypterioides*). See "New York fern" on p. 167 for more information.

Ostrich fern (*Matteuccia struthiopteris*, formerly *M. pensylvanica*). See "Ostrich fern" on p. 167 for more information.

Polypody, rock (*Polypodium virginianum*). Also called rockcap fern, this evergreen fern ranges from 6 to 12 inches tall and spreads about as far. In nature, plants grow atop and among moist rocks. Plants can be difficult to establish on a new site, but they spread easily once they adapt. Give them average, well-drained soil. They are best in soil that is somewhat poor in nutrients but rich in humus. Hardiness: Zones 2 to 8.

Royal ferns (*Osmunda regalis*) in a moss garden. Photo by Barbara Ellis; Liesfeld garden.

Royal fern (*Osmunda regalis*). This handsome species ranges from 2 to 6 or more feet in height and spreads to about 2 feet. Plants produce branched fronds and are native to swamps and other wet places. Give them rich, moist to wet soil. They tolerate extended flooding as well as partial sun with consistent soil moisture. Hardiness: Zones 2 to 10.

Sensitive fern (*Onoclea sensibilis*). See "Sensitive fern" on p. 167 for more information.

Wood ferns (*Dryopteris* spp.). Several species of wood ferns are native and easy to grow in Chesapeake-area gardens. All spread slowly and can be massed to use as ground covers. Intermediate wood fern (*D. intermedia*), also called fancy fern and intermediate shield fern, bears evergreen fronds and ranges from 1½ to 3 feet tall. Plants spread to form 2-foot-wide clumps and thrive in rich, moist soil. Hardiness: Zones 3 to 8. Marginal wood fern (*D. marginalis*) is also called marginal shield fern, evergreen wood fern, and evergreen shield fern. Plants are 1 to 2 feet tall and spread about as far. They grow in rich, moist, acid soil, but they also tolerate sandy soil and dry shade. Zones 2 to 8. Goldie's wood fern (*D. goldiana*) is deciduous and ranges from 3 to 4 feet tall. Plants spread to form 3-foot-wide clumps. They prefer rich, moist, well-drained soil. Hardiness: Zones 3 to 8.

Wildflowers for Spring

Some of the most beloved wildflowers are spring ephemerals, meaning plants that produce foliage and flowers in early spring and then go dormant over the summer months. Ephemerals are wonderful for adding early season interest to the garden, although many are best for intermediate to experienced shade gardeners. Include them with some of the wildflowers grown for outstanding foliage so that the spaces they leave in the garden will be covered once they

🍂 Grasses and Sedges

The foliage of grasses and sedges contrasts nicely with the leaves of perennials and ferns, adding interesting texture and a vertical accent to shade combinations. Consider some of the following for shade gardens.

Bottlebrush grass (*Elymus hystrix*, formerly *Hystrix patula*). Plants grow in any well-drained soil, tolerate drought, and prefer sites in part shade but will grow in full shade. See "Bottlebrush grass" on p. 202 for more information.

Sea oats, northern (*Chasmanthium latifolium* formerly *Uniola latifolia*). Also called wild oats and Indian wood oats, this adaptable 3- to 4-foot-tall grass forms clumps and self-sows enthusiastically. Use it under shrubs, since clumps will quickly outcompete most shade perennials. See "Sea oats" on p. 203 for more information.

Sedges (*Carex* spp.). These produce clumps of fine-textured grassy foliage. Pennsylvania or oak sedge (*C. pensylvanica*) is about 8 inches tall and spreads to 12 or more inches. Plants have semi-evergreen leaves and can be massed and used as ground covers or tucked in individually for accent and texture. They also make a good lawn substitute and can be mowed to a height of 2 or 3 inches. Plants grow in part sun to shade and thrive in average moist, well-drained soil but tolerate drought as well. Plantain-leaved sedge (*C. plantaginea*), also called seersucker sedge, forms 1- to 2-foot-tall clumps of crinkled, 1-inch-wide evergreen leaves that spread to about 2 feet. Broad-leaved or silver sedge (*C. platyphylla*) is very similar but features blue-gray evergreen leaves.

Both plantain-leaved and broad-leaved sedge grow in part sun to shade and prefer rich, moist soil. All of the species listed above are hardy in Zones 4 to 8. Palm sedge (*C. muskingumensis*) is native to the Midwest but is worth adding to shade gardens because of the interesting texture of its leaves. The plants have erect stems, each with many leaves arranged around them, and they resemble a clump of miniature palm trees. Plants are 2 feet tall and spread about as far. They grow in moist, well-drained soil in shade but can grow in full sun in constantly moist soil. Hardiness: Zones 3 to 8.

Plantain-leaved sedge (*Carex plantaginea*).
Photo by Nancy Ondra.

die back. As with all wildflowers, be sure to purchase them from reputable dealers. Spring ephemerals are often wild collected. Look for nurseries that offer plants propagated from seed or by dividing clumps already in cultivation. Unless otherwise noted below, all of the plants listed thrive in rich, moist, well-drained soil. They can tolerate drier soil in summer once they are dormant.

Jack-in-the-pulpit (*Arisaema triphyllum*). Photo by Neil Soderstrom; Hannelore Soderstrom garden.

Arisaemas (*Arisaema* spp.). These produce unusual-looking flowers followed by red berries in summer. Jack-in-the-pulpit (*A. triphyllum*) bears compound, 3-leaflet leaves and ranges from 1 to 2 feet in height. Plants spread to about 1 foot. The "Jack" is actually a column of flowers, called a spadix, surrounded by a leaflike spathe, the "pulpit." The spathe varies in color but is usually shades of purple and green. Green dragon (*A. dracontium*) is similar, but the leaves have 7 to 15 leaflets and the spathe and spadix are both green. Both species thrive in moist to wet soil and are best left undisturbed once planted. Hardiness: Zones 4 to 9 for both species.

Bloodroot (*Sanguinaria canadensis*). When the flowers of this lovely native appear in very early spring, each is wrapped in a leaf that unfurls after the flowers have faded. Flowers are white with a yellow center, and each opens during the day and closes at night. Individual flowers last for only a few days. The handsome, rounded, deeply lobed leaves can range from

Bloodroot (*Sanguinaria canadensis*). Photo by Neil Soderstrom; Hannelore Soderstrom garden.

8 to 9 inches across. Plants are 6 to 8 inches tall and spread steadily by rhizomes to form drifts 1 foot or more across. With even moisture, the foliage remains attractive for much of the summer. Hardiness: Zones 3 to 8.

Virginia bluebells (*Mertensia virginica*). Photo by Neil Soderstrom; George Fenn garden.

Bluebells, Virginia (*Mertensia virginica*). This clump-forming perennial ranges from 1 to 2 feet and spreads about as far. Plants produce showy, dangling clusters of pink buds that open into small, blue, trumpet-shaped flowers above oval, blue-green leaves. They grow from a deep, carrotlike taproot and are best left undisturbed once established. Bluebells will self-sow. Hardiness: Zones 3 to 8.

Bluets (*Houstonia caerulea*). Also called Quaker ladies, these tiny wildflowers produce four-petaled, blue flowers with yellow centers on 3- to 4-inch-tall plants. Plants form a matlike covering and can spread to several inches. Give bluets a site in part shade with average acid, well-drained soil. They are not able to compete with larger, more vigorous wildflowers. Bluets can be difficult to establish on a new site, but they are lovely in moss gardens, along the edges of beds, or planted with less-competitive wildflowers such as columbine (*Aquilegia canadensis*) and shooting stars (*Dodecatheon meadia*). Once established, bluets will self-sow. Hardiness: Zones 5 to 7.

Dicentras (*Dicentra* spp.). Fringed bleeding heart (*Dicentra eximia*) is a widely available member of this genus (see "Bleeding heart, fringed" on p. 226 for more information), but two other species are sometimes available from native plant nurseries. Dutchman's breeches (*D. cucullaria*) bears clusters of dainty, pantaloon-shaped, white-and-yellow flowers above ferny, blue-green leaves. Squirrel corn (*D. canadensis*) bears clusters of white, locket-shaped flowers above ferny leaves. Both plants are about 10 inches tall and wide. Hardiness: Zones 3 to 7 for both species.

Dogtooth violet (*Erythronium americanum*). Photo by Neil Soderstrom; Hannelore Soderstrom garden.

Dogtooth violet (*Erythronium americanum*). Also called eastern or yellow trout-lily as well as yellow adder's tongue, this species grows from corms and produces narrow leaves mottled with maroon and small, yellow, nodding, lilylike flowers. Plants are 4 to 6 inches tall and, once established, can spread slowly by stolons to form broad drifts. The foliage

disappears by early summer. Give plants moist, well-drained soil. Do not disturb plants once they are in the ground. Hardiness: Zones 3 to 8.

Hepatica (*Hepatica* or *Anemone* spp.). The nomenclature for these lovely natives is in flux, but by any name these are pretty native wildflowers that are sometimes available from nursery-propagated stock. Sharp-lobed hepatica (*H. nobilis* var. *acuta*, also listed as *H. acutiloba* and *A. acutiloba*) and round-lobed hepatica (*H. nobilis* var. *obtusa*, also listed as *H. americana* and *A. americana*) both produce small clumps of leaves topped by five-petaled, cup-shaped flowers in shades of blue, purple, pink, or white. Plants are about 6 inches tall and spread as far. They need moist, well-drained soil that is rich in humus and self-sow where happy. Hardiness: Zones 3 to 8.

Mayapple (*Podophyllum peltatum*). Photo by Neil Soderstrom; Hannelore Soderstrom garden.

Mayapple (*Podophyllum peltatum*). Also called American mandrake and umbrella plant, this is a 1- to 1½-foot-tall native that spreads by rhizomes to form drifts that can be several feet across. Plants, which also spread by self-sowing, produce one or two umbrella-like leaves that turn yellow and then disappear by midsummer. On plants with two leaves, a white, cup-shaped flower forms under the foliage. Flowers are followed by greenish fruit that is popular with wildlife. Hardiness: Zones 3 to 8.

Rue anemone (*Thalictrum thalictroides*). Photo by Neil Soderstrom; Mt. Cuba Center.

Rue anemone (*Thalictrum thalictroides*, formerly *Anemonella thalictroides*). This dainty wildflower is 6 to 9 inches tall and spreads about as far. Plants bear loose clusters of small but showy white flowers with yellow stamens in spring above mounds of three-lobed leaves. Hardiness: Zones 4 to 8.

Common shooting star (*Dodecatheon meadia* f. *alba*) with wild blue phlox (*Phlox divaricata*). Photo by Barbara Ellis.

Shooting star, common (*Dodecatheon meadia*). This exotic-looking beauty produces a cluster of tiny, downward-pointing, shuttlecock-shaped flow-

 Gain Some Experience

Filling a garden with rare wildflowers such as lady's slipper orchids (*Cypripedium* spp.) and trilliums (*Trillium* spp.) can be incredibly tempting, but it is best to wait to add these treasures to the garden. Native lilies, including Carolina lily (*Lilium michauxii*), fall into this category as well. One reason for caution is that these species are still widely collected in the wild. Buying plants collected in the wild—even if they are dug with the landowner's permission—is simply not sustainable or acceptable.

Fortunately, there are companies that sell nursery-propagated plants, but reputable nurseries cannot compete with those that sell wild-collected plants. Nursery-propagated lady's slippers and trilliums both take a number of years to reach sufficient size suitable for sale, so the plants are expensive. Before investing in them, develop a well-established shade garden, increase the soil organic matter, and plant a diverse selection of natives that are easier to grow and less particular about their site. Once you have some experience and are more familiar with your site, it may be time to invest in a plant or two.

ers above a low mound of rounded leaves. Flowers come in pink, purple-pink, or white. Plants are 10 to 18 inches tall and spread to 1 foot or more with time. They need average, well-drained soil and good drainage when they are dormant, especially in winter. Clumps spread slowly but can be divided, or shooting stars can be grown from seed. Hardiness: Zones 4 to 8.

🍂 Brilliant Berries

Flowers are not the only things that bring seasonal color to the shade garden. The plants listed below produce colorful berries.

Aralias (*Aralia* spp.). These have never been popular wildflowers, but in the right site they make handsome additions to the garden. All bear compound leaves, meaning leaves divided into many smaller leaflets. Their berries are attractive to wildlife. American spikenard (*A. racemosa*) is a herbaceous perennial that ranges from 3 to 5 feet tall and wide. Plants bear tiny white flowers in midsummer followed by clusters of dark purple berries in fall. They spread slowly by rhizomes and thrive in average moist but well-drained soil in part shade to full sun. Hardiness: Zones 3 to 8. Wild sarsaparilla (*A. nudicaulis*) is a 1- to 3-foot-tall perennial with white or greenish flowers in early summer followed by purple-black berries. Plants spread by rhizomes and feature maroon-purple fall foliage. Hardiness: Zones 2 to 8. Devil's walking stick (*A. spinosa*) is a large, deciduous shrub or small tree that ranges from 10 to 20 feet tall. Plants spread easily by suckers to 10 or more feet and are only suitable for large sites that can accommodate them. They have spiny stems and huge, 2- to 5-foot compound leaves that lend a very tropical appearance. Small white flowers are carried in huge panicles up to 2 feet long midsummer and are followed by blue-black berries that are very attractive to birds. Plants prefer rich, moist, well-drained soil but tolerate drought. Plant them in a site where they have room to spread. Hardiness: Zones 4 to 9.

Baneberries (*Actaea* spp.). As their common name suggests, these plants bear extremely poisonous berries. Do not plant them in gardens that are frequented by young children. White baneberry (*A. pachypoda*) ranges from 1½ to 2½ feet tall and spreads to about 3 feet. Plants bear tiny white flowers followed by showy clusters of white berries above lacy, fernlike foliage. Hardiness: Zones 3 to 8. Red baneberry (*A. rubra*), native north and west of the Chesapeake Bay area, is similar but bears showy clusters of red berries. Hardiness: Zones 3 to 9.

Cohosh, blue (*Caulophyllum thalictroides*). This 1- to 3-foot-tall species bears brownish to greenish yellow flowers but is primarily prized for its lacy, compound leaves and clusters of blue, berrylike seeds. Plants, which spread slowly to about 1 foot, require rich, consistently moist soil and are best not disturbed once planted. Hardiness: Zones 3 to 8.

(right) American spikenard (*Aralia racemosa*). Photo by Neil Soderstrom; Kathleen Nelson garden.

(left) Devil's walking stick (*Aralia spinosa*). Photo by Neil Soderstrom; National Arboretum.

Spring beauties (*Claytonia virginica*). Photo by Barbara Ellis.

Spring beauties (*Claytonia virginica*). This early-blooming wildflower bears grasslike leaves and small, five-petaled, white flowers flushed with pink. The flowers are carried on 4- to 6-inch-tall racemes, and foliage may reach 8 or 9 inches before dying back. Plants, which grow from tiny, edible corms, can spread about as far. Give spring beauties rich, moist, well-drained soil in part sun to part shade. They self-sow if conditions suit. Hardiness: Zones 3 to 8.

Toothworts (*Cardamine* spp.). These small, unassuming wildflowers with dainty, four-petaled, white flowers add appeal to spring woodland gardens. Cut-leaf toothwort (*C. concatenata*) and common toothwort or crinkleroot (*C. diphylla*) are 6 to 8 inches tall and spread about as far. Give plants rich, moist, well-drained soil. Hardiness: Zones 3 to 8.

Water is the lifeblood of the garden, and sustainable gardeners conserve and use it wisely. Installing rain barrels, converting to permeable paving, planting trees, and maintaining healthy, well-mulched soil all reduce runoff and are ways that gardeners can redirect and encourage rainwater to stay on the landscape where it fell. Rain gardens, which allow rainfall to soak into the soil to sustain plantings and replenish aquifers, are another option.

In this chapter, you will find information on building a rain garden, as well as ideas for planting wet sites that exist naturally in your landscape. There also are lists of plants suitable for constantly wet sites.

Rain Gardens

Designed to collect rainfall as it flows off rooftops, driveways, and other hard surfaces, rain gardens are a simple, extremely effective tool to prevent erosion and conserve water. They also can be beautiful additions to the landscape. The way rain gardens work is simple: Water that flows off rooftops and other surfaces is directed to the rain garden via a swale or underground pipes. The rain garden itself is a shallow depression in the landscape. The depth of the depression ranges from 3 to 12 inches below the surrounding area, depending on the slope of your property, soil drainage, and the amount of area the garden is designed to handle. Water collects in the depression after a rain and then soaks into the soil over the course of several days. This means rainfall that normally would flow off your property into rivers and streams is used to grow your garden.

(overleaf) Rain barrels collect and store valuable rainwater so that it can be used later in the garden instead of running off into streams and the Bay. Many different models are available. Photo by Neil Soderstrom; Linda Decker garden.

A rain garden collects rainfall and allows it to soak gradually into the soil. Rain garden plants must be able to tolerate soil that ranges from wet (after a rain) to dry. Photo © Roger Foley; design by Tom Mannion Landscape Design.

Plants, of course, are what make a rain garden beautiful, and the perennials, grasses, shrubs, trees, and other species used in rain gardens are tough native species that withstand heat, drought, and deluge. The best plants for rain gardens are deep-rooted species that can tolerate a wide range of conditions, ranging from temporary standing water to dry soil. In a properly designed and installed rain garden, standing water drains away in 2 to 3 days, so rain gardens *do not* create habitat for mosquitoes. (They do, however, attract mosquito-eating dragonflies!) A well-designed rain garden also helps direct water away from foundations and other structures.

Water that stands in a rain garden gradually soaks

(top) This stone-lined channel carries water away from the house, under a bridge that spans the front walk, and out to a rain garden surrounded by lawn. Photo by Barbara Ellis; Jelich garden, Denis Radford design.

(bottom) Closer to the house, the stone-lined channel was used to create a drought-tolerant garden with thread-leaved coreopsis (*Coreopsis verticillata*), butterfly weed (*Asclepias tuberosa*), eastern prickly pear (*Opuntia humifusa*), and non-native sedums (*Sedum* spp.). Photo by Barbara Ellis; Jelich garden, Denis Radford design.

Essentially, a rain garden is a shallow depression that collects water, preventing it from flowing off the property and into storm drains and waterways. Over a few days, the water soaks into the soil, recharging groundwater and reducing runoff. Plants that tolerate both wet and dry conditions will thrive in a rain garden.

into the ground below. Soil in the garden traps silt and other pollutants carried in the water, preventing them from reaching streams, rivers, and the Chesapeake Bay. Even a fairly small rain garden can handle a surprising amount of runoff. Since most storms produce less than 1 inch of rain, and since the majority of pollutants are carried off in that first inch, most rain gardens are designed to catch a 1-inch rainstorm. That is quite a bit of water for growing plants. One inch of rain falling on a 1,000-square-foot roof yields about 600 gallons of water. The average size for a rain garden on a lot for a single-family home generally ranges from 100 to 400 square feet.

Since design and plant choices depend on your goals and your site, every rain garden looks different. The garden can be designed to look just like a full-fledged perennial garden featuring dozens of species with colorful flowers. Or for a completely different look, along with lower maintenance, consider a rain garden that contains shrubs, a tree or two, and grasses or ground covers. Depending on your space and situation, more than one rain garden may be a good choice—for example, one to handle runoff in the front yard and another in the back.

Rain Gardens 101

Proper site selection, design, and soil preparation are critical to create a rain garden that handles the maximum amount of runoff with a minimum of problems. Homeowners with fairly level yards and well-drained soil can design and install their own rain gardens. However, a great many gardeners leave this to professionals—especially the construction phase—once they realize that moving and perhaps amending large volumes of soil is involved. Hiring a professional makes sense if there is any question of the site's suitability or if the physical challenge of installation will be problematic. To find a good contractor, obtain recommendations from the local Cooperative Extension or Conservation District office, local botanical gardens and arboreta, municipal government, or local garden center. Ask for *and check* references. Ideally, visit a few rain gardens installed by a potential contractor. Either way, prepare yourself to discuss options by learning basic information on selecting and evaluating sites (see p. 247). Use the online resources link in Suggested Resources to find resources on rain gardens. Consult a landscape architect or landscape

While rain gardens are easiest to design and build on relatively flat sites, designers can develop them for nearly any site. Here a series of rain gardens carries water down the slope through stone terraces, ultimately releasing it into a bed planted with Joe-Pye weeds (*Eutrochium* and *Eupatoriadelphus* spp.) and other moisture-loving plants. Photo © Roger Foley; design by Tom Mannion Landscape Design.

design professional if you are planning a rain garden for a large public site. A professional can help design a rain garden that handles runoff from parking lots, pathways, and large buildings.

Site Selection

Rain gardens can be any size or shape and can be located in sun or shade, although those located in sun or part sun dry out more quickly than gardens in shade. To determine where a rain garden would work best, start by studying where water flows on and off your property. (See Chapter 2 for instructions on analyzing your property; this is the best way to start the overall design process.) The easiest way to determine where water flows and collects is to grab an umbrella and go outside during a rainstorm. Or turn on a hose and watch where the water goes. Look for the following:

- Depressions where water naturally collects. Avoid these, since a relatively flat spot is best.
- Water that sits near the foundation of your home. You will want to direct this away from the house and toward a rain garden using a planted swale or buried pipe.
- Runoff that flows onto your yard from neighboring properties.
- Steep slopes where water washes away soil, mulch, and plants. Slopes greater than 12 percent are not suitable for rain gardens, so look for pathways to direct water away from slopes toward a flatter area.
- A site where the ground remains soggy for a few days after a hard rain. This may seem like a good choice, but wet soil and the compacted conditions that create wet spots make installation difficult. To handle water before it reaches the soggy spot, look for a level spot closer to the source of the runoff and above the existing slope that leads to the spot that is normally soggy.
- Sun and shade patterns, which will help identify the best plants for a rain garden.
- The location of buried cables, wires, and pipes. Call Miss Utility (811) or your state's "call before you dig" hotline to locate them at least 3 days before you plan to dig.
- At least 3 feet of soil above bedrock. A rain garden needs this much soil to function properly.

In addition, identify existing plantings that might be affected by a new rain garden. Depending on the design, a rain garden can be installed next to established plantings or in the middle of the lawn. Installing one directly next to an existing planting of shrubs or trees can be problematic, however, since woody plants are difficult to move and resent the amount of digging around their roots that installing a rain garden requires. Look for a site where plant roots will not need to be disturbed. One option for creating a unified design from two separate plantings is to create the rain garden near an existing bed and then visually link the two by eliminating grass between them using newspaper and mulch. Then plant the area with ground covers, perennials, or shrubs. The end result is one larger planted area, less lawn, and a rain garden that is incorporated into the overall design.

An area that is constantly wet is not a good choice for a rain garden. Since soil drainage is already inadequate, the site will likely be unable to accommodate the additional runoff. Consider a wet-soil or bog garden for such sites. See "Gardens in Wet Soil" on p. 257 for design guidelines and plants. Another option for a constantly wet spot is to install a rain garden closer to the source of the water. This will divert some of the runoff that normally flows to the wet area.

A rain garden can also be a beautiful focal point—many rain garden plants attract butterflies, for example—so think about a spot where you can enjoy it.

Pick a location that is at least 10 feet away from the house and 10 feet away and downslope from a wellhead. Locate rain gardens downslope and at least 25 feet away from septic fields. Ideally, pick a spot that is halfway between the main source of runoff and the point where water runs off the property. While locating a rain garden on the property line may seem logical, rain gardens generally require an overflow area planted with additional vegetation. This gives water more time to sink into the soil, especially when the rain garden overflows after a heavy rain. Placing the rain garden closer to the source of the runoff leaves space for an overflow area.

While nearly all sites have at least some degree of

slope, keep in mind that a relatively flat area (5 to 7 percent slope) is best. Water can be directed to rain gardens via planted swales or soil berms. Underground pipes connected directly to downspouts are another option for moving water to a rain garden. To contain water in your garden, use part of the excavated soil to build a berm along the lower edge of the garden. On completely flat sites, perforated drainage pipe set in slightly sloping ditches is an option for collecting water.

Size and Soil Considerations

The size of your rain garden depends on how fast your soil drains and how much runoff from impermeable surfaces the garden needs to handle. Use the online resources link in Suggested Resources to find websites and publications that will guide you through the design process. There you will find links that provide information on evaluating your soil type to determine how fast it drains. In addition, you will find instructions for calculating the amount of runoff your garden will need to handle—typically water from the roof of your home, paved walkways, the driveway, and areas of lawn, which are considered impermeable surfaces because of soil compaction. Both soil type and the amount of runoff are crucial factors when designing a rain garden.

Site rain gardens with the longest edge along the upper side of the slope so it can catch the largest amount of water. Ideally, rain gardens should be twice as long as they are wide with a minimum width of 10 feet.

Installing a Rain Garden

The first step in the installation process is eliminating lawn or other existing vegetation on the site. See "Deep Mulching" on p. 92 for options on clearing the site. Use a hose, stakes and string, a sprinkling of flour, or landscape paint to "draw" the shape of the garden on the ground. Once the site is clear, if you are installing the garden yourself, loosen the soil over the entire site and begin the excavation. Use soil removed from the site to build a berm on the lower side of the garden, away from the water source. As you build the berm, pack down the soil firmly every few inches. It should be highest along the downslope edge of the garden. Use the online resources link in Suggested Resources to find information on calculating slope, determining the best method for digging, estimating the amount of amendments to have on hand, and designing a berm. Once enough soil has been removed, loosen the site again and work in gravel or grit to increase infiltration. The goal is to create a completely flat surface for the garden that is 3 to 8 inches (not counting mulch) below the highest point of the berm.

To prevent erosion, cover the section where water flows into the garden with large rocks, gravel, and/or river rock, ideally placed on biodegradable landscape fabric or a thick layer of newspaper (8 to 10 sheets) to prevent weeds. Also arrange rocks on the lower edge to create a section of the berm where water can flow out when the garden is too full. Plant the berm with drought-tolerant perennials to prevent erosion. The berm can also be planted with sod stripped off the garden site or seeded with grass seed, but that means mowing and trimming, two tasks that are best avoided. To prevent weeds throughout the garden, cover it with 3 or 4 sheets of newspaper topped by 2 to 3 inches of hardwood mulch. When planting, simply scrape the mulch back and plant directly through the newspaper.

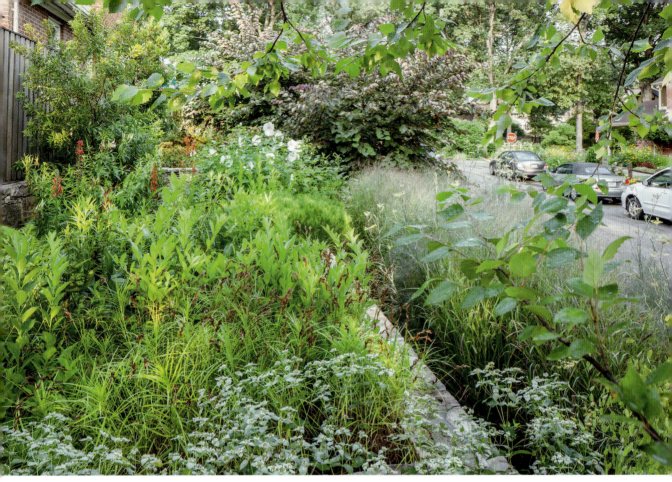

For best results, site plants in a rain garden according to the amount of moisture they prefer. The center of most gardens is wettest, and the areas around the outside of the garden are drier. Mountain mint (*Pycnanthemum* spp.), sedges (*Carex* spp.), cardinal flower (*Lobelia cardinalis*), and common rose mallow (*Hibiscus moscheutos*) are just some of the plants that fill this streetside rain garden. Photo © Roger Foley; design by Tom Mannion Landscape Design.

Plants for Rain Gardens

Design your rain garden like a conventional flower bed, a meadow, or a shrub border, depending on the style of your landscape. Use the lists of plants on pp. 251–52 for rain gardens.

Typically, new rain gardens are planted with container-grown plants. If cost is a factor, ask at your local nursery if you can purchase small plants in plugs or cell packs. Seeding or using a combination of planting and seeding is another option, although seeds will be dislodged and can wash away if the garden is flooded before they germinate and become well established.

Sun Plants for Rain Gardens

The following plants are good candidates for planting in rain gardens. See Chapter 6 for more information on the flowers and grasses listed below; Chapter 4 has information on the trees and shrubs.

Perennials

Amsonia, eastern blue star flower (*Amsonia tabernaemontana*)

Baptisia, blue wild indigo (*Baptisia australis*)

Beebalm (*Monarda didyma*)

Blue-eyed grass, narrow-leaved (*Sisyrinchium angustifolium*)

Coreopsis, lance-leaved (*Coreopsis lanceolata*)

Green-and-gold (*Chrysogonum virginianum*)

Hibiscus, crimson-eyed rose mallow (*Hibiscus moscheutos*)

Iris, blue flag (*Iris versicolor*) and southern blue flag (*I. virginica*)

Joe-Pye weed (*Eutrochium* spp., *Eupatoriadelphus* spp., and *Eupatorium* spp., all formerly *Eupatorium* spp.)

Milkweed, swamp (*Asclepias incarnata*)

Orange coneflower (*Rudbeckia fulgida*)

Sweet flag (*Acorus americanus*)

Grasses

Bluestem, little (*Schizachyrium scoparium*)

Dropseed, prairie (*Sporobolus heterolepis*)

Indian grass (*Sorghastrum nutans*)

Panic grass or switchgrass (*Panicum virgatum*)

Shrubs

Blueberry, highbush (*Vaccinium corymbosum*)

Buttonbush (*Cephalanthus occidentalis*)

Chokeberries (*Photinia* spp., formerly *Aronia* spp.), including black chokeberry (*P. melanocarpa*) and red chokeberry (*P. pyrifolia*)

Clethra, sweet pepperbush (*Clethra alnifolia*)

Dogwoods (*Cornus* spp.), including pagoda dogwood, alternate-leaf dogwood (*C. alternifolia*) and silky dogwood (*C. amomum*)

Fringetree, white (*Chionanthus virginicus*)

Hollies (*Ilex* spp.), including winterberry holly (*I. verticillata*), inkberry (*I. glabra*), and possumhaw (*I. decidua*)

Itea, Virginia sweetspire (*Itea virginica*)

Ninebark (*Physocarpus opulifolius*)

Spicebush (*Lindera benzoin*)

Sweetshrub, Carolina allspice (*Calycanthus floridus*)

Viburnums (*Viburnum* spp.), including southern arrowwood (*V. dentatum*) and possumhaw (*V. nudum*)

Witch hazel, American or common (*Hamamelis virginiana*)

Trees

Bald cypress (*Taxodium distichum*)

Birch, river (*Betula nigra*)

Buckeye, yellow (*Aesculus flava*)

Holly, American (*Ilex opaca*)

Magnolia, sweetbay (*Magnolia virginiana*)

Maple, red (*Acer rubrum*)

Persimmon, common (*Diospyros virginiana*)

Tupelo, black or black gum (*Nyssa sylvatica*)

Shade Plants for Rain Gardens

For more information on the plants listed below, see the chapter listed after each plant name.

Flowers

Bluebells, Virginia (*Mertensia virginica*) (chap. 7)

Geranium, spotted (*Geranium maculatum*) (chap. 5)

Green-and-gold (*Chrysogonum virginianum*) (chap. 5)

Groundsel, golden (*Packera aurea*) (chap. 7)

Spiderworts (*Tradescantia* spp.) (chap. 7)

This garden features a water garden at the top, near the steps, that also functions as a rain garden. Runoff collects in the water garden and flows through the beds, ultimately soaking the soil near the oak tree in the foreground. Photo © Roger Foley; design by Tom Mannion Landscape Design.

Sunflower, woodland (*Helianthus divaricatus*) (chap. 7)

Thin-leaved sunflower (*H. decapetalus*) (chap. 6)

Wood rush, hairy (*Luzula acuminata*) (chap. 6)

Ferns

Cinnamon fern (*Osmunda cinnamomea*) (chap. 5)

New York fern (*Thelypteris noveboracensis*, formerly *Dryopteris noveboracensis*, *Polypodium noveboracense*, and *T. thelypterioides*) (chap. 5)

Sensitive fern (*Onoclea sensibilis*) (chap. 5)

Wood fern, marginal (*Dryopteris marginalis*) (chap. 7)

Shrubs

Bladdernut (*Staphylea trifolia*) (chap. 7)

Dogwoods (*Cornus* spp.), including gray dogwood (*C. racemosa*) and silky dogwood (*C. amomum*) (chap. 4)

Hydrangea, wild (*Hydrangea arborescens*) (chap. 7)

Itea, Virginia sweetspire (Itea virginica)

Spicebush, northern (*Lindera benzoin*) (chap. 7)

Viburnum, arrowwood or southern arrowwood (*Viburnum dentatum*) (chaps. 4 and 7)

Trees

Hornbeam, American (*Carpinus caroliniana*) (chap. 7)

Tupelo, black or black gum (*Nyssa sylvatica*) (chap. 4)

Loose, uncompacted soil that is rich in organic matter and well-covered with vegetation is quite effective at retaining water and allowing it to sink into the soil. Here Virginia sweetspire (*Itea virginica*), ostrich ferns (*Matteuccia struthiopteris*), purple-leaved ninebark (*Physocarpus opulifolius* 'Center Glow'), and Virginia creeper (*Parthenocissus quinquefolia*) all clamor for space. Photo by Barbara Ellis.

Rain Garden Care

A newly planted rain garden will need regular weeding at first. Weed weekly for the first few months and then every other week for the first year. After that, annual attention may be all that is necessary.

Also plan on watering the garden regularly for the first few months as well, until plants become established.

The only other care that a rain garden requires is an annual haircut: Cut all the herbaceous plants back to the ground in late winter or early spring. Crumble up the cuttings and spread them as mulch or add cut-back vegetation to the compost pile.

A Chain of Water

Think of rain gardens as only part of an overall approach to reducing runoff. The most water-efficient gardens incorporate many different, interconnected features for collecting water and managing runoff. Here are some other options to consider:

Amended soil. It is easy to overlook one of the most basic runoff management tools: Deeply dug soil that has been amended with plenty of organic matter is extremely effective at absorbing runoff. Well-prepared soil acts like a sponge and can soak up large amounts of water as long as the site does not slope too steeply. On sloping sites, terraced beds filled with well-amended soil and framed by walls that allow water to flow from one level to another (through piled stone walls, for example) are also extremely effective.

Gravel grass. This is a porous surface similar to a gravel driveway covered with grass. Essentially, it is a layer of several inches of gravel mixed with enough soil (generally sandy loam or loamy sand) to provide stability and enough soil minerals for the grass or other plants growing on the site. The conditions are fast-draining and low in nutrients, so tough, drought-tolerant native grasses and clover are suitable plants. An area with properly installed gravel grass can be used for occasional parking or driving, perhaps up to once or twice per week, and it will allow up to 2 inches of water to infiltrate per hour.

In this garden, a simple gravel channel directs runoff from downspouts, around the top of the lawn, and into a garden bed where it can soak into the soil. Photo by Neil Soderstrom; design by Andie Phillips.

Green roofs. These can be installed on homes and commercial buildings, as well as sheds and smaller structures. Overflow from green roofs can be directed into rain gardens. For more information, see "Plants on the Roof" on p. 256.

Rain chains. An ornamental alternative to downspouts, these deliver rain from a rooftop to a rain barrel, outflow, or channel or onto the ground.

Outflows. An outflow, the point where a downspout or rain chain meets the earth, collects and slows water before sending it on its way. It can be creative or straightforward. For example, the outflow could be a recycled sink filled with gravel that spills into a shallow channel or gully to carry water on its way to a rain garden.

Channels and gullies. These are surface features that move water away from buildings and toward rain gardens or other infiltration features. They prevent water from spreading across walkways and other surfaces, which is essential in winter for keeping such surfaces free of ice. A channel or gully can cross pavement or a pathway and, again, can feature extremely simple or creative design. Precast forms are available, but it is also possible to create a path for water with stones or tile in concrete or an informal path that is lined with plastic and covered with river rock. When you keep water on the surface instead of piping it under paved surfaces, it is generally much easier to keep the system clear and running free.

Stormwater planters. Generally connected directly to a building, these are a cross between rain barrels and planter boxes. They collect water that flows from a downspout and reduce runoff by allowing it to soak into the ground as well as to evaporate and be transpired by plants growing in the planter. Planters are waterproofed against the building they are connected to and must be able to flow into another area once they have filled up. Plant them with shrubs, perennials, grasses, and even small trees suitable for rain gardens so that plantings can withstand both periodic flooding and drier conditions.

Planted swales. Designed to move water slowly and give it a chance to soak into the soil, these are shallow depressions planted with a mix of grasses, perennials, shrubs, and trees. They can be used in commercial settings but are adaptable to home landscapes as well. For example, a 6-inch-deep, 2-foot-wide swale could run through a meadow garden or even a conventional perennial border. In areas with clay or compacted soil, incorporate gravel and sharp sand into the soil before planting to increase its permeability. Mulching the bottom of the swale with river rock also improves drainage. To slow water and give it even more time to run off, consider installing shallow dams along the course of the swale.

Sinks. Digging sinks or holes in low spots is a very low-tech way to reduce runoff from an existing, relatively flat garden and collect it to benefit your plants. After a rain, water will sit in the sink and slowly seep out to nearby plants. Holes can be any size, but one that is 2 feet wide and deep is effective. Refill these holes with soil that has been heavily amended with organic matter, and then mulch the spots so they blend with the rest of the garden. You can change the topography around each sink to direct water toward it. Be sure to rough up the bottom and sides of the hole before refilling. If you have heavy clay soil, amending with lots of gravel and/or sharp sand is a good idea as well.

Permeable paving. Everything from driveways and patios to walkways, garden paths, and temporary parking areas can be covered with paving that lets water flow right through it to decrease runoff. Porous asphalt and concrete are suitable for driveways and other large areas. There also are structural cells, including ones made of plastic or precast concrete, that can be installed on areas where vehicular traffic is occasionally necessary. These support the

Unlike conventional paving options, the permeable pavers used to build this walkway allow water to soak into the soil and replenish the water table. Photo by Neil Soderstrom; Bill Matuszeski garden.

weight of the vehicle while allowing grass or other tough ground covers to grow in the spaces between. (Without such support, grass does not survive if it is driven on more than about one day per week.) Sites using structural cells still require mowing, but they reduce runoff and have been shown to reduce carbon dioxide as well.

These are only a few of the options. It is possible to install aboveground tanks or belowground cisterns to store large quantities of water that can then be reused. Runoff can also be directed into water gardens or ponds. As interest in managing runoff increases, designers are devising ever-more-inventive approaches to managing water.

Green roofs reduce runoff by absorbing approximately 75 percent of the rain that falls on them. Photo by Neil Soderstrom; American Horticultural Society's River Farm.

In addition to reducing runoff, a green roof protects the underlying roofing material, doubling its expected life, and also reduces heating and cooling costs. Photo by Barbara Ellis; Scott Arboretum of Swarthmore College.

Plants on the Roof

Rooftop gardens and green roofs may seem like new technology, but the earliest ones actually date back 1,000 years. These early models were built over birch bark roofs and covered with sod. While the materials have changed, many of the benefits are still the same. Green roofs provide thermal insulation and protect the underlying roofing—be it bark or a more modern material—from ultraviolet light, weather, and other factors that degrade it. A green roof can double the life of modern roofing. It can also reduce indoor temperature fluctuations, and studies have found it can reduce summertime cooling costs by 50 percent and wintertime heating by 25 percent. Green roofs reduce glare, release oxygen, store carbon, absorb carbon dioxide, and reduce pollution. They also reduce the overall heat island effect caused by too much paving in urban areas. Reducing runoff is another major benefit: A green roof can absorb up to 75 percent of the rain that falls on it. Green roofs also provide wild-

life habitat, such as nesting sites for ground-nesting birds such as kildeer.

There are two general types of green roofs: extensive and intensive. Extensive green roofs use a thin, lightweight substrate to grow plants and are planted with tough, drought-tolerant species. (In addition to a variety of tough, non-native plants, three U.S. native sedums are currently used in green roofs, *Sedum glaucophyllum*, *S. nevii*, and *S. ternatum*.) Extensive green roofs are generally designed for little or no access by people. Intensive green roofs are more people oriented. They use a deeper substrate and often feature walkways for people as well as woody shrubs and trees.

Extensive green roofs can be retrofitted onto existing buildings, from garden sheds and even bird houses to garages, homes, and larger buildings. However, it is essential to have the building's load capacity and structural integrity evaluated before starting any construction. See the online resources link in Suggested Resources to find information on green roofs.

Gardens in Wet Soil

While many plants can tolerate occasional flooding, areas that are wet on a regular basis are harder to plant. It is not unusual to see lawn—or at least a semblance of lawn—on such sites in the Chesapeake Bay region. Planting trees, shrubs, perennials, grasses, and/or ferns instead of lawn on wet-soil sites not only makes the area more aesthetically appealing; it eliminates the need to cut grass—a huge advantage on sites where mowers tend to bog down in muddy soil.

Conventionally grown nursery plants cannot necessarily be planted in a site with wet, poorly drained or flooded soil, even if the species in question can grow in wet soil. Start with species adapted for wet sites, such as the plants listed on pp. 259–63. Oxygen, which roots require to grow, is limited in wet or saturated soil, but special planting techniques can help plants adapt. See "Planting along Waterways" on p. 258 for information on techniques for planting stream banks and other similar sites.

To plant in a wet-soil site and ensure roots are able to obtain the oxygen they require, set plants with the root balls higher in the soil than typical gardening techniques dictate. This gives the plant time to adapt to the site and grow the root system necessary to survive in wet or flooded soil. Purchasing from a supplier who raises plants specifically for such installations is helpful but not always possible.

Before planting, water the root balls thoroughly. (If they will be too heavy to move once they are thoroughly saturated, water after the plants are in position.) Planting depth will vary depending on the site and the species being planted. On a site with wet or compacted soil, dig a hole that is only two-thirds as deep as the root ball and at least twice as wide. Set the plant in place with a third of the root ball aboveground and then fill the hole. Create a wide mound—five times as wide as the root ball—that slopes gently up to the crown of the root ball. Water thoroughly. One disadvantage of this planting technique is that the root ball will dry out quickly during dry weather. Mulch to keep the soil moist, and water regularly during the first growing season to ensure the plant is able to resume growing and become well established.

In sites that flood regularly or remain flooded year-round, planting with the entire root ball above the surrounding soil can be effective. Loosen the soil on the planting site, set the plant in place, and create a mound of soil around it—again, at least five times as wide as the root ball. Plants purchased from a nursery that grows them in water are already adapted to wet conditions and can be planted normally.

Butterflying the root ball is another effective technique for plants with fibrous roots. This method is recommended by Rare Find Nursery in New Jersey for planting azaleas and rhododendrons even in normal garden soil, since they are shallow rooted and require perfectly well-drained soil that remains moist. It also can be used for planting in wetter situations. Take the plant out of its pot. To divide it into quarters, cut up from the bottom of the root ball, making a deep X that severs the root ball about two-thirds of the way up. Spread out the quarters, scratching out and loosening any pot-bound roots that are in evidence. (Keep the root ball moist during this process.) To plant, depending on the site, build a mound in the bottom of the hole or on the soil surface, spread the root quarters over it, refill, and mulch. Whether used to establish species that demand moist, well-drained soil or for plants that can tolerate flooded sites, butterflying helps roots obtain the oxygen they require.

Planting along Waterways

When correctly installed, plants protect the banks of streams or other waterways and are both more effective and less expensive than bulkheads or other hardscape solutions. Several different techniques are used to help plants become firmly and quickly established so they can protect the bank and effectively prevent erosion.

Conventional plantings. Bare-root, container-grown, and balled-and-burlapped (B&B) plants can all be installed along a stream or other waterway. Choosing container-grown or other conventional nursery plants might widen your selection of species, but the individual plants cost more than the options listed below, and installation is more labor intensive.

Live stakes. These are dormant ½- to 2-inch-thick cuttings of willows (*Salix* spp.), dogwoods (*Cornus* spp.), viburnums (*Viburnum* spp.), or other species that can root quickly along a stream bank. Ideally, the cuttings are collected and installed on the same day and are driven into the ground like stakes. The stakes help hold the bank, and the plants root quickly to hold it against water flow.

Live fascines or wattles. These are 4- to 20-foot-long bundles of live, dormant branches of fast-rooting natives—willows (*Salix* spp.), dogwoods (*Cornus* spp.), viburnums (*Viburnum* spp.), or other species. The bundles, tied with biodegradable twine, are 6 to 8 inches in diameter, and the length of the branches varies so that individual branches begin and end at different points within the bundle. Live fascines are placed in shallow trenches in a stair-step pattern up the slope and are staked in place.

Replenish the soil if the site floods soon after planting. Ideally, this is a technique for sites where water rises gently. Try staking burlap over the soil to protect it from heavy rain or fast-rising water.

Plants for Wet Soil

While many of the plants in this book tolerate wet soil or occasional flooding, those in the list below can grow on sites that are flooded regularly. All the species listed below adapt readily to occasional seasonal flooding, but some can tolerate much more. You may need to experiment to determine the perfect location for a particular plant, whether that means finding a spot on the edge of a wet area or low-lying forest, a site with the right amount of sun or shade, or a location that is always flooded. From a garden design standpoint, use these moisture-loving plants much as you would other natives: to screen views, provide privacy, and create habitat for birds, butterflies, and other wildlife. Many also can be used to stabilize wet banks, swales, or the edges of streams or ponds to reduce erosion and improve water quality.

The plants listed below grow in full sun to part shade, unless otherwise indicated. Also use the following tolerances to help determine planting locations:

The white flowers of American black elderberry (*Sambucus nigra* ssp. *canadensis*) are followed by edible berries that provide valuable summer food for a variety of wildlife. Photo by Neil Soderstrom; Adkins Arboretum.

(top left) Bald cypress (*Taxodium distichum*). Photo by Barbara Ellis; Longwood Gardens.

(top right) Loblolly pine (*Pinus taeda*). Photo by Neil Soderstrom; J. Kent McNew garden.

(bottom right) Sweetgum (*Liquidambar styraciflua*). Photo by Neil Soderstrom; Adkins Arboretum.

- Species that can tolerate flooding or saturated soil for at least 25 percent of the growing season are marked with an asterisk (*).
- Species that can withstand being flooded or that will survive in saturated soil for more than 75 percent of the growing season are marked with two asterisks (**).
- A few grasses and grasslike plants tolerate salinity, and tolerances are indicated for these below. Plants that can withstand salt spray or infrequent flooding by saltwater are listed in Chapter 4.

In addition to the plants listed below, one vine, climbing hydrangea (*Decumaria barbara*), also called woodvamp, will survive in wet soil.

Trees

Bald cypress (*Taxodium distichum*)**
Birch, river (*Betula nigra*)
Hackberry, common (*Celtis occidentalis*)
Holly, American (*Ilex opaca*). Sun to shade.
Hornbeam, American (*Carpinus caroliniana*). Shade or sun.
Magnolia, sweet bay (*Magnolia virginiana*)**. Sun to shade.
Maples (*Acer* spp.). Red maple (*A. rubrum*); silver maple (*A. saccharinum*)
Oaks (*Quercus* spp.). Swamp white oak (*Q. bicolor*); swamp chestnut oak (*Q. michauxii*)*; water oak (*Q. nigra*); pin oak (*Q. palustris*); willow oak (*Q. phellos*)

Silky dogwood (*Cornus amomum*). Photo by Neil Soderstrom.

Northern bayberry (*Morella pensylvanica*). Photo by Neil Soderstrom; Environmental Concern, Inc.

Persimmon, common (*Diospyros virginiana*)

Pine, loblolly (*Pinus taeda*)

Red cedar, eastern (*Juniperus virginiana*)

Serviceberry, shadblow (*Amelanchier canadensis*). Shade.

Sweetgum (*Liquidambar styraciflua*)*

Sycamore, American (*Platanus occidentalis*)

Tupelos (*Nyssa* spp.). Black tupelo (*N. sylvatica*); swamp tupelo (*N. biflora*)*; water tupelo (*N. aquatica*)**

White cedar, Atlantic (*Chamaecyparis thyoides*)**

Willow, black or swamp (*Salix nigra*)**

Shrubs

Alder, hazel (*Alnus serrulata*)**

Azalea, swamp (*Rhododendron viscosum*)*

Baccharis, eastern (*Baccharis halimifolia*)*

Bayberries (*Morella* spp.). Southern, small, or swamp bayberry (*Morella caroliniensis*, formerly *Myrica caroliniensis*, *M. heterophylla*)*; northern bayberry (*Morella pensylvanica*, formerly *Myrica pensylvanica*)

Blueberry, highbush (*Vaccinium corymbosum*). Sun to shade.

Buttonbush (*Cephalanthus occidentalis*)**. Sun to shade.

Chokeberries (*Photinia* spp., formerly *Aronia* spp.). Black chokeberry (*P. melanocarpa*, formerly *A. melanocarpa*); red chokeberry (*P. pyrifolia*, formerly *A. arbutifolia*)

Clethra, sweet pepperbush (*Clethra alnifolia*)*. Shade.

Cranberry, American (*Vaccinium macrocarpon*)*. Wet acid soil.

Devil's walking stick (*Aralia spinosa*)

Dogwoods (*Cornus* spp.). Gray dogwood (*C. racemosa*) and silky dogwood (*C. amomum*) both grow in sun to shade; red twig dogwood (*C. sericea*)

Elderberries (*Sambucus* spp.). American black elderberry (*S. nigra* ssp. *canadensis*), which grows in sun to shade; red elderberry (*S. racemosa*)

Hollies (*Ilex* spp.). Winterberry holly (*I. verticillata*); inkberry (*I. glabra*). Both sun to part shade or shade.

Itea, Virginia sweetspire (*Itea virginica*)*. Shade.

Leatherleaf (*Chamaedaphne calyculata*)*. Wet acid soil.

Leatherwood, eastern (*Dirca palustris*)*

Loosestrife, swamp (*Decodon verticillatus*)*. This native shrub, also called water willow, is not an invasive, unlike purple loosestrife (*Lythrum salicaria*).

Lyonias (*Lyonia* spp.). Male-berry (*L. ligustrina*); Piedmont stagger-bush (*L. mariana*)

Roses (*Rosa* spp.). Swamp rose (*Rosa palustris*)*, sun to shade; Carolina or pasture rose (*R. carolina*)

Spicebush (*Lindera benzoin*). Shade or sun.

Strawberry bush (*Euonymus americanus*). Shade.

Sumacs (*Rhus* spp.). Shining or winged sumac (*R. copallinum*, formerly *R. copallina*). Staghorn sumac (*R. typhina*) prefers drier sites.

Viburnums (*Viburnum* spp.). Arrowwood viburnum or southern arrowwood (*V. dentatum*), nannyberry viburnum (*V. lentago*), and possumhaw viburnum (*V. nudum*)*, sun to shade; withe-rod (*V. nudum* var. *cassinoides*).

Willows (*Salix* spp.). Pussy willow (*S. discolor*); purple osier willow (*S. purpurea*)

Yellowroot (*Xanthorhiza simplicissima*)

Flowers

Ageratum, hardy (*Conoclinium coelestinum*, formerly *Eupatorium coelestinum*). Shade.

Anemone, Canadian or meadow (*Anemone canadensis*)*

Arrowhead, broad-leaved (*Sagittaria latifolia*)**

Arum, green arrow (*Peltandra virginica*)**

Aster, New York (*Symphyotrichum novi-belgii*, formerly *Aster novi-belgii*)

Pickerelweed (*Pontederia cordata*) and broad-leaved cattail (*Typha latifolia*). Photo by Neil Soderstrom; Environmental Concern, Inc.

Beebalm (*Monarda didyma*)

Black-eyed Susan (*Rudbeckia hirta*)

Blue-eyed grasses (*Sisyrinchium* spp.). Coastal or eastern blue-eyed grass (*S. atlanticum*); narrow-leaved blue-eyed grass (*S. angustifolium*)

Boneset, common (*Eupatorium perfoliatum*). Shade.

Culver's root (*Veronicastrum virginicum*)

Goat's beard (*Aruncus dioicus*)

Goldenrods (*Solidago* spp.). Wrinkle-leaved goldenrod (*S. rugosa*); seaside goldenrod (*S. sempervirens*)

Groundsel, golden (*Packera aurea*, formerly *Senecio aureus*)

(left) Skunk cabbage (*Symplocarpus foetidus*), green false hellebore (*Veratrum viride*), and marsh marigolds (*Caltha palustris*). Photo by Barbara Ellis; Bowman's Hill Wildflower Preserve.

(right) White turtlehead (*Chelone glabra*). Photo by Neil Soderstrom.

Irises (*Iris* spp.). Zigzag iris (*I. brevicaulis*)*; blue flag iris (*I. versicolor*)*; southern blue flag (*I. virginica*)*

Ironweeds (*Vernonia* spp.). New York ironweed (*V. noveboracensis*); giant ironweed (*V. gigantea*)

Jack-in-the-pulpit (*Arisaema triphyllum*). Shade.

Joe-Pye weeds (*Eutrochium* and *Eupatoriadelphus* spp., formerly *Eupatorium* spp.). Eastern or coastal plain Joe-Pye weed (*Eutrochium dubium*, formerly *Eupatorium dubium*); spotted Joe-Pye weed (*Eupatoriadelphus maculatus*, formerly *Eupatorium maculatum*); hollow-stemmed Joe-Pye weed (*Eutrochium fistulosum*, formerly *Eupatorium fistulosum*)

Lady's tresses, nodding (*Spiranthes cernua*)*

Lizard's tail (*Saururus cernuus*)**

Lobelias (*Lobelia* spp.). Cardinal flower (*L. cardinalis*); great blue lobelia (*L. siphilitica*). Shade.

Marsh marigold (*Caltha palustris*)*

Meadow beauty, Virginia (*Rhexia virginica*)*

Milkweed, swamp (*Asclepias incarnata*)

Monkey flower, Allegheny (*Mimulus ringens*)*

Pickerelweed (*Pontederia cordata*)**

Rose mallows (*Hibiscus* spp.). Common rose mallow (*H. moscheutos*)*; scarlet rose mallow (*H. coccineus*)*

Skunk cabbage (*Symplocarpus foetidus*)*. Shade.

Sunflowers (*Helianthus* spp.). Giant sunflower (*H. giganteus*); swamp sunflower (*H. angustifolius*)**

Turtleheads (*Chelone* spp.). White turtlehead (*C. glabra*)**; pink turtlehead (*C. lyonii*)**

Veratrums (*Veratrum* spp.). Green false hellebore (*V. viride*)*; Virginia bunchflower

(*V. virginicum*, formerly *Melanthium virginicum*)*. Shade for both.

Vervain, blue (*Verbena hastata*)

Water plantain, American (*Alisma subcordatum*)**

Grasses and Grasslike Plants

Grasses that can tolerate brackish water (0.5 parts per thousand) are indicated by the word "brackish." Saltwater-tolerant plants (30 or more parts per thousand) are indicated by the word "saltwater."

Blue joint grass (*Calamagrostis canadensis*)*

Bluestem, little (*Schizachyrium scoparium*)

Bulrushes (*Scirpus* spp.). Green bulrush (*S. atrovirens*)**; wool grass (*S. cyperinus*); salt marsh or sturdy bulrush (*Schoenoplectus robustus*, formerly *S. robustus*) tolerates saltwater, plant at mean high tide mark.

Cattails (*Typha* spp.). Broad-leaved cattail (*T. latifolia*); narrow-leaved cattail (*T. angustifolia*). Slightly brackish.

Cord grass, smooth (*Spartina alterniflora*)**. Saltwater, mid-tide to high tide mark.

Equisetum or horsetail (*Equisetum* spp.). Common horsetail (*E. hyemale*); woodland horsetail (*E. sylvaticum*). Note that these have vigorous rhizomes and are very difficult to eradicate once established.

Hair grass, tufted (*Deschampsia cespitosa*)

Panic grasses (*Panicum* spp.). Bitter or coastal panic grass (*P. amarum*); switchgrass, panic grass (*P. virgatum*)

Rice cutgrass (*Leersia oryzoides*)**

Rushes (*Juncus* spp.). Common or soft rush (*J. effusus*); needlegrass rush (*J. roemerianus*)

Salt meadow hay (*Spartina patens*). Saltwater, above mean high tide.

Sea oats, northern (*Chasmanthium latifolium*)

Sedges (*Carex* spp.). Upright or tussock sedge (*C. stricta*)**; fox sedge (*C. vulpinoidea*)*; fringed sedge (*C. crinita*)

Sweet flag (*Acorus americanus*)**

Three-square, common (*Schoenoplectus pungens*, formerly *Scirpus pungens*)**. Brackish.

Ferns

Chain ferns (*Woodwardia* spp.). Netted chain fern (*W. areolata*); Virginia chain fern (*W. virginica*). Part to full shade.

Cinnamon fern (*Osmunda cinnamomea*)*. Sun to shade.

Marsh fern (*Thelypteris palustris*). Sun.

Ostrich fern (*Matteuccia struthiopteris*, formerly *M. pensylvanica*). Part to full shade.

Royal fern (*Osmunda regalis*)**. Sun to shade.

Sensitive fern (*Onoclea sensibilis*)**. Sun to shade.

NINE ❧ Gardens for Wildlife

Welcoming wildlife to our landscapes is such an essential part of sustainable design that five of the principles outlined in Chapter 1—reducing the size of the lawn, building plant diversity, growing more native plants, managing water runoff, and gardening wisely—all serve the sixth: welcoming wildlife. Pursuing projects that relate to any of these principles makes a landscape more welcoming to wild creatures. Planting a wider variety of native trees, shrubs, and perennials adds food for wildlife in the forms of leaves, nuts, seeds, and berries while encouraging a larger, more diverse insect population—a vital food source for larger creatures. The way trees and other plants are arranged also plays a role, as does the amount of lawn. Planting islands, shrub borders, meadows, privacy screens, and other plantings that add appeal to our homes and gardens also creates safe cover for birds and other creatures, as well as sites for nests and burrows. Many of the features outlined in Chapter 8, including rain gardens, make water more available to wildlife in our yards and gardens. Gardening in a sustainable fashion also helps clean up the water that flows throughout our region, which benefits everything from fish, crabs, and mollusks to ospreys and eagles.

This chapter focuses on features that make a landscape more appealing to all sorts of creatures. It also recognizes that management is the primary objective regarding some types of wildlife, so information on reducing the influence of some creatures is included.

(overleaf) Cattails (*Typha* spp.) provide a suitable hunting ground for a hungry great blue heron. Everything from the plants in our gardens to the ways we landscape along creeks and streams affects wildlife in the Chesapeake Bay region. Photo by Barbara Ellis.

Food

Seeds, berries, insects, foliage, earthworms, nematodes, and many other creatures are menu items in a wildlife-friendly garden. Although we commonly avoid thinking about it, birds, mice, and other small animals are necessary food sources for larger predators such as hawks and owls. Native plants form the framework of a landscape that supports a rich web of life. In addition to creating areas for cover and sites for raising a family, plantings of native species offer food. Even leaf litter mulch becomes a food source, since it helps support a rich population of soil-dwelling creatures, many of which live among the leaves themselves. Native sparrows, towhees, and wood thrushes are just three of the many species that depend on leaf litter for insects.

Use these guidelines to increase the food supply for wildlife on your property.

Plant nuts and berries. Acorns from oak trees (*Quercus* spp.) are a prime source of food for wildlife, but other nut trees are suitable as well, including hickories (*Carya* spp.), walnuts (*Juglans* spp.), American beech (*Fagus grandiflora*), Allegheny chinkapin (*Castanea pumila*), and American hazelnut or filbert (*Corylus americana*). Berries also are vital for wildlife. See "Berries for Wildlife" on p. 271 for a list of berry-producing plants.

Install feeders. Birds are attracted to a variety of feeders, so install a combination of hanging feeders and platform feeders for ground-feeding birds, such as mourning doves and juncos, to attract the broadest number of species. (Squirrels visit feeders, too, but it is possible to exclude them by purchasing squirrel-proof feeders.) Different birds are attracted to different seed mixes. A basic mix of black-oil sunflower, white proso millet, and safflower seed attracts a wide range of species. Cracked corn is ap-

(top) This border, tucked up against trees, offers a wealth of flowers for butterflies and pollinators, including purple coneflowers (*Echinacea purpurea*), black-eyed Susans (*Rudbeckia fulgida* var. *fulgida*), and perennial sunflowers (*Helianthus* 'Lemon Queen'). These, plus asters and ornamental grasses, also produce seeds for winter. Photo by Nancy Ondra.

(bottom) American beech (*Fagus grandiflora*) trees have shallow roots and are effective in woodland gardens and wild areas where their nuts feed squirrels, chipmunks, ducks, foxes, and various songbirds. Photo by Neil Soderstrom; Green Spring Gardens.

🍃 Creature Comforts

Attracting wildlife can easily become the primary inspiration for a garden or landscape design. Like Bay-friendly gardening in general, creating a landscape that attracts wildlife is a process, not a single decision. To let wildlife-friendly landscaping serve as the overall focus of your design, begin by evaluating the plants on your property, along with any new ones you purchase. Your goal should be to work toward having only plants that are valuable elements in a wildlife habitat, so consider what kinds of features they offer and whether they warrant space in the garden. Determine if perennials have a long enough bloom time for butterflies and pollinators, for example, or if they produce a sufficient seed crop to feed birds in winter. Select shrubs that produce berries or other edibles, and, of course, plant an oak tree or two.

Reviewing the six principles outlined in Chapter 1 and selecting projects from all of them is another way to begin working toward a wildlife habitat garden. Plant drifts of perennials and arrange trees and shrubs to maximize cover and nest sites. Also incorporate water in the design. Every wildlife garden is unique, but a plan focused on the needs of wildlife inevitably leads to a lush and fascinating property that is fun to explore. You may want to start a list of the creatures you spot visiting your yard—just to enjoy the challenge or to inspire the addition of new plants or features.

Many features make a landscape more appealing to wildlife. Access to food—including flowers, berries, nuts, and insects—is the first essential requirement for every wildlife-friendly property. Water, whether from a stream, pond, or birdbath, is another vital component. Wildlife habitats also include dense plantings for cover as well as places to raise young.

pealing to jays, white throated sparrows, and wild turkeys. During the summer months, providing cut oranges and other fruit on a table or platform will attract orioles. For tips on attracting and feeding hummingbirds, see "Gardens for Hummingbirds" on p. 279.

Woodpeckers, chickadees, nuthatches, and Carolina wrens are among the species attracted to suet, and flying squirrels may visit suet feeders after dark. Suet cakes are available for purchase during the winter months everywhere from garden centers to grocery stores. When temperatures rise above 70°F, either avoid using suet or switch to suet cakes formulated for summertime feeding, available at garden centers and wild bird stores. Be sure to attach suet feeders securely to prevent raccoons from carrying them away altogether. A carabiner, a metal ring with an opening on one side that either springs or screws closed, makes affixing a suet feeder to a large screw eye attached to a feeder easy and allows it to be taken down for refilling. See the online resources link in Suggested Resources for more information on feeders and feeding birds.

Woodpeckers, including the red-bellied woodpecker, frequently visit suet feeders. They also appreciate dead trees, where they drill for insects and create nesting sites. Photo by Neil Soderstrom; Hannelore Soderstrom garden.

Leave snags and collect brush. Woodpeckers appreciate dead trees, also called snags, because they harbor insects. Hawks, osprey, and owls use them for perching while hunting. Snags do not work in every landscape, but try to leave them where possible. Look for snags located away from the house so they cannot do damage if they fall. Osprey and kingfishers especially appreciate snags that extend over water. Many wild animals also nest in dead trees, including flying squirrels, woodpeckers, owls, and raccoons.

Native sparrows, wrens, and dark-eyed juncos hunt for insects in brush piles, and spiders use them to fashion their nests. Brush piles also provide excellent habitat for snakes, mice, and rabbits, so choose a location carefully. To provide for these creatures, while keeping them away from your home, build brush piles on the outskirts of your property. Ideally, build them on the edge of a woodland, wild area, or shrub border.

Plant a meadow or meadow garden. Both meadows and meadow gardens contain a diverse mix of grasses and flowers that attract wildlife and feed insects, birds, and other creatures. Coneflowers (*Echinacea* spp. and *Rudbeckia* spp.) and other typical meadow flowers provide seeds. Native grasses such as panic grass or switchgrass (*Panicum virgatum*) and little bluestem (*Schizachyrium scoparium*) are valuable seed producers as well. See "Meadows and Meadow Gardens" on p. 205 for more information.

Delay garden cleanup. Leave perennials standing over winter to provide seeds for birds and other winter wildlife as well as overwintering sites for insects. Allowing fallen leaves to remain on garden

(left) Wildflower meadows with a mix of flowers and grasses provide food and habitat for a wealth of insects, which in turn feed birds and other creatures. The seeds of many meadow plants, including tufted hair grass (*Deschampsia cespitosa*) in the foreground, also feed birds and wildlife. Photo by Neil Soderstrom; design by Dave Korbonitz at Mt. Cuba Center.

(right) Even a casual meadow exploration reveals prey insects such as this katydid, which are at the base of the food chain. Photo by Barbara Ellis.

beds, along shrub borders, and in woodlands also provides essential habitat for overwintering insects. Birds, including eastern towhees and brown thrashers, commonly hunt for food in leaf litter.

Practice balanced pest control. Insects are an essential link in the food chain, and protecting a healthy insect population is an important part of managing a wildlife-friendly landscape. Switch to organic pesticides, if they are needed at all. Contrary to popular belief, insects do not overwhelm landscapes designed to attract them or where organic controls are in place for pests. While there will be insects that chew leaves or flowers, wildlife-friendly management means there also will be many predators, including beneficial insects, spiders, mice, voles, birds, and other creatures that help keep populations in balance. Damage generally remains insignificant. That is especially true where plants have been planted in a site that provides the conditions they need to thrive. Vigorous growth is

a good defense against many insects, and plants that are healthy have reserves to replace leaves or withstand damage.

When you spot an insect on a cherished plant, try to identify it and determine whether it is actually doing damage. It is most likely a beneficial or benign species that happens to be in the wrong place at the wrong time. If a group of insects are chewing leaves or doing other damage, watch them over several days to see if the population is building or whether any damage to the plant is significant. Even if there is some damage, such as a few chewed leaves, take a step back and look at the plant from a few feet away: Damage that is not noticeable is generally not worth worrying about and will not affect the plant's overall health. In most cases the network of beneficial insects and larger animals that prey on smaller ones will handle any problems that appear.

Take inventory. Broaden the types of food wildlife is able to find in your landscape. Make a list of nuts,

Wait until early spring to cut back plants instead of taking care of this task in fall. This helps wildlife by making seeds available all winter long. Standing stems also contain insect eggs and pupae—valuable winter food for birds. Photo by Nancy Ondra.

berries, and other edibles and the months when they are ripe. Use a computer spreadsheet program or make a list in a notebook or journal entry. Identify the months when little is available and look for plants that will fill the gap. Also consider using feeders, at least during lean months, to help provide an abundant supply.

Berries for Wildlife

The following trees and shrubs produce fruit that is attractive to birds and other wildlife. Two native vines, American bittersweet (*Celastris scandens*) and Virginia creeper (*Parthenocissus quinquefolia*), also produce berries that are attractive to birds. Include

Black cherries (*Prunus serotina*) pop up everywhere because the fruit is relished by so many species, including robins, brown thrashers, mockingbirds, eastern bluebirds, catbirds, waxwings, thrushes, wild turkeys, foxes, raccoons, opossums, and rabbits. Photo by Barbara Ellis.

Trees such as eastern red cedar (*Juniperus virginiana*) are important because wildlife does not eat the berries until wintertime, when food is sparse. Evergreens also provide essential cover in winter. Photo by Neil Soderstrom; Adkins Arboretum.

berry-bearing trees and shrubs in informal hedges and privacy plantings, use them to create or revitalize hedgerows, include them in island beds or foundation plantings, or add them throughout your landscape. You will find more information on most of the plants listed below in Chapter 4.

Trees

Cherries (*Prunus* spp.). American wild plum (*P. americana*); pin cherry (*P. pensylvanica*); black cherry, chokecherry (*P. serotina*), or chokecherry (*P. virginiana*)

Crab apples (*Malus* spp.). Southern crab apple (*M. angustifolia*); sweet or American crab apple (*M. coronaria*)

Dogwood, flowering (*Cornus florida*)

Hackberries (*Celtis* spp.)

Hollies (*Ilex* spp.)

Persimmon, common (*Diospyros virginiana*)

Red cedar, eastern (*Juniperus virginiana*)

Tupelo, black (*Nyssa sylvatica*)

Shrubs

Aralias (*Aralia* spp.). American spikenard (*A. racemosa*); wild sarsaparilla (*A. nudicaulis*); devil's walking stick (*A. spinosa*)

Bayberries (*Morella* spp., formerly *Myrica* spp.)

Beautyberry, American (*Callicarpa americana*)

Blueberries (*Vaccinium* spp.). Highbush blueberry (*V. corymbosum*); farkleberry (*V. arboreum*); deerberry (*V. stamineum*); Blue Ridge or hillside blueberry (*V. pallidum*, formerly *V. vacillans*)

Chokeberries (*Photinia* spp., formerly *Aronia* spp.)

Dogwoods (*Cornus* spp.). Gray dogwood (*C. racemosa*); silky dogwood (*C. amomum*)

Elderberries (*Sambucus* spp.)

Hollies (*Ilex* spp.). Winterberry (*I. verticillata*); possumhaw (*I. decidua*)

Huckleberries (*Gaylussacia* spp.)

Lyonia or male-berry (*Lyonia ligustrina*)

(left) Also called wild raisin, withe-rod viburnum (*Viburnum nudum* var. *cassinoides*) bears white flowers in spring followed by colorful berries relished by birds. Photo by Neil Soderstrom; James A. Duke garden.

(right) Nannyberry viburnum (*Viburnum lentago*) bears clusters of white flowers and fruit that can be eaten fresh by people or made into jams or jellies. Birds and other wildlife value it as well. Photo by Neil Soderstrom; Environmental Concern, Inc.

Roses, wild (*Rosa* spp.)

Snowberries (*Symphoricarpos* spp.).
   Common snowberry (*S. albus*); coralberry
   (*S. orbiculatus*)

Spicebush (*Lindera benzoin*)

Sumacs (*Rhus* spp.)

Viburnums (*Viburnum* spp.). American
   cranberry bush (*V. opulus* var. *americanum*,
   formerly *V. trilobum*); arrowwood viburnum
   or southern arrowwood (*V. dentatum*);
   nannyberry viburnum (*V. lentago*);
   possumhaw viburnum (*V. nudum*); withe-
   rod viburnum (*V. nudum* var. *cassinoides*);
   blackhaw viburnum (*V. prunifolium*);
   mapleleaf viburnum (*V. acerifolium*)

Water

Birds drink water anywhere it collects, from puddles on the driveway to streams, ponds, ditches, plant saucers, water buckets, and more. Installing a birdbath is one of the simplest ways to provide a reliable water supply for birds and other wildlife. Providing a variety of water sources attracts the widest variety of creatures. Consider the following options.

Birdbaths. Conventional birdbaths consist of a shallow basin of water set on a pedestal, and these are ideal for attracting a great many species. A basin of water placed on the ground or on a low tree stump is likely to attract different species than one on a pedestal. Another option is a shallow basin scraped into the soil that has been lined with a scrap of water-garden liner. Whatever the design, shallow water is the key: Birds prefer a depth of 1 to 2 inches and generally avoid deeper water. Clean birdbaths and refill them with fresh water daily. Scrub basins with a brush every day before refilling, and use a broom to sweep the water out of a shallow area on the ground. In winter, install an electric or solar birdbath deicer to provide a year-round source of water. They are inexpensive and are available at wild bird centers.

It is important to place birdbaths carefully so that birds have a safe place to bathe. (Their flight is impaired when feathers are wet.) Locate birdbaths near perching areas, such as clumps of trees or shrubs, but keep them at least 2 feet away from cover where cats or other predators could hide.

Water for insects. Set a few rocks in a basin of shallow water to provide a safe place for butterflies and other insects to drink. The insects can alight

A garden pond, regardless of size, provides water for birds and land-dwelling wildlife. It also becomes a rich habitat where frogs, toads, and insects such as dragonflies can lay eggs and raise young. Photo by Barbara Ellis; London Town and Gardens.

on the rocks and safely reach the water. These need regular cleaning, too. For easy cleaning, select a few large, rounded rocks that are simple to set aside and replace during cleaning.

Moving water. Water that trickles or moves in some fashion is extremely appealing to birds. Tiny fountains that emit a spray of water are available. The simplest option for adding moving water is to make a tiny hole in the bottom of a bucket, milk jug, or other container. Fill it with water, and then hang it above the birdbath. Birds will be attracted to the sound and sight of dripping water. While the container will empty itself daily, filling once a day is sufficient to ensure a steady stream of wildlife. Birds also are attracted to running water in streams or water gardens. Make sure there are branches alongside these features so birds can easily and safely reach the water.

Water gardens and ponds. Whether small or large, water gardens and ponds add sparkle to any garden. They also provide habitat for wildlife, including water-dwelling insects as well as dragonflies, frogs, turtles, and more. Sites in full sun are best, as many water-garden plants demand them. Water gardens can be installed as part of a design that handles water runoff. To attract the widest variety of wild-

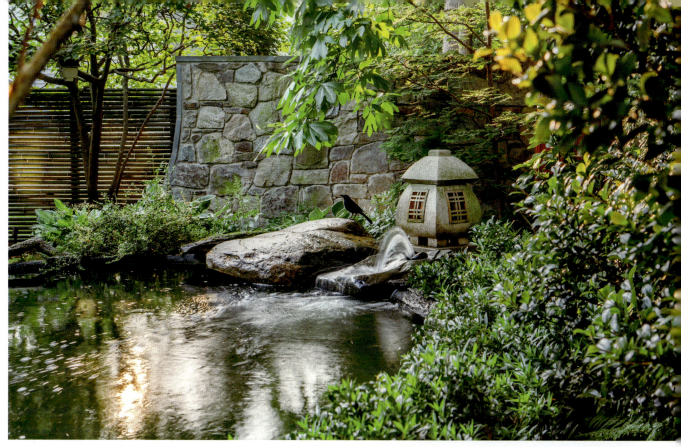

(top) Moving water is especially attractive to birds. Design water features to provide a flat area so they can access the water safely. Photo © Roger Foley; design by Green Themes Inc.

(bottom) Even a tiny water garden—this one is 2 feet by 3 feet—adds vital habitat and draws wildlife to a garden. Miniature hardy water lily 'Helvola' shades the water and helps keep it cool. Photo by Barbara Ellis.

🍂 Value Vernal Pools

Also called ephemeral pools, these small, even tiny, bodies of water are wet for only part of the year. In the Chesapeake Bay region, they typically are filled from winter to late spring and dry up by early summer. During wet years, they may remain full much longer. Despite their small size and temporary nature, vernal pools are incredibly vital and rich habitats. Spring peepers, the chorus frogs that sing on warm, late-winter nights beginning in March or even February, are one of the species that depends on vernal pools for reproduction. Wood frogs use them as well, and of the 17 species of frogs native to the Delmarva Peninsula, 15 have been found breeding in vernal pools. Five of the 13 species of salamanders use vernal pools for reproduction as well, along with countless insects and other invertebrates. In addition, wood ducks and mallards, box turtles, toads, garter snakes, and some shorebirds visit vernal pools to feed or drink. Bats frequent them to hunt the insects that fly over them at night. One reason vernal pools provide such valuable habitat is that they lack fish that readily consume eggs, tadpoles, young salamanders, and insect larvae. Because they dry up annually, vernal pools also have lower populations of fungi that infect amphibian eggs. The amphibians that live in the pools keep mosquito larvae in check.

The importance of vernal pools as wildlife habitat is often completely overlooked when properties are developed, and unknowing homeowners often view them as inconvenient or unattractive landscape features. Cutting trees or other types of disturbance can cause them to dry up too early in the season, leaving tadpoles and young salamanders insufficient time to mature. Filling them to create areas for lawn is disastrous.

Vernal pools deserve to be cherished, and gardeners who have them on their property are lucky, indeed. To protect a vernal pool, protect the plants growing around it. A well-planted buffer supports the adult frogs and other creatures that depend on the pool for breeding. Trees also shade the area, slowing evaporation and ensuring that water remains in the pool as late in the season as possible. Experts suggest protecting the vegetation 1,000 feet on all sides of the pool. Also avoid using pesticides and other chemical sprays in the area because they can be toxic to amphibians, insects, and other invertebrates. For more information on vernal pools, use the online resources link in Suggested Resources.

life, plan on using a flexible liner for construction. Conventional fiberglass water-garden liners have steep sides, which makes water access difficult for many creatures. A flexible liner (EPDM rubber is long-lasting and easy to use) makes it possible to dig a hole of any shape and nearly any size to create a garden that fits the site. Most importantly, it allows

for construction of a gradual slope into the water on at least one side. To cover the liner on the sloping side, install large rocks partway down the slope, on top of the liner. Fill in above them with smaller river rock (the larger rocks prevent the smaller ones from sliding down into the water). When digging the hole for the water garden, create shelves around

Frogs, such as this northern green frog, will move into water gardens large and small. Photo by Barbara Ellis.

water garden installed with a liner, the soil conditions will be similar to those of the overall site. Therefore, plant around the garden with species that suited the site before the garden was installed. Water-lily leaves floating on the surface help shade the water, reduce algae, and provide hiding places for frogs and other pond dwellers. Most commercially sold water lilies are hybrids, but American white water lily (*Nymphaea odorata*) is a common parent of many hardy cultivars.

the steeper sides that can be used to set containers for plants that thrive in wet or boggy soil. These include pickerelweed (*Pontederia cordata*), broad-leaved arrowhead (*Sagittaria latifolia*), and lizard's tail (*Saururus cernuus*).

To make an existing water garden with steep sides safer for wild creatures, install containers around the edges that sit with the soil surface just under the water surface. Another option is adding a log that extends from one edge across and into the water. Both options provide access to the water for smaller creatures and allow them to escape if they fall in. Cover the edges of the liner with pavers or larger rocks to lend a natural look. Dragonflies, butterflies, and frogs will use larger rocks around the garden for sunning.

Use the online resources link in Suggested Resources to find information on designing and constructing a water garden. Fish are optional, but if the garden will not contain them, add Mosquito Bits or Mosquito Dunks to the water to control mosquito larvae. They are organic and are safe for plants, fish, and wildlife. The soil around natural ponds will be wet—suitable for planting the wet-soil species listed in Chapter 8. Since water does not seep away from a

Roosting and Nesting

Landscapes that offer plantings of native trees and shrubs, minimal lawn, and an abundance of food provide wildlife with ample reasons to visit, and features such as shrub borders and wooded areas offer spaces for wild creatures to hide from predators or simply roost. Adding bird houses to the landscape will encourage more species to settle in and raise a family on newfound habitat. Use these tips to make a variety of safe nesting sites available.

Install bird houses. A great many birds, including chickadees, nuthatches, titmice, wrens, bluebirds, swallows, and woodpeckers, will build and raise families in bird houses. Even wood ducks, kestrels, and barn owls will use nest boxes, provided they are the proper size. Always install a predator guard on nest boxes that are mounted on posts or poles to prevent snakes, mice, or other creatures from gaining access to the nest.

Put up additional housing. In addition to bird houses, consider installing a bat house. Native orchard mason bees, which are important pollinators in orchards, also use houses for nesting. Mason bee houses are available at garden centers or on the Internet, but they are also easy to make. The simplest

(left) Shrub borders, clumps of trees, hedgerows, and other areas thickly planted with trees and shrubs all prove safe cover for nesting birds, such as this American robin, and other wildlife. Photo by Neil Soderstrom.

(right) Many species readily accept bird houses, including wood ducks, chickadees, bluebirds, screech owls, and more. Install predator guards beneath bird houses to exclude snakes and other wildlife that may climb into houses. Photo by Neil Soderstrom; Adkins Arboretum.

consist of a block of wood drilled with holes on ¾-inch centers. The holes need to be 5⁄16 inch in diameter and 4 to 8 inches deep.

Plant thorny thickets. Thick, dense brush makes it more difficult for many predators to access nest sites. Hawthorns (*Crataegus* spp.) with thorns provide especially effective protection. Thickets of American red raspberries (*Rubus idaeus*), black raspberries (*Rubus occidentalis*), or other native species also are effective, and many provide edible fruit for wildlife and people.

Create safe spaces. Keeping cats indoors is an important way to guarantee the safety of nesting birds and newly fledged nestlings. Cats also prey on animals of all sorts, so if neighborhood cats visit frequently, try applying scent repellents (available at wild bird stores and garden centers). Motion-sensitive heads that spray water also may be effec-

tive at keeping cats away. If feral cat colonies are the problem, work with local humane organizations to capture and then spay or neuter individuals. Although these organizations typically rerelease the cats where they were trapped, spaying or neutering prevents new kittens from being born, and eventually the colony will die out.

Unwanted Wildlife

Deer, groundhogs, raccoons, and rabbits are not welcome visitors in the family vegetable garden. The best option for keeping marauders out of the vegetable patch is to install a fence *before* they become regular visitors. Ideally, dig a trench around the garden and line it with poultry wire or hardware cloth to prevent creatures from digging under the fence. If a fence is not an option, or to protect plants in the larger landscape, experiment with deer repellents. If one is not particularly effective, try another that contains different ingredients. It also pays to switch repellents periodically, since their effectiveness can decrease over time. Motion-sensitive spray heads for the hose also have proven effective, as have motion-sensitive lights that scare away wildlife. A family dog can be another effective deterrent. Male dogs that are allowed to scent mark in the landscape can encourage deer or other creatures to move to a safer area farther away.

A fence is the best guard against unwanted deer. Photo by Neil Soderstrom; Hannelore Soderstrom garden.

Gardens for Hummingbirds

Ruby-throated hummingbirds, the only hummingbirds that nest east of the Mississippi River, are found in the Chesapeake Bay region. Like songbirds, they need food, water, cover, and nest sites. Flower nectar provides an important part of their diet. Hummingbirds have such fast metabolisms that they must feed almost constantly during daylight hours. They store food in their crops to sustain them overnight. In cool weather or during cold spring nights, they can temporarily enter a state of dormancy, called torpor, to conserve food reserves.

Tubular or trumpet-shaped blooms, especially those that are bright red or orange, are especially attractive to hummingbirds, but they commonly visit flowers in many other colors as well. Native hummingbird plants include columbines (*Aquilegia* spp.), cardinal flower (*Lobelia cardinalis*), lilies (*Lilium* spp.), and penstemons or beardtongues (*Penstemon* spp.), as well as trumpet vine (*Campsis radicans*), trumpet honeysuckle (*Lonicera sempervirens*), and

In addition to feeding from a variety of tube-shaped flowers such as penstemons (*Penstemon* spp.) and trumpet vine (*Campsis radicans*), hummingbirds eat garden insects as well. Photo by Neil Soderstrom.

Hummingbird moths visit the same types of flowers that hummingbirds do, including garden phlox (*Phlox paniculata*) and beebalms (*Monarda* spp.). Photo by Neil Soderstrom.

red buckeye (*Aesculus pavia*). Since hummingbirds need a constant supply of blooms from late spring or early summer to early fall, plant long-blooming, non-native annuals, tender perennials, and perennials to extend the supply of flowers, such as zinnias (*Zinnia* spp.), petunias (*Petunia* spp.), salvias (*Salvia* spp.), and hostas (*Hosta* spp.).

Hummingbirds also visit nectar feeders, which you can purchase from wild bird centers or make yourself. (Purchase bee and wasp guards if you don't want insect visitors at your feeders.) Feeders must be kept clean, and the solution should be changed at least weekly. Otherwise, bacteria that will harm hummingbirds will build up in the nectar. Use the online resources link in Suggested Resources for more information on feeding hummingbirds and making your own feeders.

In addition to flowers, insects are an important part of every hummingbird's diet. Hummingbirds eat aphids, gnats, mosquitoes, flying ants, leafhoppers, flies, small beetles, bugs, and weevils, along with beneficial spiders and parasitic wasps. Ruby-throated hummingbirds even have been observed picking insects out of spider webs.

Since hummingbirds guard feeding and nesting territories during breeding season, scatter plants that attract them throughout your yard instead of creating a single hummingbird garden. Or plant two hummingbird gardens, one in the backyard and another in the front, out of sight of the first.

Wooded areas provide ideal nest sites. Hummingbirds make their tiny, cup-shaped nests by fastening a variety of materials together with silk from spider webs, another reason why an organic garden rich in spiders is also good for hummingbirds. To make a birdbath or other water feature especially appealing to hummingbirds, consider adding a device that produces a fine spray or mist above it. (These are available from wild bird centers.) Hummingbirds are designed for a life in the air, and they will actually bathe by repeatedly flying through the mist. They also will alight on a twig positioned near water.

Butterfly Gardens

Butterfly gardens come in all shapes and sizes, but the best ones are much more than just a pretty patch of flowers in the backyard. That is because nectar is just one of the things butterflies need to thrive in your yard. In addition to nectar-bearing flowers, they also need plants that feed their caterpillars, or larvae. The same is true of moths, and many of the plants listed in this section attract native moths, ranging from large and showy to tiny and unremarkable. You'll find many plants listed below, and you can use Chapters 4, 5, 6, and 7 to identify which will work best on your property. To provide nectar sources all season long, strive to plant a mix of perennials, shrubs, and annuals that bloom in spring, summer, and fall. Fall-blooming asters are especially important for helping monarch butterflies fuel up for their annual migration south.

Fall-blooming flowers such as asters (*Symphyotrichum*, *Doellingeria*, and *Ionactis* spp.) help monarch butterflies build needed reserves to fuel their migration. Photo by Neil Soderstrom; New York Botanical Garden.

🍃 Providing for Pollinators

Many of the features that attract wildlife to the garden also support native pollinators. These hardworking creatures—including hummingbirds, bees, butterflies, moths, beetles, hover flies, and other insects—are vital to the health of ecosystems worldwide. They pollinate 75 percent of flowering plants in the world, including 150 crop plants such as apples, cherries, blueberries, sunflowers, and more. Use the tips below to attract and support pollinators.

Grow native plants. Native shrubs, trees, and wildflowers attract and feed many more pollinators than non-native plants. Fostering a variety of habitats is beneficial as well. For example, some pollinators require bare ground for nest building while others build clay nests. You can buy or build boxes to encourage mason bees. See "Roosting and Nesting" on p. 277 for simple directions.

Plant clumps of bright flowers. Arranging your garden with clumps of flowers rather than scattered individuals makes it easier for bees and other insects to find the flowers they need to feed on. Bees are especially attracted to white, yellow, blue, and purple shades of flowers. Also select as many different

Plant a variety of perennials and annuals to ensure that a progression of flowers is available for vital pollinators such as bees. Photo by Neil Soderstrom; Owen Brown Interfaith Center.

shapes and sizes of flowers as possible, since pollinator preferences differ.

Plan a progression of flowers. Select flowers that bloom at different times to provide food in the form of nectar and pollen throughout the growing season.

Reduce or eliminate pesticides. Eliminate the use of broad-spectrum pesticides that kill a wide range of insects. If you must use pesticides, start with the least toxic ones available.

Locate your garden in a sunny spot that is protected from prevailing winds. If possible, plant or make use of an existing barrier planting of trees and shrubs to help create a relatively windless spot where butterflies can fly without being buffeted about. Trellised vines can also help provide wind protection. Ultimately, though, you will want to add butterfly plants throughout your landscape, since the more types of habitats your yard provides, the more species of butterflies you are likely to attract. Boggy areas, shady wooded areas, woodland edges, sunny meadows, and conventional beds and borders will all attract their share of butterflies.

Also include the following in your design:

Sunning spots. Butterflies will use areas covered with low ground covers, grasses, or clovers to sun themselves. Since they are cold-blooded, sunning helps them regulate their temperatures. Providing a flat rock in a sunny, windless spot along the edge of your butterfly garden is also a good idea.

(top left) Butterflies and dragonflies use flat rocks for sunning, as do five-lined skinks, which feed on insects and various invertebrates. Photo by Barbara Ellis.

(top right) Shallow water interspersed with rocks provides safe access to water for butterflies and other insects. Ferns, iris, and native golden club (*Orontium aquaticum*) edge this small garden watercourse. Photo by Barbara Ellis; Wilbur garden.

(bottom right) Cecropia moths are among the largest and showiest of our native moths. The larvae feed on a variety of tree and shrub species. Photo © Roger Foley.

Water—and mud. There are several ways to provide butterflies with water. Fill a conventional birdbath or other shallow container with flat stones that stick just above the water to provide a safe drinking spot. The emergent stones allow butterflies to alight and drink without getting wet. A low muddy spot that remains moist or that you keep moist by regular watering provides a suitable drinking spot. Or include an extended shallow area in a water garden. Butterflies also visit muddy or sandy spots along streams and pools for water and minerals.

Darkness. If you are interested in attracting and supporting moths, turn off all unnecessary outdoor lights, which disorient moths and reduce the amount of energy they have for finding mates and reproducing. (This also benefits budding astrono-

mers!) Toss out bug zappers, too. Not only are they completely ineffective at killing mosquitoes and other biting insects, but they eliminate thousands of beneficial insects and moths annually. Mosquitoes are primarily attracted to the carbon dioxide released by people and pets and will zero in on that instead of the ultraviolet light in the zapper.

Plants for Caterpillars

While butterflies will visit flowers of many different species, their larvae, or caterpillars, are not necessarily as flexible. Many butterflies require a specific plant or group of plants to reproduce successfully, while others are more adaptable. Mourning cloaks, for example, are fairly flexible as far as butterflies go:

🌿 Butterfly Life Cycles

Butterflies and moths are insects that belong to the order Lepidoptera, which contains 82 families and an estimated 12,423 species in North America. All exhibit complete metamorphosis, meaning there are four stages in their life cycles: egg, larva (caterpillar), pupa (cocoon), and adult. Any habitat that truly supports them needs to provide plants for egg-laying adults that the caterpillars can eat. While it may seem that providing flowers for adults is the only other consideration, understanding the way a species pupates and how it overwinters is also necessary for success. Some species attach their cocoons to leaves that remain on the plant, while others drop to the ground either to pupate or after they have formed a cocoon. Still others overwinter attached to grasses or other plants, frequently those that are routinely cut back as part of annual landscape maintenance. Other species overwinter in leaf litter or plant debris as eggs or caterpillars. Raking and routinely disposing of leaf litter or cutting down plants throughout the landscape as part of fall maintenance also disposes of the next generation of many butterflies and moths. This is yet another reason why preserving leaf litter and maintaining wild areas even in home landscapes is so important.

(top) Careful use of pesticides—including organics such as Bt (*Bacillus thuringiensis*)—preserves insects, including butterfly larvae. This is the larva of pipevine swallowtail, which primarily feeds on pipevine (*Aristolochia macrophylla*). Photo by Barbara Ellis.

(bottom) Plants that feed butterfly larvae should be the cornerstone of any butterfly garden. This is an American lady caterpillar feeding on plantain-leaved pussytoes (*Antennaria plantaginifolia*). Photo by Neil Soderstrom; Owen Brown Interfaith Center.

Their larvae can feed on birches (*Betula* spp.), elms (*Ulmus* spp.), hackberries (*Celtis* spp.), nettles (*Urtica* spp.), poplars (*Populus* spp.), and willows (*Salix* spp.). Monarch butterfly larvae require plants in the milkweed family, Asclepiadaceae, while the larvae of tiger swallowtails, another popular, often-seen species, can feed on a wide variety of different trees, including American basswood (*Tilia americana*), sweetbay magnolia (*Magnolia virginiana*), birches (*Betula* spp.), cherries (*Prunus* spp.), and tulip trees (*Liriodendron tulipifera*). The flashy zebra swallowtail, on the other hand, requires pawpaw trees (*Asimina triloba*), and if you want pipevine swallowtails, you'll need to add either pipevine (*Aristolochia macrophylla*) or Virginia snakeroot (*A. serpentaria*) to your landscape. Spicebush swallowtail, another striking butterfly of summer, feeds on spicebush (*Lindera benzoin*) as well as sassafras (*Sassafras albidum*).

For a butterfly garden that attracts and supports a rich variety of species, start by building plant diversity. Flowers may be the showiest aspect of a butterfly garden, and you will find lists of showy nectar plants and other features that attract adult butterflies later in this section. But you should also include a diverse selection of woody plants—trees, shrubs, and vines—to form the framework of a garden that supports the widest variety of larvae.

Woody Plants for Caterpillars

The following lists include some of the native trees, shrubs, and vines that support butterflies and moths. There are many more, and any native plant you choose to grow will support some insects. A few of the butterflies and moths whose larvae are found on each plant or group of plants are listed after the genus or species below. Many more insects than those listed depend on these plants. In addition to the trees listed below, both maples (*Acer* spp.) and elms (*Ulmus* spp.) attract a great many species of moths and butterflies.

Use this list to begin identifying species that are already growing on your property as well as ones that might be suitable to add. In Chapter 4, you will find more information on a great many of the species listed below.

Oak trees, such as this willow oak (*Quercus phellos*), are especially valuable in butterfly-friendly landscapes because they feed more butterfly and moth larvae than any other group of plants. Photo by Neil Soderstrom; Phantom Gardener.

Trees

Birches (*Betula lenta, B. nigra, B. populifolia*). Larval food for common tortoiseshell, mourning cloak, tiger swallowtail.

Cherries and plums (*Prunus* spp.). Larval food of coral hairstreak, red-spotted purple, spring azure, striped hairstreak, tiger swallowtail, white admiral, viceroy.

Cottonwoods and aspen (*Populus* spp.). Larval food of mourning cloak, red-spotted purple, striped hairstreak, tiger swallowtail, viceroy, and white admiral, along with 7 species of giant silk moths.

Crab apples (*Malus* spp.). Larval food of gray hairstreak, red-spotted purple, striped hairstreak, and viceroy, as well as many species of moths, including 8 species of sphinx moths.

Hackberries (*Celtis* spp.). Larval food of eastern comma, hackberry butterfly, mourning cloak, question mark, snout butterfly, tawny emperor.

Hickories (*Carya* spp.). Larval food for banded and hickory hairstreak butterflies, plus many moths, including the royal walnut moth. Its harmless, 5-inch-long larvae are referred to as hickory horned devils, but they also feed on ash (*Fraxinus* spp.), sweet gum (*Liquidambar styraciflua*), cherries (*Prunus* spp.), and others.

Oaks (*Quercus* spp.). Larval food of Horace's duskywing, Juvenal's duskywing, red-banded hairstreak, striped hairstreak, white-M hairstreak. Also used by many species of moths, including cecropia moth, imperial moth, io moth, luna moth, and polyphemus moth.

Willows (*Salix* spp.). Larval food of compton tortoiseshell, mourning cloak, red-spotted purple, striped hairstreak, tiger swallowtail, viceroy.

Shrubs

Blueberries, deerberries (*Vaccinium* spp.). Larval food of Henry's elfin, spring azure, striped hairstreak, and numerous moths.

Dogwoods (*Cornus alternifolia, C. sericea*). Larval food of polyphemus moth, spring azure, summer azure.

Prickly ash, common (*Zanthoxylum americanum*). Larval food plant for giant swallowtail.

Spicebush (*Lindera benzoin*). Larval food of spicebush swallowtail.

Sumacs (*Rhus* spp.). Larval food plant for hickory horned devil, red-banded hairstreak, showy emerald.

Viburnums (*Viburnum dentatum, V. lentago*). Larval food plant for azalea sphinx, Harris' three-spot, hummingbird clearwing moth, rose hooktip moth, rusty tussock moth, spring azure.

Witch hazel, American (*Hamamelis virginiana*). Larval food of spring azure, plus a variety of moths.

Vines

In addition to the two species listed below, grapes (*Vitis* spp., including summer grape [*V. aestivalis*] and fox grape [*V. labrusca*]) and Virginia creeper (*Parthenocissus quinquefolia*) support several species of sphinx moths.

Passionflower, maypops (*Passiflora incarnata*). Larval food of Gulf fritillary, variegated fritillary.

Pipevine (*Aristolochia macrophylla*). Larval food of pipevine swallowtail.

Flowers for Caterpillars

While caterpillars do not require flowers per se, many popular herbaceous perennials and other plants support butterfly larvae. All are well worth adding to butterfly plantings. Consider some of the following:

Asters (*Eurybia, Doellingeria,* and *Symphyotrichum,* formerly *Aster* spp.) are larval food for pearl crescent butterflies.

🍃 Weeds for Butterflies

Butterflies visit the flowers of many weeds, but that is not the only reason to include them in your butterfly garden. Many are essential larval plants for butterflies and moths. In addition to the species listed here, many gardeners include violets on their weed lists. While they can be enthusiastic spreaders, violets are vital larval plants for several species of fritillary butterflies. They also make excellent ground covers. See "Violets" on p. 162 for information on the best species of violets for this use.

Carrot-family plants, including Queen Anne's lace (*Daucus carota*), a widespread non-native weed, and popular garden plants such as parsley, fennel, and parsnips are larval plants for black swallowtails. Native carrot-family plants include common cow parsnip (*Heracleum maximum*) and sweet cicely or long-style sweetroot (*Osmorhiza longistylis*).

Clovers and other legumes. Eastern tailed-blues and clouded sulphurs lay eggs on clovers (*Trifolium* spp.) and other members of the pea family, Fabaceae, including ticktrefoils (*Desmodium* spp.)

Milkweeds. While some of these plants are quite at home in the flower garden, and many adult butterflies visit the blooms, common milkweed (*Asclepias syriaca*) is a plant for meadow plantings, fields, and other wild areas. Monarch butterflies lay eggs on all species of milkweeds (*Asclepias* spp.) in addition to climbing milkweed or honeyvine (*Cynanchum laeve*). Spreading dogbane (*Apocynum androsaemifolium*) is a host plant for monarch butterflies that thrives in shade.

Monarch butterflies depend on milkweeds for feeding their larvae. This is common milkweed (*Asclepias syriaca*). Photo by Barbara Ellis.

Nettles and false nettles. Red admirals, eastern commas, mourning cloaks, and question marks lay their eggs on slender or California stinging nettle (*Urtica dioica* ssp. *gracilis*) and false nettles, including small-spike false nettle (*Boehmeria cylindrica*).

Sheep or garden sorrel (*Rumex acetosella*) and curly dock (*Rumex crispus*) are larval plants for bronze coppers, little coppers, and American coppers.

Painted lady butterflies lay their eggs on many different weeds, including both native and non-native thistles (*Cirsium* spp.), rabbit-tobacco (*Pseudognaphalium obtusifolium*), and common mallow (*Malva neglecta*), among others.

A number of butterflies, including Appalachian eyed brown, little wood satyr, common wood nymph, and various skippers, lay their eggs on grasses or sedges (*Carex* spp.).

Zebra swallowtails, which depend on pawpaw (*Asimina triloba*) to feed their caterpillars, are among the many butterfly species that visit butterfly weed (*Asclepias tuberosa*) and other milkweeds. Photo by Barbara Ellis.

Like many plants belonging to the aster family, Asteraceae, ironweeds (*Vernonia* spp.) are especially valuable for attracting pollinators and butterflies, such as this tiger swallowtail, to the garden. Photo by Neil Soderstrom; Green Spring Gardens.

Milkweeds. Showy members of this family, which provide larval food for monarch butterflies, include butterfly weed (*Asclepias tuberosa*) and swamp milkweed (*A. incarnata*).

Partridge peas and sennas. These meadow plants—sennas (*Senna* spp.) and partridge peas (*Chamaecrista* spp.), both formerly *Cassia* spp.—are larval plants for cloudless sulphur, little sulphur, and sleepy orange sulphur butterflies.

Pussytoes, pearly everlasting, and daisy-family plants. American painted lady butterfly uses plantain-leaved pussytoes (*Antennaria plantaginifolia*) along with pearly everlasting (*Anaphalis margaritacea*) and other daisy-family plants for its larvae.

Snapdragons and acanthus-family plants. Plants of two different families are larval food for the common buckeye butterfly. Members of the snapdragon family, Scrophulariaceae, include false foxgloves (*Aureolaria* spp. and *Agalinis* spp.), Allegheny monkey flower (*Mimulus ringens*), and blue or Canada toadflax (*Nuttallanthus canadensis*, formerly *Linaria canadensis*). Hosts in the acanthus family, Acanthaceae, include Carolina wild petunia (*Ruellia caroliniensis*). Baltimore checkerspots prefer white turtlehead (*Chelone glabra*).

Violets (*Viola* spp.). These are larval food for great spangled, meadow, variegated, regal, and silver-bordered fritillaries, so be sure to make plenty of room for them. (Variegated fritillaries also lay eggs on mayapples [*Podophyllum peltatum*].)

Flowers for Butterflies

Colorful flowers, of course, are the centerpiece of any garden designed to attract butterflies. While it is true butterflies visit the blooms of butterfly bushes (*Buddleja* spp.) and other non-native plants for nectar, native plants should top the list of choices for butterfly plantings because of the importance they play in the life cycles of butterfly larvae and other insects.

🍃 Annual Flowers

Because annuals bloom over a longer season than most perennials, plan on including some of those listed to ensure there are flowers open as many days as possible. Most are not native, but they will help fill in without getting out of hand. Annuals to consider include sunflowers (*Helianthus annuus*), which are native, along with cosmos (*Cosmos* spp.), Mexican sunflowers (*Tithonia rotundifolia*), marigolds (*Tagetes* spp.), and zinnias (*Zinnia* spp.).

🍃 Shrubs for Butterflies

Don't overlook the following shrubs, all of which bear flowers that attract butterflies and a wide array of beneficial insects.

Buttonbush (*Cephalanthus occidentalis*)
Devil's walking stick (*Aralia spinosa*)
Dogwood, alternate-leaf or pagoda (*Cornus alternifolia*)
Itea, Virginia sweetspire (*Itea virginica*)
New Jersey tea (*Ceanothus americanus*)
Potentilla, shrubby cinquefoil (*Dasiphora fruticosa*, formerly *Potentilla fruticosa*)
Rhododendrons and azaleas (*Rhododendron* spp.)
Viburnums (*Viburnum* spp.), including mapleleaf viburnum (*V. acerifolium*) and southern arrowwood (*V. dentatum*)

Butterflies visit literally thousands of different plants, both to sip nectar and to lay their eggs. Planting one of everything does not necessarily result in the most effective butterfly garden, however, from the standpoint of both appearance and attractiveness to the butterflies themselves. Arranging plants in drifts of three, five, or more creates an attractive mass of color for you, but it also helps butterflies find the flowers. Locate your garden in as much sun as possible. If you do not have a sunny site, use the lists in Chapter 7 to identify butterfly plants that will grow in partial shade or shade.

A few plant families are especially important to butterflies as either nectar sources, larval plants, or both. You will find the plants grouped according to these families below. Select some from each family. Also try to ensure that there are flowers—bright colors are especially effective—in bloom from spring to very late fall. It also helps to look at flower forms, because butterflies tend to prefer flowers that provide flat landing surfaces.

Daisy Family, Asteraceae

Daisies and their kin not only attract butterflies; they are very attractive to a wide variety of beneficial insects, including pollinators. Plant some of the following:

Ageratum, hardy (*Conoclinium coelestinum*, formerly *Eupatorium coelestinum*)
Asters (*Eurybia, Doellingeria,* and *Symphyotrichum* spp.)
Coneflowers, orange (*Rudbeckia* spp.)
Coneflowers, purple (*Echinacea* spp.)
Coreopsis or tickseeds (*Coreopsis* spp.)
Goldenrods (*Solidago* spp.)
Ironweeds (*Vernonia* spp.)

Joe-Pye weeds (*Eutrochium* and *Eupa-*
toriadelphus spp., formerly *Eupatorium*
spp.)

Liatris, blazing stars, or gayfeathers (*Liatris* spp.)

Sneezeweed, common (*Helenium autumnale*)

Sunflowers (*Helianthus* spp.)

Bee balms (*Monarda* spp.)

Hyssops (*Agastache* spp.)

Mountain mints (*Pycnanthemum* spp.)

Pagoda mint, downy (*Blephilia ciliata*)

Sage, lyre-leaf (*Salvia lyrata*)

Wild mint (*Mentha arvensis*)

Pea Family, Fabaceae

While clovers and alfalfa may be the best-known members of this family, other pea relatives make suitable additions to butterfly gardens, including the following:

Bush clovers (*Lespedeza* spp.)

Butterfly pea (*Clitoria mariana*)

Lupine, sundial (*Lupinus perennis*)

Partridge peas (*Chamaecrista* spp., formerly *Cassia* spp.)

Vetch, American or purple (*Vicia americana*)

Mint Family, Lamiaceae

In addition to the plants listed below, butterflies are attracted to members of the mint family typically grown in the flower or herb garden, including catmints (*Nepeta* spp.), lavender (*Lavandula* spp.), and rosemary (*Rosmarinus officinalis*).

Milkweed Family, Asclepiadaceae

While milkweeds are best known as plants for the larvae of monarch butterflies, the adults of many different species of butterflies, including swallowtails, sulphurs, fritillaries, painted ladies, viceroys, skippers, and question marks visit the flowers for nectar. Butterfly weed (*Asclepias tuberosa*) and swamp milkweed (*A. incarnata*) are most commonly planted.

Parsley Family, Apiaceae

Parsley (*Petroselinum crispum*), dill (*Anethum graveolens*), and fennel (*Foeniculum vulgare*) are herb garden plants that belong to the parsley family. All bear flat-topped blooms that are very attractive to butterflies as well as a wide variety of beneficials. While none of the above-mentioned plants are native, there are native zizias or golden alexanders (*Zizia* spp.) and angelicas (*Angelica* spp.). Also see "Weeds for Butterflies" on p. 286 for more information.

SUGGESTED RESOURCES

In this age of technology, a wealth of information on sustainable gardening and landscaping is available to readers online. Since website addresses change frequently, and excellent new ones appear regularly, readers of *Chesapeake Gardening and Landscaping* will find an online guide to organizations, websites, blogs, tools, books, and other information at www.chesapeakegardeningandlandscaping.org. The site also tracks and lists native plant nurseries that offer trees, shrubs, vines, perennials, and other natives grown and sold in a sustainable manner.

Suggested Reading

The following are among the best books on sustainable landscaping and related topics.

Native Plants

Armitage, Allen. *Armitage's Native Plants for North American Gardens.* Timber Press, 2006.

Cullina, William. *Ferns, Moss and Grasses: From Emerald Carpet to Amber Wave, Serene and Sensuous Plants for the Garden.* Houghton Mifflin Harcourt, 2008.

———. *Growing and Propagating Wildflowers in the United States and Canada.* Houghton Mifflin Company, 2000.

———. *Native Trees, Shrubs, and Vines: A Guide to Using, Growing, and Propagating North American Woody Plants.* Houghton Mifflin Company, 2002.

Eastman, John, and Amelia Hansen. *The Book of Swamp and Bog: Trees, Shrubs, and Wildflowers of the Eastern Freshwater Wetlands.* Stackpole Books, 1995.

Leopold, Donald J. *Native Plants of the Northeast: A Guide for Gardening and Conservation.* Timber Press, 2005.

Miller, Bebe. *Wildflower Perennials for Your Garden: A Detailed Guide to Years of Bloom from America's Native Heritage.* Stackpole Books, 1996.

Roberts, Edith A., and Elsa Rehmann. *American Plants for American Gardens.* 1929. University of Georgia Press, 1996.

Slattery, Britt E., Kathryn Reshetiloff, and Susan M. Zwicker. *Native Plants for Wildlife Habitat and Conservation Landscaping: Chesapeake Bay Watershed.* U.S. Fish and Wildlife Service, Chesapeake Bay Field Office, 2005.

Thunhorst, Gwendolyn A. *Wetland Planting Guide for the Northeastern United States: Plants for Wetland Creation, Restoration, and Enhancement.* Environmental Concern, Inc., 1993.

Invasive Plants

Burrell, C. Colston. *Native Alternatives to Invasive Plants.* Brooklyn Botanic Garden, 2006.

Kaufman, Sylvan Ramsey, and Wallace Kaufman. *Invasive Plants: Guide to Identification and the Impacts and Control of Common North American Species.* Stackpole Books, 2007.

Swearingen, Jil, Britt Slattery, Kathryn Reshetiloff, and Susan Zwicker. *Plant Invaders of Mid-Atlantic Natural Areas.* National Park Service and U.S. Fish and Wildlife Service, 2010.

Uva, Richard H., Joseph C. Neal, and Joseph M. Ditomaso. *Weeds of the Northeast.* Comstock Publishing/Cornell University Press, 1997.

Ecology and Gardening

Carroll, Steven B., and Steven D. Salt. *Ecology for Gardeners.* Timber Press, 2004.

Cloyd, Raymond A., Nancy R. Pataky, and Philip L. Nixon. *IPM for Gardeners: A Guide to Integrated Pest Management*. Timber Press, 2009.

Darke, Rick. *The American Woodland Garden: Capturing the Spirit of the Deciduous Forest*. Timber Press, 2002.

Eastman, John. *The Book of Swamp and Bog*. Stackpole Books, 1995.

Kays, Jonathan, Joy Drohan, Adam Downing, and Jim Finley. *The Woods in Your Backyard: Learning to Create and Enhance Natural Areas Around Your Home*. Natural Resource, Agriculture, and Engineering Service (NRAES), 2006.

Lathan, Zora, and Thistle A. Cone. *Ecoscaping Back to the Future: Restoring Chesapeake Landscapes*. Chesapeake Ecology Center, 2005.

Maloof, Joan. *Teaching the Trees: Lessons from the Forest*. University of Georgia Press, 2005.

Nardi, James B. *Life in the Soil: A Guide for Naturalists and Gardeners*. University of Chicago Press, 2007.

Pleasant, Barbara, and Deborah L. Martin. *The Complete Compost Gardening Guide*. Storey Communications, 2008.

Stein, Sara. *Noah's Garden: Restoring the Ecology of Our Own Backyards*. Houghton Mifflin Company, 1993.

———. *Planting Noah's Garden: Further Adventures in Backyard Ecology*. Houghton Mifflin Company, 1997.

Sustainable Landscape Design

Adkins Arboretum and Tawna Mertz. *The Green Book for the Bay: An Illustrated Guidebook for Chesapeake Bay Critical Area Property Owners Living on Maryland's Eastern Shore*. Native Seed Publishing, 2008.

Adkins Arboretum and the Critical Area Commission for the Chesapeake and Atlantic Coastal Bays. *The Green Book for the Buffer: An Illustrated Guidebook for Planting at the Shoreline*. Maryland Department of Natural Resources and the Critical Area Commission for the Chesapeake and Atlantic Coastal Bays, 2012.

Apfelbaum, Steven, and Alan Haney. *Restoring Ecological Health to Your Land*. Island Press, 2010.

Beck, Travis. *Principles of Ecological Landscape Design*. Island Press, 2013.

Dunnett, Nigel, and Andy Clayden. *Rain Gardens: Managing Water Sustainably in the Garden and Designed Landscape*. Timber Press, 2007.

Hadden, Evelyn. *Beautiful No-Mow Yards: 50 Amazing Lawn Alternatives*. Timber Press, 2012.

Reed, Sue. *Energy-Wise Landscape Design: A New Approach for your Home and Garden*. New Society Publishers, 2010.

Sawyers, Claire E. *The Authentic Garden: Five Principles for Cultivating a Sense of Place*. Timber Press, 2007.

Scarfone, Scott C. *Professional Planting Design: An Architectural and Horticultural Approach for Creating Mixed Bed Plantings*. John Wiley and Sons, 2007.

Summers, Carolyn. *Designing Gardens with Flora of the American East*. Rutgers University Press, 2010.

Thompson, J. William, and Kim Sorvig. *Sustainable Landscape Construction: A Guide to Green Building Outdoors*. 2nd ed. Island Press, 2008.

Thompson, Peter. *The Self-Sustaining Garden: The Guide to Matrix Planting*. Timber Press, 2007.

Zimmerman, Catherine. *Urban and Suburban Meadows: Bringing Meadowscaping to Big and Small Spaces*. Matrix Media Press, 2010.

Wildlife and Wildlife Habitat

Badger, Curtis. *Birdwatcher's Guide to Delmarva*. Sierra Press, 1999.

Beane, Jeffrey C., Alvin L. Braswell, Joseph C. Mitchell, William M. Palmer, and Julian R. Harrison III. *Amphibians and Reptiles of the Carolinas and Virginia*. 2nd ed. University of North Carolina Press, 2010

Kress, Stephen W. *The Audubon Society Guide to Attracting Birds*. 2nd ed. Cornell University, 2006.

Mikula, Rick. *The Family Butterfly Book: Projects, Activities, and a Field Guide to 40 Favorite North American Species*. Storey Books, 2000.

———. *Garden Butterflies of North America*. Willow Creek Press, 2001.

Mizejewski, David. *Attracting Birds, Butterflies and Other Backyard Wildlife*. Creative Homeowner Press, 2004.

Roth, Sally. *Attracting Birds to Your Backyard: 536 Ways to Turn Your Yard and Garden into a Haven for Your Favorite Birds*. Rodale Press, 2003.

———. *The Backyard Bird Feeder's Bible: The A-to-Z Guide to Feeders, Seed Mixes, Projects, and Treats*. Rodale Press, 2000.

Soderstrom, Neil. *Deer-Resistant Landscaping: Proven Advice and Strategies for Outwitting Deer and 20 other Pesky Mammals*. Rodale Press, 2008.

Tallamy, Douglas W. *Bringing Nature Home: How Native Plants Sustain Wildlife in Our Gardens*. Updated and expanded. Timber Press, 2007.

Wagner, David L. *Caterpillars of Eastern North America*. Princeton University Press, 2005.

Webster, Wm. David, James F. Parnell, and Walter C. Biggs Jr. *Mammals of the Carolinas, Virginia, and Maryland*. University of North Carolina Press, 2004.

White, James F., Jr., and Amy Wendt White. *Amphibians and Reptiles of Delmarva*. Tidewater Publishers, 2002.

Woodbury, Elton N. *Butterflies of Delmarva*. Tidewater Publishers, 1994.

INDEX

Page numbers in *italic* indicate photos or illustrations.

Hellebore, green false. See *Veratrum viride*
Hemerocallis fulva (daylily, common), 104
Hemlock. See *Tsuga canadensis*
Henbits. See *Lamium* spp.
Hepatica (hepatica), 239
   americana (round-lobed hepatica), 239
   nobilis
     var. *acuta* (sharp-lobed hepatica), 239
     var. *obtusa* (round-lobed hepatica), 239
Heracleum maximum (cow parsnip), 286
Herbicides
   lawn grass and, 96, *96*
   meadows and, 208
   seasons and, 105
Heuchera spp. (heucheras, alumroots), 159–60, 227
   americana (American alumroot), 159
     'Cajun Fire', 160
     'Citronelle', 160
     'Dale's Strain', 160
     'Frosted Violet', 160
     'Plum Pudding', 160
     'Silver Scrolls', 160
     'Spellbound', 160
   micrantha (West Coast native crevice alumroot), 159–60
   villosa (hairy alumroot), 159
     'Autumn Bride', *159*
Hexastylis spp. (wild gingers, asarums), 163–64, 228
   arifolia (little brown jug), 164
   shuttleworthii (large-flower heartleaf), 164
     'Velvet Queen' (mottled wild ginger), *163*
   virginica (Virginia heartleaf), 164
Hibiscus spp. (rose mallows), 200
   coccineus (scarlet rose mallow), 200, 262
   moscheutos (common rose mallow), 23, 176, 200, *200*, 250, *250*, 251, 262
     'Kopper King', 200
Hickory. See *Carya* spp.
Hieracium caespitosum (hawkweed, yellow), 72
High-maintenance plants/plantings, 32–33
Hippophae rhamnoides (sea buckthorn), 103
Historic gardens, sustainable, 75

Holly. See *Ilex* spp.
Homeowners' association regulations, 31
Honeylocust. See *Gleditsia triacanthos*
Honeysuckle. See *Lonicera* spp.
Honeysuckle, bush. See *Diervilla* spp.
Honeyvine. See *Cynanchum laeve*
Hop hornbeam, American. See *Ostrya virginiana*
Hops, Japanese. See *Humulus japonicus*
Hop tree. See *Ptelea trifoliata*
Hornbeam, American. See *Carpinus caroliniana*
Horsetail. See *Asclepias* spp.
Hosta spp. (hosta), 97, *165*, *166*, 215, *215*, 225, 280
Houstonia caerulea (bluets), 170, *170*, 238–39
Huckleberries. See *Gaylussacia* spp.
Humulus japonicus (Japanese hops), 103
Hummingbird moths, 279
Hummingbirds, 10
   feeders for, 280
   gardens for, 279–80, *279*
Hydrangea, climbing. See *Decumaria barbara*
Hydrangea spp. (hydrangeas), 120, 222–23
   arborescens (wild hydrangea), 20, 148, *111*, *112*, *148*, 168–69, 222–23, *223*, 252
     'Annabelle' (smooth hydrangea), 168–69, *168*, 223
   macrophylla (bigleaf hydrangea), 69
   quercifolia (oakleaf hydrangea), 120, *120*, 223
     'Snow Queen', 223
Hylotelephium telephioides (Allegheny stonecrop), 70, 179, 189
Hypericum spp. (hypericum), 120
   densiflorum (bushy St. John's wort), 120, *120*
   frondosum (golden or cedar glade St. John's wort) 120, 157
   kalmianum (Kalm's hypericum), 115
   prolificum (shrubby St. John's wort), 120

Ilex spp. (hollies), 28, 114–15, 119–20, 272
   decidua (possumhaw), 119–20, 251, 272
   glabra (inkberry), 70, 114–15, *114*, 141, 251, 260
     'Shamrock', 115

   opaca (American holly), 29, 114, 125, 139, 140, 154, 218, 251, 259
     'Clarendon Spreading' (dwarf American holly), 114
     'Jersey Delight', 126
     'Jersey Knight', 126
     'Jersey Princess', 126
     'Maryland Dwarf' (dwarf American holly), 114, *114*
     'Old Heavy Berry', 126
   verticillata (winterberry holly), 119, 139, 157, 251, 260, 272
     'Apollo', 119
     'Jim Dandy', 119
     'Raritan Chief', 119
     'Red Sprite', 119
     'Southern Gentleman', 119
     'Winter Red', 119
   vomitoria (Yaupon holly), 114
     'Nana', 114
Indian grass. See *Sorghastrum nutans*
Indian physic. See *Gillenia trifoliata*
Indian pink. See *Spigelia marilandica*
Indian strawberry. See *Duchesnea indica*
Indigo, wild. See *Baptisia* spp.
Informal gardens, 56, 62
   about, 61
   formal elements in, 61, 63
Inkberry. See *Ilex* spp.
Insects
   beneficial, 29, 31, 185, 187, 193, 270, 282, 288
   hummingbird moths, 279, *279*
   hummingbirds and, 280
   identifying before spraying, 30
   native plants and, 17, 22
   pesticides and, 31, 283, *283*
   prey, 270, *270*
   providing for pollinators, 280, *280*
   water for, 273–74
Invasive plants. *See also* Non-native invasive plants/trees
   control measures for, 103–5
   ground covers, 149, 151
   management of, 102–5
   pulling and cutting, 104–5
   site evaluation and, 47
   trees, shrubs, and vines, 103
Ionactis spp. (asters), 178, 193–94, 280, *280*
   linariifolius (stiff aster), 204

Small-spike false nettle. See *Boehmeria cylindrica*

Smilacina racemosa. See *Maianthemum racemosum*

Smoketree, American. See *Cotinus obovatus*

Smooth cord grass. See *Spartina* spp.

Snags, wildlife and, 29, 269

Snakeroot, white. See *Ageratina altissima*

Snakes, 30

Snapdragon family, Scrophulariaceae, 287

Sneezeweed. See *Helenium* spp.

Snowbell. See *Styrax* spp.

Snowberry, pink. See *Symphoricarpos* spp.

Snowdrop. See *Galanthus* spp.

Soaker hoses, 85, *85*, 96

Soft rush. See *Juncus* spp.

Soil
    about, 74–84
    caring for, 31
    compaction of, 82–83, 84, 93
    health of, maintenance of, 79–82, 83–84
    improvements to, 81
    in layered planting, 65, *65*, 66
    loosening and amending, 25–26
    mulch and, 31, *31*, 81
    organic matter in, 77, *77*, 79, *79*, 83
    particle types in, 76
    planting holes and, 90
    rain gardens and, 249, 253
    shade gardens and, 216
    on site, working with, 83
    readiness for digging, 86
    starting with, 74, 76
    structure of, organic matter and, 77–79
    sustainability and, 77
    texture of, 76
    tilling and digging, 79–80
    topography and, 46–47
    topsoil, protection of, 82
    turning over, 74
    unamended, 90

Soil compaction, 82–83, 84

Soil disturbance, 96

Soil moisture level, 86

Soil saucer, 90

Soil tests, 12, 25, 33, 83

Soil type, 68

Solidago spp. (goldenrods), 178, 195, 199, 288
    caesia (wreath goldenrod), 70, 73, 231, *231*
    canadensis (Canada goldenrod), 70, 73
    flexicaulis (zigzag goldenrod), 231
    juncea (early goldenrod), 187
    nemoralis (gray goldenrod), 195
    odora (anise-scented goldenrod), 195
    rugosa (wrinkle-leaved goldenrod), 199, 262
        'Fireworks', 199, *199*
    sempervirens (seaside goldenrod), 195, 262
    speciosa (showy goldenrod), 187
    sphacelata (autumn goldenrod), 195
        'Golden Fleece', 195, *195*
    ulmifolia (elm-leaved goldenrod), 195

Solomon's plume. See *Maianthemum racemosum*

Solomon's seal. See *Polygonatum* spp.

Solomon's seal, false. See *Maianthemum racemosum*

Sorghastrum nutans (Indian grass), 70, 210–11, 251

Sorrel, sheep or garden. See *Rumex* spp.

Sorvig, Kim, 81

Sourwood. See *Oxydendrum arboreum*

Southern arrowwood. See *Viburnum* spp.

Southern magnolias. See *Magnolia* spp.

Southern red oak. See *Quercus* spp.

Southern wax myrtle. See *Morella* spp.

Spartina spp. (cord grasses)
    alterniflora (smooth cord grass), 41, *41*, 263
    patens (salt meadow hay), 41, *41*, 263

Specialists, consulting, 23

Specimen plants, 176

Spicebush, northern. See *Lindera benzoin*

Spider flowers. See *Cleome hassleriana*

Spiderwort. See *Tradescantia* spp.

Spigelia marilandica (Indian pink), 227, *227*

Spikenard, false. See *Maianthemum racemosum*

Spiraea japonica (spiraea, Japanese meadowsweet), 103

Spiranthes cernua (lady's tresses, nodding), 201, 262
    var. *odorata* 'Chadds Ford', 201

Spodiopogon sibiricus (frost grass), 175, *175*

Sporobolus spp. (dropseeds), 202–3
    cryptandrus (sand dropseed), 202–3
    heterolepis (prairie dropseed), 70, 202, 203, 210, 251

Spreading dogbane. See *Apocynum androsaemifolium*

Spring beauties. See *Claytonia* spp.

Spurge, cypress and flowering. See *Euphorbia* spp.

Staking trees, 89

Staphylea trifolia (bladdernut), 221, 252

Stars of Bethlehem. See *Ornithogalum* spp.

Steep slopes, lawn reduction and, 14

Stems, twining, 137, *137*

Stewartia spp. (stewartias), 219
    malacodendron (silky camellia), 219
    ovata (mountain camellia), 219

Stinking ash. See *Ptelea trifoliata*

St. John's wort. See *Hypericum* spp.

Stokes' aster. See *Stokesia laevis*

Stokesia laevis (Stokes' aster), 180, 183

Stolons, *150*

Stormwater planters, 254

Strawberry bush. See *Euonymus* spp.

Strawberry, mock or Indian. See *Duchesnea indica*

Style. *See* Garden style

Stylophorum diphyllum (celandine poppy), 158, *158*

Styrax spp. (snowbells), 218–19
    americanus (American snowbell), 219
    grandifolius (bigleaf snowbell), 219

Suckers, *150*

Sumac. See *Rhus* spp.

Summersweet. See *Clethra alnifolia*

Sun
    or shade, 177
    shade patterns and, 44–46

Sunflower oxeye. See *Heliopsis helianthoides*

Sunflowers. See *Helianthus* spp.; *Tithonia rotundifolia*

Sun plants, rain gardens and, 250–51

Sun terms, 45

Sustainability, soils and, 76

Sustainable historic gardens, 75

Sustainable Landscape Construction (Thompson and Sorvig), 81

Wineberry. See *Rubus phoenicolasius*
Winged euonymus. See *Euonymus* spp.
Winter aconite. See *Eranthis hyemalis*
Winterberry holly, common. See *Ilex* spp.
Winter creeper. See *Euonymus* spp.
Wintergreen. See *Gaultheria procumbens*
Wise gardening practices, 4, 30–33
Wisteria spp. (wisterias)
    floribunda (Japanese wisteria), 103, 139
    frutescens (American wisteria), 18, 139
        'Amethyst Falls', 139
    sinensis (Chinese wisteria), 103, 139
Witch hazel. See *Hamamelis virginiana*
Wood fern. See *Dryopteris* spp.
Woodland garden, informal, 215, *215*
Woodland pinkroot. See *Spigelia marilandica*
Woodland planting, shady, 80, *80*
Woodpeckers, 29, 40, 269, *269*

Woodpiles, 29
Wood rush, hairy. See *Luzula accuminata*
Woodvamp. See *Decumaria* spp.
Woodwardia spp. (chain ferns)
    areolata (netted chain fern), 235, 263
    virginica (Virginia chain fern), 235, 263
Woody plants
    caterpillars and, 284–85
    defined, 112

Xanthorhiza simplicissima (yellowroot), 156, 261

Yaupon. See *Ilex* spp.
Yellow adder's tongue. See *Erythronium americanum*

Yellow archangel. See *Lamiastrum galeobdolon*
Yellow crownbeard. See *Verbesina occidentalis*
Yellow-leaved common elderberry. See *Sambucus* spp.
Yucca filamentosa (yucca), 79, *79*, 176, 178, 189–90
    'Bright Edge', 189
    'Color Guard', 189
    'Golden Sword', 189, *189*

Zanthoxylum americanum (prickly ash), 285
Zephyranthes atamasca (Atamasco lily), 234
Zinnia spp. (zinnias), 29, *173*, *174*, 280, 288
Zizia spp. (golden alexanders), 289
    aurea, 233–34